MAX LILIENTHAL

The Making of an American Rabbinate

Bruce L. Ruben

Wayne State University Press   Detroit

15 14 13 12 11   5 4 3 2 1

Library of Congress Cataloging-in-Publication Data

Ruben, Bruce, 1952–
Max Lilienthal : the making of the American rabbinate / Bruce L. Ruben.
p. cm.
Includes bibliographical references and index.
ISBN 978-0-8143-3516-1 (cloth : alk. paper)
1. Lilienthal, M. E. (Max E.), 1815–1882. 2. Rabbis—United States—Biography.
3. Reform Judaism—United States. I. Title.
BM755.L5R83 2011
296.8'341092—dc22
[B]
2011015226

Typeset by Maya Rhodes
Composed in Warnock Pro and Meta

Contents

Preface

In early March 2007, I was sitting at the Hebrew Union College Founders' Day commemoration in my new capacity as director of the School of Sacred Music. At the end of the service, I was touched to hear the name of Max Lilienthal read among the school's departed faculty. After spending fifteen years studying this man, in that moment his life came alive for me in a special way. Lilienthal had been Hebrew Union College's first history teacher. It is for this reason that he is mentioned on the Kaddish list. However, few remember the extent of Lilienthal's role in the founding of that institution and more generally in creating an American rabbinate.

Max Lilienthal (1814–82) has a compelling life story that traverses three major nineteenth-century Jewish communities: Germany, Russia, and America. Lilienthal lived through many of the conflicts inherent in the struggle for emancipation. A modern Orthodox upbringing, traditional yeshiva training, and a doctorate from the University of Munich combined to make him an advocate for German Haskalah. His early training in *Wissenschaft des Judentums* and subsequent scholarly work attracted the attention of Ludwig Philippson, who arranged for his first post in Riga. Lilienthal's subsequent controversial efforts to modernize the educational system of Russian Jewry made him famous in his 20s.

When Lilienthal landed in New York in late 1845, he was only the third ordained rabbi to come to these shores. The first, Abraham Rice, soon gave up the rabbinate altogether, and the second, Leo Merzbacher, died too soon to have a lasting impact on the American Jewish scene. Lilienthal arrived to find an American Jewry still in the throes of what Jonathan Sarna characterized as "the collapse of the unified synagogue-community" and its replacement by a more pluralistic and diverse "community of synagogues."[1] American Jews searched for new models to deal with the demands of the influx of many immigrants, who struggled to adjust to a new world and yet to save what was meaningful from the old. How were they to deal with the poor, the education of the young, and the desire to reshape the worship service to conform to American mores? How were they to respond to the threat of missionaries and to the challenge of freedom itself? As Lilienthal struggled with these issues, he evolved in his own religious ideology, embracing Reform as the most meaningful—and, for his time, the most authentic—response to the needs of this German immigrant community.

The mid-nineteenth century was a chaotic time in which the first rabbis had little real authority. An entrenched lay leadership only grudgingly gave up power to the rabbis. During that difficult transition, Lilienthal experienced humiliations and difficult power struggles. As a result he and his rabbinical colleague Isaac M. Wise (in contrast to the elitist approach of David Einhorn) developed a strategy of collaboration with lay leadership that ultimately bore lasting fruit in the creation of the Union of American Hebrew Congregations and the Hebrew Union College. Also, responding to those difficult early experiences, Lilienthal spearheaded the professionalization of the rabbinate, raising standards by creating the first rabbinic professional union.

Lilienthal broadened his rabbinate to go beyond traditional service to his congregation or even the local Jewish community. He became a community leader who served on school, university, and hospital boards, worked to alleviate poverty, and pioneered interfaith activities. He would forge a new post-emancipation model for the rabbinate, innovating in ways that were inconceivable anywhere but in the freedom that America offered. Lilienthal was therefore a seminal rabbinic leader whose experiences over more than thirty years shaped the American rabbinate.

Given these accomplishments, it is remarkable that Lilienthal has been treated as a footnote to the history of American Reform Judaism, very much in the shadow of his friend Wise. Although Wise is viewed as the founder of American Reform, Lilienthal's early contribution was critical. He surpassed his friend in scholarship and tactical savvy and in his later years was acknowledged as the elder statesman of American Jewry. This book is intended to fill a gap in the history of the development of American Judaism in the nineteenth century by reassessing a figure who, hidden in the shadow of others, deserves a more adequate portrayal.

Only one other book-length treatment of Lilienthal has been written: an uncritical tribute penned by his student and successor David Philipson.[2] Lacking critical analysis, footnotes, and bibliography, more than half of Philipson's volume presents English translations of Lilienthal's writings without any analysis. The treatment of the transitional New York period is especially weak. Philipson also wrote articles—for example, "Max Lilienthal" for the *Central Conference of American Rabbis Annual* and "Max Lilienthal, 1815–1882" in *Centenary Papers and Others*—and he discussed Lilienthal in his history of Congregation Bene Israel.[3] Lilienthal's career is briefly covered in a similarly uncritical fashion in two family memoirs.[4]

Articles dealing with Lilienthal usually focus on a particular aspect of his career. Although no one has studied his German years, several scholars have discussed Lilienthal's attempt to modernize Jewish education in Russia. Among them are Saul Ginsburg, Emanuel Etkes, Michael A. Meyer, and Michael Stanislawski.[5] Stanislawski discusses the historiographical debate concerning Lilienthal's role and motives.

There are references to Lilienthal's American career in Hyman Grinstein's *Rise of the Jewish Community of New York, 1654–1860.* However, Grinstein's book does not offer any systematic assessment of Lilienthal's German background, career, or religious evolution. In addition, Grinstein published "The Minute Book of Lilienthal's Union of German Synagogues in New York" and mentions Lilienthal in his "Studies in the History of Jewish Education in New York City." Morton Merowitz discusses Lilienthal as an educator.[6] An article by Sefton D. Temkin presents a translation and analysis of one of Lilienthal's letters to the *Allgemeine Zeitung des Judenthums.*[7] A recent article by Matthew Silver relates Lilienthal's negative experience in Russia to his later fervent embrace of the principle of the separation of church and state.[8]

Lilienthal is mentioned in biographies of several of his American colleagues. Most significant was his place in the life of Isaac Mayer Wise, documented in James G. Heller's *Isaac M. Wise: His Life, Work, and Thought.* The more recent biography by Sefton D. Temkin, *Isaac Mayer Wise: Shaping American Judaism*, makes only scant reference to Lilienthal. Recent works treating the Orthodox rabbi Bernard Illowy and the early Philadelphia hazan and editor Isaac Leeser also mention Lilienthal.[9] Finally, Lilienthal's contribution is noted in Michael Meyer's history of the Reform movement and in Naomi W. Cohen's *Encounter with Emancipation.*[10]

Many people helped me on this intellectual journey. I started my graduate work at the Graduate School of City University of New York studying European intellectual history with Gertrude Himmelfarb, Abraham Ascher, and Philip Dawson, but I was drawn into Jewish history by fascinating courses in European Jewish history with David

Berger and Robert Seltzer and American Jewish history with Naomi Cohen. Abraham Peck at the American Jewish Archives suggested to me that Lilienthal deserved more serious treatment, and my adviser, Naomi Cohen, urged me to pursue this topic. By choosing Lilienthal, I was able to combine European and American interests in my dissertation. Guided by Naomi Cohen until she moved to Israel, I was fortunate that Robert Seltzer agreed to help me finish the dissertation. His encouragement and advice throughout the process were invaluable. Through the generosity of Temple Shaaray Tefila, I was able to take a sabbatical from my cantorial duties that allowed me to transform my dissertation into the present book. In that effort I was aided by Bonny Federman, who patiently and skillfully helped me shape the material into a more compelling narrative and guided my efforts to find a publisher.

Mel Scult gave me valuable criticism of the original dissertation, as did Jonathan Sarna. Dr. Sarna has continued to share materials and suggestions that have been invaluable. Stephan Brumberg shared his knowledge of nineteenth-century Jewish education and especially his research into the Cincinnati bible war. Margaret Bloomfield helped with the nineteenth-century Southern German dialect of Lilienthal's early letters, and Almut Fitzgerald transcribed a handwritten document from the Munich archives. Many institutions were helpful, including the Leo Baeck Institute, the archives of Temple Emanuel and Central Synagogue in New York, the American Jewish Archives, the Western Jewish History Center, the Rare Book Division of the Public Library of Cincinnati and Hamilton County, and the archives of the University of Cincinnati. At Hebrew Union College, David Ellenson, Michael Meyer, Carole Balin, and Amira Meir provided valuable assistance. The support of Mark Kligman, Benjie Ellen Schiller, and Dean Shirley Idelson has allowed me to complete this project while attending to my many responsibilities as director of the cantorial program. Numerous other friends discussed the book with me and helped me clarify my thoughts, including Hollace Weiner, Leslie Curtis, Gene Guberman, and Marilyn Sladowski (of blessed memory).

Finally, without the support of my wife, Judith, and my son, Ari, this book never would have been written. Both of them aspire in their own work to the highest ideals. Their example, as well as their emotional support, has been invaluable to me. This book is dedicated to them.

1

German Origins

Between Reaction and Modernity

Maximilien Eduard Emanuel Lilienthal (known as Max Lilienthal) was born in Munich in November 1814, the same year that the family took Lilienthal as their official surname.[1] Max was the first of seven children born to Dina Lichtenstein and Loew (or Loeb) Seligmann. His birth came just as the Munich Jewish community was being officially established. His family was among the approximately thirty-four families who made up the small Jewish community, all of whom had recently migrated from their rural ancestral home in the neighboring valley of Schnaittach-Huttenbach. Other Jews had settled in Munich before the Lilienthals. By 1802, Hesekiel Hessel served the tiny community as its rabbi, but as late as the year that the Lilienthals arrived, Munich did not yet have a synagogue or a Jewish cemetery. Working closely with the authorities, Munich's Jews organized formally in January 1815, and within a year they had established a cemetery and had begun to plan for a synagogue. A site was purchased on Theaterstrasse, and a committee, which included Max's father, began raising funds. They hired an architect, Jean-Baptiste Métivier, who designed a building in the classical style. The finished synagogue was dedicated on April 21, 1826, at a ceremony attended by the king and queen and many important city and state officials.[2]

That this vanguard of thirty-four Jewish families, who had only recently been allowed residency, could afford such an impressive building, much less host the king and queen at its opening, is remarkable. They represented an elite group of court Jews and state suppliers who had long served the nobility of Bavaria. Because of their wealth and influence, the Lilienthal family qualified as part of this Jewish aristocracy. Dina came from a family of wealthy merchants; Loew was a wholesale merchant descended from a long line of court Jews.[3]

The court Jew was "a large-scale Jewish merchant-financier with court connections, a type that was to become a key feature of central European life in the century 1650–1750."[4] In Bavaria the presence of these Jewish figures represented an exception to the legal code of 1553, which theoretically banned Jews from settling in the area.[5] In that turbulent period, absolutist rulers turned to skilled Jews to add wealth and power to their states. Court Jews served the nobility as contractors, agents, bankers, masters of the mint, and even diplomats.[6]

In various regions of Germany, the Jewish communities gradually reconstituted themselves under ad hoc agreements with local officials. Court Jews often defended the interests of large Jewish communities (*kehillot*) and of small Jewish rural groups (*Landjudenschaften*) in the surrounding territory. Both the *kehillot* and the *Landjudenschaften* were essentially autonomous and self-sufficient communities, although they depended on the local secular ruler for their corporate existence. They administered synagogues, elementary schools, yeshivas, charitable organizations for the poor and sick, and a burial society. The leadership had the power to levy taxes and exercised considerable legal coercion over their members, short of capital punishment. These Jews, who lived their lives almost entirely within the Jewish community, had contact with non-Jewish society mainly when required by business.[7] In contrast, the court Jews, because of their wealth, role in international commerce, and alliances with aristocrats and governmental officials, were the Jewish communities' link to the wider world. Max Lilienthal's ancestors belonged to this illustrious group.

Lilienthal's niece Sophie claimed that one branch of their family had been prominent in the rural community of Schnaittach-Huttenbach as early as 1529. In the mid-sixteenth century this largely Jewish village boasted its own chief rabbinic court.[8] A century later, an ancestor named Loew Seligmann settled in Schnaittach; by 1710 members of his family had become community leaders. In the mid-eighteenth century, Max's great-grandfather, another Loew Seligmann, rose to prominence when he and a partner became quartermasters to the army of the elector of Bavaria during the Seven Years' War. In 1758, they contracted to supply the troops and, although it became clear that they would suffer a great financial loss because of wartime inflation, they honored the original prices in their contract. They also placed themselves in physical danger, following the army into enemy territory to help maintain its food supply. The army paymaster testified to their bravery and honesty and, as a result, Loew was made the official purveyor of provisions and subsequently Bavarian court banker.[9] After the government granted him special privileges, Loew used his influence at court to aid his people. Following a series of successful investments in 1762 that greatly enriched the Bavarian court, he was allowed to purchase property in Schnaittach. In recognition of his father's service, his son—also named Loew Seligmann—became a fiscal agent of the Bavarian court, receiving a contract in 1791 to furnish precious metals to the Upper Palatine mint.[10] This Loew Seligmann (Max's grandfather) became a wealthy man; he owned two houses and a lucrative grain business. For many years he was also head of the Jewish community and, out of his own funds, built a school and gave financial support to Jewish scholars.[11] The government allowed him to travel freely without paying the onerous poll tax, permitted him to carry firearms, and bestowed upon him the title of Court Purveyor of Fürth. Max's father, named Loew Seligmann as well, was born in Schnaittach in 1777. Also a successful merchant, he settled with his beautiful wife Dina in Munich, where he followed the family tradition by serving as a member of the community's administrative board and the governing board of the burial society. The Lilienthals were among the privileged few who gained residential status in Munich. That Max grew up among this urban elite was critical to his development.

Jewish legal status varied greatly throughout the Electorate of Bavaria that emerged in 1777. Gradually more and more Jews were settling in the area despite restrictive conditions (they had been allowed official permanent residence only since 1750). However, the Enlightenment was inspiring revolutionary theories that would destroy the ancien régime's traditional corporate structure and its hodgepodge of laws. German Jacobites tried to institute radical changes in the wake of the French Revolution.[12] As notions of equality and citizenship were debated, German Enlightenment figures argued that a modern, cohesive, centralized state demanded a uniform approach toward all its inhabitants, including its Jews. Confronted with the tangle of laws that applied to the Jews throughout the region, the Enlightenment-inspired bureaucrats sensed possible economic advantages to emancipating the Jews as well.[13]

One such enlightened bureaucrat was Count Maximilian Montgelas. Although his roots were in Alsace, he entered the Bavarian bureaucracy and rapidly rose through the ranks. He served Elector Karl Theodor and then his successor, Max Joseph. When the Bavarian kingdom was established in 1806, Montgelas strove to set up a uniform set of institutions for all citizens. The Napoleonic conquests gave new urgency to his goals, spreading revolutionary ideology in their wake. Bavaria became part of the French empire's Rhenish Confederation, as one of its largest and most important members. Bavaria dissolved Jewish corporate status and rabbinic jurisdiction in 1806.[14] Although only Westphalia and other states bordering France itself officially emancipated their Jews, in 1813 Bavaria passed a law granting certain Jews citizenship. It was this law that allowed the Lilienthals and the rest of Munich's Jews to gain residence.

However, faced with the deeply rooted hostility toward Jews, Bavaria also placed severe restrictions on that citizenship, which effectively decreased the Jewish population. Most important, the government established a Matrikel, a registration that replaced the older letter of protection. Matrikel numbers were limited and transferable only to the oldest son. Only the death or emigration of someone holding a number made another citizenship available, effectively freezing Jewish communities as they were and excluding Jews from moving into new areas. The 1813 Judenedikt (Jewish edict) also kept extraordinary tariffs and other economic restrictions in place.[15]

However, forces were gathering throughout Europe to confront Napoleon. On October 8, 1813, Count Wrede of Bavaria and Prince Henry of Reuss of Austria signed an agreement giving Bavaria "full and entire sovereignty." In exchange, the kingdom promised to renounce membership in the Rhenish Confederation, to commit at least 36,000 troops to fight Napoleon, and to make no separate peace with France.[16] The fate of the modernizing legislation, including the status of the Jews, would have to wait for the Congress of Vienna, which convened after Napoleon's defeat in 1815.

Growing up in Munich in the turbulent years following the defeat of Napoleon, Max Lilienthal's early life in Germany was forged by the tension between reactionary and modernizing forces within Bavarian society. Max was only 6 months old when Loew heard the news that Napoleon had been beaten at Waterloo.[17] Loew kept himself informed as the diplomats in Vienna decided the fate of the Jewish community. Although the "Jewish question" was only a peripheral topic of discussion at the Congress of Vienna, the major players had significant disagreements. The Prussian chancellor, Prince Karl August von Hardenberg, and the Prussian liberal diplomat Wilhelm von Humboldt strove to negotiate uniform emancipatory legislation modeled after the Prussian edict of 1812. The conservative Austrian foreign minister Clemens von Metternich, however, was determined to reverse all French advances, including civil emancipation for Jews. The Jewish issue was addressed briefly—and basically left on hold—in Article 16 of the constitution of June 1815: "The Diet of the German Confederation shall consider how improvements in the civil status of adherents of the Jewish faith in Germany can be implemented in the most broadly acceptable manner and, specifically, how the enjoyment of civil rights in return for the assumption of civic duties in the states of the Confederation can be provided and assured."[18] This vaguely worded ruling implied the promise of eventual emancipation, but because the edict of 1813 remained in effect in Bavaria, including the restrictive Matrikel, Jewish life was still severely hampered. Bavarian Jews were also held back until 1861 by a law restricting freedom of movement.[19] This law prevented Jews from taking advantage of certain liberalizations of trade laws that had technically allowed them to get training in previously forbidden occupations but effectively prevented them from earning a living in these fields. Without freedom of movement, particularly in rural regions, the opportunity to practice these more highly skilled trades was extremely limited.[20]

Anti-Jewish violence was also a reality of life in Bavaria. According to German historian Eleonore Sterling, these attacks were fueled by "German literature in the first half of the nineteenth century [which] frequently describes the Jews as the crucifiers of Christ and as the damned people. They are depicted as diabolical and sinister, close to the horrors of death, uncivilized, backward, and sub-human."[21] Even among the more educated classes, German plays such as *Unser Verkehr* (Our Crowd) found a sympathetic audience. This notorious drama mocked the desire of the younger generation of Jews to acculturate into German society. By the end of the show the message was clear: "Jews cannot acculturate; they can only degrade German culture." Christian playwrights treated Jews as the butt of ridicule.[22] Both the popular pamphlets and the more sophisticated literature helped to sustain an atmosphere of hatred and contempt toward the Jews of Bavaria.

The violence was spurred by the anxiety over the possibility of Jewish emancipation. The conservative peasants and the no less anxious artisans and merchants, who had already been through the fluctuations of the revolutionary and Napoleonic periods, feared changes that would upset their medieval corporate relationships and their monopolies. Despite Metternich's efforts to turn back the political clock, Bavaria continued to modernize its government, education system, and economy. Indeed, in February 1819, King Maximilian Joseph I called an assembly of the states to further improve the legal status of minority groups such as Jews.[23]

To make matters worse, serious crop failures in 1816 and 1817 caused bread prices to skyrocket, and German goods were no longer competing well on the international market. During 1816, various regions throughout Europe were disturbed by social violence, and by the end of the year the trouble had spread into Germany. Angry crowds gathered in Munich and other cities.[24]

Max was 4 years old when anti-Jewish riots broke out on August 2, 1819, in Würzburg in northern Bavaria. Sparked by the debate over Jewish emancipation in the Bavarian parliament, the "Hep, Hep" riots, spread rapidly through other cities and villages in Bavaria and then to Heidelberg, Frankfurt, Hamburg, and even Denmark. "Hep, Hep" is believed to have been either an acronym for the Latin phrase "Hierosolyma est perdita" (Jerusalem is lost) or a word used by peasants to call billy goats, which also alluded to the beard that many Jews wore.[25] In Würzburg, crowds also yelled "Schlagt die Juden tot!" (Kill the Jews) and "Jud' vereck" (Jews drop dead). But the mobs did not limit themselves to name-calling. Jews were abused, pursued through the streets, and shot. The home of a wealthy Jewish banker, Jacob von Hirsch, was attacked by a mob of sixty to eighty men, who turned on the police sent to stop them. The Jewish population fled the town, and it took until August 5 for the police to bring the situation under control. In two Bavarian villages, the synagogues were destroyed and the Torah scrolls desecrated. The Jewish lane was pillaged in Heidelberg, and in Danzig a crowd attacked the two synagogues on the eve of Yom Kippur.[26]

According to historian Stefan Rohrbacher, these seemingly random events had a common element. "The attacks were against the most conspicuous local symbols of Jewish aspirations for emancipation and of Christian unwillingness to accept profound changes in the status of the Jews."[27] The Hirsch family had been the first family granted a residence permit in Würzburg since the Jews' expulsion in 1642. They acquired their palatial home in an auction. To compound the problem, the home had been part of a monastery that was secularized by the government. In Hamburg, the rioting took place in a neighborhood where wealthy Jewish families had recently moved and where Jews had never been allowed before. Other violence took place at fashionable cafes where Jews had previously been excluded. The wealthy Jews who had taken advantage of governmental liberalization, such as the Lilienthals and the other new residents of Munich, were therefore the direct focus of the anti-Jewish agitation.

What was even more troubling was that in a number of cases the police either allowed the incidents to happen or even participated. Most authorities, however, were afraid that these riots could get out of hand and, fearing a wider conspiracy, usually moved quickly to reestablish order. Although the government restricted them, the Jews still looked to the police and authorities for protection and ultimately as the agents of their emancipation.

Max's family chose to embrace the dream of future equality rather than the reality of Bavarian anti-Semitism. The family grew rapidly. Samuel was born a little more than a year after Max (November 19, 1815). Sarah (Sophie) arrived a year later (January 6, 1816), followed by Seligmann (July 8, 1818), Ephraim (August 4, 1819), Heyman (February 3, 1822), and Henrietta (March 3, 1823). During this period, a fire destroyed many of the family's possessions.[28] Although the family came from an illustrious and wealthy past, the family fortune was greatly diminished by this disaster. Their hope to retrieve it lay in the success of their children, which in turn depended on one thing: education.

Throughout Central Europe it had always been the responsibility of a Jewish father to provide religious instruction for his children, traditionally until the age of 13.[29] Typically children began their formal education at the age of 4 or 5, either through private tutors if the family could afford it or in a Talmud Torah, a school run by the community. It is unlikely that the small community in Munich could support a community-run school, because it had yet to open a synagogue. In Max's case, he writes explicitly in his "Notice Biographique" that his primary education was at home under the care of tutors. He claims to have never set foot in a public school until the age of 13. It is likely that Max and his male siblings learned the fundamentals of Hebrew, Bible, and some Talmud. Max also reported that he "obtained elementary instruction in the sciences" from tutors.[30]

That Max's family chose to introduce him to the sciences is telling. As part of the privileged class that formed the German Jewish economic elite of the age of early industrialization (1800–1880), they represented the vanguard of modernization, adopting German cultural and educational norms long before their rural brethren.[31] Their willingness to integrate secular and Jewish subjects meant that they embraced the values of a small subculture within Jewish society known as the Haskalah (Jewish Enlightenment). That Max Lilienthal's family was part of this new subculture was perhaps the determining factor in his professional development.

The eighteenth century brought vast intellectual and political changes to European society. These changes would gradually break down the walls of separation between Jews and an increasingly secular world. First in France and England and then later in Germany, Italy, and elsewhere, a rational, cosmopolitan, and largely secular body of ideas revolutionized European thought. The hallmark of Enlightenment thought was its emphasis on human reason, free of the shackles of the past and of authority.[32] As noted, new concepts of equality and citizenship fostered a debate in Western European intellectual circles that would eventually lead to the transformation of the status of Jews from a segregated, barely tolerated group into individual citizens. Jews were promised an end to legal restrictions if they were willing to "totally expunge the flaws in their culture, religion and morality."[33] The impact of these developments in Bavaria could be seen through the efforts of Count Montgelas.

The Enlightenment presented a revolutionary challenge to traditional premodern Jewish society.[34] For the first time, Jews became aware of the vast chasm between Jewish and European intellectual worlds. Inspired by secular education and philosophy, an elite network of Jews developed new approaches to politics, education, culture, and religion that became known as the Haskalah. Moses Mendelssohn (1729–86), its early pivotal figure, exemplified the movement's ideals in his own life. Although traditionally observant, Mendelssohn mastered modern languages and disciplines, contributing to the philosophical discourse of his day. His translation of the Torah into German helped the Jews of his generation gain entry into the secular world.[35]

Advocates of the Haskalah in Western Europe, known as Maskilim, accepted the dominant culture's view that Jews were intellectually backward, tied to nonproductive occupations, and often illiterate in the language of the countries in which they lived. They believed that Jews had to become modernized to deserve full emancipation in European society. They published detailed proposals for the modernization of Jewish education, initiated in the tract by Naphtali Wessely called "Words of Peace and Truth" (1782). This controversial program sparked a fierce reaction from traditionalists, who were opposed to any change in Jewish education. Because they were a small minority within the Jewish world, the Maskilim's progress was slow. As a result, they relied on the state for leadership, viewing the government as a benevolent agent in liberating Jews from their medieval backwardness. Wessely argued that in recent years "merciful kings" and enlightened absolutists would bring about a new era for the Jewish people.[36] The secular ruler would be the deliverer of the Jews.[37] Writing in 1811, Yehudah Leib ben Zeev epitomized the maskilic faith in the government's virtually messianic role. "God awakened a new spirit in the hearts of kings and princes, to break the yoke that had been pressing upon us, and to remove the wall that has been separating us from them."[38] This ideology was repeated throughout the first half of the nineteenth century. Accepting the quid pro quo of regeneration for rights, the middle-class Jewish minority had absolute faith that the tutelary state would accomplish this.[39]

The Bavarian government did its part to encourage that moderniza-tion. The educational policy (*Erziehungspolitik*) offered the promise of rights in exchange for the transformation of German Jewry. As early as 1804, while still elector, Maximilian Joseph opened all the schools in his country to Jewish youths and allowed the establishment of modern Jewish schools as well. These provisions were repeated in the 1813 laws, the goal of which was to encourage Jews to enter new occupations other than trade. In 1823 Jews were compelled to attend Bavarian public or parochial elemen-tary schools; five years later modern curricular requirements for Jewish schools were legally decreed.[40] The 1813 laws also stipulated that rabbinic training must go beyond traditional religious subjects to include "Greek, Latin, logic, metaphysics, moral and religious philosophy, pedagogy, his-tory, exegesis of the Old Testament, homiletics, and Jewish history, philos-ophy, and liturgy."[41] Applicants were also required to pass a battery of state examinations that lasted eight to ten days. These requirements provided the model for the rest of Germany.[42]

Max was drawn quite early to a career in the rabbinate. Family tradi-tion relates that 11-year-old Max promised his mother on her deathbed that he would become a rabbi.[43] Dina died on December 31, 1824. Not yet 30 years old, she left behind seven children ranging from 11 to less than 2. According to Max's nephew Ernest, "Sophie who was then seven, tried to be a little mother for them all."[44] We can only speculate about Max's feelings at the time of his mother's death. His resolve to fulfill his solemn promise to her, made during those trying times, survived many challenges and disap-pointments.

At some point during this period, Max, needing more advanced Judaic study than the community of Munich could offer, attended the yeshiva in Fürth.[45] Rabbi Wolf Hamburger headed this traditional school, which was one of the most respected in Germany.[46] Supported by the community and individual donors, including Max's grandfather Loew, the Fürth yeshiva attracted students from both Eastern and Western Europe. According to Max's account, at its peak in the mid-eighteenth century, the school had as many as 500 students. In 1824 it still boasted eighteen teachers and eighty-eight teenage students.[47] These students, who boarded in local homes, were immersed in the study of the Talmud and its commentaries. They heard lectures each morning from the head of the yeshiva and studied a page of text in depth for the rest of the day. Discipline was strict, and the students were tested regularly.[48] The yeshiva was the focal point for a circle of schol-ars (*lomdim*) who lived locally and created a powerful Jewish court.[49]

Although the yeshiva continued in its centuries-old traditions into the nineteenth century, the Bavarian government, as part of its policy of *Erziehungspolitik* was seeking ways to modernize the rabbinate. The king issued a law in 1826 that sought to turn the Fürth yeshiva into a modern seminary under government supervision. The curriculum, which would include advanced secular studies, represented a direct threat to Wolf Hamburger's institution.[50]

Traditionalists like Hamburger feared that a university education was the first step toward apostasy. Likening secular learning to the evil woman in Proverbs, they said, "None that go to her return again" (Proverbs 2:19). This warning was directed at those rabbis who forsook Orthodoxy and embraced the new Reform movement. Centered in Berlin, Hamburg, and Vienna, these new leaders sought to modernize Judaism to make it more acceptable to the Christian world while holding onto younger Jews who were quickly assimilating into European society. Indeed, many young people, hoping to advance professionally, chose to embrace Christianity. Referring to them, Orthodox leaders quoted Proverbs again: "Numerous are those slain by her" (Proverbs 7:26).[51]

In 1830 Rabbi Hamburger decided to close down the Fürth school rather than add the secular curriculum that Bavarian law demanded. His students dispersed. Some, such as Abraham Rice and Seligmann Bamberger, went to the neighboring Würzburg yeshiva, run by another of Rabbi Hamburger's students, Abraham Bing. Rice, who never studied secular subjects, remained strictly Orthodox. Unable to serve as a rabbi under the new laws, he accepted a teaching job at a house of study in a town near Würzburg before becoming the first rabbi to immigrate to America. Bamberger got the government to exempt him from the secular requirements and became the head of the Würzburg yeshiva.[52] Rabbi Hamburger's fears proved true in the case of several of his students who did go on to university study; David Einhorn, Joseph Aub, Isaac Loewi, and Max Lilienthal all became prominent Reform rabbis.[53]

What was the danger in secular education that these traditional rabbis feared so much? During the nineteenth century, Germany pioneered a new approach to education, based on the concept of *Bildung*, or self-transformation. The term, which had its origins in late medieval German mysticism, became popular in the seventeenth century as a pietistic notion—that the individual realized himself by copying the prototype (*Bild*) of Christ. *Bildung* came to have a secularized meaning during the early German Enlightenment, referring instead to moral individualism based on reason and the cultivation of the heart. By the late eighteenth century, *Bildung* came to represent "a new secular form of individual salvation."[54]

Inherent in it was a new sense of human potential based on freedom and the transformative power of education.

After Prussia's disastrous loss to Napoleon in 1806, it was clear that a major overhaul of its entire bureaucracy and educational system was necessary. The leadership called on the important neohumanist scholar and statesman Wilhelm von Humboldt to carry out this task. Humboldt set up a three-stage system that became the model for education throughout much of Europe and the United States: elementary school, gymnasium, and university.

In the elementary school, all students learned basic skills. Then, in the gymnasium those students who qualified were immersed in classical languages and literature and in modern languages, mathematics, physics, natural history, geography, religion, music, calligraphy, drawing, and philosophy.[55] During this intensive nine-year course of study, the student learned specific material and how to be intellectually independent. By the time the student reached the university, he was to be given maximum freedom to learn by himself.[56] Humboldt believed that "everyone must seek out his own individuality and purify it." This cultivation of one's full potential was possible only in an atmosphere of maximum freedom. A new generation of leaders would be better educated, not by the old rote transmission of knowledge but by "science and its vital principle of freedom."[57] This critical, creative approach to learning was known as *Wissenschaft*, conceived as an organically united and ever-unfolding field of scientifically and objectively obtained knowledge.[58] Humboldt, along with Johann Fichte, F. A. Wolf, Leopold Ranke, and others, emphasized research and methodology leading to creative scholarship over pedantic memorization. The Prussian system provided the model for the reformation of university education throughout Germany and, by extension, the transformation of its bureaucracy.

This *Wissenschaft* method as applied to Judaism was both inherently and historically reformative. It posed a fundamental challenge to the assumptions, interests, and methods of traditional Jewish learning, especially in the early decades of the nineteenth century. If Judaism was to be understood "scientifically," then it was no longer a timeless set of truths received through divine revelation and interpreted by the scholars of the tradition. It was a living, evolving tradition that had to be understood in its historical context. Further, it rejected dogma and demanded from a scholar an openness of mind to all evidence, including Gentile sources.[59] Both the method and content of this approach were anathema to traditional rabbis.

When Bavaria opened the University of Munich in 1826, it also established a gymnasium in the same year.[60] Both schools followed the new Prussian *Wissenschaft* model. A long line of prominent scholars from central and northern Germany were invited to teach at the university. These scholars helped transform the institution from its eighteenth-century ecclesiastical orientation into a modern research university.[61]

When the new gymnasium opened in Munich, the Lilienthal family sent their oldest son. They immediately grasped the opportunity that this educational track offered, namely, access to a new kind of intellectual aristocracy. According to his autobiographical account, Max's work greatly pleased all of his professors. He graduated with honors in history, geography, German, and French. Armed with these tools, the young scholar enrolled at the University of Munich, recently opened to Jews, probably in 1833. He was perhaps the second or third Jew to attend the university, which was necessary to meet the state's requirements for rabbinic ordination.[62] In 1834, Max's brother Samuel finished his gymnasium studies and joined Max at the university to study medicine.[63]

Embracing the *Wissenschaft* approach, Max enrolled in the philosophy department, the equivalent of a modern college of arts and sciences, which was the heart of the new humanistic educational system. Theoretically, university students had complete academic freedom to choose their own course of study. They had no fixed curricular requirements. Humboldt and the other pedagogical theorists believed that this freedom was crucial to the development of *Bildung*, the central goal of the new institutions. Also crucial was the condition of "social intercourse" within a community of scholars. Self-transformation could be achieved only through free interaction with other students and with professors. At the university, an egalitarian environment made it possible for people from different classes to form new social bonds.[64] Although the University of Munich had attempted to free itself completely from its ecclesiastical heritage, it did not quite succeed in offering its few Jews that free environment. Max was required by law to take courses in Christian theology, although he seems to have had some choice in the subjects he selected.[65] Years later, he also recalled the difficulties his faith posed in social relationships. "I still remember today my Christian fellow students at the University of Munich; they deplored the state of my soul, they said, because of my religious profession. Several of them, young men to whom I was attached by the bonds of the most sincere friendship, believed me irretrievably lost! How ridiculous, how blasphemous this doctrine sounds!"[66] Indeed, in his autobiographical account, Max describes his university years as rather isolated and lonely. He was alienated from all the societies that made up the social life of the university, the groups through which the student body bonded.[67]

Still Max took full advantage of what the university offered. In the first year he studied philosophy intensely. The University of Munich had recruited a stellar philosophy faculty, of whom the most important was Friedrich W. J. von Schelling (1775–1854). Schelling ranked with J. G. Fichte and G. W. F. Hegel as the most influential thinkers of German Idealism.[68] Of the 337 students, Max was one of only seven to receive the highest rank on his examinations. As a result he was recommended to the minister of the interior. In succeeding years he studied theology, Hebrew, Syriac, Chaldean, and classical languages, again obtaining the highest possible grades from his professors.[69] Passing these exams was the key to a successful future, providing access to civil service and other influential positions. At this stage Max passed the examination for rabbinic candidates, again with the highest grades. For most, this was sufficient certification, but some elected to work toward a doctorate, which required independent research culminating in a thesis. Max received access to the Hebrew and Chaldean manuscripts housed in the Royal Library in Munich. This treasure, which according to his account was completely unknown to scholars, became the basis for his doctoral research.[70] His dissertation, "Ueber den ursprung der jüdish-alexandrischen Religionsphilosophie," is interesting to us because it demonstrates Max's commitment to the *Wissenschaft* approach as applied to the history of Judaism. The document, more like a modern term paper, was about twenty-two pages long and offered few footnotes or quotations from ancient writers. However, Max's treatment of the material shows that he had fully mastered the historical and philological tools of the new *Wissenschaft* methodology. Underlying his thesis was the assumption that Jewish thought developed and changed from period to period to meet the needs of each new era; therefore it was necessary to examine the historical context in which these works were created. He began his analysis with the Jewish community at the end of the Babylonian exile in the late sixth century BCE. Emphasizing the discontinuities with the past, Max argued that post-exilic Judaism developed new types of leaders, as scribes and men of the Great Assembly replaced the prophets. Direct revelation was gradually replaced by the interpretation of the received Law as the means of governance, and Jewish monotheism was clarified through its confrontation with Chaldean and Persian paganism.[71] Jewish culture and thought had evolved in response to the needs of the times.

Max next turned his attention to the Jewish community of Alexandria, which took shape in Egypt in 331 BCE, after the conquest of the region by Alexander the Great. The Diaspora Jewish community there found itself threatened by a sophisticated syncretic environment inspired by Platonism, Stoicism, Pythagoreanism, and "Egyptian mysticism."[72] Max focused on two challenges to traditional Jewish thought: the concept of an ultimately unknowable God in Platonism and its theory of evil. Teaching that human understanding was limited to knowledge of the forms, Platonism challenged the possibility of direct divine revelation. Platonism also located evil's source in matter, the opposite of the spirit, whereas the biblical view took evil to be part of God's creation. In his study Max asserted that sophisticated Alexandrian Jews, led by the philosopher Philo, created a new Jewish philosophy to maintain their traditional faith in the face of these challenges. Out of the contradiction of these opposing systems came important advances in Jewish thought. Max even suggested that this synthesis had an important influence on early Christianity.[73] Max finished the dissertation and successfully defended it on August 17, 1838. This short paper put him squarely in the camp of the modern Jewish scholarship emerging in Germany in these years.

During their university years, Max and Samuel developed romantic relationships with two sisters, both daughters of their father's friend, Isaac Nettre. When Loew first settled in Munich, he befriended Isaac Nettre, originally from Alsace. Nettre, who spoke both French and German, was the Munich agent for the international banking firm of Solomon Hirsch. This firm helped supply money for the new Bavarian kingdom's building projects. He married Elise Levy, and they had a family of five girls and a boy. The children of the two families grew up together. The two oldest children, Clara (Caroline) and Babette (Pepi), born in 1818 and 1821, respectively, were attractive girls with soft brown eyes, black hair, and olive skin. According to family accounts, Pepi was especially pretty. "As a young girl when she was walking one day on the street in Munich, the King of Bavaria (probably Ludwig I) had paused and pinched her cheek. No doubt he had been attracted by her youthful charm, for he was a great connoisseur of beauty."[74] Max and Samuel, both tall redheads, began to court the Nettre girls while at the university, and by their graduation both were engaged. Samuel would marry the oldest daughter, Caroline, and Max proposed to Pepi. Later, the youngest of both families, Henrietta Lilienthal and Philip Nettre, would make a third union.

Samuel's engagement was straightforward. After receiving his medical degree in 1838, he served a yearlong internship at the Municipal Hospital of Munich. Both families encouraged him to begin his practice of medicine in America, probably because the Matrikel laws would not allow him to reside in Munich. In 1840, after receiving Caroline's promise to follow him soon, he settled in Allentown, Pennsylvania, where he began what would become a prominent career in homeopathic medicine.

Max's personal and professional life took more complex turns. After passing his university examination, in which he ranked among the top seven students in the university, Max was offered a job in the diplomatic service. Thrilled with the opportunity and the honor involved, he briefly considered forsaking his solemn promise to his mother about becoming a rabbi. His student and biographer David Philipson claims that Max felt compelled to consider the change in career course because of the fire that had destroyed much of the family's possessions. He felt responsible, as the oldest child, to assist in the rearing and support of his younger siblings. He was deeply disappointed to learn, however, that the appointment required conversion to Christianity. He rejected the offer indignantly, prompting the minister of foreign affairs to warn him that his attitude made a Bavarian diplomatic career impossible.[75] Max returned to his original plan—to become a rabbi.

Max and Pepi's long engagement went through many tumultuous ups and downs. His early letters to Pepi are full of romantic mood swings and overblown assertions of his feelings. In an undated early letter from Munich concerning their engagement, he wrote, "Mein Suesses Kind! [My sweet child] I am sick that I must write to you." Trying to smooth over a misunderstanding, he asserted that he loved her more and more daily.[76] In another early letter, dated August 22, 1839, Max described some existential crisis that seems to have gripped him while he was studying at the traditional Würzburg yeshiva, the stronghold of Orthodoxy after Fürth's yeshiva closed in 1830. He felt as though life had grasped him with a mighty force, attacking his soul, heart, and spirit. Anxiety and fear disturbed him to his innermost being. Yet the words of a note from Pepi had a magical power to soothe and restore him to a more peaceful, harmonious frame of mind.[77] Max found the people around him difficult, and he was moody under the strains of the preparation for his ministry. He was sustained by keeping his eye on what he was "striving to attain" and by his love for Pepi. "Even though much has until now remained obscure to me, one thing is clear and sure: that I love you deeply and sincerely and that you love me fully. Oh, believe me, it is a beautiful feeling to know that in this life that tries our hearts, there is one heart that beats for us, that lives with, and in and for us, and to whom we can give ourselves feely and completely."[78] It is this knowledge that gave him the courage to fight the battles that he faced, to endure until he could truly call himself hers. Max would have to wait six long years to marry his beloved Pepi.

While still a rabbinic candidate, Max delivered his first sermons to the Munich congregation. These addresses, published in 1839 under the title *Predigten für Sabbathe und Festtage*, exhibited the characteristics of a new style, cultivated by modern rabbis during his youth. The traditional *derashah*, delivered in place of a sermon, delved into the difficulties in passages of Scripture, using exegetical complexities and arcane literature. Max would scornfully comment that old-style preachers often used to find difficulties in passages of the Scriptures where none existed in order to show their ingenuity in solving them. They were full of rabbinic sophistries and kabbalistic subtleties.[79] This style was no longer understood by the majority of the rapidly Germanizing congregants. Meanwhile, Jews who visited Christian churches were impressed by both their decorum and edifying addresses. Many of the early Jewish preachers read works on homiletics, were friendly with their Christian colleagues, and even received critiques from their non-Jewish counterparts.[80] Despite its formal style, the sermon became the principal means to a spiritual end, namely, to exalt the heart of the worshiper. Its goal can be seen as the religious equivalent of *Bildung*, transforming and edifying the listener through moral reasoning. It was from the pulpit that the modern German rabbi would most effectively fulfill his task—to inspire his congregation to live according to divine law and to love one's neighbor, country, and humanity.[81]

At first, modern rabbis slavishly followed Christian structural models in their sermons. As community after community embraced the vernacular sermon, however, they were growing dissatisfied with the overly Christian style of the new Jewish homiletics. By the late 1830s, when Max first preached, there was a strong feeling that sermons should reintegrate some elements of the older exegetical style. Jewish themes and examples were used within the new homiletic structure.[82] Moses and Abraham, for example, might become exemplars of moral reasoning and the source of Jewish edification.

Max appealed often to the faith and "higher nature" of his listeners, admonishing them to be virtuous while adopting a severe, pietistic tone. In the first address, "Der Herr und sein Name der Einig-Eine," he suggested that the millennial suffering of the Jewish people had purified them, bringing them wisdom and virtue.[83] In "Die Beruf," Lilienthal contrasted the life ennobled by a higher calling to the slothful and meaningless pursuit of pleasure and sensuality.[84] The final sermon in the collection, "Unsterblickheit," contrasted those who lived with the awareness of their immortality and ultimate judgment with those who doubted these truths. The former were pilgrims, he claimed, who did not overvalue either the discomforts they encountered or the wealth and wisdom they might accumulate. The latter lived only for the moment, immersed in meaningless sensuality.[85] He played on the emotions of his congregants with graphic descriptions of the decay of the body in the grave, plundered by worms.[86]

As depressing as these passages were, they were part of a rhetorical technique whose goal was the uplifting of the listeners to holiness, piety, faith, and fear of God.[87] Each sermon ended with the triumphant assertion of a central Jewish belief, such as the unity of God and his name, the ultimate value of a life in harmony with God's will, or the immortality of the soul.

The sermons also drew on traditional Jewish sources. The addresses were replete with appropriate scriptural references. In the second sermon, Moses was offered as a paradigm for a life inspired by a divine calling. In the third, Max conjured up the patriarch Jacob's deathbed as a springboard for his discussion of immortality. Each sermon had a biblical proof-text from the Torah, Prophets, Psalms, and liturgy.[88] Max consistently used Jewish texts in the service of the contemporary goal of moral and spiritual edification.

While stylistically modern, Max's sermons were theologically traditional, in harmony with the religious conservatism of the congregation he addressed. He strove to impart spiritual edification, giving no hint of the sophisticated scholarship evident in his dissertation and certainly no reflection of the reformist currents of his time.[89] In a passionate passage that touched on the contemporary debate between reformers and traditionalists of the 1830s, Max blamed the arrogance of his era for the polarization that threatened the Jewish community and urged the parties to overcome the quarrels and strife that divided them.[90] When he asserted that contemporary Jews had placed their will above God's will and their reason above God's reason, he seemed to favor a traditional position. He urged the congregation not to abandon the Torah that had been revealed on that first Shavuot.[91] Invoking the words of Deuteronomy 29:9, he declared, "You all stand here today before the Eternal, your God."[92] He told them to unite to build Jewish institutions and schools and to sanctify God's name through righteousness. Then "the Jewish name would be cleansed of all stains and shame" and, true to the ancient faith, Jews would be prepared for the great day when all would recognize God as Father and Lord."[93] In these sermons, Max appears as a traditionalist rather than a reformer, advocating adherence to Torah as the basis for unity.

Max completed his rabbinic studies under Hirsch Aub, the rabbi of Munich and a moderate in the conflict between Reform and tradition. Aub had studied Talmud in Prague, but from 1826 to 1827 had enrolled in philosophy courses at the University of Munich to qualify for a rabbinic position under the new laws. In 1832, Aub established a synagogue choir in the new Munich synagogue and reorganized the traditional liturgy. His willingness to fight for these innovations showed that he had some sympathy of the modernizing trends within Judaism.[94] When Max published his dissertation in 1839, he dedicated it to his mentor and ordaining rabbi. Having attained both ordination and his doctorate in philosophy, he became one of about sixty rabbis in all of Germany with these credentials.[95]

The acquisition of a doctorate became the most conspicuous mark of the new type of rabbi that emerged in the mid-nineteenth century. The traditional rabbi interpreted the Law. He was responsible for all matters involving the life cycle, kashrut (dietary laws), and other legal decisions. If he was associated with a yeshiva, he would teach the advanced scholars but rarely young children. The occasional sermon was usually a legal discourse. The new, university-trained rabbi taught both the young and the old through sermons and lectures. He was in charge of the administration of charity, comforted the suffering, and represented the congregation in the broader community. Zacharias Frankel, leader of the Positive-Historical school, claimed in 1835 that the new rabbi constituted the lifeblood of the community. In his view, the modern rabbi represented the higher moral principle that transformed it into a spiritual whole.[96]

Although eager and well qualified, Max Lilienthal was unable to find a position in the modern German rabbinate. According to the family memoirs, he was rejected because of his progressive orientation. His nephew Ernest Lilienthal suggested that "the government had issued an order forbidding congregations from selecting candidates with liberal views. The order had been pushed by older rabbis, who regarded the Reform movement as the destruction of traditional Judaism."[97] The same government whose laws had created the new rabbinate by demanding university education now banned them from serving the Jewish community. Jews faced further restrictions concerning residency and were excluded from joining the army and from practicing law, and rabbis who were too modern were not eligible for pulpits. David Philipson confirms this view of a period of retrenchment on the part of the government. "In this bitter opposition to all religious reform they were playing with fire, for the government was not satisfied with legislating against this alone, but in 1838 an edict was issued which reenacted all the harshest restrictive measures against the Jews."[98]

The young university-trained rabbi suffered from this discrimination even though he was not associated with the Reform wing of German Judaism at this point. Max's rabbinic training had been traditional and, as noted, his rabbinic mentor, Hirsch Aub, was considered a moderate. Nothing in Max's dissertation indicated a particularly reformist orientation in practice. His choice of a historical topic allowed him to avoid any critical analyses of either biblical or talmudic documents, which would have been problematic to observant readers. His early sermons also expressed only traditional sentiments.

Nevertheless, there are hints from his circle of scholarly colleagues and friends that Max was sympathetic toward some reforms. A new mentor, Ludwig Philippson, was a moderate reformer. Born in 1811, just a few years before Max, Philippson attended the gymnasium and during his university years also studied Philo. After completing his dissertation on Plato and Aristotle in 1831, Philippson became a preacher and rabbi in Magdeburg; in 1837 he founded the weekly Jewish paper *Allgemeine Zeitung des Judenthums*, which he would edit for more than fifty years. Active in the fight for Jewish emancipation and an organizer of the Reform rabbinic conferences in the 1840s, Philippson emerged as an energetic and influential figure in progressive German Jewish circles.[99]

Max also conducted a correspondence with Isaac Noah Mannheimer, who became the "first teacher of religion" in the state-supported Viennese synagogue in 1825. Facing an ideologically divided community, Mannheimer introduced ritual and liturgical modifications in his synagogue by omitting some of the medieval poetry (*piyyutim*) from the services and by formulating a series of rules to foster decorum. At the time of Max's correspondence, Mannheimer's cantor, Solomon Sulzer, was composing his groundbreaking *Schir Zion* (1839), which combined Western musical traditions with traditional Jewish musical motifs and modes. The two created a liturgy and musical service that would unify their polarized community along the lines of moderate Reform.[100] It may be that, in the reactionary years immediately following his graduation, Max's association with these men made him suspect in the eyes of the conservative government as well as of the older rabbinic leaders.

The pressure to find a position was compounded by Max's engagement to his childhood sweetheart, Pepi, and by his desire as the oldest child to help support his family. Further, he needed employment to qualify for Matrikel status in Munich. As he continued to look for a pulpit, Max made use of his training in *Wissenschaft* by cataloging the collection of Hebrew manuscripts in the Royal Library in Munich that he had used in writing his dissertation. Between May 19, 1838, and November 16, 1839, Max wrote a series of "bibliographical notices" for Philippson's journal, the *Allgemeine Zeitung des Judenthums*. Published in the literary supplement, these reports described 313 manuscripts in varying detail, including Hebrew Bibles, prayer books, medieval Jewish philosophy treatises, traditional commentaries, kabbalistic texts, and grammatical discourses. Max also began a history of the Jews of Bavaria, which was never completed.[101]

Max's scholarly work impressed Philippson. Despairing of the political future for Jews in Bavaria, not to mention his own professional prospects, Max was pleased when his mentor recommended him for rabbinic posts in

Leipzig and Szegedin, Hungary. While Max negotiated with these congregations, Philippson received a letter from the congregation in Riga requesting help in finding a modern rabbi and teacher to serve in Russia. According to the letter from Russian minister of education Sergei Uvarov, "a German teacher and preacher" was preferred, "since German was the mother tongue of the Jews of Riga." The letter continued, "Such a man was not to be found in Russia where there was no modern education and no modern enlightenment among the Jews. The leader they desired must be a man of modern culture, but of conservative religious tendencies."[102] Philippson immediately recommended the 24-year-old Max for that position as well. Rabbi Mannheimer of Vienna convinced the young rabbi to take the Russian post, arguing that something had to be done for the backward Russian Jews. Looking back on this fateful decision, Max admitted that he was thrilled with the opportunity to contribute to such an important undertaking as the modernization of Russian Jewish education. "The sphere of activity in such a vast empire flattered my youthful vanity, and hoping for the best results of my sincere endeavors—to raise millions of Jews to a higher standard—I asked the Russian ambassador at Munich for my passport."[103] As historian Steven Aschheim noted, German Jews often believed that they had a mission to remake all other Jews in their image, based on the values of secular education and *Bildung*. By implementing modern education, these missionaries sought to uplift their unemancipated brethren, transforming them into useful citizens. In Aschheim's view, "Max Lilienthal's famous attempt in the 1840s to modernize Russian Jewish schools . . . is the classic example." Max's mission came to represent an epochal encounter between German Jewish and Russian Jewish cultures at an important moment in Russian Jewish history.[104] With a missionary's zeal, Max set off for the East, confident that modern education would create the conditions necessary for the emancipation of the masses of downtrodden Russian Jewry.

2

Exporting Haskalah

The Russian Misson

The young rabbi may not have been so enthusiastic about going to Russia if he had truly understood the political drama into which he was naively walking. The cast of characters, most of whom only partly understood each other, had contradictory motivations. The most powerful player was the emperor, Tsar Nicholas I, who rose to power in December 1825. From the beginning, he sought to create a personal absolutism so pervasive that it would control the lives of everyone in Russia.[1] Ruling over a vast and diverse empire, the tsar strove to create uniformity under the slogan "Orthodoxy, autocracy, and nationality." The Jews were among the most isolated, unassimilated people within the empire, separated by religion, lifestyle, language, and education. Nicholas resented their differences and accepted the common anti-Semitic critique of their destructive role in Russian life. In his 1816 diary, he blamed them for the impoverishment of the peasants in the provinces, calling them leeches that completely exhausted the area.[2] His solution was to convert them by any means possible. Tsar Nicholas was served by a group of ministers who came almost exclusively from a military background and who were dedicated to fulfilling his will.

Under the reign of the previous tsar, Alexander I (r. 1801–25), Russian officials used a combination of carrot and stick to assimilate their recalcitrant Jewish subjects. In 1804, Jews were allowed to attend all state schools and universities. Few availed themselves of the privilege, though, remaining true to the traditional system of heder and yeshiva. At the same time, the code of 1804 restricted their residence to the Pale of Settlement—former Polish and Baltic lands acquired by the Russian empire—and ordered their expulsion from villages.[3]

In 1827, soon after Nicholas took the throne, the government passed the Recruitment of the Jews legislation. This oppressive law set high quotas for Jewish recruits, ranging in age from 12 to 25. Believing all Jews to be cowards, Nicholas urged that they be put in the navy so that they would have fewer opportunities to desert. Those under the age of 18—and as young as 12—would join special units called Cantonist battalions, which were made up of criminals, vagabonds, political prisoners, gypsies, and illegitimate children. These units were a means of social and police control. That the conscription had a conversionary goal was clear from the beginning. In July 1829 Nicholas ordered commanding officers to separate Jews who would convert from those who would not. Further, army priests could baptize Jews without prior authorization from their bishops. Given the age and vulnerability of these children, it is not surprising that baptisms occurred at a steady rate.[4] Conscription and conversion through the military became the crux of Nicholas's Jewish policy. The Jewish community responded with bitterness, distrust, and further alienation. Moreover, the harsh draft quotas caused internal strife in Jewish communities because they fell disproportionately on the sons of the poor, whose families could not offer bribes for their freedom.

In 1835, Nicholas ordered the governmental Jewish committee to standardize the tangle of Jewish policies in the realm. The resulting statutes reaffirmed the 1804 education law and extended it. The following year a new censorship law set up a commission of rabbis to examine all books before publication. Yet the general thrust of the government opinion on the eve of Lilienthal's arrival was still deep dissatisfaction with the progress of Jewish assimilation. Worse, local officials were pressing the government to enact further repressive measures against the Jews, believing them to be responsible for poverty in Ukraine and Belarus because of their occupations as traders and middlemen. Recent access to the Soviet archives has shown that this rising group of Jewish capitalists, a new elite, was able to exercise considerable influence on the Russian government, especially in the generations following Lilienthal. Ironically, the emergence of wealthy Jewish entrepreneurs was an inadvertent effect of Nicholas's economic policies.[5]

Although the Jewish community was not monolithic, the vast majority was deeply traditional, made up of two major groups with a history of confrontation: the Hasidim (followers of the eighteenth-century mystic known as the Baal Shem Tov) and the Mitnagdim (strictly Orthodox Jews but opponents of Hasidism). Both groups remained immersed in the world of Jewish sacred texts. Most knew little Russian, had never studied any secular subject or foreign language, and had little interest in anything outside their intensely Jewish world.

When Lilienthal entered Vilna for the first time, he recalled Napoleon's words: "Gentlemen, I think we are in Jerusalem."[6] All the businessmen, craftsmen, and day laborers were Jews. Lilienthal was also struck by how all the activity came to a standstill on the Sabbath. Every aspect of life was permeated with Jewish study and practice. These Jews, living essentially the same way they had for centuries, profoundly mistrusted the motives of the Russian government.

A much smaller group of Jewish intellectuals had emerged in the 1820s and 1830s. This was the nascent Russian Jewish Enlightenment (Haskalah). Inspired by the example of Moses Mendelssohn in Germany in the previous century, these individuals saw the promise of combining secular studies with traditional learning. They denigrated the backwardness of their coreligionists, disparaged the Yiddish language that was spoken by the Jewish masses, despised their mysticism, and lamented their lack of worldly knowledge. Following the political theories of the German Haskalah, they also believed that by aligning themselves with the government, they could both bring Enlightenment (secular learning) to the masses of Russian Jews and in the process earn emancipation—or at least, civil equality—for their people. According to Shmuel Feiner, "They truly believed that the 'benevolent emperor' would 'heal the wounds and end the tribulations of the Jewish people.'"[7]

With virtually no power base and unable to get even rabbinic censors to publish their books, the Russian Maskilim turned their attention to educational reform. Overcoming traditional opposition, they opened a series of modern schools that taught secular subjects along with traditional Jewish texts. In Odessa, for example, a modern school opened in 1826 with an enrollment of 63 students; within a year it had grown to 250.[8] In 1829, a Maskil named Bezalel Stern took over the administration; by 1835 the school boasted 289 students. The six-year curriculum, based on the Central European Haskalah model from Galicia, combined modern languages, history, archaeology, geography, literature, mathematics, and sciences with study of the Bible (with Mendelssohn's translation and commentary), Hebrew grammar, and some Talmud.[9] In 1835, a girls' branch was opened with an enrollment of sixty pupils. Encouraged by this success, Stern opened another school in Kishinev in 1838, modeled after Odessa's curriculum. In 1838, the officials of the Jewish community of Riga received permission from the national government to invite an enlightened German rabbi to head a German-style school in their community,[10] a position Max Lilienthal eagerly applied for and accepted.

Lilienthal left Munich on October 8, 1839, armed with his passport and letters of recommendations to education minister Count Uvarov from the Russian ambassador in Munich and the Bavarian minister, Prince Wallerstein. In his memoirs, published over a decade later in the Cincinnati Jewish paper the *Israelite* in 1855–57, Lilienthal remembered leaving "with an easy heart from my sweet home." The letters he sent home during that period, however, tell another story. In a letter to his family from St. Petersburg, dated October 25, 1839, he exclaims, "Tears of the warmest, deepest longing fall from my eyes as I try to write these lines to you, which are to inform you of my arrival at this place." A year and a half later, in a letter to his brother Samuel he recalls "the pangs of separation," which he is loath to reopen.[11] As he reminds us in his memoirs, he was only 25 years old. No amount of missionary zeal could compensate for his anxiety at leaving his family and his fiancée. As his letters home reveal, Lilienthal had left a tight-knit family circle.

Before taking leave of Germany, Lilienthal planned his trip so that he could meet some of the leaders of German Jewry. First he visited Ludwig Philippson in Magdeburg, from whom he received letters of recommendation to present to the congregation as well as travel expenses for the trip, which the Riga community had sent to him through Philippson.[12] Meeting his mentor for the first time, Lilienthal told his brother that he was very taken with this "tall, lanky young man, with a face made aged by the deep lines of study and experience."[13] After spending an exciting day at his home, he felt Philippson would remain an inspiration in the challenges he would face.

Leaving Magdeburg, Lilienthal sailed up the Elbe River to Hamburg, where Reform Judaism had first struck permanent roots. Dedicated in 1818, the Reform temple in Hamburg had developed the first Reform liturgy and became the epicenter for fierce polemical battles between traditionalists and reformers. Although he was unimpressed with the building itself, which would be replaced a few years later, Lilienthal enjoyed meeting its two preachers, Eduard Kley and Gotthold Salomon. The two men, he recalled, were a study in contrasts. He found Salomon "a well-proportioned, competent man, whose conversation was fascinating, witty and genial," with a full household of sons and an attractive daughter. Although an autodidact, he was a charismatic speaker who played an important role in early Reform. Salomon was one of the first rabbis to emulate Christian sermon style and had also been an advocate for Jewish emancipation. In 1837 he had collaborated with Isaac Noah Mannheimer to publish a Bible translation for Jewish schools.[14] In contrast, according to Lilienthal, Kley was a "small, sniveling man, without children and with much money, with little heart but with all the more intellect." Armed with a doctorate from the University of Berlin, Kley was more pedantic than Salomon. His sermons, Lilienthal observed, spoke to the mind rather than the heart.[15] Lilienthal also met the more traditional but university-educated chief rabbi of the Hamburg community, Isaac Bernays, who was seeking to modernize the community synagogue within the parameters of Jewish law. Bernays formulated the basis for "Modern Orthodoxy," which influenced the views of his disciple, Samson Raphael Hirsch, who became its leading spokesman.[16]

Lilienthal's next stop was in neighboring Altona, whose synagogue far exceeded his expectations. He met there with Solomon Steinheim, whom he called "the Maimonides of our day," presumably because Steinheim was a physician who wrote on medical subjects and theology and composed music and poetry as well. In 1835, Steinheim had published the first of four volumes of a theological defense of Judaism. A champion of Jewish emancipation, he also supported the ritual reforms of the Hamburg temple. His home was a meeting place for leading contemporary writers, artists, and musicians.[17]

After a short stay in Lübeck, which he characterized as "a free imperial city of no significance and without special spirit," Lilienthal boarded the large steamer *Nicolai* on October 19, bound for St. Petersburg.[18] Coming from landlocked Bavaria, he was excited by the voyage, even though he suffered from seasickness an entire day of the journey. He found some distraction in the company of several high Russian officials on board who were initially friendly but became cold and distant when they reached Russian waters. On October 24 the *Nicolai* arrived at Kronstadt, a fortified island base serving St. Petersburg. No sooner had the ship cast anchor when customs and police officers came on board and seized the passengers' belongings and passports. The foreign visitors were told the items would be returned in St. Petersburg at the Bureau of Police for Strangers. The travelers were transferred to a small steamboat on which they made the hour and a half trip up the Neva River to St. Petersburg. Along the way they passed majestic views of the imperial summer residence of Peterhof. The young man's excitement grew as he arrived in the magnificent city. He reacted like a tourist to the famous sights: the Peter monument, the senate, the Admiralty, the imperial palace, and the columns of Nevsky Prospect.[19] In his first letter home, written the day after his arrival, Lilienthal reveals his youthful enthusiasm. "St. Petersburg! This exceeds all expectations. A city five miles in circumference—nothing but palaces—surely this is to be seen nowhere else. Whoever has not seen St. Petersburg has not seen the world."[20] After paying a fee to get his baggage and documents back, Lilienthal found lodging at a German hotel on the beautiful main thoroughfare, Nevsky Prospect. He received a friendly reception from Baron Falkenberg, whose sister his family knew in Munich. The next morning he brought his letter of recommendation to the Bavarian ambassador, Count Lerchenfeld, who promised to personally introduce him to Count Uvarov by the next Sunday. The inexperienced youth believed all was going smoothly. Within a few days he would learn that Lerchenfeld's promise was in vain. Uvarov had gone to Warsaw on business the very day that Lilienthal had arrived. Lilienthal had been advised by the Bavarian ambassador not to leave St. Petersburg until he had met with Count Uvarov, because the education minister was the key to the success of his Russian career. His letter home, dated November 1, optimistically predicted that he would be delayed two weeks longer, but as his memoir reports, Lilienthal waited six weeks. He recalled that the news dampened his enthusiasm to begin at once "the great work of the civilization of the Russian Jews."[21] Because Lilienthal had some time on his hands, he was determined to learn as much as he could about this country.

Lilienthal gravitated toward the scant Jewish life in the capital—all of it associated with the Jews in the army. St. Petersburg—in Russia proper, outside the Pale of Settlement—was prohibited to Jews without a special permit; all the Jews he met there had ties to the military. He visited the home of the *gabbai* (sexton) of the synagogue associated with the fortress,[22] where he had a wonderful meal and taught them a passage from the Mishnah (the third-century compilation of Jewish law). He witnessed a Jewish soldier's wedding as well, a joyous traditional ceremony that he described in detail in his memoirs. Lilienthal also attended Sabbath services, where soldiers from the various regiments prayed in full uniform. He was impressed by the fervent devotion of the cantor and the precision with which the Torah was read.[23]

Lilienthal's level of religious observance during this period is revealed in his letters home and in his memoirs. Because few Jews were permitted to live in St. Petersburg, Lilienthal initially had trouble getting a kosher meal. Converted Jews sought him out and invited him to dinner, but he would accept only tea, not a meal, at their homes. He soon began to feel lonely in the immense capital. Finally, a member of the congregation of Riga arrived and introduced him to a Jewish soldier and his family who offered him dinner. His host, a tall, decorated soldier with a big mustache, and his Polish wife served him a sumptuous, if rather unclean meal. Lilienthal recalls that he stuffed himself on fish, soup, poultry, and pie after having fasted about fourteen days. (This is clearly self-dramatization by Lilienthal, writing in Cincinnati years later.)[24] Later, when he left St. Petersburg for Riga, Lilienthal refused to continue his journey on the Sabbath. "I declared to my fellow travelers that I had to leave them, for, as I professed Judaism, it was forbidden me by law to travel on the Sabbath."[25] These passing remarks, taken together, show that the young rabbi was willing to go to some lengths to follow Jewish law. At this stage of his life, he seems to have been relatively traditional by German Jewish standards, despite his shaven face and modern clothes. In an early encounter with a Russian general, Lilienthal declared, "I feel myself as sound a Jew as the strictest in the whole empire." As he would find out in Russia, levels of observance were relative.[26]

Despite urgent messages from the congregation in Riga asking him to come as soon as possible, Lilienthal remained in St. Petersburg, determined to meet with Count Uvarov. It was not easy to remain in the capital because foreign Jews were not allowed without a Russian passport and Lilienthal was not yet installed in his job. Without legal recourse, he was called to the Bureau of Police for Strangers, where he obtained an extension by offering a bribe. Lilienthal learned quickly that this was standard procedure in Russia. Petty officials regularly demanded bribes; refusal to pay cost more money and trouble in the end. The second time he was called, he had to go to the general of police, who reluctantly granted him a further extension. In the meantime, the congregant from Riga who was there to escort him to his rabbinic post got into trouble with the law because his passport had expired. Lilienthal was implicated in this affair and avoided arrest only because of his acquaintance with the Bavarian minister.[27]

While he waited, Lilienthal picked up more information about his new pulpit. He wrote home that his school would have eleven rooms, five for his personal use. He was told incorrectly that the rabbi was to be dismissed that winter, with his functions passing to Lilienthal. Revealing his youthful cockiness, he bragged to his family that he would be a rabbi before many Bavarian candidates back home. He looked forward to officiating at six weddings that winter. He confided to his father that he would be glad to get away from St. Petersburg, with its "dreadful excitement" that robbed him of his sense of balance. He longed to begin his work in Riga.[28]

Finally Lilienthal's patience was rewarded when Count Uvarov returned from Warsaw. Lilienthal rushed to see the Bavarian ambassador for a letter of introduction, only to be told that the ambassador had been transferred to Berlin. Fortunately, the ambassador's chargé d'affaires wrote Lilienthal an official letter of recommendation. Armed with this note and one from the Russian embassy in Munich, Lilienthal took his carriage to the minister's palace. The Ministry of Education was built in a half-circle, divided by three immense porticos. The count lived in the right wing, consisting of 120 apartments. The left wing housed about 100 officials, divided according to the seven districts of the empire. One can only imagine the young rabbi's mood as his sleigh stopped and he climbed the marble stairs leading to the minister's palace that Friday morning. Believing that his fate in Russia depended on the impression he made at this meeting, Lilienthal remembered feeling uneasy. He waited less than ten minutes before he was ushered into Uvarov's presence. The count worked in a large room adjacent to an immense salon covered in red silk and decorated with many paintings. Lilienthal's anxiety melted the minute they met. "Instead of a Russian bear, whom I had expected to meet, I found a thorough gentleman, whose highly intellectual features made the most favorable impression on me. Uwaroff is a man of middle size, lean and thin; but his high forehead, sharp eyes, aquiline nose, and fine mouth, showing at once the philosopher, the shrewd statesman, and kind-hearted disposition, win for him at once the heart of everyone who comes in contract with him."[29] Lilienthal bowed as Uvarov came up to shake his hand and greet him in German. He asked about his birthplace and education and read his testimonials. Telling him that the emperor was establishing a committee to study the condition of Jews in Russia, he invited Lilienthal to return the next evening so that he could discuss his ideas for the reform of Jewish education. In the meantime, he wrote a letter of recommendation to the minister of the interior so that Lilienthal might meet him. The young rabbi left so elated that he recited all the psalms he knew by heart.

Lilienthal's interview with the interior minister, Count Stroganoff, went just as well. Dressed in a military uniform, he addressed Lilienthal frankly about the need for "the regeneration" of the Jewish people. He advised him to cooperate with the government but warned him that his task would not be easy and invited him to return anytime he might need advice.

It seemed that the long wait had finally borne fruit. Lilienthal had met and established relations with key officials at the highest levels of the Russian government. The Jews, who were anxiously awaiting his return, congratulated him on the success of his first interviews. During the Sabbath that followed, they shared their advice and opinions as to what Lilienthal should say to the minister at their next meeting.

That Saturday evening, according to his later account, Lilienthal and Count Uvarov discussed the backward state of Russian Jewry and what needed to be done to modernize it. Uvarov began by telling him that the emperor had just established a committee to address that challenge and frankly expressed the government's frustration with Jewish recalcitrance.

He listed a series of rights and privileges that the emperor had granted, including exemption from the military to those who would become farmers or the opportunity to study classics in the Russian schools. Nicholas was impatient, Uvarov warned, and demanded substantial results. He hinted that bad times would be in store for the Jews if they resisted modernization, but the brightest future was possible for this "highly gifted people" if they seized this opportunity.

Uvarov also listened to the young rabbi, insisting that he was eager to hear his views. Lilienthal, a zealous representative of Haskalah, advocated the introduction of Russian language and secular subjects into modern Jewish schools. Uvarov agreed and directed him to write up a plan for higher and lower schools. Citing the model of France, Lilienthal concluded with a bold plea for Jewish emancipation. "Let the emperor at once proclaim the emancipation of the Jews, and let him then issue any ukase whatever to begin the work of Jewish reform in earnest, to cut short the exclusive study of the Talmud. . . . I dare avouch that in ten years hence they will surpass the most sanguine expectations of the imperial government."[30] Lilienthal made his case by pointing out that there was nothing stopping Tsar Nicholas, an autocratic ruler, from setting "a magnanimous and liberal example to Europe," for which he would be applauded by all good men.

Uvarov enjoyed Lilienthal's enthusiasm but demurred with regard to immediate emancipation. The Jews had to earn the favor of the emperor first, he warned. Lilienthal remembered sighing and thinking to himself, "The same old game was to be played here too." He had grown up in a country that also demanded that Jews prove their worthiness for emancipation. As he reported in his memoirs years later, he knew then that his mission would be difficult.[31] Still, the relationship had gotten off to a favorable start. Uvarov had been pleased with Lilienthal's enthusiasm for modernization on the European model, and Lilienthal felt embraced by a father figure who seemed to take his ideas seriously. More important, Uvarov's position joined perfectly with the maskilic belief in the benevolent tutelary state.[32]

This crucial relationship has been interpreted in different ways. Some historians cast Uvarov as a villain. The Lubavitcher biographer Joseph Schneersohn claimed that Nicholas had instructed Uvarov to cultivate the friendship with Lilienthal "to learn whether he and his companions who had abandoned Judaism would be the proper medium for bringing the Jews into the Christian fold."[33] Israel Zinberg, in his multivolume *History of Jewish Literature*, characterized Uvarov as a "crafty courtier, an unprincipled careerist with enormous ambition and narcissism" who manipulated the young Lilienthal to further the tsar's agenda, namely, to promote "the unified spirit of Orthodoxy, Autocracy, and Nationality." He points to a "secret memorandum" that revealed a conversionary intent behind the goal of educational modernization.[34]

Historian Michael Stanislawski challenged this accepted view, claiming that Uvarov's intellectual and cultural home was in Germany. He spoke French, German, Italian, and English fluently and preferred them to Russian, especially in his writing. He wrote essays in the classics and Oriental studies that were published in Paris in the 1840s.[35] In fact, in his own ministry journal in 1835 Uvarov wrote sympathetically about the Jewish people. "The existence of a nation dispersed over the face of the earth for centuries, persecuted and despised by all, but energetic and industrious, to whom we are all indebted for many important discoveries, must occupy an important place in the history of European enlightenment."[36] Uvarov, a romantic nationalist, had an unconventional understanding of his Orthodox Christian faith, viewing it as a "statist, nonpartisan Christianity" in which each nation must find its own separate development based on its unique spirit.[37] Uvarov did hold a general view that civic society, true culture, and Christianity were all linked. Presumably he believed that the ideal citizen would be a Christian. Even so, Uvarov "does *not* say that the Jews will or should be converted to Christianity" in the proposed modern schools.[38] Rather, Uvarov wanted to Europeanize Russian Jews, not convert them. If Lilienthal understood himself to be an ambassador of German Jewish culture to the backward Russian Jews, he could have found no one more sympathetic toward his views at the Russian court than Count Uvarov. Lilienthal was not the only Maskil who thought well of Uvarov. Isaac Baer Levinsohn (the leader of the Russian Maskilim) characterized him as "the 'selfless helper' who decided to drive away the deep darkness which prevailed over the Jewish quarter through light and enlightenment."[39]

Uvarov wanted Lilienthal to meet Counselor Duksta-Dykshinski before he left for Riga. Duksta-Dykshinski, who was fluent in French and German, was the chief clerk for the affairs of the kingdom of Poland and for the Jews, a member of the imperial committee of censors, and an employee of the Ministry of Education. He warned Lilienthal, after an otherwise pleasant conversation, not to be too self-confident. "You are still very young," he added, "unacquainted with the sly and slippery ways of the art of government."[40] The counselor was clearly well disposed toward Lilienthal, because he invited him to his home to meet his family. Lilienthal was asked to put his views on the regeneration of the Jews in writing. After submitting his report to the counselor later that week, Lilienthal encountered one of the less tolerant members of the Russian government: Count Pratasoff, president of the Imperial Synod. Pratasoff wondered why someone who had actually studied Christian theology had not converted. Lilienthal, offended by the question, defended his faith but was left troubled by the conversionary impulse of this important leader. The young ambassador of Haskalah could not tolerate the missionary zeal of the Russian Orthodox official. Lilienthal invariably reacted in anger whenever Russians tried to convert him during his years there.

Having fulfilled his duties in St. Petersburg, Lilienthal was finally ready to depart for Riga. In a final meeting with Uvarov, he received a letter of recommendation to his future chief, Mr. Napierski, director of the state of Livonia, and a final encouraging talk. Uvarov urged Lilienthal to raise the young school to perfection and not to be discouraged by difficulties and assured him of the support of the government and of the promise of rewards for his success. Uvarov embraced Lilienthal and kissed him on both cheeks. Lilienthal was overwhelmed by this honor, which he took as evidence of the minister's favor.

Lilienthal left St. Petersburg on December 28, 1839, after a productive stay of a little over two months. He boarded a sleigh, along with other passengers, after giving his passport to the conductor. In the frigid Russian winter, everyone was wrapped in fur from head to foot. The sleigh traveled quickly across the countryside as the passengers conversed in German. Unfortunately the roads were in terrible condition, and the sleigh was jarred and rocked and came close to turning over. Lilienthal, who had a problem with motion sickness, felt so tired from the rocking that he begged to be left behind. The passengers convinced him to continue, promising to stop the sleigh whenever he needed to have some relief. After about an hour and a half, he had such a violent attack that he had to dismount, fainting to the ground. When he awoke, the sleigh was pulling away into the night. He ran as fast as he could, attempting to overtake it, but soon lost its tracks in the deep snow. Taking the wrong turn, he became lost in the knee-deep snow, alone in the woods without his passport or any provisions. He wandered through the cold until he finally sat down and recited his evening prayers. Too cold to remain stationary, he continued walking for hours until he realized he had been going in a circle. Finally, feeling feverish and unable to walk any farther, he sat down on a huge stone and recited the prayer for the dying. He sat there remembering his family and his fiancée, sure that he would never see them again. Finally he fell asleep. In the meantime, the sleigh driver, realizing his mistake, had gone to the next village where he recruited the local farmers to bring torches to search for Lilienthal.

A Russian serf, who happened upon Lilienthal along the road, saved his life. The kindly peasant took him to an inn, where Lilienthal thawed out before a fire, warmed by a considerable amount of brandy. Early the next morning a driver brought him to the next inn, where he met his original group. After a hearty breakfast the travelers continued their trip without incident.

They reached Dorpat (Tartu), Estonia, the seat of the only German university in Russia, on Friday afternoon. Here Lilienthal insisted that the travelers leave him behind, because he would not travel on the Sabbath. While in Dorpat, Lilienthal explored the university and its library but foolishly neglected to visit one of his future chiefs, Lieutenant-General Kraftstroem, who was regent of the university and in charge of upper and lower schools in Livonia, Kurland, and Estonia. Lilienthal admitted in his memoirs that, coming from the free academic environment at Munich, he was unable to reconcile himself to the fact that his new superior was a military commander. Lilienthal felt alienated by the military rules and discipline that permeated the school and by the uniforms that both students and faculty wore. Snubbing his superior revealed his immaturity, allowing his sense of German superiority to override appropriate behavior in the present circumstances.[41]

On Saturday evening, when the Sabbath had ended, Lilienthal continued by sleigh, using his trunk as a seat. Managing to fall asleep, he awoke to find himself deep in a snow bank. This time he was not abandoned because the driver had also fallen asleep and had been thrown from the sleigh in a near-collision with a passing vehicle. Gathering his luggage, Lilienthal remounted and they continued without incident, changing sleighs at every station.

Lilienthal saw the steeples of Riga in the distance by Sunday afternoon. Again his youthful insecurity asserted itself as he worried about the reception he would receive. He recalled the "antipathy of the Russian and Polish Jews" toward their German coreligionists. "I knew very well how little they [Russian Jews] think of their [German] abilities, and how far superior they fancy themselves." He feared that they would judge him for his strange dress and that he would not be able to understand the Yiddish they spoke. Most of all, he feared that he would not be taken seriously in a society where only the experience that comes with old age is revered.[42] Fortunately his fears were unwarranted, because the welcoming committee was dressed in European garb, spoke correct German, and was eager to engage him. In fact, Riga had been part of the German cultural sphere since its origins, dating from 1226, when its charter was modeled on that of the German Hansa towns. The Germans remained the social elite and determined Riga's political, economic, and social life even after its annexation by Peter the Great in 1710. Consequently, in the early nineteenth century, Riga, the fifth largest city in the Russian Empire, had the characteristics of a northern German city; German was still the language of business and culture, even for the Jews.[43]

The next morning, Lilienthal was met at his hotel and taken to the schoolhouse. Situated in the center of the city, it consisted of eleven rooms. The sexton greeted him at the door with genuine warmth. This 68-year-old man with a silvery white beard would be his host, because the trustees thought that Lilienthal, being a bachelor, should board with the sexton's family. After touring the small school, the young rabbi admired its open, airy feeling and comfortable furnishings. The ladies of the congregation brought in cakes, wine, and brandy to welcome him.[44]

That evening the trustees took him to meet the old rabbi, whom Lilienthal believed he was replacing. He recalled, "I never saw a more patriarch-like man." With his long silver-white beard and high stature, the rabbi evoked a feeling of true reverence in Lilienthal as he shook his hand. In the description, written years later, one can still sense the younger man's feeling of intimidation. He knew that the rabbi "enjoyed the unbounded confidence of his congregation in religious affairs, being an eminent Talmudist"; even Christian merchants preferred his judgments to those of the Russian courts. The older man graciously greeted Lilienthal, saying, "I will be your father, and whenever you want my advice please call on me."[45] Evidently he was unaware of the plan to relieve him of his duties. Lilienthal thanked him and met his wife, who greeted him as her husband's new assistant. The young rabbi managed, inadvertently, to insult her by refusing some of the food she offered him, a violation of local hospitality. They patched things up over a Sabbath meal, after which the rabbi again promised to be his friend and advocate.[46]

Upon his arrival, Lilienthal had to negotiate a series of political landmines. First he met Counselor Napierski, director of schools in Livonia, to whom he delivered Count Uvarov's letter of recommendation. Although the director greeted him warmly enough, he feared that Lilienthal had secret instructions from St. Petersburg, based on the Russian government's continuing attempts to Russianize this German province. In addition, as a fervent Protestant, he worried that Lilienthal's influence would undermine his missionary efforts among the Jews of Riga. Fortunately, Napierski, though never very helpful, never actively obstructed Lilienthal either. Lilienthal also met the bishop of the Greek Orthodox church. The bishop hoped that the young rabbi would help him gain influence over the German-oriented leadership in Riga, which had long opposed allowing him an official palace within the city limits. He had supported the establishment of a Jewish school to further his own fight against the German hegemony of the local leadership. The Russian bishop made the mistake, several weeks later, of trying to convert Lilienthal. He even offered to give Lilienthal the necessary instruction. Lilienthal reacted indignantly, as he always did when attempts were made to convert him. The two saw each other only once more during his entire stay in Riga.[47]

Gradually, Lilienthal came to understand that the Jewish community also had a political motivation for founding the modern German Jewish school. The old Swedish and German commercial elite of Riga wanted to protect their lucrative trade privileges in the thriving city by excluding Jews from residency, in direct contradiction to recent changes in Russian law. The Jews, embroiled in a five-year lawsuit in which they were fighting for the right to live in Riga, hoped that the new school would give them a foothold that would lead to this right.[48]

The formal opening of the school on January 15, 1840, was a festive event, attended by the governor of the state, the director of schools, other local aristocrats, the Catholic and Protestant clergy, and the Russian bishop. After the older rabbi said a short prayer, Lilienthal delivered the inaugural sermon. The entire audience congratulated him, urging him to publish the address. Lilienthal sent copies to the imperial family and other high functionaries in St. Petersburg. In spite of his youth, Lilienthal knew how to promote himself. Clearly his instinct had been correct, because six months later he received a valuable diamond ring from the tsar in acknowledgment of his address.[49] The community also published Lilienthal's later sermons, which he dedicated to Count Uvarov. In the preface, Lilienthal articulated his mission to raise the level of Russian Jewry to that of the Jews of Western Europe. He compared Russian Jewry to a sick man who cannot heal himself. In the fawning manner of the Haskalah, he declared that "no other government . . . has so earnestly and energetically undertaken to regenerate Judaism and to organize it as 'Russia's great monarch' and his ministers."[50]

From the outset, Lilienthal threw himself into the work of making the school the success that he had promised Uvarov it would be. In February 1840 he wrote to Pepi that he began his studies at five in the morning. He taught school from eight until four and, after a short break, he conducted a confirmation class for boys and one for girls. Most evenings he was busy with a variety of meetings, as head of the Orphan Association and a member of the school commission, the congregational board, and the synagogue committee. Otherwise, he received visitors at home until nine at night. He also kept the school's records and accounts. In addition, he preached every three weeks. In letters to his family and fiancée, he complained that he had many visitors every day and still more letters to write. He received petitions and requests from a wide area. He had to visit the sick and care for the poor, all in addition to his daily teaching.[51]

Included in this description of his duties were some innovations that Lilienthal introduced into the community. Especially important was the institution of confirmation for both girls and boys. Confirmation was "adopted from Christianity, where it represented the culmination of a course of study intended to prepare the young person for adult status in the church."[52] The first Jewish confirmation had been performed in Dessau in 1803 under Israel Jacobson, an important early Reform leader. The rite was among the reforms that spread throughout various German states in the 1820s and 1830s, when it took on a more Jewish character. Despite the criticism of its detractors, many believed that confirmation was more successful as an educational device than the ceremony of becoming a bar mitzvah because it emphasized intellectual understanding over rote learning.[53]

Lilienthal began his class of seven young women in the spring, four months before Shavuot, but soon the number grew to twenty-five. Some parents apparently sent their daughters, hoping that Lilienthal would be interested in marriage. They were amazed that the *apikores* (atheist) actually desired to teach them about theology. At first Lilienthal met resistance, but eventually he told his brother Samuel, "They saw that this thing called confirmation consisted of nothing but instruction in the holiest, highest interests of mankind." Lilienthal reported to Samuel that the first confirmation service was an inspiring celebration.[54]

Lilienthal hoped to introduce other changes into the service. He complained that even the most enlightened members of the congregation believed that devotion and heartfelt prayer were impossible without "loud ejaculations and violent motions." Through "unwearying persistence" Lilienthal succeeded in removing only the "crassest abuses."[55]

After hearing about some destitute orphan boys wandering around the city, Lilienthal convinced the board of trustees to transform a number of empty rooms in the schoolhouse into an orphanage. He galvanized the community into action as they furnished the rooms, gathered the children from the shanties in which they were hiding, bathed and clothed them, and contracted the sexton's wife to provide them with board.[56]

Despite his busy schedule, Lilienthal could not obliterate his sense of loneliness and alienation from those around him. He felt like a "stranger in a strange land," constantly aware of his differences from the Russian Jews he served. He wrote to his father and future father-in-law of his alienation. "I have no other joy here, exiled from all that I hold dear in my native country."[57] He thought that they judged him to be a heretic, based on his shaved face and modern ways. He was the *Datshel*, a slang term for a German Jew. They did not understand his sermons and mistook the motivations for his innovations. It did not help that Lilienthal disdained them as well.

In his letters home, he described the backward state of the Jewish community he served. "The Jew with his dirty *fischke*, or cap, and his long, torn coat (*schebitze*) considers himself above king or emperor; he combats all education, hates all culture, opposes all customs, misunderstands every attempt at enlightenment, does not comprehend a word of German, or, consequently, my German sermons. It often hurts me to my innermost soul when I stand before my congregation . . . and I confess to myself that two-thirds of them do not know what I want."[58] It is unclear how objective the young man's perceptions of his relationship with his congregation were. He approached them with the secret condescension of a missionary among savages. Despite the lengthy passages in his memoirs praising the scholarship and charitable traits of Russian Jewry, his letters home conveyed his powerful sense of German Jewish elitism. One wonders how much of the hostility he perceived directed against him was his own projection and how much of his secret condescension came through in his interactions.

In addition, Lilienthal was desperately homesick. He told his family that the only thing that sustained him were their letters to him. He reported to his father and Isaac Nettre, his future father-in-law, that he had learned by heart the six letters he had received. He wrote to Pepi of his longing for her. "Never have I loved you more truly, never yearned for your presence with more intense longing. . . . Often when I sit alone and my heart feels as if it would break with longing, lost in thought I open my arms and clasp only an empty shadow." He worried if she would really follow him to this distant land, as they had planned.[59]

Lilienthal worked himself into a state of exhaustion. He explained his long silence in an apologetic letter home in September 1840. He revealed to his father and Nettre that he had worked so relentlessly that he had developed constant headaches and a burning in his chest and felt faint. Finally he was forced to rest, taking sea baths that seemed to cure him, but thrown back into his hectic schedule, he came down with a high fever. Even after he recovered, he still had occasional chest pains. In spite of it all, he expressed a strong sense of pride in what he had accomplished in seven months.[60]

Soon after his recovery, Lilienthal was notified that his superior, Lieutenant-General Kraftstroem, would be coming from Dorpat to inspect the new school. The staff rushed to prepare the boys for what would be a military-style inspection. The moment the general descended from his carriage, he asked Lilienthal sternly why he had not called on him when he had been in Dorpat. The young rabbi excused himself, citing the sleigh accident he had suffered on the trip. Letting the slight go, the general toured the school. He was quite impressed with the clean and orderly appearance of the boys. The next morning a professor, the commissioner of the university, came to examine the students. After four hours of rigorous testing, he left pleased. Four weeks later, Lilienthal received an official paper from Count Uvarov, informing him that the emperor was happy with the professor's report. He told Lilienthal that his efforts would be duly rewarded. Five weeks later Lilienthal received an order to go to St. Petersburg to meet with the minister. Uvarov wanted Lilienthal to head the proposed reform of the entire Russian Jewish educational system.[61]

Lilienthal's congregation was upset to see him return to St. Petersburg to consult with Uvarov. They warned him that he was too young and a foreigner unacquainted with the sly and cunning diplomacy of the Russian government. Further, they argued that the government would use him as cover for proselytizing schemes. Although Lilienthal promised to confront the minister with their concerns, they did not expect any good to come from his visit to the Russian capital.[62]

Other more mundane considerations were on Lilienthal's mind. In his letter home in September 1840, he seemed convinced that he did not have much of a future in Riga. He complained bitterly about how hard he had to work and how the job had driven him to become ill from exhaustion. But beyond the conditions of the job itself, the position seemed tenuous on many levels. If the Jews of Riga lost their five-year legal battle with the city, not only would they be denied residency but they would also not have the financial resources to pay his meager salary. The community was already quite poor. He told his family that the poverty of the Russian Jews exceeded their wildest imagination. His salary amounted to about 300 thalers a year, with an extra 100 thalers from preaching, and the entire budget of the school including his salary, collected from a tax on meat, was only 1,000 florins a year.[63] The school was really quite modest, with only thirty-seven students in three grades. It was conceivable that at some point the congregation would not have enough money to pay him. His future, as well as the future of the Jews of Riga, hinged on the outcome of the lawsuit.

Lilienthal's correspondence with his father and Nettre also indicates that they were highly critical of his financial arrangement with the congregation. In his defensive answer to their queries Lilienthal admits that he had considered the possibility of other positions, but where? "Do you think that in this country every city has its ordained rabbi, its educated preacher, its competent religious teacher? Do you think that here one can make application for ten different places at the same time?" he wrote them. Implicit in the letter was the question of whether he really felt secure enough to invite Pepi to join him. Lilienthal wrote of his concern more directly in a letter to his fiancée. "God alone knows what will be the position I hope to attain; a position that will enable me to come to you with honor, that will support you and my dear ones in comfort."[64]

Yet Lilienthal did not want to give up and go home. He told his father and future father-in-law, "Shall I believe that God in mere capricious mood has taken me as a blind puppet of fate, thrown me into Russia in order, in another mood, to throw me out again?" When the invitation to St. Petersburg came, Lilienthal hoped it signified an opportunity to establish a meaningful career in Russia and finally vindicate himself in the eyes of his family.[65]

During the year in which Lilienthal was working to establish his school, the tsar's government had been moving forward with its Russian Jewish program. By mid-1840 Nicholas, disturbed by reports from local officials blaming Jews for the poverty in the western provinces, asked the State Council to review the existing Jewish legislation. After the Council agreed that no further oppressive measures were called for, Nicholas turned to Count P. D. Kiselev, a gifted general and reformer. Kiselev, who was in the midst of a reform of the status of serfs, wrote a memorandum that would change Russian Jewish history. In the report Kiselev rehashed many of the old misrepresentations of Russian Jewry, but he also realized that further repressive measures would not end that community's alienation from the mainstream. Rather, Kiselev, under the influence of Uvarov, recommended applying the approach that Western Europe had used to bring about a social metamorphosis of its Jews. Its new goals were to be the moral and religious reeducation of the Jews and the abolition of legal impediments to their integration into Russian society. A key element in the new approach was to set up a network of Jewish schools that emphasized Russian language and history and inculcated patriotism, loyalty to the state, and the superiority of "useful" occupations. The report also recommended importing "enlightened Jews" from Prussia and Austria to teach in these schools.[66] Uvarov, in charge of the key educational element in the new policy, had been working in this direction for years. In 1838 he had met with members of Vilna's Jewish intelligentsia to discuss the possibilities of collaborating on a new educational program. He also had conferred with influential German Maskilim.[67] In 1840, Uvarov had tried to set up regional committees made up of governors-general and Jewish leaders to discuss future educational and rabbinic policy. Of the six committees that were set up, only one, Odessa, submitted the report Uvarov requested. Most of the Jewish communities boycotted the committees. Frustrated by these disappointing results, Uvarov turned to Lilienthal, convinced that the enlightenment of Russian Jewry would have to spearheaded by the Jews of the West.[68]

Lilienthal and Uvarov conferred for five weeks, beginning on January 15, 1841. Uvarov greeted the young rabbi warmly and let him know how pleased he had been to get the fine report on the school in Riga. Uvarov told Lilienthal about the Committee of Ministers plan to modernize Russian Jewry. He asked Lilienthal to draw up a plan for primary and higher schools, including curricular and pedagogical details. According to Lilienthal's memoirs, it was at this point that Lilienthal reported the fear of the Jewish community concerning the intent of Nicholas's policies toward them. He needed to be sure that this reform effort was not "a farce, a pretext for wholesale proselytism." He warned Uvarov that the Russian Jews would endure any misery rather than give up their religion. The minister interrupted him angrily and demanded to know why they had these fears. Lilienthal listed the various onerous taxes placed on Jews and the discrimination within the military and the university system that allowed advancement only to converts. Still pressing their case, he asked that they be offered emancipation or, short of that, some favors that would convince them that conversion was not the aim of the government. Uvarov somehow managed to appease the worried Lilienthal and ordered him to get to work on the report.[69]

In addition, Uvarov asked Lilienthal to extend invitations to other German Jews to teach in the proposed schools. Lilienthal wrote to the most influential Western European Jewish intellectuals of the day, including the *Wissenschaft* scholar Leopold Zunz, the Reform leader Abraham Geiger, Ludwig Philippson, and Samuel David Luzzatto, requesting their help in finding teachers. His letter to Luzzatto, head of a modern rabbinic college in Padua, gives us a sense of the gist of his appeals. Lilienthal wrote of the dire need to "avoid the collapse of the elementary and secondary schools of our coreligionists in Russia and Poland." He asked Luzzatto to send a detailed plan of his seminary to serve as a model for modern schools in Russia. Further, he wanted Luzzatto to provide a list of his recent graduates to serve as directors of the "eight hundred schools" that were to be founded. Not only would they enjoy good fortune and success, he wrote, but they would also be "part of a great mission of *Kiddush haShem* [the sanctification of the Divine Name]." In closing, he urged that "haste is necessary" to save the 2 million Russian Jews from "a misery of which we have no conception." He called on Luzzatto's help in the name of suffering Jews at a critical moment. "Their chains are to be broken and their need is to cease. This is an opportunity and a cause the like of which has never before arisen in the history of Israel. Once they have attained culture they are offered emancipation; in the wake of knowledge—the rights of man."[70] The letter captures Lilienthal's earnest belief in the Russian minister's promise of emancipation as well as his missionary fervor for the cause of Enlightenment. He emphasized the need for haste, yet warned Luzzatto that Uvarov expressly forbade making the plan public. If Uvarov's promises were sincere, what was the problem with publicizing the plan? Perhaps, in the minister's defense, Uvarov knew how slowly the Russian government moved in these matters.[71]

The letters show both the best and the worst of what the young rabbi brought to this task. Lilienthal's youthful idealism, his sense of mission, and urgency were effectively communicated to the Maskilim in the West and indeed succeeded in galvanizing their support. According to Jacob Raisin, a historian of the Haskalah, these letters made Lilienthal a famous man. "For more than three years Lilienthal was one of the most popular personages in Europe. The eyes of all who had the amelioration of the lot of the Russian Jew at heart, it may be said the eyes of the civilized world, were fixed upon him as an epoch maker in the history of the Jews."[72] Lilienthal's call to action caused a major stir in Western Europe. Luzzatto had few graduates from his Italian seminary to send, but Ludwig Philippson and other German Maskilim soon sent lists with more than 200 names of modern scholars who were ready to teach in the Russian schools. Philippson and historian Isaac Marcus Jost expressed the determination to come themselves.[73] At the same time, Lilienthal's tendency to overdramatize the situation, to exaggerate his own importance, and to naively trust the Russian government all reveal his immaturity and inexperience.

In Lilienthal's defense, the Russian Maskilim, who should have known better, were equally enthusiastic about this government-sponsored education plan. Believing in the benevolent nature of the Russian emperor, Odessa's Bezalel Stern proclaimed, "Now our master, the emperor, has taken upon himself to be tiller of our soil, to uproot from it all rank and bitter weeds, to cleanse the hearts of the Jewish people of all evil schemes and to sprinkle blessed dew upon the thirsting, yearning soil."[74]

Several weeks later, after working closely with Uvarov, Lilienthal finished his report. In it he emphasized the need for German teachers and suggested that the language of instruction therefore be German, at least in the beginning (to accommodate the foreign teachers). He recommended that the schools be free and offer occupational training in such areas as horticulture, agriculture, and technical drawing. The graduates should be allowed to go on to university or to join the civil service. He also argued that the graduates be allowed to live outside the Pale of Settlement after their graduation. Uvarov agreed to all but the last, which he said was impossible.[75] The minister, pleased with Lilienthal's efforts, had them translated into Russian. They became the basis for the papers sent to the Committee of Ministers. Later the council submitted its own report to the tsar, titled

"Decrees for the Jews," which included Lilienthal's educational proposals. The tsar gave the document his stamp of approval, indicating "the principles are sound." Uvarov sent Lilienthal back to Riga on March 6, promising to remain in constant touch.[76]

The Jews of Riga were thrilled to see Lilienthal upon his return. They feared that he would be retained indefinitely in St. Petersburg while they still badly needed his services. For the rest of the year, with the exception of a brief trip to nearby Mitau, Lilienthal continued to serve the congregation and teach in its school. Although faced with ongoing financial shortages, Lilienthal found the work more satisfying. The school was flourishing, he had established a circle of close friends, and he had even won over the confidence of the old rabbi, who apparently was not fired. The congregation even accepted his "improvements," such as regular German sermons and confirmation.[77]

Toward the end of 1841, Lilienthal received new orders from Uvarov's department. He was to accompany the Maskil Nisan Rosenthal to Vilna to help him establish another new modern school there. He was also to test the receptivity of the community to the plan for "enlightened" education. Rosenthal, who had recently been appointed an honorary citizen in recognition of his services during the Polish uprising, was in the midst of a power struggle over control of Vilna's educational institutions.[78] Considered a "Berliner," or reformer, he was hated by the Polish Jews. Lilienthal described him as a handsome, modern man yet admitted that he did not like him either, characterizing him as a schemer.[79]

The two men traveled south from what is today Latvia into Lithuania. At each town along the way they had to present their passports to the authorities. In his memoirs Lilienthal sees this trip as the beginning of the second act in his Russian drama. As he traveled, he came in contact for the first time with Jews untouched by Western culture. Finally Rosenthal and Lilienthal reached Vilna and established themselves in a Jewish hotel. Lilienthal could not get over the high concentration of Jews, having only lived in places where Jews were a small minority. Jews owned all the stores; they were the carpenters, masons, mechanics, shoemakers, tailors, and even the day laborers. Jews certainly practiced "useful occupations" here. They were strictly Orthodox as well, wearing a leather or velvet yarmulke (head covering) and the traditional *arba kanfot* (an undergarment with fringes on the four corners).

Lilienthal was not given much time to adjust. Within two days of his arrival, the representatives of the community gathered to hear the plan for the modernization of Russian Jewish education. Here Lilienthal would test the waters in this first public announcement of the government's new policies. He stared out at the sea of Polish Jews, feeling uncomfortable. He told them that Minister Uvarov wanted him to make them aware of the changes that the imperial government intended to introduce into Jewish education. By supporting this modern school in Vilna, they would gain the favor of the government and would also set an important example, because of the immense influence that Vilna had on the rest of Russian Jewry. Members of the younger generation, those who had been touched by the spirit of Haskalah, were excited by the prospect. The elders, pointing out Lilienthal's inexperience with Russian government, told him that they could not trust the proposals of the ministerial council. They were convinced that the new proposals had the goal of conversion. Lilienthal admitted that he could not offer them a guarantee. Instead he promised that he would quit if he became convinced that conversion was the true purpose of the new program.[80] According to Lilienthal's memoirs, this personal promise won them over. Even though reservations remained, the Vilna leadership tentatively agreed to collect the money (5,100 rubles) for the establishment of a new school. Lilienthal was swept out of the hall on the shoulders of the young Jews of Vilna.[81]

Lilienthal spent the next few days soliciting further support for the new school. On Monday morning he received a new order, signed by the regional director of Uvarov's ministry, Prince Schichmatoff. Lilienthal was to visit all the Hebrew schools in Vilna and submit a report to the government. After he informed the *parnass* (president of the community) of the order, they arranged that he would begin his inspections that Thursday in order to give the schools time to clean house. He visited the whole range of schools, starting with the elementary schools for the poor, where children (perhaps a hundred) crowded into dark, dank rooms with low ceilings. The poor and hungry teachers controlled the room with a rod, teaching the children basic prayers and Bible. Then Lilienthal moved on to the yeshiva, five rooms containing more than 200 students, where the men studied in the traditional manner, rocking their bodies as they studied in a singsong chant. The yeshiva had a graded curriculum that emphasized Talmud and its commentaries. In the afternoon, Lilienthal visited the elementary school of the Maskilim Hirsch Klatzcko and Rosenthal. In contrast to the heder, the rooms were large and clean; the eighty to ninety students were taught Hebrew, Russian, German, and French by an efficient corps of learned teachers. Lilienthal expressed tremendous respect for these self-taught scholars, who finally felt validated for their efforts. Finally, Lilienthal visited an adult education class (*beth hamidrash*), returning to the traditional world of talmudic commentary. Thinking over all that he had experienced during the day, Lilienthal naively recorded in his memoirs that progress would inevitably come and that these obsolete schools would be replaced. "Even if the Russian government would not close them . . . they soon would disappear of themselves, giving way to the improved institutions of our age," he predicted.[82]

Lilienthal tried to make good use of his time while he waited for the decision of the Vilna community. He lobbied various rabbis and local officials to gain support for his plan, and he marveled at the intensely Jewish atmosphere in which he found himself. After three weeks, the Vilna community remained deadlocked out of fear of taking the lead in such a radical departure from tradition. The idea occurred to Lilienthal to try to gain the support of another important Jewish city to help move the plan forward. Having received an invitation from the leaders of the Minsk community to explain his position, Lilienthal decided to go there. Some of the Maskilim of Vilna warned Lilienthal against accepting the invitation. Minsk had few "enlightened" figures (Lilienthal puts the figure at less than ten); traditionalists and a substantial Hasidic community dominated. With little to no chance of success, some of the Maskilim saw the invitation as a plot to derail the government's reforms. It seemed to them that Lilienthal was walking into a trap.[83]

Indeed, the rabbinic scholars and the Hasidim, usually at odds with one another, had made common cause to defeat their enemy. Even before Lilienthal arrived, they had stirred up all the hostility they could muster to thwart this potential threat to their way of life. Unlike in Vilna, where he had been treated respectfully, in Minsk Lilienthal was given "cold and reserved treatment." Meetings were held throughout the city in which all firmly resolved to defeat the plan. Declaring that they were unafraid to face the consequences of opposing the government, they were "ready for martyrdom" to set an example for their sister cities. Such was the mood of the crowd that gathered in the synagogue that Sunday evening. The rabbis threatened to excommunicate anyone who supported this modernization scheme. One after the other, they rose to quote texts proving the wickedness of studying secular subjects, which, in their view, inevitably led to apostasy. In the face of their fanaticism, Lilienthal followed the advice of friends and left the meeting before its conclusion. His few enlightened allies in Minsk agreed that all was lost. The last thing Lilienthal heard as he left the city was the taunts of Hasidic children: "We don't want any [secular] schools!"[84]

Back in Vilna, Lilienthal reported his experiences and commiserated with his friends. Some reproached him for going; others berated themselves for advising him to go. Inspired by the "manly" opposition of the

Jews of Minsk, the traditional forces in Vilna mobilized their forces, overwhelming the modicum of support that Lilienthal had previously enjoyed. The confrontation was postponed awhile longer by the imminent approach of Passover; Lilienthal had been away from Riga for three months by this point. As soon as the first two days of the festival had been completed, the community met in the main synagogue to take final action on the plan. Lilienthal (wildly exaggerating) estimated that the attendance exceeded 40,000,[85] most of whom were inflamed with righteous indignation. Speaker after speaker rose to denounce the scheme as "godless and sinful" and to utter daring threats. The Maskil Benjamin Mandelshtam playfully described the vivid scene.

> The tailor said, "Gouge out his eyes with a needle"; the cobbler: "Pierce his ears with an awl"; the butcher: "Bind him like a goat to the slaughter"; the locksmith: "Lock his mouth so that he cannot open it." . . . The teachers in the forefront said: "Be strong for the sake of our nation and youth! Strengthen the customs of our fathers. We want no part of Lilienthal and his followers and their ways." The crowd chanted: "We don't want, we don't want!"[86]

The chief of police, present to keep order, feared that a riot was developing. He arrested the *parnass* and ordered the fire department to come and disperse the crowd with their hoses. Within a half-hour the synagogue was empty; Lilienthal knew his case was "lost irretrievably." Even after the meeting the animosity toward him continued to grow until he feared "being stabbed by fanatics." The governor-general of the region told him that a full report had been sent to St. Petersburg concerning the deportment of the Jews of Vilna. Despite everything, Lilienthal feared that the government would punish the Jewish community, so he resolved to rush to the capital as soon as the Passover holiday was over.[87]

Lilienthal hurried north to try to catch the mail coach from Warsaw. He missed it by two hours but was told that if he traveled nonstop all day, he would reach the coach that evening. As his driver raced over the terrible roads, Lilienthal's motion sickness came back. The only respites from the torturous pace were the stops at each station to have his passport registered. Finally he reached the coach, only to be told that it was completely full. Lilienthal, forced to wait until the next morning, slept soundly at an inn despite its terrible bedbugs. The next morning he continued his journey to St. Petersburg.[88]

Count Uvarov received Lilienthal that afternoon, greeting him warmly. Lilienthal was introduced to the director and vice-director of the department and to the chief aide-de-camp of the emperor's brother, the Grand Duke Michael. He gave a short report and was ordered to return early the same evening for a full discussion. According to his memoirs, Lilienthal tried to deflect the blame away from the Russian Jews onto himself. He argued that because he was only 25 (by then Lilienthal was 27, but perhaps he was exaggerating for effect) and also a foreigner, the local Jews did not trust him. He suggested that the count needed to enlist men that they would trust to garner support for the modernization plan. Lilienthal invoked the model of Napoleon's Sanhedrin, which had gathered the leadership of French Jewry together to forge the consistory system. If Uvarov would convene a convention of rabbis, chosen by the communities themselves, the suspicions surrounding Lilienthal himself would be circumvented. He suggested that this synod be composed of a rabbi from each of the seventeen provinces in which Jews were allowed to live, in order to ensure a representative body. His proposal pleased Uvarov, who after all, wanted to emulate Western Europe in Russia's approach to the Jewish question. It also played into his desire to increase the power of his ministry, divesting the Ministry of the Interior of some of its jurisdiction.[89] The minister presented Lilienthal's proposal to the Committee of Ministers, who approved it and passed it on to Nicholas. The emperor approved of the synod but limited the number of delegates to four. Although disappointed not to have broader representation, Uvarov and Lilienthal worked out a new system of representatives, analogous to the four governors-general: in Vilna, Kiev, Odessa, and Vitebsk. Lilienthal pressed the minister to agree to allow each group to choose its own representative, ensuring their legitimacy.

Uvarov gave Lilienthal a new task: to tour the entire Pale of Settlement as an official of the government to inform the Jewish communities of the ministry's plans and to find appropriate delegates for the synod. Lilienthal was understandably anxious at the prospect of returning to the scene of his humiliation and ill treatment. Uvarov reassured him that he would have the protection of the government, through a general order to the governors-general to grant him any assistance required as well as the support of the Ministry of Police. Further, the count would provide all the necessary letters of introduction and recommendation to the officials in each province. Lilienthal was to contact the local officials in each community, explain the minister's plan, and keep track of possible resistance. Along the way, he would visit respected local Jewish leaders, examine the most important schools, identify gifted teachers, and note young people with some modern knowledge who might be potential teachers. Uvarov gave Lilienthal a week to prepare for the journey.[90]

Lilienthal was still quite anxious about the reception that he would receive. He insisted that the written orders contain a clause assuring the Russian Jews that the new plan would in no way infringe on their religion. Point 4 of the orders accomplished this: "New schools will be established at the expense of the government, to be no other than, without infringing upon their religion, to prepare them for a truly civil and moral life, which consists merely in the approach to universally acknowledged civilization."[91]

To further hold the Russian government to its word, Lilienthal sent a detailed account to the *Allgemeine Zeitung des Judenthums* that was published on October 8, 1842. He commented in his memoirs, "By this stratagem I intended to confront the Russian policy with the public opinion of Europe, assured that if the European press would hail the good intentions of the Russian government in behalf of my brethren, the same would not dare back out, and make of the reform of the schools a missionary scheme."[92]

Finally, Lilienthal composed a polemical tract titled "Maggid Yeshu'ah" (Herald of Salvation) to announce his tour, in which he repeated his earlier arguments concerning the benefits of the new education system. In it, he stated that Nicholas had granted the Jews the opportunity to improve themselves, to bring themselves prosperity and security. The changes would not violate either the laws or customs of traditional Judaism. At the same time Lilienthal asserted that this tour was not meant to air the various opinions on the new law but rather to inform them of the government's benevolent will in this matter. If there were further incidences like the ones in Vilna or Minsk, he warned, the consequences would be most serious. Only if the communities followed the recommendation for the proposed rabbinic synod would they be safe. The government printed thousands of copies of the pamphlet and distributed it throughout all the communities that Lilienthal would be visiting. Lilienthal had learned well the carrot-and-stick approach of the Russian government. Although one Hasidic group burned the document, the rest of the Jewish communities showed no resistance to his visit or to the instructions to nominate delegates.[93]

Ironically, the person who was most offended by Lilienthal's manifesto was the Maskil Mordecai Aaron Günzberg, who rebutted the document in his *Maggid Emet* (Herald of Truth), published in Leipzig under a pseudonym. Günzberg expressed indignation that the government was empowering a German doctor to fulfill its will. It was degrading to Russian Maskilim that this upstart serve as a mediator between the government and the Russian Jews rather than one of their own.[94] Günzberg noted, "Our land is not devoid of wise men. . . . The kingdom need not seek out wise men in a distant land." Further Günzberg argued that German rabbis were not great scholars in Torah.[95]

The Maskilim were not united in their opposition, however. Abraham Baer Gottlober (1811–99) urged that the Jews accept this initiative. He saw Lilienthal as the "people's shepherd." He proclaimed, "May you be the father to the children of Israel until they have grown to manhood. . . . May Menahem [the comforter, and Lilienthal's Hebrew name], restorer of our soul, grow old in peace [among us] and be our comforter! In his light we will walk confidently and never falter, he will lead us unerringly to life."[96] Benjamin Mandelshtam (1805–90), reflecting on this initiative, compared Nicholas favorably to the great liberal rulers of the past, such as Frederick the Great and Joseph II.[97]

Having done everything he could to guarantee that the tour would go smoothly, Lilienthal set off in July, following the instructions in the ministry's itinerary. "The line of your journey goes through Riga, Mitau, Kovno, Vilna, Minsk, Grodno, Byalystok, Zhitomir, Berditchef, Kaminiecz-Poldolsk, Kishinef [Kishinev], Odessa, Cherson; from there you will go to the province of Kief [Kiev], pass Uman to the city of Kief, and further to Chernigof, Mogilef and Vitebsk back to St. Petersburg."[98] The orders gave him discretion to visit any other places he deemed important without leaving the basic route.[99]

The first stop, Riga, set the tone. The congregation was happy to see Lilienthal, expressing their pride in his new mission. At the general meeting, the resolutions in favor of the plan were unanimously adopted. There was a similar result in Mitau. The next stop, Vilna, would be the first real test. If Lilienthal was anxious about returning, the community was even more so, expecting retribution for its past behavior. Rather than berating them, Lilienthal assured them that he had pleaded their cause in St. Petersburg. As the secretary read the documents, their suspicions vanished; their mistrust gave way. They rushed forward to shake Lilienthal's hand and ask his pardon. Even the *melamdim*, the traditional teachers, were silenced. The community informed Lilienthal that the representative they had selected was the head of the prestigious Voloshin yeshiva. Lilienthal decided he would go to confer with this leader of Lithuanian Jewry. Rabbi Yitzhak ben Haim was the head of the moderate wing of rabbinic Judaism, thus he was somewhat receptive. According to Lilienthal's memoirs, ben Haim told the younger man that he understood that the reform of the schools could not be delayed any longer. Later during the visit, which lasted a couple of weeks, Rabbi Yitzhak and Lilienthal discussed the details of the mission. Lilienthal begged him to accept the nomination as a delegate and the rabbi agreed. This rather benign description of the discussion apparently glosses over the fact that Lilienthal made it very clear that Nicholas might impose forced penal service upon the Jews if they resisted these educational re-forms.[100]

The recruitment of this great rabbinic scholar was a great coup that gave Lilienthal's mission much added credibility. As he moved on to Minsk, he encountered no opposition. Celebrating the fall festival of Sukkot in Minsk, Lilienthal was even honored by the Hasidim. He had been so wor-ried about meeting this group that he had asked Rabbi Yitzhak for advice. Yet the Hasidim invited Lilienthal to accept a prestigious honor (*Chatan Torah*) on the holiday of Simchat Torah. After chanting the blessing and reading the final sentences from the Torah, Lilienthal was treated to wild dancing and a large cup of brandy. The Hasidim later came to his host's house late that night and again sang and danced with him. After offering them in turn brandy and cakes, they departed "highly pleased with the Datsch-Rebbi, who had treated and entertained them with so much cour-tesy." Although this breakthrough boded well for Lilienthal's relations with the Hasidim, rumors of a plot to poison him caused him to have a servant taste all his food.[101]

In Bialystok, Lilienthal was impressed with a wealthy merchant, Itzele Sabludowski, who had created a luxurious palace for himself, modeled after the finest in Western Europe. The merchant introduced him to the gov-ernor and other high officers of the state. Lilienthal experienced no op-position at all from the Jewish community, especially after his successes in Vilna and Minsk. Representatives of the community of Berdichev wrote an effusive letter to Lilienthal's father, which he proudly published in the *Allgemeine Zeitung des Judenthums*. The letter acclaimed Lilienthal as a deliverer who was "announcing help to his oppressed people," and the writ-ers expressed the community's honor in having "this brilliant star" in their midst.[102]

Lilienthal's welcome was equally enthusiastic in Brest-Litovsk, where young people sympathetic to Haskalah entertained him. It was there that Lilienthal came in contact with the family of Pauline Wengeroff, whose memoir offers a taste of the excitement surrounding Lilienthal's tour. Her father rushed home from *mincha* (the afternoon service) with the wonder-ful news that Lilienthal was coming to announce the impending reforms in Jewish education. As a young girl, Wengeroff witnessed the reactions to Lilienthal's visit in her home.

> My father, a strictly observant Jew, was not too upset about the im-pending reforms; he himself had long been dissatisfied with the poor methods of instruction in the Jewish schools of Brest, and been wish-ing for many improvements. My two eldest brothers-in-law and the

other young men of the town also received the news with great anticipation, although they dared talk about it only in whispers. As for the *melamdim* themselves—they were simply in despair.[103]

The young people of the town in particular were excited by Lilienthal's arrival. Wengeroff writes, "Dr. Lilienthal made it a point to gather many of Brest's young people around him every day, speaking to them of acquiring West European learning. . . . He won the hearts of these impressionable young people."[104] For Wengeroff, Lilienthal's arrival in her town marked the beginning of "the Lilienthal epoch," referring to the cultural revolution that began among Russian Jews.[105] Her deeply traditional mother, however, did not trust the new phenomenon; Wengeroff comments, "She saw more deeply, as was confirmed in the end." In retrospect, Wengeroff felt that "the dazzling brilliance of European culture burst upon our amazed young people without a mediating dawn." The old ways of life were destroyed precipitously.[106]

Throughout his tour, Lilienthal inspected schools, interviewed teachers, and formed alliances with Jewish leaders. In Odessa, for instance, he spent three days touring the modern school, "testing students in a wide range of subjects." Lilienthal was impressed with both the level of the students and the skill of the teachers. He called the school a model for the government-sponsored system.[107]

Yet, despite all his precautions, everything did not go smoothly on the trip. Lilienthal had been right to fear the Hasidim. One of the low points in the trip was the reception he got in the Lubavitcher community. It was here that Rabbi Schneersohn told his followers to burn Lilienthal's pamphlet, "Maggid Yeshu'ah."[108] According to the Lubavitcher account, Lilienthal later told the commission that he was verbally assaulted when he tried to speak to Rabbi Schneersohn's community. Many Hasidim gestured angrily and called him the "apostate from Riga" or "filthy German apostate." Gangs of children chased him, calling him a "builder of *shmad* [conversionary] houses (missions) for Jewish children."[109] To support the claim that Lilienthal was an apostate, the Hasidim dug into his family background, asserting that his grandfather had renounced Judaism. This jumbled account did contain a grain of truth. According to Sophie Lilienthal's memoirs, Bavaria's Max Joseph IV raised one of Lilienthal's ancestors to noble status on the condition that he embrace Christianity.[110]

Sadly, Lilienthal managed to alienate some of the Russian Maskilim as well. At first, the local Maskilim welcomed him with enormous enthusiasm as he toured. He was called "liberator and redeemer" or an "angel of God." Benjamin Mandelshtam, who was deeply involved with Lilienthal's mission, had high praise. "[He] was in my eyes virtually like a new Moses through whom God had chosen to aid his people." The euphoria was short-lived, however. Through a series of slights and misunderstandings, Lilienthal lost the support of the constituency closest to his position, those who should have been his natural allies. He neglected to visit Isaac Baer Levinsohn, the acknowledged head of the Russian Maskilim, during his visit to Kremenets, yet he spent weeks courting the Orthodox and Hasidic Jews. Israel Zinberg, who has studied the literature of the Maskilim, suggests that Uvarov's cold attitude toward Levinsohn influenced Lilienthal's decision to snub him. Mandelshtam complained that he "plays at being a deeply pious man who must say his prayers twice a day with the congregation. The enlightened, therefore, consider him a hypocrite."[111] In fairness to Lilienthal, it was crucial to the success of his mission to win over the vast majority of Orthodox and Hasidic Jews. He had to devote attention to them. Nevertheless, Bezalel Stern, head of the modern school in Odessa, made a point of being away on an archaeological study-tour during Lilienthal's visit to his city because of his intense dislike for the young rabbi.[112]

Behind the miffed feelings was a deeper disappointment on the part of the Russian Maskilim. They had labored for years in their cause; many lived in dire poverty, only to find out that the new schools would be importing teachers from abroad. They sent many letters to Levinsohn begging him to intercede with Lilienthal and the government to recommend them for the teaching positions. Yet Lilienthal referred to them in communications to Uvarov's ministry as "dirty, bearded Jews who are barely touched by the rays of enlightenment."[113]

In December 1842 Lilienthal returned to St. Petersburg and presented his report. The commission would be made up of Rabbi Yitzhak ben Haim, Rabbi Menahem Mendel Schneersohn (representing the Hasidim), traditionalist financier Israel Halperin, and Bezalel Stern. Uvarov, his assistants, and Lilienthal represented the government, and the Maskil Leon Mandelstamm served as interpreter and scribe.[114] The commission met in secret from May 6 to August 27, 1843; there is no official record of its deliberations. The combination of personalities represented an explosive mix of viewpoints. Rabbi Schneersohn, one of the most vocal opponents of Lilienthal's modernization program, was there under duress. He told his followers that he was on a holy mission to save the traditional Jewish way of life against the designs of the government. Rabbi Yitzhak, perhaps a little more open to the government's ideas, was also motivated by government threats. Stern, though a Maskil, had considerable personal animosity toward Lilienthal.

Minister Uvarov opened the conference; other important Russian officials took the roles of chairman and secretaries. Lilienthal recalled feeling hopeful about the outcome.[115] Shockingly, just one week into the proceedings, the tsar announced an edict that would banish Jews from the region near the western frontier. This cruel ukase, which would displace more than 100,000 Jews, promised terrible suffering for the Jews of the Pale. According to Lilienthal's account many years later in the *Jewish Times*, the members of the committee were stunned by the tsar's duplicity.[116] The timing could not have been worse, because it undermined the basic premise in Lilienthal's argument. The case for educational modernization depended on Nicholas's benevolent intentions with regard to Russian Jewry. That is why Lilienthal defended Nicholas's motives over and over in his speeches. In an early address in Riga he proclaimed, "No other government has so earnestly and energetically undertaken to regenerate Judaism and to organize it as 'Russia's great monarch and his ministers.'"[117] Lilienthal went immediately to confront Count Uvarov with this betrayal, only to find that he had left for Germany. Although other officials counseled patience, believing that such an order would never be put into effect, the ruling cast a dark shadow over the commission's work.[118]

One of the only existing accounts of the meetings other than Lilienthal's brief recollections was the hagiographic Hasidic biography of Schneersohn. It portrayed the commission as a series of confrontations during which the Hasidic leader heroically defended the faith, taking positions for which he was imprisoned numerous times. The biography claims that the two traditional rabbis were often at odds, as were the two Maskilim, Lilienthal and Stern, and that Uvarov frequently lost his temper with the participants.[119] After many months of heated disputation, in the end, perhaps under the threat of coercion, they all signed the document that established basic guidelines for all Russian Jewish education. One of Uvarov's assistants, who worked with the commission on a daily basis, praised the Jewish members of the commission for their loyalty, stating that their work supported the government's goals and deserved reward. Each commission participant received the title of Honorary Citizen, a kind of minor nobility, and a gold medal to be worn around his neck. As the Jewish participants left, the other rabbis pleaded with Lilienthal to try to do what he could to reverse the ukase.[120]

Lilienthal's hope that the commission would successfully unify the Russian Jewish community behind his vision for modern education was not realized. Instead the commission's work exacerbated the division between traditionalists and modernist factions. Rabbi Yitzhak told his closest followers that the conference was a failure. He hoped that there would be no further evil decrees, because "a wind of destruction is now prevailing over our nation."[121] Rabbi Schneersohn met with other prominent rabbis shortly after his return "to discuss the Petersburg conference and measures to be taken to stem the plague of Haskalah." He spoke disdainfully of the "intentions of the 'Berlintchikes' to poison Jewish youth with the venom of heresy."[122] Although the Maskilim generally celebrated the law as their final victory over the traditionalists, not all were convinced. Commission member Bezalel Stern was skeptical, believing that reformed education could work only if it reflected the wishes of an already enlightened community. His experiences had taught him that reform imposed from above would be rejected by the Jewish community and would collapse in failure.[123]

In the year and a half following the commission, Lilienthal worked tirelessly to bring the educational program into being. He wrote to his father and Isaac Nettre in July 1844 about the many meetings, the provisions that had already passed through the bureaucracy, and the weekly inquiries by the tsar about the status of work. He predicted that the law would be finalized by the end of the year.[124] Countless memorandums from Lilienthal to the Ministry of Education reveal how, with regard to both purpose and method, Lilienthal's views were reflected in the legislation.[125] According to Michael Stanislawski, when the commission's work became law on November 13, 1844, "Haskalah was now the official policy of the Russian government."[126]

The law set up a new modern system of primary, secondary, and rabbinic schools alongside the older heder and yeshiva system. The government would administer the traditional system, demanding lists of students and regular reports, but the focus was on the new schools. The law detailed the curriculum for the new schools, greatly increasing the emphasis on secular subjects, such as Russian language, mathematics, the sciences, and commercial and technical subjects. Provisions were made for the importation of teachers from Central Europe. Provincial and district-level committees, made up of Jews and Christians, would supervise the new system, but all directors of rabbinic seminaries would be Christian. Strong incentives for Jews to attend these new schools included a ten-year exemption from the draft for secondary students. The decree concluded, "We hope that this new demonstration of Our concern for the moral improvement of the Jews will convince them to cooperate with these plans aimed at their true benefit."[127]

This education law should have been Lilienthal's crowning achievement, the culmination of almost six years of effort. It should have guaranteed the success of his career. Yet, in July 1845, about eight months after its promulgation, Lilienthal suddenly left Russia. The glorious career that he had hoped for had not materialized. Not only had he alienated the various constituents of Russian Jewry, but his position as "first learned Jew" was that of a bureaucrat at the Ministry of Education, with a salary equivalent to that of a skilled laborer in St. Petersburg. His salary was never raised during his entire service to the government.[128] As the oldest son, he had felt responsible for recouping some of the family's fortune lost in the fire while he had been at the university. He must have also realized that he would never support Pepi in a manner to which she was accustomed. This is the conclusion that Stanislawski arrived at after examining a variety of possibilities. "Realizing his failure in creating in Russia the future he envisioned, he submitted to the primary personal and familial demands of life and abandoned the Russian mission—through the back door."[129] Stanislawski correctly argues that this theory is unprovable because of Lilienthal's silence at the time. Further, Lilienthal's later reconstructions of the decision can be seen as attempts to present himself in the best possible light. What Stanislawski does not take seriously enough is the young man's missionary zeal for the transformative hope of German Haskalah. The strength of his maskilic faith meant that his disillusionment developed slowly. Further, Lilienthal was terrified to express his true feelings in letters home because of censorship. This fear meant that his frustration came out fitfully, especially to his elders, whose approval he craved. In what follows I offer an explanation that is perhaps no more provable than Stanislawski's claim, but it takes into consideration more of Lilienthal's psychological motivations.

Unlike Stanislawski, I believe it is clear that Lilienthal did become disillusioned while he was still in Russia. He had come to Russia imbued with a missionary's zeal to help the poor, backward, and oppressed Jews of Russia. Based on his educational experience, he believed deeply in the central faith of the Haskalah—that education would lead to intellectual and moral enlightenment as well as to civic betterment for the Jews. This regeneration of the Jewish people would help them earn emancipation through the agency of a benevolent absolutist government. It was that faith that inspired the Maskilim throughout Central Europe to patiently work for their own emancipation in the countries of their birth. It was this shared faith that caused the European Maskilim to become so excited by Lilienthal's call for teachers.

Lilienthal's naive belief in the benevolence of the Russian government received a severe jolt as a result of the 1843 edict threatening to banish Jews from the region near the western frontiers of the empire. When on January 10, 1844, the emperor rejected all appeals to overturn the ukase, Lilienthal decided to leave Russia. "[Councilor Wrontshenko] told me that the emperor had rejected the petition of the council and that all hope for a repeal was gone. I then made up my mind to leave the imperial service, and in July 1845, I left St. Petersburg for the shores of the land of human right and liberty."[130] This reconstruction of events prompts some questions. If Lilienthal had made up his mind in January 1844 with the promulgation of the ukase, why did he wait a full year and a half to leave Russia? And why was there no mention of this decision in his letters home during that period?

Glimpses of the reasons for his delay can be gleaned from these letters. For more than a year and a half Lilienthal petitioned the Russian government for permission to return to Munich to get married. In the letters he set a series of dates and made plans with Pepi, only to have to back out because of obstacles created in St. Petersburg. In November 1843, Lilienthal told Pepi that his request to leave in early 1844 was denied because Uvarov was out of town.[131] In July 1844 he explained to his father and Isaac Nettre that the work on the education law made it impossible to leave. Further complicating the situation was the fact that he would not have an official position until the education law was enacted. Without that position, he was unable to marry Pepi in Munich under Bavarian law.[132] At the end of 1844 Lilienthal wrote home that he had finally received the appointment and was making plans to come to Munich. "I will take the first steamer to Stettin, from there to Berlin, then by railroad to Leipzig, and from there to Munich. My stay there will be at the most three weeks; my work will not permit me to remain longer. . . . Make all necessary preparations; get your trousseau ready."[133] Even then Lilienthal was unable to leave until July 1845.

If Lilienthal was so disillusioned, why had he never written to his family of a desire to give up his Russian mission? Indeed, late in 1844 Lilienthal wrote to Pepi suggesting that she purchase a fur coat in order to survive the Russian winters when she joined him after their marriage.[134] It is likely that he wrote this for the benefit of Russian officials, whom he feared were reading his letters. In his memoirs, Lilienthal wrote about the coercive and invasive power of the secret police. As early as September 1840, he had written to his father and Nettre, "I have risked a good deal writing this to you, for the mail is opened. However, you have driven me to such desperation that I will take the chance of putting it into words, although the secret police keep strict watch over correspondence, and would like to get knowledge of my opinions."[135]

In a December 1840 letter to his brother Samuel, Lilienthal explained, "My position is so difficult, the circumstances are so varied and interdependent, the whole requires so much subtlety, suppleness and, alas, dissimulation, that one cannot give expression to it in a correspondence by letter, for various and many reasons."[136]

It is likely that Lilienthal could not express his disillusionment directly for fear that his mail was being read. Nevertheless, his letters home during this period idealized the freedom of France and America. In a letter to Isaac Nettre in July 1843, while the harsh law was being reviewed, Lilienthal wrote, "You will want to move to France and pass the quiet evening of your life in the land of freedom and equality." In the same letter he asserted, "I hope nothing for the Jews in Europe, everything in America."[137] On November 23, 1843, Lilienthal wrote to his father about how fortunate his siblings Samuel and Sophie were to be settled in America. In the same letter he told his father, "Seligmann [Lilienthal's brother] must in any case, I think, sail [to America] in May, 1844, for there is no future for him in Munich." Still later in that letter he advocated sending his sister Henrietta (Jette) to America as well.[138] In July 1844, Lilienthal dared to write of his deep dissatisfaction with his situation. "Since the sad ukase that has proclaimed the banishment of the Jews from the boundaries, the future of the Jews has become so bad that unless the Lord, in whose hands the hearts of kings are like running water, takes pity on them, I would not wish to become a Russian Jew for any price in the world."[139] Finally allowed to leave St. Petersburg in July 1845, ostensibly for a short vacation to marry Pepi, Lilienthal sent his resignation to the Russian court after the ceremony. The timing was crucial because had he resigned before the ceremony, he would not have qualified to marry Pepi under the Matrikel rules in Bavaria.[140]

The rabbi left Russia heartsick and disappointed. Some critics in Europe joined the chorus of Russian Jews who condemned him for the failure of his mission. One journalist criticized him relentlessly, even going so far as to blame him for the evil ukase.[141] Objectively, Lilienthal had accomplished something significant through the work of the commission and the passage of the education law. During his tenure as "learned Jew," the number of modern Jewish schools doubled from four to eight. After his departure the state-sponsored Jewish school system really became established. By the end of Nicholas's reign, in 1855, between 62 and 103 modern schools were established throughout Russia. Their curriculum followed the commission's guidelines, with an emphasis on secular studies. Gradually, especially after Uvarov was dismissed following the European revolutions of 1848, the schools moved further from Lilienthal's vision toward an emphasis on practical and commercial subjects. Still, Lilienthal had initiated a process that would open the door of secular studies to many Russian Jews.[142]

Lilienthal's disillusionment was slow to emerge, because of his illusions about the benevolence of the tsar and his inflated conception of his own mission.[143] Eager to recapitulate his family's illustrious past, in his role as "maskilic redeemer" of the Jews of Russia, Lilienthal was like a court Jew in many respects, interacting with the highest levels of government. That mission, founded on Haskalah dogma, was hard to give up. What almost everyone underestimated—including Lilienthal and possibly even Uvarov—was the difficulty of applying the Western European model to both the rigid autocracy of Nicholas's Russia and the deep traditionalism of its Jews. After leaving Russia, Lilienthal would look back on the tsarist government with much bitterness. In his first correspondence from America he bemoans the "terrible Jew-hatred of Russia." In a series of articles in the Jewish periodical the *Occident*, called "Sketches of Jewish Life in Russia: A General Survey of the Conditions of the Jews in Russia," Lilienthal traced the history of anti-Jewish tsarist policy from the eighteenth century on.[144] Within a year of his departure he had clearly lost his illusions about the nature of the emperor and his Jewish policy.

Lilienthal was not the messianic figure that he and those around him wanted him to be. Haskalah's rhetoric about the redemptive nature of the modern state was, especially in Russia, an act of faith, a reflection of the need for optimism under terrible oppression.[145] All the players in the drama had expectations that were neither realistic nor realizable at that historical moment. Yet that does not mean that Lilienthal's six years in Russia were unimportant. On the contrary, they marked an important moment in the relationship between Western European and Russian Jewry. In this dynamic clash between German Haskalah and Russian Jewish traditionalism, Lilienthal was the main actor in a drama that changed the course of Russian Jewish history. As Stanislawski notes, Haskalah did become the official education policy of the Russian government toward its Jews. The disgruntled Russian Maskilim did, in fact, get jobs as directors and superintendents of modern schools.[146] The number of schools increased over the next years and decades. Jacob Raisin notes:

> It should not be forgotten that, if Lilienthal met with mighty opposition, he also had powerful supporters. There were many who, though remaining in the background, strongly sympathized with his plan. Indeed, the number of educated Jews, as proved by an investigation ordered by Nicholas I, was far greater than had been supposed. Not only in the border towns, but even in the interior of the Pale, the students of German literature and secular science were not few. . . . Before the reign of Nicholas I drew to its end, Haskalah centres were as numerous as the cities wherein Jews resided.[147]

Max Lilienthal's years as an international Jewish leader or "epoch-maker" (Raisin's term) were over by the time he reached 30. What would he do for an encore? No longer trusting in benevolent absolutism to provide emancipation, Lilienthal would wholeheartedly embrace the freedom that America offered. In America the rabbi would continue his quest to modernize Jewish life and create, in the process, a post-emancipation model for the rabbinate.[148]

On to America

Congregational Rabbi

Leaving Russia in July 1845, Lilienthal sailed homeward. On the way, he stopped in Magdeburg to give a full report to his mentor, Ludwig Philippson, who had originally recommended him for the mission.[1] Nothing could deter Lilienthal for long, though, from the much anticipated reunion with his beloved Pepi. They had missed each other desperately during the six years of separation, often quarreling through the mail out of frustration over the many delays of their wedding date. The marriage ceremony, which took place on August 27, 1845, was an occasion for a celebration in Munich, thrown by two pillars of that Jewish community. The love between the two, deepened through the years of painful separation, remained a constant throughout their lives together.

Following the wedding, Lilienthal preached several times in the Munich synagogue. These sermons made a lasting impression on many listeners, according to family memoirs, but unfortunately did not lead to any job offers. Without a rabbinic position Lilienthal could not qualify for the Matrikel, and he feared that his family would be considered illegal residents in Munich.[2] Ruling out a return to Russia, on October 25, 1845, Lilienthal resigned his position in the imperial government.[3] After conferring with their elders about their options, Max and Pepi decided to join their siblings in America.

Apart from the pull of family already in America, Lilienthal was excited by the promise of American freedom. He had written about it in letters from Russia and had been getting detailed accounts about the New World from Samuel as early as 1840, when the young physician had emigrated to establish a career.[4] Lilienthal's favorable opinion of America is already evident in a July 1843 letter to his future father-in-law, advising him to send his son Philip there. In making his case, Lilienthal knowledgeably commented on the American situation and explained why he thought the young lawyer would have greater opportunities in the New World. "Now that Germans of high character are gaining an upper hand in the North American free states, now that the monetary crisis seems to be passing and credit is being reestablished, now that the western colonies or states are making such rapid strides forward, a future of industrial and commercial activity is to be looked for, such as is not likely in Germany and in Europe where narrow-minded nationalism is on the increase."[5] Meanwhile, Lilienthal's growing pessimism about the Jewish future in Europe contrasted sharply with his optimism about America. Feeling that the Bavarian government had betrayed the promise of emancipation, he would soon follow the lead of an increasing number of German Jews who chose emigration rather than wait for civil equality in Europe.[6]

Lilienthal came to the United States possessed by an idealistic love for the religious liberty that this country offered. As a foreign correspondent for Philippson's journal, the *Allgemeine Zeitung des Judenthums*, he urged German Jews to come to America, anticipating the "On to America" movement of Leopold Kompert and others by several years.[7] Love of America became an important early theme in many of Lilienthal's addresses and was also the focus of a lengthy three-part article in Philippson's periodical.[8] Calling the United States the embodiment of the promise of Jewish emancipation and full of potential for greatness, Lilienthal never lost this admiration for America despite the many problems he faced in his adjustment to this new country.

Max and Pepi were part of a wave of Central European immigration to America that commenced in the early 1840s. Economic depression and a reactionary political climate provided the push for many Jews and non-Jews.[9] In this period, German Jews faced particular obstacles to making a living, getting married, or raising a family. Along with their non-Jewish countrymen, who emigrated in far greater numbers, Jews were drawn by the promise of better economic opportunities, but they also sought the personal freedoms that America offered: freedom of speech and religion, privacy, freedom from military service, and equality before the law.[10] Europeans, who closely watched the American experiment as it unfolded, created an idealized image of this country. America became a popular subject in German Jewish literature as early as the 1820s. Many books, pamphlets, and articles in Jewish periodicals as well as letters from family members in America all inspired immigration.[11]

Numbers increased dramatically in part because the ocean voyage had become less risky as a result of technological advances. In the early nineteenth century, ships carried better instruments for navigation, increasing the safety and speed of voyages; ports developed signaling beams to warn of hazards in harbors. After 1815, the transport of emigrants became a regular feature of an expanding transatlantic commercial trade network. By midcentury ships had been designed especially for the emigrant traffic; in the 1840s sailing ships were gradually replaced by steamships that could cut the journey's duration from months to two or three weeks.[12]

The voyage was still fraught with dangers, as travelers had to cope with weather delays and unscrupulous agents, innkeepers, and con artists at the points of embarkation.[13] Because many ships were still primarily freighters, passengers had to bring their own cooking utensils, food, and rat-proof storage containers on the journey. The poor traveled in steerage, a hold below deck whose ceiling was usually four to six feet high. They hung cheese and sausages from hooks, slept on double wooden bunks, and got fresh air from a hatchway to the deck that was open only during fair weather. The steerage passengers were crowded into one room with no privacy, subject to hunger, unhealthy conditions, and diseases such as typhus, cholera, smallpox, and dysentery. They sometimes experienced neglect and brutal treatment at the hands of the captain and crew and witnessed frequent fights on board.[14] Vere Foster, an Irish philanthropist, traveled to America as a steerage passenger in 1850 to investigate the hardships involved. It took him several years to fully recover his health after the voyage. Indeed, some died during the journey.[15]

Max and Pepi Lilienthal, still newlyweds, traveled to Paris in the early fall, where the rabbi conferred with French Jewish leader Albert Cohn about his Russian experience.[16] Then, in late October, they embarked from Le Havre on the *Sully*, having reserved a stateroom.[17] The Lilienthals did not have to endure the indignities of steerage, being able to afford more comfortable accommodations in an individual cabin. Still it would not likely have been an easy trip, especially given the rabbi's predilection for seasickness. Charles Dickens, who also could afford a stateroom, visited the United States in 1842. He provided a colorful picture of the rigors of ship travel from the bewildering tumult of boarding to the stark and gloomy feeling on the ship after it had weathered a storm. Planking was torn away, masts were crusted white with salt. Rigging was knotted, tangled, wet, and dripping; "a gloomier picture it would be hard to look upon."[18] Dickens was ill for a good portion of the rough trip.

Conditions were not much better upon arrival in New York. In the 1840s the city posed numerous challenges for the newcomers. According to the *New York Times*, the port presented dangers of its own. "When a ship arrived everyone in the great city, who can make a living from the arrived immigrants is here (i.e. *im Hafen*): runners, sharpers, pedlars [*sic*], agents of boardinghouses, of forwarding offices and worst of all, of all the houses where many a simple emigrant girl, far from friends and home, came to a sad end."[19] Runners, little better than ruffians, were known to steal luggage and misdirect new arrivals.[20] One observer, reporting in 1845, compared the swearing, fighting, shouting of passengers, and crying of women and children to the confusion of Babel.[21] Concerned German Americans wrote books and pamphlets advising prospective émigrés of the pitfalls involved. A Boston pastor, F. W. Bogen, advised them to keep their luggage with them at all times and to avoid engaging a runner or even asking one a question. Newcomers were warned never to ask directions, pretend to know where they were going, and avoid bargain-rate inns, because these lodgings were often dirty and the owners cheated the clientele. In 1847, the state set up a commission of immigration to help regulate the chaos and control corruption in the New York harbor. In 1855, New York finally opened Castle Garden, the nation's first official entry point.[22] The Lilienthals' arrival preceded these reforms by a decade. Fortunately Lilienthal's sister Sophie and her husband, John Lehrmaier, already lived in the city and helped them negotiate the dangers of the harbor. No unpleasant experiences are recorded in the family histories.

The Lilienthals arrived in America during a time of rapid national expansion as new towns grew up throughout the South, Midwest, and far West. Many of the new Jewish immigrants bypassed the established Jewish centers along the eastern seaboard to take advantage of the economic opportunities offered by this growth. Often among the first white settlers, they established trade links between new settlements and the older cities of the East. Jews were pioneers in the development of cities such as St. Louis, Kansas City, Cincinnati, Milwaukee, Minneapolis, Omaha, and San Francisco.[23]

Thousands of other immigrants like the Lilienthals chose to remain in New York, which was burgeoning rapidly from the influx of new arrivals. Manhattan grew from 166,000 inhabitants in 1825 to 630,000 in 1855.[24] The immigrants, most of whom were poor, settled in overcrowded, squalid tenement housing. Both Jewish and non-Jewish immigrants chose their neighborhoods largely based on nationality, language, and religion. Living in compact, cohesive neighborhoods allowed the immigrants to maintain their traditions and customs in relative isolation, affording them a safe place to adjust to American life.[25] By the 1840s, the largest concentration of German-born immigrants in New York had settled in "Kleindeutschland," Little Germany, a neighborhood that eventually stretched from Division Street north to East Fourteenth Street and west to east from Mott Street to the East River.[26] There, one could hear the German language spoken and find German stores.

> A visitor to Little Germany noted that the Germans were "satisfied, happy and contented," and, most significantly among their own people, they enjoyed life in the city where they "could speak their own language and live according their own customs." He added that "according to the standards of the German workingman one can live like a prince for ten to fourteen dollars a month." Despite their shabby apartments, he believed that "they would never willingly leave their beloved *Kleindeutschland.*"[27]

German Jewish immigrants settled at the southern end of this emerging German neighborhood in the 1840s, in the area that in later decades would become known as the Lower East Side.

German Catholic, Protestant, and Jewish immigrants shared a common language and cultural background that made their adjustment to America comparable in general terms. Each group tried to adapt Old World institutions and models to the American scene to keep their faiths viable. For German Catholics, the German language represented the old culture, which they wanted to pass on to the next generation.[28] Because of pressure from new Lutheran immigrants, the New York Ministerium reversed an 1807 decision and reestablished German as an official church language.[29]

Like Catholics and Lutherans, the German Jews in America consciously sustained a dual German and Jewish ethnicity. German Jews spoke German in their homes, often taught their children that language, established German Jewish newspapers, and developed social, cultural, and service societies for which German was the official language.[30] In the early years of his ministry, Lilienthal preached in German, attended board meetings conducted in German, and taught German in his school.[31] He valued the cultural heritage and common memories shared with other German immigrants. Because German Jews had a reputation for honesty and hard work, Lilienthal wrote in the *Allgemeine Zeitung des Judenthums* that to be a German Jew in America was a matter of great pride.[32] Even five years later he would speak movingly of the Fatherland. "How should we remember it otherwise than with love and gratitude; Fatherland . . . it brings back the joys of our sports of childhood, the loves of youth and the earnest hopes and struggles of manhood."[33] Further, in contrast to the dirty, crowded tenements of lower Manhattan, Lilienthal recalled the natural beauty of the land of his birth. "Truly, it is a great and beautiful country. Behold its nature, like God's garden it is situated in the very bosom of Europe."[34] Still, Germany lacked the one thing Lilienthal prized most: liberty. Shortly after his arrival he wrote in the *Allgemeine Zeitung des Judenthums*, "How like a dream does the memory of old Europe lie behind me, with its restrictions. How hazy is the image of the memory of the terrible Jew-hatred of Russia."[35] In pursuit of America's promise, Lilienthal willingly tackled the challenges of his new environment.

The influx of Central European immigrants would drastically alter the religious composition of the American people. At the time of the American Revolution, Catholics and Jews together constituted at most 0.1 percent of the population.[36] The vast majority of American colonists (perhaps 80 percent) were affiliated with religions of British origin: Congregationalists in New England, Anglicans in the South, and Presbyterians in the Middle Colonies. By midcentury Catholics would represent the largest church in America with approximately 1.6 million members, served by 1,800 priests in about 1,600 churches.[37] Besides Catholics, the German migration brought large numbers of Lutherans, members of the Reformed Church, and adherents of many sects. In 1790, there were perhaps 1,500 Jews in the United States; by 1825 the number had reached 3,000, and by 1848, 50,000. By 1860 the Jewish population had increased to 150,000, and by 1880, a quarter of a million Jews lived in the United States. Catholics, Lutherans, and Jews would struggle, each in their own way, for several generations to accommodate their traditions to the American situation.[38]

Growing numbers of Jewish immigrants placed increasing pressure on the traditional *kahal* system. In Europe the *kahal* signified an all-inclusive communal organization that served the needs of all the Jews in a given locality through a variety of institutions. In the United States, the synagogue, instead of being one institution within the *kahal*, absorbed most of its functions. So long as there was only one congregation in a city, the *kahal* system remained intact.[39] The Spanish-Portuguese congregation, Shearith Israel, the long-established *kahal* in New York, dominated the scene until 1825, when English and German immigrants split off to form Bnai Jeshurun.[40] This marks the beginning of what Jonathan Sarna has characterized as the collapse of the unified "synagogue community" and its replacement by a more pluralistic and diverse "community of synagogues."[41] In 1828, a group of German, Dutch, and Polish Jews seceded from Bnai Jeshurun and formed Anshe Chesed. Two other significant splinter congregations from Anshe Chesed were Shaarey Hashamayim (1839) and Rodeph Shalom (1842). By 1845, the year of Lilienthal's arrival in the city, ten synagogues served New York's Jews.[42]

This process of "multiplication by division" created many new challenges for the New York Jewish community. Each synagogue tried to create its own educational and social service societies to serve its congregants. The result was a confusing array of social service organizations that duplicated each other's efforts. Even as basic a service as burial plots became an issue. When Bnai Jeshurun separated from Shearith Israel, the parent congregation refused to share its cemetery. Each newly created synagogue was forced to purchase land to provide a final resting place for its members. At the same time, nobody was serving the needs of the community as a whole. With so many poor immigrants pouring into New York—people who lacked food, fuel for heat, schools for their children, health care, and burial plots—many were falling through the cracks. Community-wide needs for adequate educational materials, kashrut supervision, and a Jewish court (*beth din*) were not being met. The need for communal cooperation increased precisely at a time when intersynagogue competition was rampant.

The New York Jewish community fractured along lines drawn by differences of *minhag* (ritual customs). Each group worshipped according to the traditions they had brought from their country of origin. In one case the division was based on Reform ideology. In the spring of 1845, young members of Anshe Chesed and their rabbi, Leo Merzbacher, seceded to form Temple Emanu-El. Merzbacher (1809 or 1810–56) had received ordination in Europe from the arch-traditionalist Rabbi Moses Sofer and then had studied at the universities of Erlangen and Munich. He arrived in New York in the early 1840s, where he briefly served Anshe Chesed and Rodeph Shalom. The mild reforms that he instituted at Temple Emanu-El included an all-male choir and the first American Reform liturgy, *Seder Tefilah*. Although the temple was still traditional enough to separate men and women during services, these changes created controversy and division in the Jewish community.[43]

With the disintegration of the *kahal*, Jewish congregations struggled to find new ways to provide for the life-cycle, educational, and charitable needs of their members and the larger community. For example, the mass migration of German Jews placed new demands on the community's educational system. Under the Sephardim, Jewish education had been sporadic at best, dependent on private tutorials and local synagogue schools. The few established Jewish schools in America offered minimal Jewish education along with secular studies. Jacob Rader Marcus, in his study of colonial Jewry, explained that early American Jewry had no interest in extensive Jewish education.[44] Dissatisfied with the status quo, the new immigrants formed synagogue schools and private Jewish day schools.[45] They thought that there was a pressing need for improved Jewish education to maintain the continuity of faith while facilitating acculturation in what was still a predominantly Protestant society. The rapidly growing and rapidly splintering Jewish community in America called for strong and creative religious leaders who could bring order to other areas as well, such as the ritual and liturgical practices of the community, care for the sick and needy, and the creation of a viable communal structure to replace the outmoded *kahal* model. This was the chaotic landscape that the young Lilienthal entered with his arrival in 1845.

Until the middle of the nineteenth century, there were no ordained rabbis in the United States. The early clergy, called ministers or sometimes hazanim, were often poorly trained and poorly paid. With little status or power, they were firmly under the control of the lay leadership. In the *Asmonean*, an early Jewish publication, editor Robert Lyon wrote of the need to elevate the status of Jewish clergy to make them more than mere hirelings of the moment, the tools of the powerful *parnassim* (synagogue presidents).[46] It is no wonder, Lyon argued, that few respectable families educated their children to become ministers. Isaac Leeser (1806–68), one of the early nonrabbinic leaders of American Judaism and editor of the Jewish monthly the *Occident*, commented frankly on the frustrations of the clergy serving these congregations.

> He may be reminded to his cost that he has no rights as a minister, that he can be treated at the pleasure of the congregation like a servant, like one employed to perform certain duties merely, and that he can be browbeaten by all who please to arrogate the mastery over him in quality of their being electors of the congregation, not to mention that he is under the absolute control of the ruling elders, without any redress.[47]

The moderate traditionalist Leeser came to know this from bitter personal experience. He served the Sephardic Mikveh Israel congregation in Philadelphia from 1829 until his acrimonious dismissal in 1850.[48]

This absence of clergy power and status perpetuated the domination of a lay leadership ill-equipped to meet the challenges created by the influx of immigrants. Historian Leon Jick compared the Jewish leadership crisis with the centralized, hierarchical Roman Catholic Church, whose immigrants were also adjusting to American society. In their case, responsibility for reformulating the church's role was left almost exclusively up to the clergy. American Jewry, structureless and leaderless, could not even create a forum in which crucial problems could be addressed, much less establish an ecclesiastical authority to provide structure. In this chaotic situation each congregation went its own way, directed only by its board of trustees.[49]

Lilienthal could offer a great deal to this young American Jewish community. With his elite university education and his traditional rabbinic ordination, he was eminently qualified to provide the leadership the Jewish community so sorely lacked. He also had remarkable professional experiences, particularly for a young man, having already created a successful modern school in Russia. Working side by side with the highest officials in the Russian government and with the cream of Russian Jewish rabbinic and lay leadership, he had attempted to implement his Haskalah agenda within the largest Jewish community in the world. Regardless of the outcome, the experience had been invaluable. Now, forced to start anew, he came to America with this wealth of experience behind him and a powerful optimism concerning the future of Judaism in the New World.

Lilienthal was already rather well known when he and Pepi arrived in New York in November 1845. His Russian exploits had been reported in the *Occident* as early as 1843. Upon his arrival, the paper hailed him as an eminent scholar, an "experienced and tried laborer in the vineyard of the Lord."[50] Six feet tall and thin, with red hair, blue eyes, and fair skin, Lilienthal was an imposing figure who wasted no time making his presence felt.[51] On November 19, he was invited to speak at the second annual banquet of the German Hebrew Benevolent Society. According to the *Occident*, Lilienthal spoke forcefully in German about how gratified he was to be in this free land where Christians and Jews could unite in charitable causes. He compared it with the deplorable sufferings of the Jews of Russia and other lands suffering under the cloud of despotism.[52]

This occasion was soon followed by an invitation to preach at Congregation Anshe Chesed, the largest German congregation in New York, on November 29. Lilienthal's talk was even announced in a non-Jewish local paper: "Dr. Lilienthal, chief rabbi of Russia [*sic*] will give a lecture in the

Synagog [*sic*] Anshe Chesed next Saturday."[53] Presented to a capacity crowd, Lilienthal delivered a sermon that the *Occident* described as both eloquent and fervent. Making a deep impression on the congregation, Lilienthal asserted that Judaism was the one true faith. In affirming this exclusivist claim, he was expressing an idea at odds with the liberal Protestant ethos, particularly its denominational theory that repudiated the theory of one true church. The tension between these two positions was a challenge for all immigrant religions, all of which were used to traditional monopolistic pretensions.[54] Facing the issue head on, Lilienthal discussed the difficulties in maintaining Judaism in an American environment where religious pluralism gave every religion equal rights. The following Sabbath, he preached at Shaarey Hashamayim and Rodeph Shalom, two other German congregations.[55] James K. Gutheim, whose summary of the Anshe Chesed sermon appeared in the *Occident*, expressed the wish that Lilienthal be given many opportunities to preach, or better yet, that a local congregation offer him a job.[56]

The boards of Congregations Anshe Chesed, Shaarey Hashamayim, and Rodeph Shalom concurred with Gutheim's sentiments. In early December they met to draw up a plan whereby Lilienthal would be hired as the rabbi of their united congregations, choosing a joint board of officers made up of members from each congregation to work out further details.[57] Anshe Chesed, the oldest and largest of the three congregations, agreed to contribute $500 to Lilienthal's salary, and the other two congregations pledged $250 each. Relative to salaries of other Jewish clergy in America, this was a reasonable offer.[58] By way of comparison, Rabbi Merzbacher received $200 from the newly formed Temple Emanu-El in 1845. Hazan Lyons of Shearith Israel received $1,250 yearly. Two years later Reverend Samuel Isaacs earned $5,000 a year.[59] Lilienthal's appointment was contingent on receiving proof of his rabbinic certification. A number of immigrants came to the United States claiming rabbinic credentials. Among them were plenty of charlatans—adventurers, apostates, even former missionaries who applied for clerical positions in antebellum America.[60]

The list of Lilienthal's rabbinic duties, described in one of the earliest extant contracts for an American rabbi, was formidable.[61] The original German agreement of the three synagogues stipulated the following tasks:

1. He was to be the teacher of the Jewish religion in the three congregations.

2. He was to supervise religious services and was to rule on all questions pertaining to Jewish worship.

3. He was to preach in one of the three synagogues each Sabbath and festival.

4. He was to rule on all other questions of law based on specified codes.

5. He was to supervise the kosher meat and the baking of matzah for the congregation.

6. He was to supervise the school and be involved in religious instruction of the children.

7. All post–bar mitzvah boys and twelve-year-old girls would study religion with him and be examined on Shavuot to show their true devotion to Judaism.

8. He was to give an oration at all weddings, pending the permission of the president of the respective congregation.

9. He was to visit the sick, comfort the bereaved, and deliver funeral orations when desired.[62]

It is likely that Lilienthal helped to draft this contract. In theory, it gave him the responsibilities and the authority of the new modern rabbis emerging in Germany. Although the minutes often referred to Lilienthal by the exalted title "Sein Hocherwurden Herr Rabbiner" (in the English minutes, Reverend Doctor), in reality he could do little without the approval of the joint board. Indeed, before he began the job, the board added an amendment to Lilienthal's contract that stipulated which code of Jewish law he should consult for his rulings.[63]

The speed with which the leadership of the three synagogues developed the details of their unprecedented union was remarkable. The basis for the union may have already been established by Merzbacher, who had served Anshe Chesed and Rodeph Shalom simultaneously. The minute books do not provide a reason for the haste. One observer suggested that Lilienthal was hired in a time of crisis for the traditional German congregations: the threat of competition from the new Reform Temple Emanu-El, which had just broken away from Anshe Chesed. Although small, the new congregation did have the services of Rabbi Merzbacher.[64] To compete, the traditional German synagogues were eager to acquire the talented Lilienthal.

In little more than a week, the three congregations forged a loose confederation that would meet jointly on a regular basis and develop policy on common issues. The Union of German Synagogues in New York represented an experiment in communal unity—a middle ground between the old *kahal* system and the congregational atomization that was asserting itself through the proliferation of synagogues in America.[65] In this union, each synagogue kept its autonomy, and religious services were held separately. Moreover, each group retained its own board and officers, and no important matter could be resolved without the consent of the membership of all three constituents. This system allowed the synagogues to share resources when it benefited them, for example, in paying the rabbi's salary or running a combined school.

A careful look at the plan, however, reveals the pitfall in the system: Each synagogue could go its own way if the leadership deemed it was in its best interest. This arrangement was a complicated situation for the new rabbi, who would sometimes be caught in the crossfire of conflicting demands. In December 1845, however, optimism canceled out any doubts about the plan. On December 29, the day after the general meeting at which his appointment was approved, the Union board unanimously ratified their choice. The three synagogues officially declared Lilienthal to be their joint rabbi as of January 1, 1846.[66] In the *Allgemeine Zeitung des Judenthums* Lilienthal described his new position in enthusiastic terms. He reported that the combined congregations consisted of 700 families, but he had predicted that within three years there would be at least 1,000. Calling himself the *Oberrabbiner* (chief rabbi), he claimed that he was the first rabbi to be established in the United States. Evidently, he was carried away by his enthusiasm because at least two other ordained rabbis preceded him (Abraham Rice and Leo Merzbacher). Further, although he referred to himself as chief rabbi, his authority was limited to his three constituent synagogues. This hyperbolic style is characteristic of many of Lilienthal's early reports to the Jewish leadership back in Germany, whom he evidently hoped to impress after his Russian debacle. Still, it is understandable that he rejoiced that God had given him, as he termed it, another opportunity to serve the Jewish people.[67]

The Lilienthals set up their first family home at 21½ Eldridge Street, slightly south and west of the early center of the emerging German community, where the major concentration of German Jews settled in the late 1830s and early 1840s. Lilienthal's congregations were spread out over the neighborhood. Anshe Chesed was on Henry Street, just south of the German district. The newer Rodeph Shalom and Shaarey Hashamayim congregations were located on Attorney Street, closer to the center of Kleindeutschland. Probably the determining factor in the Lilienthals' choice was the location of John and Sophie (Lilienthal) Lehrmaier on Forsyth Street, one block over.[68] Despite his relatively modest income, the Lilienthals chose a large home, capable of accommodating visitors.[69] Lilienthal's daughter-in-law Sophie (wife of their son Theodore) would recall in her history of the family that at first the financial struggle was hard, noting that Pepi "willingly undertook to do all the work of the household."[70] When the couple arrived in New York in 1845, Pepi was already pregnant with their first child, Eliza (born June 4, 1846). Although a block away from Sophie and John, it seems that the young couple depended more on the emotional support of Max's brother Samuel and Pepi's sister Caroline, who were living in Charleston and with whom they were in constant touch through letters.[71]

The couple quickly began to socialize with prominent New York German Jewish merchants and professionals, often entertaining them in their home.[72] It was clearly important to them to associate with the social and intellectual elite because both Max and Pepi came from wealthy, well-educated families. Pepi, in particular, had been brought up in luxury. Sophie recalls, "Pepi drew beautifully, spoke French well and in all her bearing, gave evidence of her fine breeding and culture. Their children remembered their father reading French aloud to his wife, while she was busy with some household duty."[73]

After their long years of frustrated waiting, the two were finally able to create a home together. Neither would have imagined that it would be in New York City when they announced their engagement in 1838. It is a testament to their optimism and love for one another that they transferred their dreams so willingly to the New World. In fact, their daughter-in-law Sophie later wrote that they had an ideal marriage, so devoted were they to one another.[74]

Lilienthal's installation was celebrated on January 10, 1846, at the largest of the three synagogues, Anshe Chesed, following the end of regular Sabbath services. An enormous crowd was present, filling every available space in the sanctuary. The presidents and other officers of the three synagogues had seats of honor, and the three cantors intoned a psalm to begin the ceremony. After a few preliminary speeches, the "Right Reverend Chief Rabbi" gave one of the most moving addresses that *Occident* correspondent James Gutheim had ever heard.[75]

In his speech, titled "The Vocation of the Minister," Lilienthal articulated a vision of the modern professional rabbinate, one that had begun to emerge in Germany during his youth and many aspects of which he had implemented during his ministry in Riga. Going well beyond the traditional model of the rabbi as interpreter of Jewish law, Lilienthal outlined the role he intended to play in the congregations, in worship services, in education, in the community, and in pastoral activities. In doing so, he deliberately redefined the balance of power between the rabbi and the lay leadership of the synagogue. Yet, rather than confronting the issue aggressively, Lilienthal framed his relationship with his new congregations as a marriage covenant, invoking the traditional vow *"Harei at m'kudeshet li*—I wed thee unto me, my flock as that being to whom my life and thoughts, my feelings, and my labours shall be devoted for evermore."[76]

With regard to his duties in the congregations, Lilienthal addressed the controversy between Reform and Orthodoxy that had already erupted in the American Jewish community. He diplomatically restated the position of both the traditionalists and the reformers in a sympathetic manner.

> The one exclaims: "Hold fast to the ancient institutions, hold fast to the venerable customs, hold fast to that which has been transmitted to us by our pious fathers. The law which Moses has instituted must eternally, eternally remain the inheritance of the congregations of Jacob." The others say: "Onward, onward, is our motto; onward is the watchword of the times, onward is the spirit of the age, we cannot, we will not, we dare not remain behind, if cold indifference shall not seize every heart, if all shall not be abandoned. Whoever will not follow the wheels of Time and history, will be crushed by the wheels of Time in its might, all-powerful revolutions, and then all will be lost."[77]

Lilienthal asserted that his duty was to rise above the controversy and reconcile all parties according to Jewish law. He maintained that any changes should be made on the basis of halakhic precedent, that is, on Jewish law.[78] Gutheim was therefore happy to report to his readers that Lilienthal was a traditional leader. "The Chief Rabbi cherishes no sympathy with the so-called reforming Rabbis of Germany; but is adverse to their movements, and fully determined to uphold our religious institutions and be guided only by the law, as it is laid down in the Bible and explained by our sages."[79] Indeed, in an 1847 letter to the *Allgemeine Zeitung des Judenthums* Lilienthal asserted, "Germany's reformatory aspiration, which has its roots, in all leading instances, in the striving for emancipation, likewise finds little approval here, since men are free from the outset."[80] Lilienthal seems to be arguing that there was no need for Reform in America.

The congregations also understood the address as representing an Orthodox point of view. They heard Lilienthal commit himself to Jewish law and were reassured, not fully grasping the modernizing agenda behind Lilienthal's words. Lilienthal's lifelong friend and colleague, Isaac M. Wise, also characterized Lilienthal as an Orthodox leader at this point.[81] In Wise's assessment, based on many private conversations, Lilienthal began his American career as a proponent of traditional Judaism who struggled over a long period of time to divest himself of inherited views. Wise also alluded to pragmatic reasons for Lilienthal to expound a traditional position at the start of his tenure. The three congregations that hired him were home to those who had rejected the innovations of Rabbi Merzbacher, who had recently broken away to establish a Reform congregation. Lilienthal was quite aware of their opposition to change. As Wise summed up in retrospect, "The doctor was elected Rabbi of three German congregations; he was bound in duty to operate *with* and not *against* them."[82]

Still, Lilienthal's stance was not merely a pragmatic nod to the ideological orientation of his new congregations. His theoretical position of finding legal precedent for moderate change is similar to that of Zacharias Frankel, the German rabbi who broke with the reformers to initiate the school of Positive-Historical Judaism and who would soon set up his seminary in Breslau along these lines. Beyond any specific ideology, Lilienthal's goal was to reconcile all parties. Finding a basis for unity remained a constant element in his thought throughout his rabbinic career.

Lilienthal did not claim the authority to make changes alone, but he wanted to establish a *beth din*, a traditional court made up of learned rabbis who would study legal precedents and issue rulings. By basing his authority on law and setting up a *beth din*, however, Lilienthal seems to have wanted to remove such decisions from the hands of the lay leadership. To mollify the laity, he pledged to listen to the advice of the respected heads of the congregations as well as individual members.[83] He made clear that his main concern was that he and the congregation would work together harmoniously.

Next in his installation address, Lilienthal changed his tone abruptly from conciliation to denunciation and took the opportunity to condemn disorder during religious services. Like other modernized German Jews who wanted to imitate the decorum of Christian worship, Lilienthal was embarrassed by the chaotic cacophony that characterized traditional services, during which congregants prayed out loud at their own pace. Calling such chaos an "iniquity," he said that the synagogue worship had "become an object of scorn, contempt and mockery to all nations."[84] Invoking the Talmud, Maimonides, later rabbinic writings, and the *Shulhan Arukh*, Lilienthal insisted that it was a sin to show such disrespect before the Holy One. He promised to form a special committee, in conjunction with his *beth din*, to bring order and dignity to the worship. In addition, as rabbi he promised to preach God's law and expound eternal truths at every solemn occasion.[85]

Next, turning his attention to the school, Lilienthal revealed his Haskalah vision in his commitment to education. "To educate our children as Jews, as good men, as useful citizens is the highest and most excellent commission we have received of the Lord," he declared.[86] This formulation was in harmony with Haskalah pedagogical goals in Germany: creating Jews who were also ethical and productive members of the broader community. However, in America, Lilienthal acknowledged, there were new challenges that pertained specifically to Jewish education. "But our children, who are brought up in this, to Israel so unaccustomed, liberty; who go forth into the distant parts of the country where the Jews live sparsely and scattered, what will become of them, if Jewish principles are not deeply planted into their minds, if religion is not deeply engraved on their hearts?"[87] Freedom and assimilation, he asserted, threatened to undermine Jewish identity in the younger generation. For all his idealization of American freedom, Lilienthal immediately grasped the new challenge that it presented to Jewish survival. Here, Jewish education must have more than a modernizing and socializing function. It also must help sustain Jewish identity in a society more open than any Jews had encountered before. For this reason Lilienthal promised to supervise the work of the schools, urging the directors and teachers to work with him to help Judaism flourish in America. He also assigned to himself the task of instructing post–bar mitzvah boys and girls beyond the age of 12 in religious principles to ensure their dedication to Jewish ideals as they matured.[88]

Finally, Lilienthal told his congregants that he wanted to share their joys and sorrows, to treat each as a friend regardless of financial status. He promised to help the widow and orphan and to plead the cause of all in need. His door, he said, would always be open to all who sought his advice or help. He prayed that ties of love would knit them into a close, trusting community, working toward a thriving future.[89]

Lilienthal concluded with a prayer that he could not then have uttered anywhere else in the world. It revealed how deeply he appreciated what the United States offered to the Jewish people. "Like no other country on earth, O Lord, has this one received us; like no other land, it has generously removed from our shoulders contumely, and cruelty, and oppression, and with equal rights and equal privileges it has hailed us as brothers."[90] How far he had come from the tyranny of the Bavarian Matrikel and from the cruel autocracy of Tsar Nicholas! Already Lilienthal loved his new country and was determined to serve his people there to the best of his ability.

As he had in Riga, the rabbi wasted no time launching into his agenda with great energy. Even before his installation, committees were set up to work out systems and procedures for a host of issues facing the community. Lilienthal combined a traditional approach with the desire to bring both order and professionalism to the various aspects of ritual life. In a number of ritual areas the young rabbi in fact demanded stricter adherence to Jewish law. A comparison with the rulings of the Reform rabbinic conferences, which took place in Germany in roughly the same period, helps to show Lilienthal's traditionalism at that time. These proceedings, reported in detail in the *Allgemeine Zeitung des Judenthums* and in the *Occident*, were well known to Lilienthal.

One area Lilienthal immediately tried to address concerned the supervision of kosher meat. At the time of Lilienthal's arrival, Jews were purchasing meat directly from Jewish or Christian butchers who employed *shohetim* (ritual slaughters) without synagogue control. Abuses were rampant. When he learned that serious violations of Jewish law were common, Lilienthal called a meeting of the *shohetim*. Meat was not being properly washed or labeled, kosher and nonkosher meat were occasionally mixed, and inspection was lax. The butchers told the rabbi that they would not tolerate any interference in this free land and threatened to sue him for libel if he called attention to their violations of Jewish law. Further, if Lilienthal tried to declare any of their meat nonkosher, they would lower their prices and Jewish women would buy it anyway.[91] Lilienthal was not an easy man to intimidate. With almost 720 members behind him, he attempted to set up rules and force the butchers to enter into agreements with the synagogues. He threatened to make public announcements exposing noncompliers. It is not known to what extent he was successful.[92]

In this regard Lilienthal adopted a much more traditional position than some of the radical reformers in the Frankfurt *Reformfreunde* who called for a complete end to dietary laws. This was a radical position even among reformers, who privately may have been lax in their observance but were reluctant to address the issue publicly. In general, early Reform leaders in Europe concentrated on changes in the public realm rather than on issues pertaining to home observance.[93]

Lilienthal also demanded higher halakhic standards with regard to the baking of matzo for Passover. In the 1840s bakers solicited synagogues for matzo-making patronage, and, as a concession, they allowed the synagogue to send one or two men to supervise the baking. The bakers also agreed to donate a certain number of pounds of matzo to the poor.[94] Not satisfied with the standards, Lilienthal formulated a set of regulations for the proper baking of matzo. At a meeting of the Union board on March 1, 1846, he clarified the regulations in seventeen points, each with a legal source indicated.[95] Robert Spier, the baker contracted by the synagogues, claimed to have attempted to follow Lilienthal's regulations, but the rabbi was not satisfied and suggested that the three synagogues buy their own equipment. Requiring each member to place a two-year matzo order at a price slightly higher than the baker's, he proposed, would cover the cost. It was unlikely that his idea was successful because the community was at that point overrun with matzo bakers who sold their wares directly to the public.[96]

The rabbi reported to the *Allgemeine Zeitung des Judenthums* that he performed about 100 weddings during his first year of service to the three synagogues.[97] On February 8, 1846, Lilienthal presented a series of rules for uniform procedures for weddings, for which he provided halakhic justification.[98]

1. The bride and groom had to submit their names, addresses, positions, and birth dates to the rabbi.

2. The rabbi was to question the groom to make sure the marriage was in no way in violation of Jewish law.

3. Weddings were to take place only in the synagogue, unless an exception could be justified.

4. The wedding was to be announced in the three synagogues on the Sabbath before the event.

These regulations reflected the chaotic conditions within the fluid immigrant population in which few had deep roots, known histories, or family connections. Careful probing by a rabbi versed in Jewish law was crucial to avoid illegal unions, such as those involving someone who had not legally divorced a spouse living in Europe. Some traditionalists objected to his last rule—the public announcement of a forthcoming wedding—claiming it was an imitation of Christian practice. Lilienthal based his ruling on a New York law, dating back to 1684, that required names to be publicly announced, but he silenced his critics by specifically citing precedents in Jewish law to prove such announcements were allowed.[99]

Some of the earliest reforms to take effect in Europe concerned marriage procedures; the goal was to harmonize civil and religious law in this area. Israel Jacobson had used his brief period of consistorial power in 1810 to rework the marriage contract and ceremony; several of his innovations found wider usage.[100] Although the rabbinic conferences discussed wedding regulations at length, they put off detailed recommendations. At the Brunswick conference in 1844, though, the group ruled that marriage between Christians and Jews was not forbidden if the couples brought up their children as Jews.[101] Lilienthal, concerned for the continuity of the Jewish people, fought this manifestation of assimilation in America.

One ancient Jewish legal tradition was that of the levirate marriage, which required the brother of a deceased groom to marry his widow if the couple had not produced an offspring. (The basis for this law is found in Deuteronomy 25:5–10.) The only legal way that this obligation could be avoided was for the brother to go through a ceremony called *halitzah*, in which he renounced his duty to the widow. In front of witnesses, the widow would remove his shoe, throw it some distance, spit in the direction of the brother-in-law, and recite a formula. Only after this ceremony was she free to remarry. This archaic law presented many practical problems for Jewish communities, not the least of which was the distance between families in America and Germany. A woman could be bound forever if her husband's brother did not release her. Lilienthal introduced a regulation, already used in Europe, whereby the brother of the groom would sign a release before the wedding (a prenuptial agreement), or the release would be sent to Germany for the necessary signature. This document, produced in the *Minute Book of the Union* on March 18, 1846, guaranteed that, in the case of the death of the groom before the couple had a child, the brother of the groom would automatically release the bride so that she could remarry.[102] Lilienthal's prenuptial agreement was an effort to solve a difficult legal problem. In spite of this procedure, Lilienthal performed only one ceremony of *halitzah* during his first year, for which he commissioned a special sandal needed in the ritual.[103]

On this issue, in particular, it is clear that Lilienthal was more traditional than the German Reform rabbinic conferences, which rejected *halitzah* at the Breslau conference in 1846. "At the closing meeting the commission on marriage laws recommended that the old institution of Chalitzah be declared unsuited to modern conditions, because 'the levirate marriage and the Chalitzah were instituted in a time when the views on the position of woman, the family rights, and the perpetuation of the individual were entirely different from what they are now.'"[104]

With the breakdown of the *kahal* system, each synagogue had to create its own burial society and cemetery. The Union board asked the chief rabbi to create an order for funeral and burial practices.[105] Following the general practice in the city, funerals were often accompanied by elaborate processions. Funeral notices were printed and sent to all synagogue members informing them of the time of the service.[106] In November 1846, Lilienthal instructed the sexton in the law concerning new burial grounds and listed various articles he would need.[107] Early in 1847, the rabbi supplied the president of Anshe Chesed with written regulations regarding the ritual washing, dressing, and interring of the deceased, which the board accepted.[108]

In contrast, in the previous year German Reform leaders at the Breslau conference had rejected many traditional mourning customs. Practices such as the tearing of clothes, refraining from shaving, washing, or wearing leather footwear were deemed artifacts from earlier periods of Jewish life that had lost all significance and religious meaning.[109]

In his installation address Lilienthal had harshly condemned the lack of decorum in services. He advocated changes from the status quo. Perhaps because he had taken a strictly traditional stand on some issues, he could advocate for some modernization here. Lilienthal's concern for decorum represented a combination of German antecedents and American trends. In Europe, decorum during services was a major focus for early reformers. Familiar with orderly Protestant services in which the congregants sat in respectful silence, these Jews became embarrassed by the old style of Jewish worship, with its loud and disorderly services. Typically, congregants prayed out loud, each at their own rate, swaying in their prayer shawls, calling out responses, and often mumbling the Hebrew they no longer understood. Others carried on conversations about their business affairs or exchanged gossip during the service. The early reformers sought to make the Jewish service more dignified by emulating Christian styles of worship; their reforms tended to minimize active congregational participation and elevate the leadership of the professional clergy.[110]

Had increased decorum been a strictly Reform issue, Lilienthal would never have been able to advance this portion of his agenda. In Europe, some ritual reforms were even advocated by the leader of Modern Orthodoxy, Samson Raphael Hirsch, who wore a black robe and introduced into his synagogue a regular German sermon based on Christian models, a male choir, and a heightened sense of propriety. In France, England, and Germany, the Orthodox countered the Reform threat by adopting much of its program in this area. England's chief rabbi, Nathan Marcus Adler, instituted a series of regulations to bring order and solemnity to the service.[111]

In addition, decorum was a concern of American Jews long before the Reform movement became a force. During the colonial period, congregations tried to limit noise and interruptions in the service by fining disruptors, denying them a seat, depriving them of ritual honors, or even revoking membership in the community.[112] Leaders tried to curb loud, excessive talking during the prayers and disruptive coming and going. In 1805, Shearith Israel enacted punitive ordinances to establish better order at services, giving the president the power to fine or expel a guilty congregant. As early as 1809, some members of Shearith Israel tried to curtail the selling of *misheberach*s (blessings recited during the Torah reading) because the custom involved interrupting the service for a raucous bidding for honors. Because this auction provided income for the congregation, the change was rejected.[113]

The newer synagogues of the city tried to strike a balance between tradition and decorum. In 1842, Anshe Chesed required mourners to recite the Kaddish in unison. When Leo Merzbacher was rabbi of Anshe Chesed, he made changes in the sale of honors distributed during the service, introduced a choir to lead the congregational responses, and required that all notices be posted on blackboards at the entrance instead of having them read out loud during services.[114]

Lilienthal vigorously continued Merzbacher's efforts. The Union board set up a committee on synagogue order at a meeting in January 1846.[115] On March 3 the Anshe Chesed trustees resolved that notice be posted at the entrance of the synagogue. "For the purpose of getting more order in the service . . . during the prayers, there will be several gentlemen who will recite the prayers with the *hazzan* [cantor] for the purpose of showing the congregators the way the prayers are required to be read and all others are requested to read the prayers silently until they have learned the way to read them."[116] Although Lilienthal had board support for increased decorum, progress was slow. A Dutch Jew who befriended the rabbi in his first years reported that "he introduced a few innovations; in the synagogue he already made enemies on the spot and they said that he was newfangled. Because these fellows believe that if one makes another niggen (melody) of 'Jigdal' . . . than they are accustomed to, that this is as bad as one of the worst trespasses of the Sabbath!"[117] This Dutch Jew was upset with the level of liturgical ignorance in the congregation. He wrote that they regularly mispronounced the Hebrew prayers. He suggested to the rabbi that he "introduce no innovations whatsoever, since his congregations are too ignorant and not amenable to any reform." Lilienthal disagreed, saying he would arrange things as he wanted them. In retrospect Lilienthal admitted that his Dutch friend had probably been right.[118] Wise, visiting Anshe Chesed in July 1846, reported that

the congregation was orthodox, and just as ill-behaved as in Germany. The cantor had on a Christian gown, trilled like a mock nightingale, and leaped about like a hooked fish. After the selling of the so-called *mitzvoth*, I lost patience with the intolerable sing-song with which the reader intoned the portion and read from the *Torah* and with the innumerable *Mi-sheberakhs*. "Why is this nuisance tolerated in a metropolis?" I asked my neighbor.[119]

Whereas Wise was impatient for change, Lilienthal was willing to work patiently toward his goals from a position based on legal precedent. He established a detailed set of rules for decorum that were published in the *Occident*. The reporter noted that the chief rabbi based the rules on the Code of Jewish Law and claimed that order now prevailed in the synagogues. The congregations chanted Hebrew liturgy properly, using appropriate melodies for hymns or reciting prayers responsively. This was said to have had the beneficial effect of keeping the congregants awake![120]

The rules were not always followed. In March 1847, the trustee minutes reported that Joseph Bachman, a member, behaved improperly during services. He was summoned to come before the board. Bachman did not appear and was fined 5 dollars.[121] The board also decided that proclamations be made in the synagogue on the next Sabbath to remind the members to keep order and that fines would be enforced for noncompliance. The Anshe Chesed board later added further rules, backing up its stand with sanctions. "The Directors hope that every member will see how necessary it is for a congregation to have its Divine Service performed with dignity and good order and for that reason the Directors flatter themselves that every member will act in accordance with the above rules, so that the board may not have occasion to impose a fine on those acting contrary to the above rules, which in no instance, will be remitted."[122]

In liturgical matters the congregation turned to their rabbi as well. In February 1846 Rabbi Lilienthal replaced the traditional prayer Ha-Notein Teshu'ah (He who gives salvation) with Ribbon Kol Ha-Olamim (Master of all the worlds), a prayer he himself had composed. He considered the traditional prayer suitable in countries where Jews had to humble themselves before monarchs, whereas his own prayer was more appropriate for citizens of a republic. Unlike the traditional prayer, which adopted the typical Diaspora tone of subservience toward earthly kings, Ribbon Kol Ha-Olamim reflected self-confidence, optimism, and the hope of redemption. According to American Jewish historian Jonathan Sarna, Lilienthal's prayer was an early and bold attempt to show that "America is different." More than just another Diaspora land, it represented the hope of all humanity. The prayer urged, "Look down from Your holy dwelling and bless this land, the United States of America, whereon we dwell. Let not violence be heard in their land, wasting and destruction within their boundaries, but You shall call its walls 'Salvation' and its gates 'Praise.'"[123] This prayer was reprinted in an Orthodox prayer book for American Jews called *Tefilot Yisra'el*, published by Henry Frank in 1848/9. Other congregations in Albany, Syracuse, Boston, and Newark also adopted this liturgical change.[124]

Lilienthal had long believed in the central place of the sermon in an edifying religious service. Sermons, which were so central in the modern German synagogue, had only recently been introduced in American congregations. There was no tradition of Jewish preaching in colonial America because the scarcity of Jews made it hard to draw the kind of crowd that would warrant a sermon and because no preachers or rabbis were sufficiently trained in Jewish sources to give sermons.[125] The first Jewish preacher of note in America was Gershom Mendes Seixas of Shearith Israel in New York. Seixas, who adopted the sermon in imitation of Protestant models, would often give a sermon on a patriotic occasion, such as a national day of thanksgiving, or for a charitable cause. These secular holidays were opportunities to link Judaism with American values such as liberty, individualism, and voluntarism.[126] The sermon became more accepted as a regular feature in Jewish congregations in the early nineteenth century.

With the influx of German Jewish immigrants, many newcomers expected sermons of the type they had come to appreciate in Germany in the 1820s and 1830s. Isaac Leeser, the major advocate of traditionalism during this period, was actually the first American Jewish leader to give an English sermon at a regular Sabbath service; he did so every two weeks and on special occasions as part of his duties as hazan. Leeser was consciously influenced by the Unitarian minister Henry Furness (1802–96). Samuel Isaacs gave monthly addresses at Bnai Jeshurun starting in 1839, and Rabbi Abraham Rice delivered regular talks in both English and German to his congregation in Baltimore.[127] For Leeser and his traditional colleagues, the sermon represented an element in the Americanization process.[128] Lilienthal's congregation therefore took his insistence on regular sermons in stride.

Moreover, Lilienthal was considered an excellent orator, having preached in Riga and Munich to large crowds.[129] Although he originally preferred the more intellectually and morally serious sermon favored by many of the early German Maskilim, while in Riga Lilienthal had learned to instill powerful feelings in his addresses. He knew he was successful when he saw their tears.[130] James Gutheim, moved by Lilienthal's emotional delivery, reported in the *Occident* that it was not possible for him to do full justice to Lilienthal's first New York address. "It was delivered with an eloquence and fervor that did not fail to make a deep impression on the minds of the audience, and the effects of which were reflected in many a tearful eye. I could but wish that frequent opportunity to preach would be given to Dr. L."[131]

Isaac M. Wise, who was thoroughly trained in the German rhetorical tradition, heard his friend preach on many occasions. His first impression was favorable. "He pleased me very much, for he was an excellent and popular pulpit orator, used a glowing diction, and had a dignified carriage."[132] The chief rabbi used this talent to bring dignity and edification to his congregations.

Lilienthal was not as successful in other attempts to bring order and dignity to the worship service. Merzbacher had formed a choir at Temple Emanu-El, and Lilienthal wished to do so as well.[133] Wise reported that Lilienthal ordered a copy of Solomon Sulzer's *Shir Tsiyon*, a compendium of cantorial and choral music that blended ancient synagogal melodies and contemporary compositional techniques. *Shir Tsiyon* had a powerful impact in Germany, France, and eventually even in Eastern Europe and America. Because Sulzer's music was for an all-male a cappella choir, it could easily be integrated into even the most traditional synagogues. It should not have been difficult to justify the innovation in Lilienthal's synagogues, but it was not to be. As Wise remembered, "His mighty *Parnass* declared obstinately that he was opposed once and for all to its introduction into the chief synagogue. . . . I listened to the bitter war of words, and put an end to it by buying the *Shir Tsiyon* and taking it home with me."[134] Lilienthal also attempted, unsuccessfully, to have the sale of synagogue honors abolished and to limit the number of *misheberach*s.[135]

In his installation sermon, Lilienthal made it clear that his most important rabbinic duty was the education of the next generation. His Haskalah ideology had advocated *Bildung* (self-realization) through education as the prerequisite for emancipation. Because the United States gave the gift of citizenship without these preconditions, Lilienthal had to translate this commitment to learning into an American context. Lilienthal's main concern was the continuity of Jewish tradition, and education was necessary to maintain Judaism in the face of secular and Christian influences.

In the 1840s and 1850s new Jewish immigrants to New York were reluctant to send their children to public school. They were eager to preserve both their Jewish and German heritage, which public schools threatened because, for the most part, instruction took place in English. However, the Public School Society of New York City set up a German-language school in 1839. Some Jewish families sent their children to this school, located near Congregation Bnai Jeshurun in the center of New York's German Jewish district. Because religiously neutral schools that taught in German were the exception, however, many new immigrants still chose Jewish schools, which better met their needs. German Catholic immigrants, who also wanted to retain their German language and heritage, opted for bilingual parochial schools.[136]

The immigrants were even more concerned by the Protestant character of the public schools. Native Protestant civic leaders, motivated by a desire for social homogeneity and fear of immigrant influence, thought that the best way to rid their cities of social deviance was through public education infused with Christian values.[137] Accordingly, the Bible was read daily in public school and "religion" was taught. To the Protestant majority, Americanization meant learning English, understanding the Constitution, and adopting middle-class values associated with a nondenominational Protestantism.[138]

In New York Catholics led a spirited debate over the Protestant nature of the public schools. An assertive bishop of New York gave a series of speeches on the insidious dangers of using the King James Bible, Protestant catechisms, and the glorification of Protestant heroes.[139] Jews added their voices to the dispute, causing the *New York Herald* to remark ironically, "The battles over textbooks had made Jews and Catholics allies for the first time in 1,840 years."[140] Both groups turned to the creation of parochial schools as an alternative.

The new German Jewish immigrants were also dissatisfied with the minimal level of Jewish education supplied by existing day schools. From the 1830s through the 1850s, the immigrants, usually poorly educated but religiously traditional, created their own Jewish day schools, either attached to their synagogues or as private Jewish institutions.[141] The Judaic content of their curricula was substantial, even though the curriculum included secular subjects to ensure a full adjustment to American society.[142] Secular studies had been part of the curriculum of American Jewish schools since 1755, when they were introduced by Shearith Israel in New York. Unlike in Russia, the inclusion of secular subjects was not controversial, even in traditional synagogues. This was one battle Lilienthal would not have to fight.

In 1842, Bnai Jeshurun formed the New York Talmud Torah and Hebrew Institute, an all-day school that taught a mixture of Hebrew and religious and secular subjects to its thirty male students under the leadership of Samuel M. Isaacs, preacher and hazan of the congregation. Isaacs hoped to make his school a community-wide project, but the other New York synagogues turned him down. Despite his success, he was forced to close the Bnai Jeshurun school in 1847 because of financial troubles.[143]

Isaacs's main competition was Anshe Chesed's all-day school, established in May 1845 with a student body of forty. Rodeph Shalom and Shaarey Hashamayim quickly followed suit with day schools of their own. When Lilienthal was hired, the Union board made it clear that education was its top priority; the rabbi went to work with the school committee immediately.[144] Proposing a fusion of the three schools, Lilienthal recommended that the congregations hold a fund-raising dinner to establish a fund for building a schoolhouse.[145] The idea was approved with the understanding that the three congregations would share the financial risk equally. The individual boards worried about having enough funding for fuel, sufficient furniture, and upkeep. They also agreed to subsidize the tuition for poor students. The Union board set up a school committee made up of two members from each synagogue. This committee evolved into the Hebrew Union School Society, to be administered by Lilienthal and nine directors.[146]

Lilienthal's school opened in September 1846 on Ludlow Street. Calling it Union School #1, Lilienthal hoped to create a system of similar schools in other sections of the city.[147] The initial student body came only from Rodeph Shalom and Shaarey Hashamayim, because the trustees of Anshe Chesed did not think that the facilities measured up to the cost of the new venture and decided not to join the merger. Anshe Chesed's leaders did promise to use their influence to obtain students for the Union School and to join as soon as the School Society was financially solvent.[148]

The Union School increased its enrollment by forty boys and girls between February and September 1847. The coed nature of the school was a departure from Bnai Jeshurun's school, where boys and girls were educated separately as late as the 1850s. It was apparently not a controversial point, though, because when Isaac Leeser visited the Anshe Chesed and Union schools, he mentioned their coed student bodies without comment. The elementary department taught biblical history, Hebrew, translation of liturgy and Genesis and Exodus, catechism, and standard English subjects. Lilienthal supervised this division and publicly examined all boys of age 13 and girls of age 12 on the first day of Sukkot.[149] A high school began with eighty pupils, offering a Jewish and secular curriculum similar to that of Bnai Jeshurun's school.[150] High school subjects included Bible, Jewish history, Hebrew language, and selections from the *Shulhan Arukh*.[151]

The committee also planned an upper school that offered classes in mercantile and polytechnical studies, a unique feature for its day. (It is unclear whether this portion of the school ever functioned.)[152] In addition to mercantile and vocational studies, Lilienthal introduced instruction in needlework. He also introduced school vacations and abolished corporal punishment.[153] Changes in the public schools, including sewing for girls and some vocational skills, may have inspired these innovations.[154]

Isaac Leeser, who visited the Union School in 1847, provides the following description.

From the synagogue we went with Dr. Lilienthal, who was also present to attend the examination, to view his Union School, No. l, in Ludlow Street, where we found about 160 scholars engaged in their studies, under four teachers in three different rooms, opening one in the other. We hastily examined the first class, male and female, in Hebrew translation and reading, geography, English grammar, and German; and we must acknowledge that the proficiency displayed was excellent, and all that could be expected, if not more, from the short time the school has been in operation.[155]

When Anshe Chesed finally did join the Union School on October 31, 1847,[156] the New York Jewish community had "the largest and best-conducted Jewish school of its day; two hundred and fifty children were in attendance, and Lilienthal, the best Jewish educator of the age, was in full charge."[157]

Confirmation had long been an important element in Lilienthal's program for modern Jewish education. Besides being an important part of his educational agenda, Lilienthal saw confirmation as a status symbol both for himself and for his congregations. As he explained in the *Allgemeine Zeitung des Judenthums*, confirmation would serve "to place our young congregations here, in all things that touch our holy religion, on an equal footing with the best organized congregations in the old world."[158] This educational innovation would also help to enhance Lilienthal's standing among the enlightened rabbinic circles of Europe.[159]

By January 14, 1846, the chief rabbi had prepared an extensive report proposing a class for post–bar mitzvah boys and girls over the age of 12 who would meet with him two hours weekly over a six-month period. The detailed course of study would cover basic Jewish theology, ethics, and the study of biblical verses. Lilienthal also described the service of confirmation in great detail. To be held on the first day of Shavuot, it would include a public examination, a vow of faith, and the blessing of the confirmands. The following day, the second day of the holiday, the confirmands would all be called to the Torah.[160] With minor amendments, the Union board accepted his proposal. They instructed the rabbi to defend the legal basis for the ceremony of confirmation to the three congregations in a series of sermons. It seems that the rabbi encountered criticism from some traditional members who feared this "destructive innovation" would replace or diminish the bar mitzvah ceremony.[161] Even at the first confirmation ceremony, the rabbi felt compelled to justify the practice with proof-texts from the Talmud and the Code of Jewish Law.[162]

Nevertheless, the chief rabbi's first confirmation ceremony in New York in 1846 was a success.[163] In a report to the *Allgemeine Zeitung des*

Judenthums, Lilienthal described how sixteen boys and girls participated in a moving ceremony at Anshe Chesed on Shavuot witnessed by 1,500 guests.[164] A correspondent for the *Occident* commented, "No one doubted the excellent effect it had on the whole assemblage. The Rabbi delivered an impressive sermon, which drew tears from all, and satisfied every one, that far from being a destructive innovation, 'confirmation' was an earnest appeal to every Jew to rally with heart and soul round the standard of our holy religion."[165]

Lilienthal also developed an adult education program in the synagogues that reflected both traditional Jewish study and *Wissenschaft* learning. Besides his regular sermons each Sabbath morning, he led a *chevrat shas* (Talmud study group). After each session, he delivered lectures to a large audience on the history of the Jews from the destruction of the First Temple to the present. This study group format reveals Lilienthal's traditional tendencies. The lectures allowed him to share his expertise in modern historical studies. In that way he introduced his modernizing agenda in a manner palatable to his traditional congregation.[166]

A number of articles that Lilienthal wrote for the *Occident*, called "Sketches of Jewish Life in Russia" (mentioned in Chapter 2), could also be considered an extension of adult education. These articles gave Lilienthal an opportunity to share his firsthand knowledge of the Russian Jewish situation without dwelling on his own failure. In his colorful narratives, Lilienthal portrayed Jewish life in Russia and its key personalities, balancing his admiration for the discipline of talmudic study with his disdain for the community's prejudice against Western knowledge.[167] Lilienthal discussed various types of Jews he had encountered, including talmudic scholars, Hasidim, and the progressive Jews of Odessa. These articles were sharply critical of Tsar Nicholas and his government, reflecting Lilienthal's own negative experience.

As a result of Lilienthal's strong leadership and successful school, the Union of German Synagogues flourished. Its growing prestige attracted the attention of the leadership of Temple Emanu-El, which began secret negotiations to merge with the other German synagogues. They envisioned a single congregation with seating for 1,200 congregants and a joint school that would share expenses and staff. The plan failed because the three traditional synagogues feared Emanu-El's reforming influence.[168]

Mass immigration and urban poverty created social welfare needs in the Jewish community far beyond the capacity of the old institutions to fulfill. As a result, a new network of benevolent societies, women's charities, and organizations to bring relief to indigents, educate orphans, assist in burials, and provide coal for the poor slowly took shape. The synagogues also had collections for the poor, yet these uncoordinated efforts resulted in duplication as well as neglect. In 1822 the Hebrew Benevolent Society was formed. By the 1840s and 1850s it was the outstanding philanthropic group in the city, led by the elite of New York Jewry. In 1844 a break-off group called the German Hebrew Benevolent Society was formed specifically to aid German Jewish immigrants.[169] Within weeks of his arrival, Lilienthal spoke at the second annual meeting of that organization. More than 200 Jews and Christians attended the dinner, including a number of wealthy merchants, who pledged generous contributions. From the beginning Lilienthal regarded involvement in such communal endeavors as an integral part of the modern rabbi's role.[170]

Also shortly after his arrival, Lilienthal convened a conference to discuss the "deplorable condition of our brethren" in Russia. At that meeting, in January 1846, a memorial statement was drafted, signed by the leaders of all the synagogues, and sent to Sir Moses Montefiore, to support his efforts to intervene on behalf of Russian Jews. In another international effort, Anshe Chesed collected money to be sent to Jerusalem during the fall of 1846.[171] Even as the Jewish community struggled to provide services for its own needy, Lilienthal encouraged and supported their concern for Jewish communities all over the world.

When Isaac M. Wise, the future leader of American Reform Judaism, came to America in July 1846, only seven months after Lilienthal, he had just suffered the agonies of a 63-day ocean voyage and had arrived penniless along with his wife and child. Depressed by what he found in New York, Wise recalled his first impressions in his *Reminiscences*. He described New York as "a large village," with only a few hints of the beginnings of a metropolis. The unimpressive houses, shops, and institutions, he wrote, greatly disappointed him.

> I had never before seen a city so bare of all art and of every trace of good taste; likewise I had never witnessed anywhere such rushing, hurrying, chasing, running. In addition to this, there was the crying, blowing, clamoring, and other noises of the fishmongers, milkmen, ragpickers, newsboys, dealers in popcorn, etc.—earsplitting noises, which were even often drowned in the rumblings of the wagons and the cries of the street gamins.[172]

After a series of discouraging job interviews and ready to give up, Wise brought letters of introduction to the Lilienthal home on Eldridge Street.

Lilienthal opened the door himself and greeted Wise in a dressing gown and a black velvet cap. After reading a letter Wise brought from one of Lilienthal's school friends, he welcomed the younger man enthusiastically. He called to Pepi, "Wife, bring coffee and cigars. I have received a guest."[173] Meanwhile, Lilienthal encouraged the uncertain Wise to continue in the rabbinate. Soon Pepi came into the room and Wise was smitten with her beauty and charm.

> After a few minutes *she* came into the room; *she* whom later I had the frequent opportunity of admiring as the most lovable and amiable of wives and mothers; she who surpassed even Munich's daughters in charm; who with clear insight penetrated into the very heart of conditions and persons, and cast a glamour of love on all about her. I mean the sainted Peppie Lilienthal.[174]

Wise claimed that the impression that he received in the Lilienthal home decided his career in America.[175] Beyond emotional support, Lilienthal helped Wise in practical ways, introducing him to important people "of a better type." Through the chief rabbi, Wise met prominent lawyers, merchants, and professors. Out of money, Wise was desperate for a position. Lilienthal asked him, "Are you a good preacher?" Getting a positive answer, Lilienthal arranged preaching opportunities for Wise in New Haven, Albany, and Syracuse. From this exposure, Wise was hired to officiate in Albany for the High Holy Days, which subsequently became his first pulpit. Lilienthal and Wise—representatives of the new type of rabbi, products of the yeshiva and the German university—enjoyed long intimate conversations and theological discussions and remained close friends for life.[176]

Wise's arrival gave Lilienthal the opportunity to move forward with one of his more ambitious projects, the creation of a rabbinic court, or *beth din*. In his installation address, Lilienthal had promised to form a *beth din*. As Sefton Temkin notes, a *beth din* was an essential feature of a traditional Jewish community, a communal source of legal authority.[177] By setting up this court, the chief rabbi intended to give legitimacy to his rulings.[178] Lilienthal may also have wanted to create some independence from his congregation. Despite his title and the ambitious agenda he set forth, in many respects Lilienthal was controlled by his synagogue board. He needed special permission to visit a school, preach a sermon, or deliver a legal decision.[179]

In October 1846, the chief rabbi established his *beth din*, made up of Rabbi Isaac M. Wise, Dr. Herman Felsenheld (a teacher in the Anshe Chesed school), and a rabbinic student named Kohlmayer. As its head, Lilienthal presented the judges to his congregation and delivered a sermon to explain the functions of the court. This *beth din*, he explained, would differ from the traditional court in that it would be only an advisory council, and, in deference to the strong spirit of autonomy among the various American congregations, it would not issue binding legal decisions.[180] With quarterly meetings planned, the court also went beyond the traditional judicial function of a *beth din* because the tasks it set itself included the preparation of a Jewish history textbook and a Hebrew grammar for schools.[181]

Lilienthal, Wise, Leeser, and other early leaders dreamed of unity among American Jews. Wise used the forum of the *beth din* to advocate for his goal of unifying the various customs of the widely separated communities into a single American prayer ritual. The creation of such a liturgy, which Wise termed *Minhag Amerika*, would be one of his goals for many years.[182]

In his introductory remarks to the court on April 18, 1847, the chief rabbi expressed his hope that the *beth din* would play a great and beneficial role in the free development of the young congregations of North America. In addition to liturgy and textbooks, the court discussed letters from European rabbis that raised issues of law as well as questions received from American congregations.[183] Future agenda items were to include principles for the general organization of the young congregations of America and a plan for the education of their congregations' children.[184]

The court met only once. Leon Jick was probably right in affirming that "the American Jewish setting was too anarchic to support even a modest experiment with authority."[185] However, it is also likely that Wise's proposed liturgy was too radical for Lilienthal and Felsenheld, forcing them to find a method to postpone action on it.[186] Wise's *Reminiscences* gives us further evidence of an ideological split within the group itself. Upset with the group's "all talk, no action" approach, Wise was even more disgruntled at the cancellation of further meetings after he had spent the entire winter preparing his liturgy.[187]

Isaac Leeser expressed skepticism with regard to Wise's liturgical proposal. Although he had not seen the details, he feared that a common liturgy would replicate the efforts of the German Reform rabbis, whose conferences he had been reporting with great displeasure. Moreover, he doubted that the Sephardim (Spanish-Portuguese congregations) would be willing to replace their traditional liturgy with a crude, poorly formulated system devised by these German newcomers.[188]

Lilienthal defended his Orthodoxy to Leeser when Leeser lumped him together with the reformers. Leeser apologized to Lilienthal and issued a retraction later in an article. "He [Lilienthal] has never done, or authorized anything to be done, since his arrival in this country, which could authorize us to suppose that he would sanction any departure from the strict standard of orthodoxy."[189] Throughout his tenure, Lilienthal consistently maintained his traditional stance. He continued to advocate only those reforms that he could support on traditional legal grounds. Although Wise was quite bitter after the *beth din* fiasco, he apparently understood his friend's position, and the two remained close.

Despite his obvious talent and many successes, all of Lilienthal's proposals were subjected to severe scrutiny and amendment by the Union board and its largest constituent, Anshe Chesed. Indeed, unless specifically invited, the board did not even admit the chief rabbi to its meetings; the rabbi and the board had to communicate by letter.[190] Exclusion of Lilienthal from the meetings of the largest and most powerful constituent within the Union seriously limited his effectiveness in establishing his program and vision.[191]

The minute books of Anshe Chesed clearly reveal tensions between rabbi and board. On March 25, 1846, the board wrote to Lilienthal reminding him that he was required to announce weddings ahead of time. Lilienthal's reply is not recorded, but the incident demonstrates that the board did not hesitate to reprimand Lilienthal or other officials for suspected lapses. For instance, on November 15, 1846, Anshe Chesed accused Cantor Hecht of eating at a public feast with an uncovered head. He was given a two-week suspension. Similarly, the board asked the rabbi why he did not attend a certain funeral. He replied that he had not been asked to preach a funeral sermon and that his contract did not require attendance per se. At the next meeting, the board decided that in the future, Lilienthal would be asked to deliver a funeral sermon at every congregational funeral.[192]

The board also took the rabbi to task for his alleged lack of attention to the Anshe Chesed school. When the Union School opened in September 1846, Lilienthal's energies were directed toward that new endeavor. Anshe Chesed had decided not to join the Union School. On November 29, 1846, the secretary wrote Lilienthal to find out why he did not visit the Anshe Chesed school more often. The rabbi replied on December 13 that he was busy with the many duties of his office, stating, with obvious annoyance, "If the board of trustees thought that he did not do enough, he was ready and willing to resign, as he did not wish to have it thought that he gets his money for nothing."[193] The incident was smoothed over when Lilienthal appeared before the board in early January 1847.[194]

On October 10, 1847, tension erupted again when Lilienthal was accused of injuring Anshe Chesed's school by calling it inferior to the Union School. Felsenheld, a teacher at Anshe Chesed and a member of the ill-fated *beth din* that had met the previous April, brought the complaint before the board. Apparently Lilienthal had told Felsenheld that the trustees and the school committee of Anshe Chesed were not satisfied with their school. Further, the board charged that he was still neglecting their school in favor of the Union School. Lilienthal reminded the board of the circumstances connected with the establishment of the Union School, reviewing his work with both. He believed that his first duty, according to his contract, was to the children in the Union School. After a long debate, it was moved and seconded to drop the subject and focus solely on the future improvement of the Anshe Chesed school.[195]

This series of confrontations illustrates the attempt by Anshe Chesed's leadership to treat Lilienthal as a hireling. Lilienthal's response showed that he would not tolerate such treatment; he was a thoroughly trained and conscientious professional who demanded appropriate respect. The school incident also brought into relief the conflict between Lilienthal's duties to the Union board and its constituent parts. Anshe Chesed's decision not to join the Union School weakened it because without Anshe Chesed, the Union School lacked the support of its most powerful member. However, the larger synagogue still expected equal attention to its own school.[196] The issue was resolved at the end of October 1847, when Anshe Chesed finally decided to join the Union School.

Intercongregational tension surfaced on other occasions, as when Shaarey Hashamayim requested that the rabbi preach at its synagogue on a certain holiday. Anshe Chesed vetoed their request because they insisted he was contracted to preach for them on that occasion.[197] In such cases the rabbi was caught in the middle of a struggle between two synagogue boards.

Beginning in March 1847, Lilienthal had begun to receive less money. Previously the minutes recorded $125 as Anshe Chesed's contribution to his salary. After early spring, however, $83.33 became the regular amount. The minutes do not indicate any reason for this cut in his pay. Not surprisingly, Lilienthal confided to Wise that he had become disheartened. Wise wrote in his autobiography that Lilienthal informed him of his negative experiences and revealed his decision to renounce the ministry to devote himself entirely to education. When Wise shared his own professional difficulties, Lilienthal's bitter response was, "There is no help for you. . . . If you want to be the Christ, you must expect to be crucified. I will not. I shall do something else for a living."[198] This shocking expression, especially for a rabbi, reveals the depths of Lilienthal's dissatisfaction.

The final showdown between Anshe Chesed and their rabbi came about as a result of a seemingly minor event. On December 14, 1847, a Mr.

Nordlinger brought a complaint against Lilienthal. His child was sick, and he wanted to organize a minyan (prayer quorum) to have a prayer recited on the child's behalf. Because only five men were present for the service, one of Nordlinger's friends went to Shaarey Hashamayim, where the board and rabbi were in the middle of a meeting, and asked them to interrupt their meeting to complete the quorum. Although the *parnass* agreed to do so, Lilienthal objected, observing that there were enough Jews in the neighborhood who could help make a minyan. By the time the friend returned to the distraught father, the required number for a service had indeed gathered. However, following the service, Mr. Nordlinger submitted a formal complaint to the Anshe Chesed board criticizing Lilienthal for refusing to adjourn the meeting to achieve the quorum. The rabbi replied that he had nothing to say because the complaint was true. By not responding, the board thought that Lilienthal was not taking a congregant's concern seriously. After Lilienthal left, the board wrote to their rabbi saying that he had offended them by not making a defense, and they ordered him to appear before the board the following Sunday.[199]

The sexton, Mr. May, personally delivered this letter to Lilienthal; the rabbi declined to accept May's letter and gave him one to take back to the board. When May warned Lilienthal that he would have to report to the *parnass* that the rabbi had not accepted the letter, Lilienthal encouraged him to do so. On December 16, the board decided by secret ballot that Lilienthal was guilty of Mr. Nordlinger's charge by a vote of 5 to 1. The rabbi was suspended for three weeks from his services to the congregation, not only based on Nordlinger's case but also for what the Board of Trustees perceived as an insult directed at them.

On December 21, a number of congregants came before the board asking why their rabbi had been suspended. They wanted a resolution of the dispute, as their minutes book indicates. "Everything with respect to Dr. Lilienthal [should be] peaceably arranged so as to put an end to general talk of it among members and even among strangers to this congregation, considering that the high station of the Rev'd Dr. Lilienthal should command the greatest respect for him on the part of the congregation, as well as the Trustees."[200] Mr. Walter, speaking for the group, further expressed the opinion that the form in which the complaint was made was insulting to Lilienthal.[201] The president defended the actions of the board, claiming that they had tried to avoid extreme measures but that Lilienthal's refusal to cooperate forced his suspension. The president added that the suspension was lenient, given the triple offense: against Mr. Nordlinger, against the trustees at their meeting of December 14, and against the whole congregation. Another member, Mr. Hoffman, remarked, "The best the congregation could do, to promote peace, would be, to beg forgiveness of the Rev'd Dr. Lilienthal."[202] After much debate, the board agreed to annul their action if the rabbi would make amends before the board that evening. The board was told that Lilienthal was indisposed. They then agreed to dispense with a personal appearance and informed Lilienthal that they were not averse to reconciliation. Members who had been waiting outside the room presented a note from Lilienthal saying that he too would consent to reconciliation provided that he could get full satisfaction. Although the board considered this response to be vague, they accepted it, making the resolution of the crisis contingent on Lilienthal's acceptance of their letter. He refused it and the suspension stood.

On January 20, 1848, May reported to the board that Lilienthal had told him that he would not officiate in that synagogue until the case was settled. Consonant with this position, the rabbi refused to perform a wedding at Anshe Chesed. An irate board again wrote to Lilienthal asking him why he had not given a sermon that Saturday or performed at the wedding. Lilienthal's response was obviously unsatisfactory because, on January 25, the board called a general meeting for February 13. After that meeting, the board terminated his contract. "On motion: Resolved to inform Dr. Lilienthal, by a letter from the Board of the Resolution passed at the General Meeting of this day concerning the refusal of the members to give him any satisfaction and of the declaration of vacancy of the office of raby [sic] to this congregation."[203] On this note, the first period of Lilienthal's career in New York City came to an end. It would seem that at several points the parties might have peacefully resolved the confrontation. Although the congregation was concerned about its honor, it was willing to compromise, whereas Lilienthal was not. To be sure, the minutes present only the board's point of view. Because of the frustrations that the rabbi had experienced and his strong sense of personal honor, he did not want to capitulate. Soon afterward, Lilienthal resigned from the other two synagogues. The Union of German Synagogues did not survive his departure, having lasted only a little more than two years.[204]

Looking back on the incident, Robert Lyon, editor of the *Asmonean*, suggested that more than honor was involved. The leadership found Lilienthal's efforts to impose order on them to be unacceptable and created a confrontation in order to remove him from office. "The discipline he introduced became irksome to some few and they eagerly sought an opportunity to question the Rabbinical authority which controlled them. Prompt in his decisions the Rev. gentleman immediately concluded to resign the spiritual charge of the conjoint congregations of New York."[205] Lilienthal's treatment at the hands of his lay board was not an isolated case. Leo Merzbacher had lost his position at Anshe Chesed in 1844. A few years later, Isaac Leeser would lose his position after many years of service. In Baltimore, after much frustration, Rabbi Abraham Rice left his congregation and opened a dry goods store.[206] Within a few years, a *parnass* would physically attack Isaac M. Wise, leading to his departure to form a new Reform synagogue.[207] Even within the more hierarchical Catholic Church, immigrant clergy suffered from lay domination. When Father Gabriel Rumpler took over St. Nicholas parish in 1842, the trustees treated him like a hired hand. They dictated to him how many candles he might light for mass and even threatened him with bodily harm at one point.[208]

These conflicts were symptomatic of the anarchy of a rapidly growing community where lay governance predominated. Religious communities were in flux, searching for leadership while clinging to lay prerogatives of power and status. In his congregation, Lilienthal tried to change the balance of power between clergy and synagogue boards, asserting the role of the rabbi in a community that saw him as their servant. Even leaders as energetic and able as Lilienthal did not yet have the professional status or clout to bring order or sustain institutions crucial to the future of the American Jewish community.

4

The Evolution of a Reformer

A little more than two years after Lilienthal's arrival in America he found himself unemployed and needing to support his wife, 1½year-old daughter Eliza, and a newborn son, Theodore. The chief rabbi, who had so recently reported his successes back to Germany through his articles in the *Allgemeine Zeitung des Judenthums*, had to reinvent himself yet again. He himself had warned potential immigrants that the transition to America was not easy but that the opportunities were great. "One who brings with him the desire and capacity for work, who is not discouraged in overcoming the first difficulties which everyone encounters in a strange country, who also leaves in the old country dreams of the old pomposities—he will certainly find his livelihood here, and have every opportunity to make of it something very suitable for him."[1] Lilienthal would have to follow his own advice to overcome the difficulties he faced.

Even before the final break with Anshe Chesed, Lilienthal vowed to his friend Wise that he would renounce the rabbinate to devote himself entirely to Jewish education.[2] He moved quickly to actualize his new plan. On April 30, 1848, after meeting with the directors of the Union School, he agreed to take over the school's lease and pay the yearly rent of $400.[3] Lilienthal found that his expenses were too great to cover operating costs.

In January 1849 he relocated the school to his home at 21½ Eldridge Street and renamed it Dr. Lilienthal's Hebrew and Classical Boarding School.[4]

The educational values expressed in the name of his school were in harmony with those of the German Jewish community he served. Jews were attracted to the school to avoid the Christian influence that still permeated the public schools. They also shared Lilienthal's concern for passing on Jewish religion and values.

Most Jews in America knew little about Judaism. Lilienthal saw young Jews as particularly vulnerable to indifference or even apostasy. In a lengthy article on Jewish education, Lilienthal emphasized the need for an intellectual understanding of Judaism.[5] Although it bothered him that most American Jews could not read the prayers or understand Hebrew, he was more concerned about their grasp of the doctrinal essence of Judaism. Because most children finished their education by early adolescence, he advocated the use of a catechism—a summary of principles in question-and-answer form—to supply students with a creed to compensate for their limited formal Jewish training. This approach also reflected the nineteenth-century tendency to teach Judaism as a "Konfession," parallel to Christianity. "Religion" was in fact included as a new and distinct subject in the modern Jewish school.[6] In 1839, Rebecca Gratz of Philadelphia introduced a catechism at her Hebrew Sunday School; Samuel Isaacs introduced a catechism into the curriculum of the afternoon school at Bnai Jeshurun in 1842.[7] Thus Lilienthal was advocating an important religious and educational innovation based on a pedagogical technique that had already taken hold in the United States.

This educational approach underlines how different the situation in America was from what Lilienthal had encountered in Riga. There he had students with strong Jewish backgrounds. He was impressed with their minds, sharpened by years of talmudic study. What they lacked was any knowledge of modern studies. As a result, Lilienthal could tailor his curriculum to help them learn Russian, history, mathematics, and so on, along with their Judaica. In America he had to teach the secular subjects to give his students the tools they needed to be effective in the modern world, but he also had to give an introduction to Judaism—all in a limited number of years.

To fulfill his Judaica goals, Lilienthal created a two-tiered curriculum, based on his conception of the stages of a child's cognitive development.

> The first one, according to the yet undeveloped faculties of the mind, should be a brief and preparatory one; the second should enlarge, complete and explain the foundations laid down in the former

course. Catechisms, written after the same plan, should be used in both courses, with the difference only that the first must be short, simply and plainly written, in order that the child may easily comprehend and learn by heart his task, and the second, enriched with verses and other explanations and adapted to more developed faculties, must try to give a full and complete system of religion.[8]

The catechism covered major themes of Jewish theology and ethics: the attributes of God, immortality of the soul, revelation, messianism, and moral law. Instruction was to be enlivened with stories and examples borrowed from daily life. The core of the lessons was the central principle of the oneness of God. The student "must learn to understand, that herein lies the difference of our religion from all others surrounding us," Lilienthal wrote.[9] By refuting both paganism and the doctrines of Christianity (i.e., the Trinity, God's incarnation, dying, and redemption), the student gained an understanding of God's oneness, forming in his view "an insurmountable barrier against apostasy."[10] To counter Hebrew illiteracy, Lilienthal adopted a Hebrew-language primer titled *The Hebrew Language Demonstrated on Ollendorf's Method*, which he also endorsed in the local Jewish papers. Along with a comprehensive treatment of the rules of grammar, the primer provided vocabulary and translation exercises.[11] The goal of Lilienthal's program was to educate American Jewish children to become faithful and knowledgeable Jews in a predominantly Christian environment.

Well-educated German Jews were also inclined to send their sons to Lilienthal's school because it allowed them to perpetuate the humanistic traditions they had admired in the old country. Having himself been a product of a gymnasium and university, Lilienthal recreated this model for these upwardly mobile young American Jews. The tuition fee of $200 excluded the less affluent; compared to the synagogue-supported schools that charged from $9 to $24 a year, the cost of these private boarding schools was significant.[12] Like the gymnasium, Lilienthal's New York school was an upper middle-class institution that focused on the classics. Its advertisements claimed that the school taught Greek and Latin. Judging from the areas covered in the school's public examinations, classical studies were actually given little attention; the curriculum emphasized commercial or practical subjects, such as German, French, English, arithmetic, and bookkeeping. The school was more like the German *Realschule*, which prepared middle-class students for jobs in commerce and normally ended when the students reached age 13 or 14.[13]

There were American models for Lilienthal's school as well. Various Christian denominations developed private religious schools, called institutes, that also followed European models with regard to curriculum and structure. These schools went beyond the limited curriculum of the public schools, which focused almost exclusively on the three R's. Jews emulated these Christian private schools.[14]

The first American Jewish "institute" was the Boarding and Day School for Young Ladies of the Jewish Faith, in New York City. Founded in 1841 by the Palache sisters, it had a close association with Shearith Israel.[15] Teaching English and Hebrew studies, the school drew on the same upper middle-class clientele that Lilienthal's school would attract. Some of the most respectable families of the city paid $200 per year for board and tuition. The school promised to provide female students with a combination of religious and secular training. "The accomplishments and other languages are taught on the usual terms. Parents and guardians may rest assured that the greatest attention will always be paid to the religious and moral instruction of the pupils, combined with their mental improvement, every family being afforded with the aid of the best master in the various branches of study."[16] A description of a public examination in December 1849 revealed a fuller picture of the course of study at the Palaches' school, which included Hebrew, biblical history, liturgy, French, and English.[17] Lilienthal knew about this boarding school from his first days in New York. In January 1846, when he was beginning to formulate plans for the Union School, the rabbi in fact had toured the girls' school. In March of the same year, he served as one of three examiners for the school's public examination.[18]

Lilienthal assembled an excellent staff of teachers and personally took an active role in the education of his wards. The students, former pupils of the Union School, ranged in age from about 7 to 13 or 14 years old.[19] An early advertisement promised that the young boys, who were to live and study with the Lilienthals, would be treated as members of the family. Careful attention was paid to their religious and moral training as well as to their comfort.[20] One early graduate testified to its supportive atmosphere. "I felt as if I was in my own father's house, and I saw by the manner in which you took care of your pupils, that I should be as safe as in my parent's arms. . . . Every scholar will look upon you as a second father; and as our warmest friend."[21]

Lilienthal's private school flourished and, by the spring of 1850, moved to new quarters at 307 Tenth Street. The old neighborhood had become packed with bars and saloons, attracting a rough element looking for crude amusements. In addition, by the 1850s the Jewish community was moving north, vacating the older center. The new district was the least industrial and most desirable neighborhood in Kleindeutschland.[22] The area boasted first-class brick and stone houses, broad boulevards, and a gracious feeling.

Tompkins Square, called the Weisse Garten by the Germans, provided an expansive, airy, open public space. Located on the square in a large and handsome house, the school was equipped with every modern improvement, including a safe and ample playground.[23] With the new location came a new element in the name: Dr. Lilienthal's Hebrew, Commercial, and Classical Boarding School. Committed in principle to the humanistic ideals of the Enlightenment, Lilienthal also clearly understood the pragmatic thrust of American life. "In our times . . . we are accustomed to judge everything from its practical side; our children have to learn a great many things at once, and this in but a short time. At thirteen years, the education is in a majority of instances said to be finished; the boy, if it is required, shall then be able to enter business, and shall know at least English, Arithmetic, French, German, and a little Bookkeeping with a host of minor things."[24]

Lilienthal's institute soon attracted an elite group of students, ranging in age from 7 to 14, from New York, Rochester, Philadelphia, Baltimore, St. Louis, Cincinnati, and New Orleans.[25] Mordecai Noah, a prominent New York Jewish communal leader who sent one of his sons to the school, praised it in an article in the *Occident*. "I recommend the school of Dr. Lilienthal's with entire confidence to my co-religionists . . . and believe that every confidence may be reposed in the fidelity and character of the Doctor, for the improvement and comfort of the children entrusted to his care."[26]

Lilienthal set high educational standards. Using examinations as much to measure instructors' ability to teach as to test the students' grasp of the material, he would test, teach, and test again.[27] In addition, Lilienthal instituted public examinations, at first yearly and then semi-annually. Because no record of the curriculum has survived, these tests give us the best overview of the ambitious course of study in Lilienthal's school. Parents, friends, and the general public as well as correspondents from the *Occident* and the *Asmonean* attended the first examination, held in August 1850. Part test, part performance, these presentations included musical recitals and dramatic readings in German, English, and French. Students answered questions on a wide range of subjects, including religion, American history, English grammar, bookkeeping, German and French translation, Hebrew, geography, arithmetic, and English literature. The quality of the student performances bolstered the reputation of the school and resulted in a dramatic increase in the student body in the next academic year.[28]

The emphasis on English subjects increased at about the time the school moved to Tenth Street. A new advertisement appeared in the *Asmonean* with this addition: "Particular attention is paid to the English education of the pupils, five hours daily being devoted to the exclusive study of the various branches of that language."[29] In May 1851, examination subjects also included how to write commercial letters in English, grammar, composition, and penmanship.[30] This change reflected an increasing recognition by both Lilienthal and his clientele of the importance of mastering English for success in America. Five hours a day represented a major portion of the time spent in class, but this commitment was a notable sign of acculturation within the immigrant community.[31]

Physical education was an important ingredient in Lilienthal's program.[32] By 1851, Lilienthal had expanded his school again, constructing a spacious and lofty detached building on the lot that extended to Eleventh Street, with a covered area for recreation during poor weather. The *Asmonean* reported that the students were "hale and hearty."[33] Lilienthal also built a large schoolroom with high ceilings and good ventilation. One observer estimated that the addition would allow the school to accommodate nearly 100 boys, but Lilienthal stipulated that the number never exceed 70 in order to give each student proper attention.[34] Lilienthal also added new faculty and course offerings, including music and art.[35]

Moral training was always a central concern for Lilienthal. Its emphasis reflected the core value of *Bildung* or moral development that Lilienthal had brought from Germany. He wrote that *yirat shamayim* (fear of God) was the basis of religion and that the knowledge of God's qualities would provide inspiration for his young wards. For instance, learning of God's kindness and omnipotence would teach the students to trust God's mercy and to rely on the divine; meditation on God's justice would teach them to despise vice.[36] To inculcate the habit of charity, Lilienthal encouraged the boys to form a juvenile philanthropic society. The students made a contribution to the German Hebrew Benevolent Society at its annual banquet in 1852.

A serious challenge facing private Jewish institutions was to achieve an appropriate level of discipline. Apparently other private schools were not very successful in this area. To this end, Lilienthal required the students to wear uniforms. Noah commended the school for its strictness, contrasting it with the indulgence that the children experienced at home, as did Robert Lyon, editor of the *Asmonean*, who also praised the school's excellent discipline. Lyon added that graduates received an education "which will fit them to be ornaments to society, from a religious, social, and political point of view."[37]

By 1852, Lilienthal's school was so large that the public examinations took three evenings to complete and the audience was limited to friends and family. There were musical performances and dramatic productions of Schiller and Shakespeare, complete with costumes. The lower or junior department was questioned on German, geography, American history, German and English diction, French dialogues and verbs, translation of the Hebrew Bible, and arithmetic. The upper or senior department was quizzed about religion, bookkeeping, and arithmetic, English grammar, American and world history, and geography.[38] Lilienthal showed his pedagogical savvy when he introduced the use of maps and other visual aids as part of the curriculum. He may also have been the first American Jewish educator to formulate lesson plans.[39]

The success of Lilienthal's school inspired others to use it as a model. For instance, Adolph Loewe formed a boys' school in New York in 1849. He began modestly, without even his own site, to teach classes in Hebrew, German, and English.[40] By February 1851, he announced the opening of a "Hebrew Seminary" in addition to his day school. Originally the school accepted only twelve students, but by 1852 the school had grown to forty.[41] Taking a cue from Lilienthal's advertisement, Loewe promised that the students "would be treated in all respects as members of the family." Like the other schools, Loewe also had annual public examinations covering Hebrew studies, English reading, rhetoric, astronomy, physiology, and geography.[42] The Greene Street Educational Institution was another local boarding school that followed Lilienthal's lead. Its formal opening was announced in January 1853 with a curriculum similar to Lilienthal's. The Greene Street school was coeducational, with 100 boys and girls between the ages of 5 and 13 years, four teachers, a governess, and a monitor.[43]

Robert Lyon called Lilienthal a pioneer among those who founded Jewish schools in America. He asserted that, although Lilienthal was not the first to establish a private school, he was the first to succeed in establishing it on such a firm basis, despite many obstacles.[44] A number of reasons explain this achievement, not least of which were Lilienthal's reputation and his skill as an educator. Moreover, Lyon noted that Lilienthal willingly risked his own money to launch his enterprise, because the school did not have the backing of a synagogue or any other Jewish institution. Even schools with institutional support were on shaky financial ground during this period.[45] Although Lilienthal struggled in the first year, his astute business sense and ability to meet the needs of the growing German Jewish community enabled the school to grow and prosper in these years.

Lilienthal's school and those like it served a segment of upper middle-class German Jews in the 1840s and 1850s who tried to maintain the educational values of the German Jewish society while adjusting to America. Others thought public schools could do a better job of Americanizing immigrant children. For instance, the liberal newcomer Isidor Busch, an intellectual who had recently fled counterrevolutionary violence in his native Austria, spoke out strongly in favor of Jewish participation in public education and prophesied the downfall of all-day Jewish schools. He argued that, as good republicans, Jews ought to support public school education. He also asserted that public schools had better facilities and were more convenient.[46] The debate in New York Jewish circles was gradually resolved through legislation that secularized the public schools by banning sectarian books (1851), made the reading of Scripture discretionary (1855), and allowed local wards to choose their own textbooks (1856). As a result, Jews began flocking to the newly secularized free public schools by the late 1850s, causing many of the expensive private schools to fold.[47] The mid-1850s marked the beginning of a long-lasting love of American Jewry for public schools.

When Lilienthal chose to leave his school to become the rabbi of Congregation Bene Israel of Cincinnati in 1855, he did so at the right moment. His successor, Reverend H. A. Henry, preacher at Congregation Shaarey Zedek, who brought students from that synagogue's school, had to make repairs to the school building when he took over, suggesting Lilienthal may have faced financial difficulties during the last years of his tenure as students gravitated to public schools. In the competition for the shrinking pool of parochial students, Henry underlined the traditional Jewish emphasis of the school in his advertisements and offered a limited number of openings for girls.[48] Henry struggled to maintain the boarding school until 1857, when it closed permanently.[49] After 1857, a marked lethargy characterized the approach to parochial education in the New York Jewish community.[50]

Even as Lilienthal labored to build his school, he was still called on to serve in rabbinic functions. Despite his bitter break with the three German synagogues, he was invited to preach, often in these same congregations, to issue rulings on Jewish law, and to work for their charitable causes. Apparently his rash promise to give up the rabbinate was short-lived, because he continued to serve, albeit on his own terms. Nor did the friction between Congregation Anshe Chesed and Rabbi Lilienthal last for long. As early as half a year after his departure, a number of congregants petitioned the board to reengage him as their rabbi. This effort at rapprochement was premature; the leadership rejected the proposal on procedural grounds.[51]

The relationship began to improve as the congregation made plans to move. A number of important reasons were behind Anshe Chesed's decision in 1850 to build a large new building in a better location. Between 1846 and 1855 the Jewish population of New York grew from 12,000 to 30,000, which contributed to the increase in membership in the local synagogues.

In addition, Anshe Chesed was driven by rivalry with Temple Emanu-El, which was becoming more influential. Emanu-El had moved into a large converted church on Christie Street in 1848, opening with a festive consecration marked by choral music and sermons by Rabbis Merzbacher and Lilienthal.[52] It would move further uptown to the elegant northern end of Little Germany on Twelfth Street in 1854. In the 1850s the Jewish community was rapidly abandoning the southern section of Kleindeutschland, along with other more prosperous New Yorkers who relinquished the downtown wards to the poor. Anshe Chesed's move to Norfolk Street would place them in the center of Little Germany. The population of this now distinctly German community was surpassed only by Berlin and Vienna.[53]

The impending move seemed to breathe a new spirit into the congregation. Anshe Chesed's minutes are full of the excitement entailed in planning, financing, and consecrating its new home. The board was concerned that its consecration ceremony make a good impression on the city. To keep its wealthier members, it had to satisfy some of their demands for ritual changes.[54] The board began modernization in several areas, further increasing decorum and focusing especially on revising the liturgy. For guidance, Anshe Chesed turned to Lilienthal, whose Committee on Divine Service presented its recommendations at the time of the opening of the new building. The committee members suggested that the congregation adopt the moderate Reform ritual of Vienna, that the cantor face the congregation during services, and that women be included in the choir.[55]

The institution of a mixed professional choir was surprising, considering that only two years earlier the president had argued with Lilienthal over the purchase of four-part synagogue music.[56] The lay leadership had not changed, but their desire to acculturate to American worship style overrode their earlier caveats. Now the board agreed not only to a four-part choir but also to a professional one, which required a significant outlay of funds. The choir director, Mr. Cohn, was engaged at an annual salary of $225.[57] Even more surprising, the board agreed to engage a professional female soloist who would be paid $50 a year.[58] This innovation marked a significant movement in the direction of Reform for this traditional congregation, because according to Jewish law it was forbidden for a man to hear the voice of a woman during religious services.

The *New York Daily Tribune* and the Jewish press covered the consecration of Anshe Chesed's new building on May 16, 1850, during Shavuot. The ceremony featured German sermons by Dr. W. Schlesinger, Samuel Isaacs of Shaaray Tefila, and Rabbis Lilienthal and Merzbacher and choral and orchestral performances.[59] Lilienthal spoke briefly in German, taking as his text Psalm 112: "I rejoiced when they said unto me, Let us go into the house of the Lord." He described the small room, heated only by a wood stove, which had originally served as the sanctuary for the congregants. He expressed gratitude that they could now worship in a beautiful new building, fulfilling the promise made to their parents back in Germany, who pleaded for them to keep their ancient faith. This well-received sermon led to two more, prompting the board to send Lilienthal a special letter of thanks.[60]

Lilienthal preached at several other synagogues while Anshe Chesed continued to maintain an informal relationship with him that continued into 1851.[61] After Lilienthal delivered a series of sermons for Passover, the Anshe Chesed board fully reversed its earlier opposition to the rabbi. "The Reverend Dr. Lilienthal shall have the privilege to preach in our synagogue any Shabbat [Sabbath] whenever the same may feel inclined to do so, provided that notice thereof be given to the Parnass in the time to have it published the week previous."[62] The association became even more cordial when the board asked the rabbi to act as superintendent of their school's examination.[63] At the same meeting the president urged the board to formalize its relationship with Lilienthal by making him their honorary rabbi, in recognition of the "many valuable and gratuitous services he had rendered the congregation." This proposal was sent to a meeting of all the members of the congregation, who unanimously elected Lilienthal to this position.[64] Lilienthal responded:

To the President and Trustees of the K. K. Anshi [*sic*] Chesed.

Gentlemen:
The letter sent to me by your secretary conveying the information of my having been unanimously elected Honorary Rabbi to your congregation has been duly received.

It is with much pleasure that I accept this honorable office, feeling that the appointment is the best proof I could receive of the confidence reposed in my feeble powers. I am truly happy that such an available opportunity is presented to me to labor for the advancement of our sacred faith and to promote the spiritual welfare of your thriving congregation.

Though much engaged in my professional duties, I will not cease to devote my best energies for the interest and prosperity of your congregation so as to justify the confidence reposed in me. Devotedly wishing that the Almighty will be pleased to direct you, and now again, my congregation to the much deserved happiness by a continuance in the good path which they have previously entered, I subscribe myself very respectfully.

SIGNED,

M. LILIENTHAL, DR. RABBI.[65]

Although he seemed pleased, Lilienthal reminded Anshe Chesed that he had professional duties in his private school. Because the appointment was honorary, he could maintain an acceptable degree of autonomy.

Rapprochement with the larger and more influential Anshe Chesed opened the way for a similar arrangement with Rodeph Shalom and Shaarey Hashamayim. The *Asmonean* reported that "[Lilienthal] has been reinstated in his important functions of Rabbi to the three congregations."[66] At that time, its editor, Robert Lyon, offered this assessment of Lilienthal's New York career: "The activity of this reverend gentleman is at length producing its effect upon the community. No matter what reputation a man may have achieved in Europe, upon his arrival here, he has to undergo a probation before he finally settles down in his proper position."[67] According to Lyon, when Lilienthal was reinstated as rabbi of the three synagogues in October 1851, he had found his niche.

This was a rich and successful time in Lilienthal's life. Two more children, Philip and Esther, were born in these years. Lilienthal's brother Samuel and Pepi's sister Caroline moved to Haverstraw-on-Hudson, within easy reach of New York. Samuel would become a member of the staff of the United States Homeopathic Dispensary and later its medical college in New York. It gave the families great mutual support and pleasure to finally live so close to one another.

Lilienthal continued to serve the synagogues without any salary for the remainder of his time in New York. The Anshe Chesed minutes record that he supervised their school examinations, ruled on Jewish law, performed life cycle functions, gave sermons, spearheaded charitable causes, and even made voluntary offerings and personal contributions to the synagogue.[68] In gratitude Anshe Chesed gave him several gifts and published formal resolutions of acknowledgment in the *Asmonean*.[69] It also offered free burial lots in its cemetery to him and his family.[70] This unusual relationship, made possible as a result of the success of his school, allowed Lilienthal to continue to serve as rabbi on his own terms.[71]

Lilienthal remained active in the wider community as well. He preached at consecration services at Congregation Anshe Emeth in Albany (1851) and Congregation Ohabei Shalom in Boston (1854). He was a regular speaker at the annual German Hebrew Benevolent Society dinners. He participated in the inauguration of the New Jewish Hospital (later renamed Mt. Sinai) in June 1855. In 1854, the New York Supreme Court asked Lilienthal to explain Jewish divorce and its relationship to civil law. He informed the court that a Jewish divorce (*get*) could not be given before the granting of a civil divorce.[72] He also continued to work on behalf of Jews abroad, advocating for Ludwig Philippson's scheme for educating Turkish and Palestinian Jews, in an attempt to make these communities self-sufficient and less dependent on charity from abroad.

Lilienthal had found a way to realize the vision of the rabbinate that he had first presented to his congregations during his inaugural sermon. He had done so by sidestepping the lay-rabbinic power struggle that had doomed his earlier efforts. The success of his school gave him the financial autonomy he needed from congregational control. He could stand on his own feet, become the type of rabbi he wanted to be, and speak his mind on the issues of the day. It was also this freedom that allowed him to emerge as a spokesman for Reform Judaism in this period.

As Lilienthal was working to reestablish himself in New York, dramatic events in the Old World gripped the immigrant community. The year 1848 was characterized by revolutionary upheavals throughout Europe. Middle-class liberals desiring representative government, civil liberties, and an unregulated economy joined forces with the working class to overthrow conservative governments in France, Austria, Prussia, and elsewhere. Because civil emancipation was linked with liberalism, many Jews allied themselves with the revolutionary cause. Jews fought at the barricades, participated in revolutionary parliaments, political clubs, and rallies, and wrote as activist journalists. In Germany and Austria, revolutionaries promised freedom of religion and the granting of civil and political rights irrespective of religious affiliation.[73]

The upheavals also gave rise to a new round of violent anti-Semitic disturbances. In the years leading up to the revolutions, anti-Jewish rioting sharply increased. In the revolutionary months of March and April 1848, Jews were attacked in at least 180 localities; the violence was motivated by both economic frustration and resistance to the idea of Jewish equality.[74]

In New York the rapidly expanding German community was gripped by the tumultuous events in their homeland. The revolutions and their aftermath dominated the politics of Kleindeutschland for the remainder of the decade, as the vast majority of German New Yorkers poured their energy into supporting their compatriots back home. Revolutionary organizations, fraternal orders, singing societies, and newspapers arose in support of the political events in Berlin, Vienna, and Frankfurt. Organizations such as the Turnverein, a gymnastics group with roots in German post-Napoleonic nationalism, began to advocate republicanism and free thought as thousands of immigrants joined the club upon their arrival in America.[75]

The Jewish immigrant community became caught up in the revolutionary fervor as well. When Kleindeutschlanders mobilized in support of the German revolutions of 1848, a number of German Jewish societies marched in the grand parade, and the Harmony Society (a German Jewish library association) held a public poetry fest for German freedom.[76] In Albany, Isaac M. Wise recalled the excitement of those days. "The months of February and March, 1848, agitated me to such a degree, that it was long before I returned to a state of normal calm. . . . Moses Schloss entered the synagogue, and whispered in my ear, 'Paris is in a state of revolution; Louis Philippe has abdicated.' I jumped up electrified, repeated the portentous words, rushed out of the house toward the post office, where the bulletins were usually posted, and found the report confirmed."[77] Fully expecting the proclamation of a European republic, Wise made preparations to return to Europe. He became even more agitated as the news of the establishments of liberal regimes in Vienna, Berlin, Hungary, and Italy filtered across the ocean. In his patriotic fervor, he informed his synagogue president that he was resigning to return to Germany and take part in the rebirth of Europe. Great torchlight celebrations were held, as thousands gathered in Albany to hear speeches proclaiming the realization of the universal republic and the brotherhood of man. Cooler heads ultimately prevailed upon Wise to give up his plan to return to Germany.[78]

The revolutionary zeitgeist inspired Lilienthal as well, although it is unlikely he ever dreamed of returning to Europe. Lilienthal addressed the plight of those fleeing the upheaval in Europe on November 13, 1849, in a speech at the joint dinner of the New York and German Hebrew benevolent societies.[79] He noted that Jews, who had been oppressed for ages, were particularly excited by the struggle for liberty in Europe. Sadly, the struggle ended in favor of the powerful and the "friends of freedom" were forced to flee. Lilienthal urged that the refugees be received with a hearty welcome, with ready assistance, because they were thrown, bereft, upon these shores.[80] The next year Lilienthal spoke at a meeting of the German Relief Committee called to aid political refugees. In that speech he praised the fact that Jews and Christians had come together to respond to German calls for assistance. He reminded his listeners, "[Those] who have struggled and suffered for liberty, call upon those who enjoy all its blessings and its happiness."[81] He urged support for the martyrs in the cause of liberty. Although Lilienthal spoke in nostalgic terms about the beauties of Germany, he used the speech to point out the superiority of America. Here, he asserted, tyrants do not rule by caprice, excessive taxes do not rob you of the fruit of your labor, humans are not reduced to machines, and education teaches liberty rather than blind obedience. His appeal was successful, and the highly acclaimed speech was published in the new periodical, the *Asmonean*.[82]

The high hopes of the revolutionaries were soon dashed all throughout Europe as conservatives retook the reins of power. With the speedy collapse of the liberal governments, Jews were among the political refugees fleeing from the reactionary regimes.[83] German Jewish immigration reached new heights as disenchanted liberals, joined by thousands motivated by persecution and economic concerns, gave up waiting for emancipation in Europe. The liberals, or 48ers, as they were called, were not large in number, but they were in general well educated and brought an infusion of talent, intellectual sophistication, and enlightened leadership to the American Jewish community.[84] Their presence in New York also had a powerful effect on Lilienthal, spurring his development and emergence as a Reform leader.

While the Jewish community was swept up in the excitement of the momentous events in Europe, American Jewish leaders knew that there were many organizational, educational, and poverty-related problems to solve in their own young congregations. Lilienthal was drawn into efforts by Isaac M. Wise and Isaac Leeser in 1849 to organize a national convention to work toward the goal of uniting Jewish congregations throughout the United States. In April 1847, Wise had returned to Albany disappointed by the failure of Lilienthal's *beth din*. To articulate his vision for Reform and unity, he wrote two lectures in English that he delivered to a circle of friends. One friend sent these lectures to Isaac Leeser without Wise's knowledge, and Leeser published them in the *Occident*. Although Leeser criticized the lectures' Reform tendency, the moderate traditionalist Leeser began a long correspondence with Wise that culminated in their first face-to-face meeting in the fall of 1847.[85] The two found common ground in the need to bring together representatives of the nation's synagogues to confront American Jewry's many problems. They used the *Occident* to announce plans for a national conference to take place in Philadelphia in May 1849.

Laying the groundwork for the first meeting, Leeser and Wise divided up the task of inviting congregations. Leeser was to promote the plan in Philadelphia, the West, and the South; Wise was responsible for the East, especially New York. Wise immediately went to New York to enlist the help of Rabbis Lilienthal and Merzbacher; Merzbacher opposed the plan, anticipating Orthodox recalcitrance, but Lilienthal endorsed it.[86]

With Lilienthal's backing, Wise gave a speech before a large crowd at Shaarey Hashamayim on February 1, 1849, advocating the plan.[87] Lilienthal and Wise then spoke to a joint meeting of the boards of the three German synagogues, gaining their unanimous support.[88] To further reawaken enthusiasm for the cause, Wise returned to New York on March 3, where Lilienthal arranged for him to speak again at Shaarey Hashamayim. In his talk Wise drew an analogy between the light in the biblical tabernacle and the need for spiritual light in the congregations of Israel. He called on the congregants to choose representatives to this conference to prepare for a national union of congregations.[89]

Inspired by Wise's address, a number of German Jewish intellectuals formed a group called the Society of the Friends of Light (Lichtfreunde). The society may have been modeled on a similar Jewish group formed in Germany in 1792, whose chief aim had been to support one another in the spread of culture and Enlightenment, taking a quote from Moses Mendelssohn as its motto: "To seek for truth, to love the beautiful, to desire the good, to do the best."[90] The gathering of Maskilim inspired by Mendelssohn never became a driving force in German Jewish life, but this type of organization reappeared in the succeeding generations. Not limited to Jewish circles, the Lichtfreunde associations were also organized in early nineteenth-century Germany among radical Protestants and Catholics (Deutschkatholiken) who advocated the need to overcome denominational barriers. In some cases liberal Jews were allowed to be members of these organizations.

The Lichtfreunde was one of many organizations that arose in Little Germany in the wake of the European revolutions. Some of those who joined the New York Friends of Light had come to America in the aftermath of the failed liberal revolutions of 1848. They met once a week to hear lectures on such topics as the existence of God, the history of pagan worship, the immortality of the soul, and Jewish history.[91] American Jewish historian Jacob Rader Marcus suggested that some members of the group believed that a messianic age was about to dawn, albeit in universalistic terms. Like their European counterparts, they embraced the dream of a universal religion that emphasized a spiritual unity in which denominational antagonisms would disappear.[92]

Lilienthal became an ardent supporter of the society. His inaugural address to the group articulated its agenda: to spread light and Enlightenment among Jews in America.[93] His address was published in the new liberal periodical *Israels Herold*, the short-lived publication of Isidor Busch, one of the intellectual Jewish leaders who arrived after the failed revolutions of 1848.[94] The Lichtfreunde address is significant because it marked Lilienthal's first public espousal of Reform ideology. A widely quoted statement from that speech also created quite a stir: "We feel that we have broken with the past of Judaism, and that the bridge which would make a retreat possible is cut off."[95] Lilienthal also gave a second lecture, "Essence of Religion," that tackled issues surrounding freedom of the will.[96] Present at the genesis of the Lichtfreunde, Wise gave his full support to the group, which was inspired in part by his own stirring address.[97] He also gave a fiery lecture, titled "Principles of Mosaic Religion" (*Die Grundlagen des Mosaismus*), that went far beyond Lilienthal's inaugural address. In it Wise claimed that ceremonial law had lost all value and significance. What mattered was striving for moral perfection.[98] The rhetoric of those and other Reform-oriented addresses frightened traditionalists who had been considering Wise and Leeser's proposed union. Hence Lilienthal and Wise unwittingly helped to drive a wedge into their fragile coalition for unity.

The Lichtfreunde became a lightning rod for dissension. In mid-April, when Wise returned to New York, he came to believe that its existence was a deterrent to his convention. Forgetting his own role in its origins, he complained that

> all the enthusiasm which had been enkindled for the progress in, and the union of, the congregations was directed by skilled manoeuvering into a marsh, where it threatened to be extinguished and disappear forever. A Society of Friends of Light . . . was organized by an influential element, rich in words, but poor in energy. . . . Enthusiasm was diverted to and all attention turned towards this society, instead of being given to the movement for congregational union.[99]

Wise reported to Leeser that when he conferred with the synagogue boards, all the congregational support for his conference had evaporated.

> As for New York, said one [board member], "progress will have to emanate from the Society of the Friends of Light. No other movement is advisable for the present." Another one said that if any one listened to the plans and purposes of the apostles of reform, as set forth in the Society of the Friends of Light, he would become very orthodox, and would strive earnestly to oppose every reform movement. A third one said: "If the bridges are burnt behind us, and nothing can be effected with the Judaism of the past, as has been claimed in the Society of the Friends of Light, then let us attempt nothing, and leave everything as it has been."[100]

When Leeser told Wise that the plan could not work without the support of New York, Wise replied that the New York congregations no longer wanted the union and that nothing more could be done.[101] Wise and Lilienthal conferred after it became clear that the union effort had failed. Wise confided his deep anger to his friend and vowed to "divide this American Judaism into two inimical camps."[102] He expressed no rancor toward Lilienthal, however, as he prepared to return to an embattled pulpit in Albany.

Although Wise felt no animosity toward Lilienthal, in a letter to the *Occident*, Joseph Beckel, one of Wise's avid supporters and a member of Wise's German literary society in Albany, attacked the Lichtfreunde and Lilienthal specifically. He called Lilienthal "the first and greatest opponent to a convention."[103] The Lichtfreunde, and Lilienthal's speech in particular, was a convenient scapegoat for the convention supporters, but Sigismund Waterman, the secretary of the society, defended both Lilienthal and the Lichtfreunde, declaring that Lilienthal had strongly supported the convention at their meeting.[104] Rather than blaming the Lichtfreunde, Waterman correctly pointed to the passionate divergence of opinion as the true cause of failure of the Wise-Leeser plan. As in the earlier case of Lilienthal's *beth din*, the dream of unity would constantly elude Jewish leaders as a result of ideological divisions.[105]

What is surprising about Lilienthal's Reform position in his Lichtfreunde speech is that it seemed to come out of nowhere compared to nearly all his public positions to date. Some later accused him of hypocrisy in his earlier, traditional stands in New York.[106] In fact, the address represented a significant change in Lilienthal's thinking. In Germany he had shown interest in corresponding with early Reform leaders, indicating sympathy with their agenda while remaining a traditional Jew in the context of German Jewish practice. When Riga had sought a head for their school, they chose a man of modern culture but with conservative religious tendencies. Lilienthal remained observant by Orthodox standards throughout his six-year Russian mission while championing the principle that there was no conflict between modern education and traditional observance. In New York Lilienthal advocated only those moderate reforms that could be justified by Jewish legal precedent. In many instances, he actually pushed the congregations in a more traditional direction.

What had changed? Lilienthal's negative experience in the New York German synagogues may have been a catalyst. His congregations had been primarily made up of young, poorly educated immigrant Jews from small towns and villages.[107] As Lilienthal himself noted in an 1847 article in the *Allgemeine Zeitung des Judenthums*, "We lack the great educated class of city-dwellers."[108] Although he praised their faith and commitment, his congregants did not have the benefit of the modern education that had so profoundly shaped his career and worldview. According to his friend Wise, reflecting back on the incidents leading to Lilienthal's dismissal, the chief rabbi had felt constrained from criticizing their beliefs, even superstitious beliefs, for fear of repercussions. Privately Lilienthal told Wise that he had come to despair of the present generation and therefore would devote his energy to teaching the next.[109] In a pattern that would be repeated later in his life, bitter controversy caused him to retreat into himself. He would emerge each time less committed to traditional Jewish positions.[110] With the remarkable success of his school, Lilienthal finally found financial security and independence, which in turn afforded him the freedom to develop a more liberal personal ideology.

At the same time, the air was full of radical ideas inspired by the revolutions of 1848. A new wave of highly educated, liberal Jews were arriving in New York in sufficient numbers to create a new circle of friends for the rabbi. Excited by the intellectual stimulation of this group, Lilienthal began moving in a more liberal direction.

Lilienthal's embrace of Reform was also motivated by his observation of trends in American Jewish life. Lilienthal was disturbed by what he saw as growing indifference, alienation from tradition, and poor Jewish education, and he believed that these problems could no longer be treated passively. In his Lichtfreunde speech, he had bemoaned the materialism and self-interest that motivated American Jewry to the exclusion of any interest in spiritual concerns. By 1849, Lilienthal had come to believe that the old Jewish world was collapsing in America and, out of his love for Judaism, he adopted a more activist Reform position.

For those who looked behind the headlines, it was clear that the speech was far from a radical break with Jewish tradition. Throughout Lilienthal acknowledged the power and beauty of traditional faith, which had provided consolation and had protected Jews in the stormy battle of life; he praised the sea of Jewish literature that had sharpened Jewish minds and had provided courage and inspiration; he openly regretted the loss of faith and fervor in the modern world. This speech, if anything, was a reflection of the anguished process by which he himself had come to embrace Reform.

At one point in his address, Lilienthal asked rhetorically, Are we not rashly trading away our rich spiritual heritage for the sake of civil freedom? Was not the destruction of that heritage comparable to the bloodletting of the guillotine during the French Revolution? Was there some higher principle to justify that sacrifice? Lilienthal answered emphatically, "Science [*Wissenschaft*] sanctions the break and calls it good; science excites the thirst for knowledge and stimulates our holiest interest in the All-Powerful."[111]

Lilienthal's analysis of the powerful trends leading to this break revealed his deep grasp of Jewish and European intellectual history, told from a maskilic point of view. The very notion of a historical break from the past comes from Naphtali Herz Wessely (1725–1804), who in his *Divrei Shalom Ve'emet* (Words of Peace and Truth, 1782) first articulated "a strong sense of a contemporary historical shift."[112] The modern age, with its consciousness of radical change, became a hallmark of maskilic history.

Lilienthal traced European intellectual history from the Protestant Reformation to the present. Luther, he explained, had challenged medieval Catholicism by giving the German people a vernacular translation of the Bible. The ensuing religious wars undermined Catholic spiritual hegemony, leading to the rise of religious skepticism. Voltaire's attack on religion and Kant's *Critique of Pure Reason* raised further doubts. The Young Hegelians continued the skeptical trend, shaking the foundations of Christianity with their dialectical analyses.[113] The remarkable growth of the natural sciences also undermined faith.

Jews were not immune to these challenges to tradition, Lilienthal argued. They too had their Luther—Moses Mendelssohn—who had given them a German translation of the Hebrew Bible. That translation had helped Jews to learn German, making European culture accessible for the first time. Mendelssohn had long been the harbinger of the modern age in maskilic history. Isaac Euchel (1758–1804), in his biography of Mendelssohn (*Toldot Harav*), established him as the key figure that marks the end of the dark period and the beginning of a new era of light, reason, and tolerance.[114] Knowing the nascent Haskalah movement needed a "maskilic pillar of fire," Euchel depicted Mendelssohn as the embodiment of the German *Bildung* ideal, someone who, in his own life, bridged the divide between the German and Jewish worlds.

At the same time, Jewish isolation was being eroded as secular law replaced Jewish law in courts, schools, and business. The "feeling of exile was extinguished," to be replaced by the promise of equal rights and dignity.[115] To earn civil emancipation, Judaism had to be modernized to adapt to the new conditions; it had to be exalted and defended so that Jews could fulfill their destiny as a light of religious truth to all peoples. Here, too, Lilienthal relied on received maskilic historical theory.[116]

All this raises the question: If Lilienthal had known and believed all this since his student days, why only now was he using it to justify a Reform position? Had he harbored these reformist tendencies and only revealed them when the conditions were right, namely, when he was no longer beholden to the three traditional German congregations and had found a group of like-minded intellectuals? What was the connection between this maskilic history, his *Wissenschaft* education, and his current espousal of Reform?[117]

I believe that Lilienthal had not dissembled or concealed reformist tendencies earlier in his life.[118] Although always committed to a maskilic embrace of modernity, Lilienthal underwent a genuine transformation in his views in these early years in America. How had he reconciled traditional attitudes with Haskalah and *Wissenschaft* earlier? Historian Ismar Schorsch sheds light on this issue by delineating the goals of different generations of *Wissenschaft* scholars. According to Schorsch, *Jüdische Wissenschaft* (Jewish science), in its earliest stage, was inherently and historically reformative. It served as the cutting edge of a concerted effort to revamp Judaism to harmonize it with a new legal and social context.[119] At this early stage *Wissenschaft* was often virulently antirabbinic, using its scholarly methodology as a destructive tool. Yet within a few decades a more conservative style of Jewish scholarship evolved that sought to bolster Jewish self-confidence by advocating a more favorable assessment of traditional Judaism. Even some Orthodox scholars, such as Esriel Hildescheimer, head of the Orthodox Seminary in Berlin, believed that it was necessary to engage in *Wissenschaft* as a matter of prestige and competition with the reformers.[120] This conservative approach had allowed more traditional exponents, such as Lilienthal, to understand Judaism within a historical context—and see it as a dynamic, evolving religion whose wisdom and beauty could be revealed to the world through *Wissenschaft*. Lilienthal took this tack in his Lichtfreunde address when he asserted that Jewish *Wissenschaft* had done much to exalt the Jewish religion in the eyes of the world.[121]

In an article in the *Asmonean*, Lilienthal himself stated that, although all historical scholars had concluded that Jewish tradition was the product of a long evolution, he recognized that disciples of *Wissenschaft* held a variety of positions regarding Reform. He noted that some of these scholars still argued that Jews should retain the whole system of traditional observance, fearing any change would undermine the whole structure. "A great scholar once remarked to me [Lilienthal related]: 'Do not touch these things, although they seem to be an immense palace, they are all but ashes; if you move them, the whole structure will tumble down and crumble.'"[122] Other traditional representatives of *Wissenschaft* had been raised in strict observance of the tradition and continued to live this way, despite their intellectual understanding. Another group waited for the masses of Jews to mature intellectually, believing that the demand for reforms should arise from the people themselves.[123] The reformers, however, refused to wait for the masses to be ready and wanted to eliminate a "heap of observances and ceremonies" and develop new forms. They insisted that Judaism should use *Wissenschaft* scholarship to identify all customs that were not of divine origin and that had simply accrued over time. By abolishing them, they maintained, Judaism would be purified and reformed, culminating in the universal reign of monotheism predicted by the prophets.[124]

Lilienthal probably began his career in America as one of those *Wissenschaft* scholars who, despite his intellectual understanding, wanted to retain the bulk of the tradition. As he became more liberal, he would use the same methodology to support a more reformist agenda. Lilienthal declared, "Science has grasped its mission that it must teach and preach to Jewry, and Jewry cleansed, has to give it to the world."[125] Stripped of archaic elements, he maintained, Judaism could be reconciled with the demands of modern times and thus be exalted in the eyes of the world.

There are indications that Lilienthal was moving away from traditional religious modes at the school as well. Although all private Jewish schools included Hebrew and the Bible in addition to secular subjects, Lilienthal's school seems to have been less observant than the others with regard to religious practice. The Palaches' school set a religious tone at its public examination by beginning with the unison singing of the hymn *Ein Keloheinu* and concluding with Psalm 29.[126] At the annual examination of the Loewe school, each student chanted a portion from the Torah with the ancient cantillation.[127] Lilienthal never included any traditional religious observances in the public presentations. Although the Greene Street school made a point that prayers were part of the daily schedule, Lilienthal never advertised this practice in his school. In contrast, his successor Henry emphasized these elements, including daily services and a Sabbath afternoon lecture.[128] Historian Morton Merowitz may be correct when he suggests that the level of observance in Lilienthal's boarding school revealed Lilienthal's growing liberalism. "The boarding school phase of Max Lilienthal's pedagogical career marked a transitional period: although not yet a spokesman for Reform Judaism, he was becoming less dependent on traditionalist modes and patterns of education and life."[129]

Lilienthal was given another opportunity to articulate his views when he was invited to speak at the consecration of Anshe Chesed's new building in 1850. Delivered in German and printed in an English translation in the *New York Daily Tribune*, the speech addressed the need for reforms. As he had in the Lichtfreunde speech, the rabbi characterized Reform as a natural consequence of historical forces. "Progress in religious views and forms cannot be prevented; its march cannot be forcibly stopped."[130]

In 1854, Lilienthal found a regular vehicle for expressing his views when he became a contributing editor to the *Asmonean*. Isaac M. Wise, who had previously held this position, had left Albany when he was offered a life contract to be the rabbi of Bene Yeshurun in Cincinnati. In his new editorial role, Lilienthal wrote a series of columns under the pseudonym L. D. in which he presented his developing Reform ideology with erudition and sophistication. Although he had advocated some of these reforms earlier, in the columns he fleshed out the details of his positions. A sampling of his articles reveals his approach to Reform, based in equal measure on Jewish legal thought and *Wissenschaft* principles.

In some articles, Lilienthal used the same conservative criterion for advocating change as he had during his early years in New York, namely, Jewish legal precedent. He considered the custom of purchasing a *misheberach* during the Torah service a "great nuisance"; such a transaction in which honors and blessings were sold to the highest bidder made him want to cry "Going, going, gone!" like an auctioneer. He harshly condemned this practice as a desecration of God's name, in which the rich showed off their wealth while the poor were humbled. He quoted the *Shulhan Arukh* to prove that there should be no profane conversation during the prayers.[131] In another article Lilienthal suggested that the Torah could be read in a three-year cycle rather than in one year. He cited the Talmud to prove that this practice was no innovation because ancient Palestinian Jewry had long ago read the Torah in that fashion.[132] In a defense of the elimination of certain prayers from the Reform service, he cited legal precedents as well as medieval sages from Ibn Ezra to Maimonides, who criticized some of the *piyyutim* (poetry) in the traditional prayer book. Further, there were precedents in the Talmud for saying the prayers in languages other than Hebrew. There was even traditional support for not repeating the central prayer of the service, the Shemoneh Esreh.[133]

In some cases Lilienthal combined legal precedent with *Wissenschaft* to argue for change. Contemporary Jewish merchants of Mantua had petitioned their *beth din* to abolish the second day of Jewish festivals in the Diaspora, arguing that the celebration of a second day was a custom detrimental to their businesses. The chief rabbi of Mantua asked for opinions from rabbis in Palestine and Europe. Lilienthal was pleased that the impulse for Reform arose in this case out of the need to reconcile what he called a contradiction between the demands of active life and the dead forms of religion. In this instance, Orthodoxy was forced by the people to confront the realities of changed times.[134] Lilienthal agreed with the Jewish merchants of Mantua that the observance of the second day of the festivals should be abolished.

Lilienthal used the methodology of *Wissenschaft* to trace the history of second-day festival observance. The Bible clearly dictated one day of observance (the first and last days of weeklong festivals) as the core legal requirement. However, central to the biblical system for setting the Jewish calendar was the need to establish the time of the new moon visually. Messengers carrying the announcement of the new moon in the land of Israel could not reach all the far-flung Jewish communities soon enough to ensure simultaneous observance of all festivals, so a second day was added in regions outside Palestine. Although the sages of the Talmud subsequently developed a mathematical method for calculating the calendar, they continued to insist on observing the second day.

On what basis could contemporary rabbis overturn the weighty precedent of the Talmud? Lilienthal drew on traditional Jewish legal reasoning to argue that it was permissible, quoting a Reform rabbi, Leopold Stein, who pointed out an inconsistency in the traditional ruling. Stein (1810–82) was a moderate reformer who served as the second rabbi of the Frankfurt community. He noted that Yom Kippur was always an exception to the two-day observance because of the difficulty involved in fasting for forty-eight hours. This proved the principle that the necessities of life were more important than theoretical concerns.[135] Lilienthal also cited Maimonides, who had ruled that two days of observance had the status of *minhag* (custom) rather than law. Further, Maimonides had ruled that a law could be abolished if urgently demanded by the times. If a law could be overturned, then certainly a custom could be as well.[136]

By combining historical methodology with legal precedent, Lilienthal revealed that he had moved beyond the conservative position of his early years in New York. In this respect he shared the approach of Zacharias Frankel (1801–75), the spiritual leader of Positive-Historical Judaism, who argued that a flexible, historically informed approach to Halakha was crucial to sustaining Jewish religious life. Lilienthal also shared Frankel's belief that change must come from the people.[137]

In other articles Lilienthal showed that he was willing to go further still when he used *Wissenschaft* arguments to challenge the divine status of Jewish law itself. He insisted that critical scientific investigation divested the Talmudists and their successors of the supernatural halo that surrounded them. *Wissenschaft* biographers presented the rabbinic sages as mortal men.[138] In response to the Orthodox claim that such historical treatment of the Talmudists and their successors was sacrilegious, Lilienthal responded, "Better no religion than such that cannot stand the trial before the forum of science, knowledge and common sense."[139] If the Talmudists themselves were not the semidivine figures that tradition had made them out to be, then their rulings could also be judged through the lens of historical criticism. Citing Abraham Geiger (1810–74), Lilienthal asserted that not all of talmudic law was of divine origin; indeed, many rabbinic rulings dealt with the exigencies of their times. Historical research helped to sift the "divine"—or what was derived from a biblical commandment—from the "human," that is, manmade rulings for a given time and place.[140]

Like many *Wissenschaft* scholars, Lilienthal assumed that there was an essence of Judaism, an unchanging yet evolving spiritual core that gave a sense of continuity to Jewish history. These scholars used the concept of essence to weed out those elements of tradition that were deemed irrelevant in the new social context. Those objectionable elements were dismissed as mere "accidents of history" and thus could be discarded.[141] Lilienthal concluded that historical research would separate what was essential to Judaism from what he regarded as "grafts upon the tree of our creed."[142]

An application of this methodology was the sharp distinction *Wissenschaft* scholars made between custom (*minhag*) and law (Halakha). If customs were merely accretions or accidents developed to meet the needs of specific historical conditions, then they had a lower degree of obligation than law, which was essential to Judaism.[143] Lilienthal posed the issue as follows:

> Is it not ridiculous to assert that the *minhag* of Israel is equally binding as the Torah? The Rabbis of old had to sanction those customs because the people had become accustomed to them, but in our age, where manners and customs and habits are totally changed, where the cause of such an antiquated *minhag* has become quite incomprehensible, who, if not blinded by ignorance, or by fanatic hypocrisy, will urge the necessity of observing those laws?[144]

Lilienthal believed that many of the onerous restrictions under which Jews labored were imitations of indigenous customs that had become out of tune with the spirit of the times. Judaism, he asserted, had to purify itself of these antiquated *minhagim* to "stand upon the solid rock of Mosaic Law."[145]

In 1854, the debate between Reform and Orthodoxy had not yet solidified into permanent denominations. Lilienthal still hoped that all Jews could unite through the embrace of biblical law. Although some radical reformers rejected all but the ethical teachings of the Bible, Lilienthal, like many other reformers of his day, accepted the divine nature of the revelation at Sinai and the biblical commandments that flowed from that sacred moment. As a moderate reformer, he believed that the rabbinic law derived from biblical precedents was also holy. This represented the essential core that he wished to preserve. Where he differed from the traditional camp was his willingness to do away with elements in the post-biblical legal corpus that critical scholarship identified as historical accretions or customs. He particularly rejected those practices he deemed archaic or out of harmony with the spirit of the modern age. He apparently did so out of a fervent desire to create a revitalized and relevant Judaism that would speak to a generation that was quickly assimilating and falling away from observance.

Lilienthal blamed Kabbalah (Jewish mysticism) for giving rise to most of the nonsensical *minhagim* and superstitious prejudices that hindered Judaism's ability to harmonize with the zeitgeist.[146] Like many Maskilim and *Wissenschaft* scholars, Lilienthal disdained Kabbalah as an alien plant that borrowed from Greek, Christian, Babylonian, and other religious traditions. In a long Jewish literature column, "Kabbalah and Philosophy," Lilienthal asserted that historical research had proved that Kabbalah was not nearly as old as it claimed to be. Based on his own work with Jewish manuscripts in the Munich Royal Library, later scholars proved that the *Zohar*, the seminal mystical text, was written by a thirteenth-century mystic named Moses de Leon and not by the second-century sage Rabbi Simeon Ben Yohai, to whom the text was attributed. Lilienthal claimed that the *Zohar*—and by extension the mystical tradition in Judaism—was neither ancient nor authoritative.[147] Through historical research, Lilienthal tried to dispel the aura surrounding Kabbalah to purge Judaism of its superstitions.

In another lengthy article, Lilienthal claimed that the historical role of philosophy was to "make up for the mischief that she [Kabbalah] has committed."[148] The Jewish mind, he thought, was peculiarly adapted to analytical thinking so that the philosophy of the Bible was not burdened by incomprehensible doctrines, such as the New Testament's notion of the Trinity or the necessity of faith as a prerequisite for salvation. Unfortunately, from his point of view, Jewish thought had later tried to read the philosophical systems of other nations into the Holy Scriptures, failing to recognize that biblical philosophy surpassed all those systems.[149]

At the same time, Lilienthal recognized the contributions of Jewish philosophers to philosophy in general. His survey of Jewish philosophy demonstrated his knowledge of primary sources and his ability to use modern research. He discussed the contributions of Philo and the role of Jewish thinkers in the development of Gnosticism.[150] Later articles covered such medieval thinkers as Saadya, Ibn Gabirol, Bahya ibn Pakuda, Judah Halevi, Abraham ben David, Joseph ibn Zaddik, Abraham ibn Ezra, and Maimonides. Lilienthal was especially enamored of Maimonides, whom he discussed at length.[151] He saved his highest praise for the "great and immortal

Baruch Spinoza," whose original philosophical system, Lilienthal claimed, pervaded all of modern philosophy.[152] No general intellectual movement of any importance, he asserted, was devoid of a Jewish contribution to its development. Nor was this contribution exhausted, because mankind had yet to achieve its destiny. "The wheels of time do not need or adopt the advice of mortal man; ruled and moved by an external power, they pursue their onward march, and whatever has to give way to new forms and ideas, they will inexorably remove. Man may remain behind; but the genius of humanity, though sometimes retrograding, knows but the motto: Onward!"[153]

Lilienthal did not define what he meant by "an external power" or "the genius of humanity." He may have been alluding to God or to the Hegelian Absolute in which History was the vehicle for the progressive manifestation of Spirit or Reason or to a generalized nineteenth-century notion of progress. In sum, Lilienthal asserted that history itself created an inevitable impetus for Reform and that Jews and their religion still had a crucial role to perform in bringing about that ultimate fulfillment of human history.[154]

While everything that we have analyzed in the *Asmonean* articles until this point shows the influence of Lilienthal's German Jewish background, his concern for American conditions helped to shape his emerging Reform views as well. In an overview of America written in 1854, at the time of the Jewish New Year, Lilienthal spoke about religious freedom in America. He obliquely refers to religious fanatics who wanted to shape America according to their own principles. America, he countered, was a part of God's plan, a shelter against tyranny for the oppressed of mankind.

Although American Jewry was prospering, many problems still had to be overcome.[155] The pressure to succeed materially in America was the central challenge that the German Jewish immigrants faced. It meant that religious affiliation, education, and institutional development were relegated to a secondary priority for them. Lilienthal declared, "We, in this country, sink under the burden of commercial competition and valuing and appreciating everything, but after the profit it will yield."[156] Only a Judaism that recognized the implications of this pressure would be successful. One important implication was apathy. According to historian Stanley Nadel, most of the German Jews living in Kleindeutschland were religiously unaffiliated.[157] Responding to an article by Isaac Leeser titled "What Good Have They [Reformers] Ever Done for Our Cause?" Lilienthal asserted that Reform was the answer to the spiritual malaise of American Jewish life. "Reform has tried its utmost by constant improvement to reconcile these masses, to bring them back to the sacred religion of our ancestors, and it can fairly boast that many . . . feel now proud of their Jewish name."[158]

How far Lilienthal has already traveled from his view in 1847 that the only reason for Reform was to earn emancipation. American Jews, already having freedom, had no need of Reform.[159] Now, after almost ten years in American, Lilienthal began to see that Reform had much more to offer American Jewry.

Reform had countered Jewish hypocrisy and self-deceit, he argued. "We are tired of seeing men violate the Sabbath until they accumulated an independent fortune, calling themselves orthodox anyway."[160] The solution was to separate God's law from the rulings of mortal men. Through scholarship and historical research it would be possible to resolve the contradiction between life and religion. Lilienthal believed that Judaism, restored to its primitive purity and simplicity, would unite Jews in the firm belief in one God and inspire them with the fervor of their ancestors.[161] Stripped of onerous traditional practices, Reform would presumably offer a way for these immigrants to reconcile their need to work on the Sabbath, for example, and feel authentically Jewish.

Another reason for apathy and alienation from Jewish observance was the lack of relevance of the traditional worship. Arguing that much of the liturgy was no longer understood and that many prayers were "unfit for the times," Lilienthal asserted that Reform would modernize the service, increase decorum, and raise the level of edification to make religious services meaningful again.

Lilienthal was realistic and understood that he could not convince the traditionalists of his positions in these articles. Although agreement was a fervent dream, he at least hoped for cooperation. He bemoaned the lack of unity among American Jews. With many pressing needs, he decried the inability of the various factions of America's Jews to work together peacefully. He declared, "A union of these scattered forces, for clerical, pedagogical, synagogal, and charitable purposes, by which many great aims might be attained, is still a pious desideratum.[162] Lilienthal's belief was that moderation and peaceful exchange would further this goal.

In an article titled "Parties—Keep Peace!" Lilienthal outlined the divisions that plagued American Jewry. "We mourn, we regret this disunion, but we cannot deny its existence. What remedy now is to be applied to this evil? *Keep peace and nothing but peace!*"[163] Noting the debates in the Talmud, Lilienthal pointed out that there had always been a diversity of opinions within Judaism. Jews, who were so often in need of tolerance from other peoples, should be tolerant of one another. Threats of excommunication and inflammatory speech, he warned, only served to create a disastrous gulf between the parties.[164]

Lilienthal returned to this need for peace in an article titled "About What Are You Quarreling?" In a position close to that of Moses Mendelssohn, Lilienthal argued that no one disagreed concerning the fundamental biblical truths or the oneness of God.[165] With regard to ritual issues, adherents to "kosher housekeeping" and the observance of the Sabbath were found among the reformers as well as among the traditionalists. Moreover, the ritual innovations of the Reformers—such as the triennial cycle of Torah reading, editing the prayer book, and praying in the vernacular—all had legal precedents. Even the introduction of organ and mixed choir could be justified on the basis of religious need. "All these innovations are nothing new . . . all these debates and discussions were heard centuries ago."[166] As the different customs of the Portuguese, German, and Polish rites proved, there had never been absolute homogeneity in worship. "What is new is the cry and clamor and tumult that is raised about such triflings," Lilienthal wrote. "I consider it but a variety of *minhagim*, but a reform not at all."[167] He concluded with an admonition to allow diversity and work for peace.

The rabbi's contributions to the *Asmonean* were not limited to articles articulating his Reform position. The column provided an opportunity to do what he loved best—teaching. Lilienthal shared the fruits of his university learning with an increasingly sophisticated American Jewish readership. In a series of articles called "Jewish Geographical Sketches," he discussed Jewish communities throughout the world, such as the farmers of Palestine and the Falashas (Ethiopian Jews).[168] In a lengthy article called "The Jews in Russia Under Nicolai I," Lilienthal departed from the style of earlier articles on Russian Jewry in the *Occident*, in which he had maintained an objective, historical voice. In the new article he revealed his personal feelings concerning his encounter with Nicholas's regime. Beginning his sketch under the reign of Alexander, whom he portrayed positively, Lilienthal then turned to Nicholas, his old nemesis. Citing the trinity of principles behind the tsar's regime—autocracy, Russian church, and Russian nationality—Lilienthal asserted that Nicholas hated every liberal idea. No longer disguising his contempt and disappointment, he accused Nicholas of clothing the most atrocious crimes in the garb of human and benevolent words. Charging that the modernization effort was merely a cover for Nicholas's desire to convert the Jews to Russian Orthodoxy, Lilienthal claimed that all of Europe had been duped by the tsar's betrayal of Russian Jewry.[169]

Lilienthal's columns in the *Asmonean* stopped abruptly in September 1854, when he accepted a corresponding editorial position for the *Israelite*, Isaac M. Wise's new, Reform-identified Jewish weekly in Cincinnati.[170] During the next months Lilienthal would contribute long English articles on a weekly basis. By that time, his writing on *Wissenschaft* and Reform had established him as an important new liberal spokesman. Having had to produce so many articles over the months he served as an editor of the *Asmonean* also had given him a fluency in written English. Apparently his spoken English was improving as well. In September 1854 Lilienthal preached at the consecration of a Boston synagogue. The reporter covering the event for the *Israelite* wrote that Lilienthal's English in the short sermon was broken but fully comprehensible.[171] This report helps us remember that Lilienthal had arrived in America just nine years earlier.

An article in the *Israelite* written in November 1854 gave the rabbi an opportunity to address a major concern of the American Jewish community: Christian missionaries. Evangelical Christians devoted great energy and funds to conversion through groups such as the Society for Meliorating the Condition of the Jews. Prominent leaders, including politicians and university presidents, associated themselves with these efforts. In addition, well-meaning individuals—especially women—privately attempted to convert their Jewish neighbors.[172] Robert Baird, a contemporary representative of evangelical Protestantism, linked missionary work with the "voluntary principle," which called for complete liberty of the individual to choose their religious affiliation.[173] Relishing the competition this freedom created, Lilienthal boasted in the *Israelite* that he had converted thirty-seven Christians to Judaism in the years he had been in America. He also reconverted several Jews who had been enticed by missionaries. For example, one woman, after being converted by the Methodists, felt remorse and returned to Judaism. Lilienthal also reconverted a man and his sons after they began coming to services at his New York congregation. Confronted by a group of missionaries at his home, the rabbi bluntly told them that, with the exception of a miserable minority, no Jew could ever believe the unintelligible doctrines of Christianity. He warned them that their efforts would prove ineffective.[174] According to Jonathan Sarna, one of American Jewry's most original and important responses to the missionary challenge was insisting on their right to compete on a level field with "no holds barred."[175]

On May 13, 1855, the president of Anshe Chesed called a board meeting to discuss a letter from their rabbi informing them that he had been offered a lifetime contract to serve as rabbi for Congregation Bene Israel in Cincinnati, at the yearly salary of $1,500.[176] The board reacted by calling for a general meeting of the electors of the congregation on May 27 and by setting up a committee to meet with the reverend doctor to investigate under what conditions he would be willing "to remain as Rabbi of this congregation."[177]

The minutes recorded neither the motivation for Lilienthal's letter (did he expect a counter offer?) nor the results of the deliberations. After the committee informed him of the decision of the electors, he proceeded with his planned departure.[178]

A number of factors made the Cincinnati offer attractive for Lilienthal. The salary was generous and gave him financial security at a time when his wife was ill and his school may have been less successful than previously.[179] The lifetime contract was an important feature of the offer. Years later Lilienthal bitterly recalled the early short-term contracts that forced rabbis "to flatter and humble themselves before every ignoramus who had a right to vote at the annual election."[180] He also had had an ongoing relationship with the Cincinnati synagogue's leadership, as several sons of prominent members had attended his private school.[181] In addition, Bene Israel, the oldest and most prestigious synagogue in Cincinnati, was moving in a more liberal direction, as can be seen in their advertisement for the position.

> K. K. Benai Israel, Cincinnati, O., is desirous of engaging a lecturer (in the English and German languages), and superintendent of their school. Salary $1000 per annum with a prospect of an increase to $1500. Candidates being endowed with the following qualifications:
>
> 1. Good theological learning and a general scientific education.
> 2. Liberal principles, progressive and in just accordance with our age. (No radical reformer!)[182]

In Cincinnati, seemingly, Lilienthal would be free to speak his mind and lead his congregation according to the dictates of his developing vision. In addition, Cincinnati was becoming an important center of commerce to which many German immigrants were drawn. A Little Germany existed in Cincinnati as early as the 1830s and had already emerged as a cultural center for German Americans.[183]

Finally, Lilienthal would be able to continue to work closely with his close friend, Isaac M. Wise, the rabbi of Bene Yeshurun in Cincinnati. When the choice of Lilienthal was announced, Wise asserted that the congregation had chosen the best man available. With his usual ebullient enthusiasm, he proclaimed, "Cincinnati is the Zion of the West, from which 'the Law shall go forth.' Here is a large and pleasant field for the devout laborer in the field of Judaism and enlightenment, and Dr. L. has the ability to verify our ardent wishes."[184]

Wise suggested that Lilienthal's reason for leaving New York was the shoddy treatment he endured from the German congregations. He thought it was a disgrace that they did not pay Lilienthal for his services to them. He also vilified Anshe Chesed's lay leaders for perpetuating an archaic traditional approach to Judaism, counter to their rabbi's agenda.[185] Wise misconstrued Lilienthal's situation on both counts. Despite his fondness for his colleague, Lilienthal wrote a stern reply.

> Personalities should be avoided at any price, and will do no good, neither to the paper, whose editor you are, nor to the sacred cause, you so manfully defend. I can assure you, that Mr. H. Moses, since his reappointment to the Presidency of the Norfolk Str. congregation, has afforded me any aid in his power, to carry out the improvements I proposed to the board of Trustees. If acting in perfect harmony, we were unable always to attain the aim and purpose we had in view, it was not his fault; but difficulties of the most different kind prevented the desired result. It is but justice on my part to give publicly this explanation, and I hope you will immediately insert it in the *Israelite*, in order to repay the unjust charge, made against the presiding officer of the respected *Congregation Anshe Chesed*.
>
> BY DOING SO, YOU WILL GREATLY OBLIGE,
>
> YOURS TRULY
>
> RABBI DR. LILIENTHAL.[186]

Wise had accurately reported Lilienthal's frustration but had incorrectly identified the forces at Anshe Chesed that had opposed him. As his Reform position developed, Lilienthal became increasingly impatient with the slow pace of change in the New York synagogues, especially in liturgical matters. However, it was not the lay leadership who opposed his reforms but the cantors. As late as April 1855, Lilienthal complained again about the ritual of *misheberach*s, the slowness of ritual responses sung by the choir, and the hollering of the cantor. In his letter of resignation to Anshe Chesed, Lilienthal stated that his grounds for leaving were feeling estranged from the other Jewish clergy, who, in his opinion, exposed Jewish worship to scorn.[187] He could have left quietly, without comment or controversy, but he did not resist the temptation to level a final critique upon those who had blocked his attempts at liturgical reform.

Although the New York synagogues had not paid their rabbi, they had often given him expensive gifts to express their appreciation. Before the *Israelite* had announced Lilienthal's appointment, Anshe Chesed had set up a committee to purchase another gift for their rabbi to thank him for the many voluntary services he had rendered. The committee chose three dozen silver tablespoons, two dozen teaspoons, a silver ladle, and a silver cup, valued at $200.53, which they presented to the rabbi before the June 24 meeting. The gift, originally meant as a show of gratitude, became a farewell present, for which Lilienthal graciously thanked the board.[188]

The ten years that Max Lilienthal spent in New York were pivotal to his development as an American rabbi. In this time he went through the difficult processes of both adjusting to the New World and self-realization. As he discovered the needs of the young American synagogues and how to serve them, he also moved in a more liberal direction. Freed from the confines of service to Orthodox synagogues by his successful private school and inspired by revolutionary events and liberal newcomers, he drew on his maskilic and *Wissenschaft* background in new ways to arrive at Reform conclusions. He found his ideological voice, which he expressed with increasing confidence and intellectual acuity. Lilienthal, having fully emerged as a moderate Reform leader in his own right, was ready to help Wise create institutions that would bring the German Jewish immigrant community into harmony with mainstream American trends.

Max Lilienthal at age 12. Photo courtesy of Jacob Rader Marcus Center of the American Jewish Archives of the Hebrew Union College–Jewish Institute of Religion.

Max Lilienthal, c. 1860s. Photo courtesy of Jacob Rader Marcus Center of the American Jewish Archives of the Hebrew Union College–Jewish Institute of Religion.

Samuel Lilienthal, Max's brother, at age 11. Photo courtesy of Jacob Rader Marcus Center of the American Jewish Archives of the Hebrew Union College–Jewish Institute of Religion.

Dr. Samuel Lilienthal, Max Lilienthal's brother. Photo courtesy of Jacob Rader Marcus Center of the American Jewish Archives of the Hebrew Union College–Jewish Institute of Religion.

Pepi Nettre as a young woman. This watercolor portrait was sent to her fiancé, Max, while he was in Russia; a letter from him dated May 28, 1841, thanks her for the picture. Photo courtesy of Jacob Rader Marcus Center of the American Jewish Archives of the Hebrew Union College–Jewish Institute of Religion.

Pepi Lilienthal (née Nettre), Max Lilienthal's wife, c.1860s. Photo courtesy of Jacob Rader Marcus Center of the American Jewish Archives of the Hebrew Union College–Jewish Institute of Religion.

New York City (Wall Street) in the nineteenth century. Image courtesy of Jacob Rader Marcus Center of the American Jewish Archives of the Hebrew Union College–Jewish Institute of Religion.

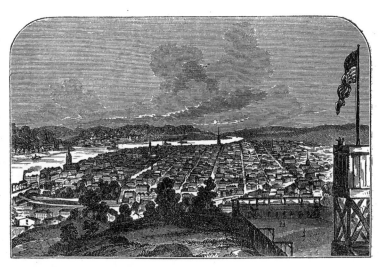

Cincinnati in the nineteenth century. Image courtesy of Jacob Rader Marcus Center of the American Jewish Archives of the Hebrew Union College–Jewish Institute of Religion.

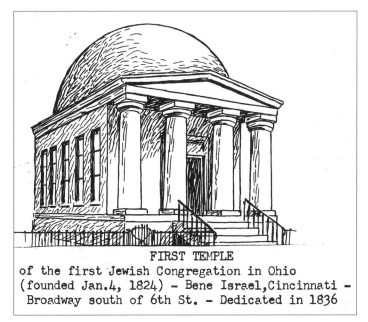

FIRST TEMPLE
of the first Jewish Congregation in Ohio
(founded Jan.4, 1824) - Bene Israel,Cincinnati -
Broadway south of 6th St. - Dedicated in 1836

The original building for Congregation Bene Israel, Lilienthal's first pulpit in Cincinnati. The temple was located on Broadway, south of Sixth Street, and was dedicated in 1836. Image courtesy of Jacob Rader Marcus Center of the American Jewish Archives of the Hebrew Union College–Jewish Institute of Religion.

Broadway Synagogue, constructed in 1852, was the second building for Congregation Bene Israel. Image courtesy of the Jacob Rader Marcus Center of the American Jewish Archives of the Hebrew Union College–Jewish Institute of Religion.

ק. ק. בית תפלה, סינסיננאטי, א.

Synagogue Beth Tephilah,   Cincinnati, O.

Mound Street Temple (Bene Israel), dedicated 1869. temple was constructed after Lilienthal threatened to leave Cincinnati following the death of his wife, Pepi. Image courtesy of Jacob Rader Marcus Center of the American Jewish Archives of the Hebrew Union College–Jewish Institute of Religion.

Rev. Dr. M. Lilienthal

This picture originally hung in the home of a Southern admirer of Lilienthal. (The rabbi would travel to various parts of the country to dedicate synagogues and preach.) With the advent of the Civil War, the outraged Southerner—resentful of Lilienthal's support of the Northern cause—defaced the picture and sent it to the rabbi with a death threat. Courtesy of the Magnes Collection of Jewish Art and Life, Bancroft Library, UC Berkeley.

MENU

HUÎTRES	De l'Est.

POTAGES	A la Royal.	A la Rahel.

HORS D'ŒUVRES	Salade d'Anchois.	Olives.
	Salade de Crevettes.	

POISSON	Sole à la Normande.
	Truite à la Venezien.

ENTRÉES	Bouchéese à la Reine.
	Grenouilles en Caise.
	Poulete à la Toulouse.
	Filets du Boeuf à la Godard.

LÉGUMES	Artichaus à la Perigole.	Petits Pois.
	Asperges à la Anglaise.	

ROMAIN PUNCH.

RÔTIS	Selle d'Agneau.
	Turkey Truffé.
	Salade de la Saison.

PIÈCES FROIDES	Galantine de Dinde à la Parisien.
	Pain de Fois Gras en Bellevue.

ENTREMETS	Gelée Macedoine.
	Oranges au Marasquin.

GÂTEAU DE NOCE.

PIÈCES	Corns d'Abondance.
MONTÉES	Chateau sur Socle.
	Charlotte Napolitaine.
	Corbeille en Merengues.
	Ruge d'Abeilles.

GLACES	Corbeille Jardiniere.
	Fort sur Socle.

DESSERT	Bonbons et Mottoes Francaise.
	Fruit Frais et Glacés.
	Gateau de Soirée etc.

Menu from the wedding of Ernest Lilienthal (Max's nephew) and Bella Sloss. Max Lilienthal officiated at the wedding, which was held in San Francisco in May 1876. Courtesy of Jacob Rader Marcus Center of the American Jewish Archives of the Hebrew Union College–Jewish Institute of Religion.

5

Fighting for a Moderate Reform Agenda

Cincinnati, situated on the northern bank of the Ohio River, was founded in 1788. The long river, the major highway connecting the settled East with the new Northwest Territories, was the settlement's lifeblood. As the frontier town grew from a few log cabins to a major city in southern Ohio, its history remained intimately tied to the river.

Cincinnati had long been a congenial place for Jews. The first Jew to settle there was Joseph Jonas, who came from Plymouth, England, in 1817. The earliest Jewish settlers to join him in this frontier outpost were also mostly English and Dutch. That Jews were among the pioneers who helped develop Cincinnati from its earliest days meant that they had earned a respected place in public life. In a way that was not possible in older, more established cities, Jews were welcomed into the economic, cultural, and political elite. Jonas himself, a successful watchmaker and silversmith, later became a state legislator. Far from experiencing prejudice, Jonas found that Jews were appreciated as good citizens. In fact, he believed that the Almighty had caused the Christians to look with favor on the Jews of Cincinnati.[1]

In the mid-nineteenth century, Cincinnati was a city on the rise with an idealized sense of its own future. From the mid-1820s to the mid-1850s, when Lilienthal arrived, Cincinnati was the premier boomtown in the United States. Its population nearly doubled every ten years, its economy expanded dramatically, and it quickly developed from a rough frontier village into one of the country's most urbane cities.[2] Some contemporaries enthusiastically claimed that it was only a matter of time before Cincinnati, already the "Queen City of the West," would become the greatest city in America, or even the world.[3] Charles Dickens, who visited in 1842, praised its beauty and cleanliness and its broad, well-paved streets and elegant private homes. He reported that Cincinnati was a thriving and interesting place, a city that its inhabitants took great pride in.[4]

German immigration did much to shape Cincinnati's character. From its frontier beginnings in the early nineteenth century, Germans held key municipal offices. They were early business leaders, forming banks, trading companies, and utilities, but they were also key figures in the development of cultural institutions, such as libraries, literary societies, and newspapers.[5] In the 1830s, as the stream of German immigrants increased dramatically, they entered the city's diverse businesses and professions. New streets and boroughs multiplied, creating the boomlike quality of the city's growth. By 1848, the German population was estimated to be between 33,000 and 50,000 out of a total population of 111,435.[6] The Germans formed schools, clubs, theater and singing groups, and lecture societies that added substantially to the cultural life of the community. Cincinnati was the first city in the country to introduce German bilingual education in the public elementary schools, an option that continued to be offered for more than seventy-five years.[7]

This strong German ethnic and cultural environment made Cincinnati a hospitable destination for German Jewish immigrants as well. The German Jewish immigration drastically changed the character of Cincinnati's Jewish community, which grew from 100 in the 1830s to 7,500 in 1860, when the immigration numbers stabilized as a result of the Civil War.[8] Throughout this period, about 82 percent of the Jewish immigrants came from Germany; of these, 66 percent came from Bavaria, Lilienthal's birthplace. Fleeing the insecurity and pauperization of their communities, these predominantly young men were searching for freedom and prosperity.[9] First, fellow Jewish villagers arrived and then virtually entire communities were transplanted, making for cohesive groups of transplanted immigrants.[10]

Of course, the existence of a thriving German community was not a sufficient cause in itself for German Jewish settlement.[11] The city's proximity to Kentucky and Indiana and its location on the Ohio River positioned it as an important trade center.[12] In addition, the development of canals and a railroad system solidified its economic position. The vast rural areas needed a wider trade network, and German Jewish immigrants eagerly filled this niche. Forced by Old World economic restrictions into peddling, Jews found their skills welcome in America. Hundreds of these peddlers came to Cincinnati in the 1830s and 1840s; some of them made their fortunes when they became merchants or bankers.[13] Operating with their own internal credit system, they created a complex system of distribution that connected retailers and wholesalers to manufacturers and importers. By 1850 half of Cincinnati's Jews were proprietors, brokers, and traders.[14] With the advent of the Singer sewing machine, the ready-made clothing industry more than tripled in the 1850s. In 1860, Jews owned sixty-five of the seventy wholesale clothing firms in Cincinnati; these companies employed over half of the Jewish workforce.[15] The upward mobility of the Jewish community was remarkable, and the median wealth of Jewish merchants more than doubled in the 1850s. The majority was now among the upper middle class, with an elite group among the truly wealthy of the city. Two important local successes, Philip Heidelbach and Jacob Seasongood, both from Bavaria and each possessing a net worth of more than $200,000, were important lay leaders in Lilienthal's synagogue.[16]

Given this dramatic success, it is no wonder that the Jews developed their own version of the prevailing Cincinnati optimism. More than just optimistic, Cincinnati Jewry believed it had a divine mission, as Joseph Jonas articulated in his memoirs. "The fiat had gone forth, that a new resting place for the scattered sons of Israel should be commenced, and that a sanctuary should be erected in the Great West, dedicated to the Lord of Hosts."[17] Lilienthal, Wise, and other local religious leaders would continue to develop this sense of mission in the second half of the nineteenth century. They confidently believed that a new vision of Judaism would issue from this new Zion, one more compatible with the new American milieu than the traditional forms they had brought from Europe.[18]

The first Cincinnati synagogue, Bene Israel, was established in 1824 as a traditional *kahal*, an all-inclusive Jewish community. The founders procured a room for worship services, and several of the early leaders took turns leading services.[19] Having bought land in 1829 on Broadway near Sixth Street, they solicited donations from wealthy Jews in New Orleans, New York, Philadelphia, and Baltimore. In that period, more established communities saw it as their duty to help fledgling congregations. Surprisingly, fifty-two Cincinnati Christians each donated $25 toward the building as well. The rest of the funds came from selling seats in the sanctuary. Although a modest building (80 × 33 feet), it had a Doric façade with pillars and a portico, a handsome central dome, and an elegantly decorated interior. In September 1836, when the congregation consecrated its opening, a band accompanied a mixed choir of twenty men and women of the congregation who sang hymns composed for the occasion. So many Christians wanted to attend that they could not admit them all. As the first synagogue west of the Allegheny Mountains opened its doors, its Christian neighbors warmly welcomed it.[20]

Bene Israel attempted to fulfill all the ritual and communal needs of the still tiny Jewish settlement, providing a cemetery, a school, a ritual bath, and a place to worship and socialize. Bene Israel supervised the sale of kosher meat and the baking of matzo, dispensed charity to the needy, and hired a Torah reader to lead services. The community exerted jurisdiction over its members in ritual matters, levying fines and disciplining members of the community. The lay leadership was generally knowledgeable enough to run the community without the assistance of a rabbi.[21]

When the large German Jewish immigration overwhelmed the small *kahal*, a group broke away to form Bene Yeshurun in 1841. These German Jews were not rejecting the traditionalism of Bene Israel; rather, they wanted to replicate their own regional customs and rituals, as is evident in their constitution of 1841.[22] In effect, they set up another *kahal* that attempted to serve its subgroup in much the same manner as Bene Israel had. Both congregations built new buildings, supported religious schools, and maintained cemeteries; and each congregation thought of itself as more observant than the rival congregation.[23]

The hiring of Isaac M. Wise as rabbi by Bene Yeshurun in 1854 precipitated a crisis at Bene Israel. As this charismatic young reformer moved his congregation in a more progressive direction, he drew members from the older synagogue and attracted newcomers. Wise promised to make his congregation a model for the entire West and South.[24] He described the effect that his arrival had on Bene Israel. "The result of all this was not long in appearing. The *B'ne Yeshurun* synagogue was crowded every Saturday, and the large and costly *B'ne Israel* synagogue became the gathering-place of the English-Polish-German orthodox, who exerted themselves to the utmost to perpetuate all of the old indecorum in the service. The *bona fide* members of the congregation became convinced that a change must take place, or else the congregation would soon dissolve."[25] Although Wise's arrival was a factor, the decline of the older congregation was also due to heavy debt, poor administration, and high dues. In 1852, Bene Israel had completed a new, larger building on the same site when many Jews were moving away from the now seedy downtown area.[26] By 1853 (before Wise's arrival), Bene Yeshurun had already surpassed Bene Israel in membership.[27] In desperation, Philip Heidelbach, the president of Bene Israel, called a general meeting and by a vote of 93 to 12 the congregation elected Wise to serve them as well.[28] Until then, they had relied solely on their knowledgeable lay leadership to conduct services, even regarding Bene Yeshurun's need for a minister as evidence of weakness. (Bene Yeshurun had had seven different ministers in ten years.)[29] Wise, an outspoken reformer, in contrast to the traditional orientation of most of Bene Israel's congregants, saw the vote as an ideological triumph. "It was a fairly won battle, a victory for the cause of progress in Judaism, for the B'ne Israel congregation was looked upon as the mother congregation of Western Jewry, and as the camp of Simon-pure orthodoxy."[30]

Wise served Bene Israel for about six months and during that time preached on Saturday afternoons; he opened the Noyoth Institute (a day school), and worked with its officers to challenge the Orthodox faction. Samuel Bruel, a spokesman for the Orthodox faction, provided a different picture of Wise's tenure, however. "The ruse gained him a present of one hundred dollars for lecturing three or four times on Sabbath afternoons, but finding nearly empty benches, he abandoned the task."[31] The solution was not permanent, in any case, because Bene Yeshurun was adamantly opposed to sharing their rabbi with Bene Israel. Bene Yeshurun's board demanded that Wise resign after Passover, forcing the Bene Israel leadership to look for another rabbi who could stem the decline of the congregation. According to Wise, the president of Bene Israel informed him that their congregation could secure Lilienthal and asked his permission to begin negotiations. Wise assented to the move enthusiastically.[32] With the way cleared, the congregation approached Lilienthal, whom they saw as a distinguished, progressive leader who could enhance their eroding status in the community and enable them to compete against Bene Yeshurun. Here was a leader with the credentials and experience worthy of the "oldest Jewish Congregation in the West."

In late April 1855, Wise trumpeted the news of Lilienthal's election as Bene Israel's rabbi for life at a salary of $1,500 per year. He informed his readers in the *Israelite* that there was no doubt they had obtained the best man for the job, lauding Lilienthal's qualifications as a scholar and orator who would help the congregation flourish.[33] Samuel Bruel, representing the Orthodox, complained that Lilienthal had been elected without an opportunity for the congregation to get to know him, a procedure contrary to the bylaws of the synagogue. He also argued that, given the financial condition of Bene Israel, it would be a burden to pay the rabbi a yearly salary of $1,500. Wise's premature announcement mobilized opposition to the rabbi even before his arrival. Given the awkward situation, the leadership invited their new rabbi to come for a carefully choreographed visit during which they would finalize the contract. Lilienthal arrived by train on the evening of May 29 and was met by the president and other members of the vestry (the executive committee). He preached in German on Saturday morning and in English on Saturday afternoon so that all sectors of the congregation could hear their prospective spiritual leader. Lilienthal claimed that the problems plaguing Jewry could be solved only by embracing Reform. He promised to work hand in hand with his beloved friend Isaac M. Wise in all matters, especially to create a Reform liturgy for American congregations.[34] Lilienthal had laid out his agenda in a clear and uncompromising manner, fully expecting that it would be in harmony with the views of a congregation that had advertised for a reformer.[35] Bruel claimed that the rabbi's remarks were not well received. "Those who visited him at the house where he was a guest assailed him in a manner which he did not expect, and he intimated to his host that he had no idea of meeting with so many adverse to his notions, and that he would not promise to return to Cincinnati."[36] After examining the school on Sunday morning, the trustees invited the rabbi to attend a meeting that afternoon for the purpose of finalizing the agreement.[37] At this meeting, Lilienthal pressed the board for a commitment to minor liturgical reforms. Lilienthal wanted to be sure that he had support for his agenda. That settled, the board demanded that Lilienthal sign the contract immediately, but he hesitated, saying he had promised to confer with his wife first. The board, genuinely concerned that the rabbi would make good on his threat not to return, insisted that he sign immediately. After more discussion, Lilienthal accepted the office.[38]

Most contemporaries agreed that when Lilienthal began his Cincinnati pulpit, Bene Israel was still a traditional synagogue.[39] During Wise's short tenure a reformist faction had been mobilized at the congregation, particularly among the leadership, but a large traditional contingent remained hostile to changes.[40] Lilienthal, faced with a major challenge to his Reform agenda, eagerly threw himself into the ideological battles.

According to Wise, the move to Cincinnati transformed Lilienthal. "In the year 1855 Dr. Lilienthal experienced a rejuvenation of the spirit. His poetic nature, obscured for so many years under the clouds of disappointments and the prosaic combat of existence, broke the spell, and Lilienthal was himself once more. . . . In the *American Israelite* and the *Deborah* also he proclaimed himself in many essays, with ardor and cheer, a friend of progressive Judaism, an enlightened man and an earnest teacher in Israel."[41] Lilienthal became a champion of the moderate Reform that he and Wise fervently believed would unite American Jews. He worked tirelessly alongside Wise on the local, national, and international levels to make their vision a reality. It was, according to Wise, the happiest period of his friend's life.[42]

During the summer of 1855, Lilienthal took a series of controversial steps that alienated Orthodox members of Bene Israel. The rabbi worked persistently for liturgical reforms. As early as mid-June 1855, the board met to act on his proposals concerning the selling of *mitzvot* and *misheberach*s.[43] By the end of the month, a special committee presented a long report that the board approved.[44] Lilienthal also proposed minor alterations in the Sabbath prayers, which the board debated without coming to any conclusion.[45] Lilienthal, now an associate editor of the *Israelite*, was writing and printing articles by others that supported his liturgical agenda. The periodical was a better vehicle for discussions of issues than the pulpit, which he thought should emphasize devotional and edifying topics.[46]

The rabbi also formed a society for the organization and support of a mixed choir. Bruel reported that they collected almost $500 for this purpose.[47] Long before Lilienthal's arrival, in the earliest days of the predominantly English congregation, a congregational chorus of mixed voices had been a staple of Sabbath services. At the consecration of the first building, a mixed choir had helped celebrate the event. Joseph Jonas reported, however, that since the emigration of many German brethren, "the sweet voices of our ladies are seldom heard."[48] The congregation had rejected the idea of a mixed choir for the occasion of the consecration of the new building as recently as 1852.[49] After Wise instituted a choir and organ at Bene Yeshurun, Lilienthal felt the need to bring a higher level of edification to his services as well. Wise reflected on why the choir was so important to their efforts. "It is scarcely conceivable now what a victory for culture and progress the introduction of a synagogal choir was at that time. No reform of the Jewish religion was possible until the Jewish ear had again become accustomed to harmony and beauty. The service would have disappeared gradually altogether if it had not been reinstated in its old dignity and uplifting solemnity by song."[50]

The institution of a choir was not a problem per se for the Orthodox at Bene Israel; it was Lilienthal's insistence that it be a mixed choir of men and women. The Orthodox claimed that it was against Jewish law for men to hear a woman's voice during prayer. In support of Lilienthal's agenda, the *Israelite* published an article that asked, "Does the canon law permit ladies to sing in the synagogue?" The editors' first line of argument was the halakhic principle that widely held customs eventually gained the status of law in Judaism. Although Lilienthal had argued that customs were not binding in his *Asmonean* articles, in this instance the editors used the opposite argument to justify the innovation of women choristers. Their reasoning was that because many respectable synagogues did have female singers, this sanctioned the use of a mixed choir.[51] Perhaps sensing the weakness of this argument, the editors turned to an examination of the legal passages that traditionalists cited to prohibit hearing women's voices at services, mainly the concern that a woman's voice would arouse "impure affections" in male worshippers. They argued that because these sources were not themselves supported by passages from the Bible, they were not intended to be legally binding.[52]

Bruel criticized these arguments in the *Israelite*, claiming that their reasoning was faulty and that they had perverted the meaning of the law code they had cited.[53] Lilienthal pressed ahead anyway, going door to door to recruit new members and offering seats at bargain prices to raise funds for the choir. The congregation hired an architect to make room for the ensemble by removing some of the ladies' gallery. This caused some temporary difficulties when Mrs. Jonas, wife of the synagogue's founder, was forced to give up her customary seat. A mixed choir, which performed for the first time during the festival of Sukkot, became a permanent feature of the synagogue.[54]

On July 24, Lilienthal's refusal to observe Tisha B'Av, the fast day commemorating the destruction of the First and Second Temples, provoked a confrontation between Reform and traditional forces at Bene Israel.[55] When the rabbi failed to appear at the evening and morning services, his friends claimed that he was unwell. Lilienthal, however, gave a sermon the next week in which he explained the cause of his absence. Bruel, his Orthodox critic, reported, "He gave us to understand that the fall of our nation and temple should be to us rather a source of rejoicing than otherwise; for mankind are now in our day more enlightened, and by far better in all respects."[56] Lilienthal's view was supported, however, in a series of articles in the *Israelite* by D. Etienne de Lara, a Jewish educator in New York, who asserted, "Few people now a days yet look back with regret to lost independence and political nationality. . . . Let the truth be told: the day is kept as a mere matter of form."[57]

On Sunday, August 5, the board called a general meeting to adopt proposed changes in the bylaws to accommodate the reforms Lilienthal sought. At this meeting Reform and Orthodox forces fought over the future direction of the synagogue. Lilienthal insisted that the changes he proposed were of a mild character and were sanctioned by the highest legal authorities. Nevertheless, he promised to abide by the will of the majority. The *Israelite* described his stated position in the following way: "If they wished for Reform he was satisfied; if they wished to remain Orthodox he was equally satisfied; he was their servant."[58] This approach encapsulates the leadership style that the rabbi cultivated after his disastrous confrontation with the German synagogues in early 1848. He strove for consensus and unity, even though he must have been disappointed that his new congregation was not as solidly behind reform as he had imagined it would be. Much was at stake because both Reform and Orthodox forces were threatening to leave if they lost the confrontation.[59]

The congregation adopted Lilienthal's changes point by point: the sale of *mitzvot* was abolished, the number of *misheberachs* was limited, and alterations in the service were adopted that would increase decorum and eliminate some *piyyutim* (medieval liturgical poetry).[60] According to the *Israelite*, a majority of the members approved all of Lilienthal's moderate Reform agenda.

Again Bruel's report to the *Occident* helps to clarify the dynamics of the meeting. Bruel admitted that the changes were approved 40 to 38, but he claimed that a two-thirds majority was required to amend these statutes. From a legal standpoint, the introduction of the reforms was in opposition to the charter. The Orthodox refused to acknowledge Lilienthal as their rabbi or to adopt the reforms in the service that he and his supporters had pushed through. The group concluded, "We can no longer enjoy the benefit of the Synagogue, which was heretofore orthodox, and now converted into a reformed temple."[61] When the meeting adjourned, the reformers went to Sylvester's Tavern for a victory party sponsored by the synagogue president, Jacob Seasongood. The disenchanted Orthodox met at a local hotel, where they unanimously resolved to rent a room and form a new synagogue, Congregation Shearith Israel.[62] The *Occident* reported these events with the following dig: "These are the first fruits of modern reform, *division* and *disunion*, as elsewhere; and our fears are fully realized."[63]

The synagogue had lost members and revenue, but Lilienthal persevered because he believed that Reform was the only long-term answer to the synagogue's problems. In recognition of the trials that the new rabbi faced in his first months, the ladies of the synagogue presented Lilienthal with a new "clerical suit" as a "testimonial to their high regard and esteem" for him and in appreciation for his "services rendered to our congregation." The ladies urged him, "Proceed unflinchingly and fearlessly in the path you have chosen and thus far successfully pursued, and with our prayers and influence, and above all with the assistance of our great Father, we have no doubt of your ultimate success."[64]

During the busy first months, Lilienthal was also trying to build a successful day school at his synagogue. One reason that Lilienthal had been such an attractive candidate for Bene Israel was his reputation as an educator.

Several prominent members had sent their children to Lilienthal's New York school and, as a result, recommended him highly. Bene Israel wanted to compete with Bene Yeshurun's day school, Talmud Yelodim, which was thriving under the supervision of Rabbi Wise.[65] During his brief joint tenure with Bene Israel in 1854, Wise had set up a day school, the Noyoth Institute, in addition to the synagogue's ongoing weekend school.[66] The members of the school board, who were also the officers of the congregation, wanted the school to be financially independent. By late April 1855, the school minutes reported that seventy-five students attended the day school.[67] Wise, who was serving two synagogues and already running Bene Yeshurun's school, did not attend meetings of Bene Israel's school board or participate in day-to-day decisions in running the school.

Lilienthal had a different approach. Even before accepting the job, he asked for the opportunity to hold an examination at the school, and the school board ordered the teachers to prepare the students to receive him on Sunday, June 2. In July the school board made him an honorary member, allowing him to attend to the many details of shaping and running the school. The school board was actively involved in the school's daily activities in such matters as cleanliness, discipline, punctuality, educational materials, furniture, and even the purchase of coal. They hired teachers, set salaries, and responded to the complaints of parents. Lilienthal immediately took control of the school, indicating that he would soon complete a plan for its reorganization.[68] By September the rabbi presented a complete list of seventy-seven students to the school board, categorized by grade and tuition.[69]

Following the pattern he had established in New York, Lilienthal made public examinations central to his pedagogical system. He invited the trustees to attend two days of testing in early October. After another set of tests in November, he reported that he was pleased in most curricular areas except for arithmetic. The first annual public examinations, which took place on December 26 and 27, were a source of great satisfaction to both the parents and the board. They acknowledged Lilienthal's experience and untiring efforts as invaluable in the success of the school.[70]

The topics covered in the annual examination indicate the ambitious curriculum that Lilienthal, as the new superintendent, formulated for his pupils. The children were tested in Jewish catechism, Hebrew grammar, their ability to translate the Bible and prayers, and biblical history. They also had to show their proficiency in English grammar and syntax, United States history and geography, arithmetic, business skills, and German grammar, dictation, and translation. The highest class debated the topic "Was Julius Caesar a Good Man?" before an appreciative audience.[71] As a result, ten new pupils applied for admission; by January 1856, Lilienthal requested more rooms in the synagogue for the school.[72]

In "The Aim of Our Schools" in the September 1855 issue of the *Israelite*, Lilienthal outlined his educational philosophy, continuing to apply Haskalah theory to the American situation. The purpose of the school was "to make our children dutiful sons and daughters, useful members of society, respected citizens, and good and enlightened Jews . . . an ornament to society, and the pride and glory of our nation."[73] In this article, Lilienthal argued that Jews must inculcate American values in their children by teaching them its history and its Constitution and laws and by inspiring them with patriotic accounts of its founders. Jews needed a thorough modern education to be worthy of their newly won rights and liberty. They had to show the whole world that Jews could be fine citizens who would contribute to the welfare of the community at large.[74]

A new Reform dimension in Lilienthal's educational philosophy was an emphasis on individual autonomy. It was important to teach students to think independently, in order to be good citizens and good Jews. This new emphasis, the most striking departure from his earlier pedagogical approach, showed the growing synthesis of Reform and American values in his thinking. In an earlier *Asmonean* article written in his New York days, Lilienthal had advocated the use of a catechism to impart the full system of Judaism, noting the brief period available for Jewish education. In this way, with all questions and doubts erased, he asserted that true belief would be inculcated in the young minds.[75] In the 1855 *Israelite* article, however, Lilienthal urged that the time be taken so that children are encouraged to exercise their own abilities and not to rely on either the teacher or a "dead formula" to tell them how to think.[76] Lilienthal concluded, "As soon as our children will know for themselves, how to discriminate between good and bad, right and wrong, divine and human, they will exercise their own judgment, will not abide by blind authority, will try to be good Jews with heart and soul."[77] Individualism had become central for Lilienthal as he grew to appreciate American freedom and its implications for Judaism.[78] Lilienthal may have been the first Reform educator to explicitly articulate this pedagogical goal.

In the fall of 1855, Lilienthal and Wise also teamed up to promote their Reform agenda on a national level. Hoping to fulfill their long-held dream of national unity, they convened a conference in Cleveland in October 1855. In calling this conference, Wise and Lilienthal were consciously following the model of the German reformers who had staged a series of rabbinic conferences (in Brunswick 1844, Frankfurt in 1845, and Breslau in 1846) to forge their ideology.[79] Like their German counterparts, Wise and Lilienthal hoped to develop principles that would guide the practical work of reforming Judaism. The goal of the Cleveland conference, however, was far more inclusive, inasmuch as Lilienthal and Wise strove to find common ground between traditional and Reform factions to unify American Jewry. Believing that effective changes in areas such as Jewish law, liturgy, and education were possible only through national unity, they forged a platform that would transcend the polarization of the various tendencies.

Embarking on this initiative, Wise and Lilienthal were in tune with national trends among immigrant Protestant and Catholic churches as well as native Protestants, who were also organizing on a national level. By mid-century all American religions were moving toward national denominational unions that provided standardized liturgies, doctrines, curricula and materials for local religious schools, and colleges to train modern ministers and religious educators.[80]

Lilienthal took an active role as an organizer, leader, and defender of the conference.[81] At the Cleveland conference the two Reform leaders established their working relationship with regard to the ideological battles unfolding on the national stage. Rabbi Bernard Illowy, an Orthodox rabbi, dubbed Wise the Generalissimo and Lilienthal his first aide-de-camp.[82]

The relationship was dictated by the contrasting personalities of the two men. Wise was short, sickly, and insecure and prone to egotistical and abrasive behavior. He felt compelled to defy the world and recognized in himself an inability to resist fighting back against the many attacks that he provoked. Wise needed to be the leader of any cause to which he devoted his considerable energy.[83] Lilienthal was described by one contemporary as vigorous and energetic, frank in the expression of his ideas, always courteous, and good-natured. Another described him as "a most lovable man, handsome, tall, and of great intellect, a peace-loving person widely known as a 'prince of peace.'"[84] As early as 1847, when Lilienthal told Wise how frustrated he was in the three German congregations, Lilienthal renounced the desire for a leadership role.[85] Lilienthal continued to avoid taking the lead on the national stage, happily allowing Wise that distinction.

Despite their contrasting characters, the two rabbis worked well together, effectively complementing each other's strengths and weaknesses. Lilienthal, the stronger scholar, helped Wise, an autodidact, to develop the rationale for many of their positions. Wise, more of a popularizer, softened Lilienthal's tendency toward elitism. A columnist for the *St. Louis Jewish Tribune* would later characterize their relationship this way: "What Wise suggested, Lilienthal supported, and what Lilienthal pacified, Wise promoted. What Wise wounded, Lilienthal healed, and what Lilienthal white-washed, Wise exposed. Where Wise wanted to lead, Lilienthal gracefully followed, and where Lilienthal wisely warned, Wise laudably obeyed."[86] Lilienthal helped the impulsive Wise plan the strategy for their various projects and attempted to smooth over the inevitable controversies that Wise became embroiled in. They were able to work closely because they shared the same moderate vision of Reform, which they pragmatically adapted to the conditions of American Jewry.

Lilienthal was involved in the planning of the Cleveland conference from its inception.[87] Isaac Leeser would later claim that Wise and Lilienthal "concocted" the entire outcome before leaving Cincinnati; he was basically correct in this assessment.[88] Lilienthal wrote lengthy articles to lay the groundwork for the approach that he and Wise would advocate in Cleveland. In an article called "The Reformers Want to Uproot All!" Lilienthal tried to calm the fears of the Orthodox party by reassuring them that the Reform party wanted to end the divisions within Judaism and to replace indifference with a new love for their religion.[89] He also began a series of articles in the *Israelite* called "Minhag America" to show the methodology that he and Wise applied to the process of Reform. Reform, he explained, was not an all-or-nothing proposition but one that tried to harmonize religion with the needs of the times through changes that could be justified by a critical and historical study of the sources. He explored various Reform issues from prayer book reform to burial customs and invited other learned leaders to respond.[90] Lilienthal cited the legal positions of Maimonides, Joseph Caro, and other venerable authorities as precedents for the changes he advocated. To bridge the widening gap between the Orthodox and Reform camps, he announced that the approach of the moderate reformers in Cleveland would be based on biblical and talmudic authority. The inclusion of the Talmud as a source of authority was a deliberate attempt to allay Orthodox fears.

Lilienthal and Wise wanted the Cleveland conference to represent a wide cross-section of views among the leadership of American Jewry. Lilienthal proudly claimed, "There is no doubt that the gentlemen who have promised to be present at the next Convention in Cleveland will represent the most diverging opinions. The Ultra-Orthodox, Orthodox, moderate Reformers, Ultra-Reformers, all these parties have already declared to send their representatives and we feel really gratified that this is the case."[91] Lilienthal thought that all sides must be represented to harmonize the diverse points of view. He hoped that the Orthodox signatories, Rabbis Henry Hochheimer and Aaron Guenzburg of Baltimore, Dr. Bernard Illowy of St. Louis, and Isaac Leeser of Philadelphia, would attend. Unfortunately, by the time the conference began, all but Leeser had backed out.[92] At the other extreme, Dr. David Einhorn, the radical reformer who had only just arrived in America, also refused to attend.

The Cleveland conference, therefore, did not encompass the full spectrum of viewpoints. According to Leeser, the reformers had a clear majority when Lilienthal called the proceedings to order on October 17, 1855. They easily elected Wise as president, Dr. Elkan Cohn (Wise's successor in Albany) as vice-president, and Lilienthal as secretary.[93] The choice of officers reinforced the conviction of the radical Reform and Orthodox factions that the Cincinnati moderate reformers controlled the agenda of the conference.

Leeser had said before leaving for Cleveland, "If our Reformers are now honest, let them bring forward a system, whatever it be, which rests on Scripture and tradition, and we assure them that they will be listened to, and their arguments dispassionately weighed."[94] Despite his misgivings, this is what they did, to his surprise and pleasure. The first order of business was to establish a common platform as the basis for their union and all future synods. After some debate, Wise read a prepared paper that listed four principles.

1. The Bible as delivered to us by our fathers and as now in our possession, is of immediate divine origin, and the standard of our religion.

2. The Talmud contains the traditional, legal, and logical exposition of the biblical laws, which must be expounded and practiced according to the comments of the Talmud.

3. The resolutions of the synod, in accordance with the above principles, are legally valid.

4. Statutes and ordinances, contrary to the laws of the land, are invalid.[95]

This platform, which acknowledged the importance of the Talmud, attempted to harmonize Reform and Orthodox positions. Later, Leeser wrote that he believed Lilienthal had been the real author of this revised version, even though Wise presented it. He called Lilienthal a tactician of rare power and penetration.[96] After Wise spoke, Lilienthal strongly supported the platform in a speech that cited the deplorable confusion, disunion, and lack of religious observance that characterized American Jewry as a whole and the powerful need for unity.[97] Isaac Leeser was thrilled. "The 17th of October [is] a day of joy for Israel, if all Jews would adopt in sincerity the Bible as the inspired word of God and the Talmud as indicating the rule of life by which they would be governed."[98] Wise was also excited, believing the two parties to be fully reconciled.

After the platform was refined and approved, Leeser urged that the conference adjourn, publicize the platform widely, and reconvene the following summer in a centrally located eastern city. He promised that they could then expect the cooperation of the other Orthodox leaders who had stayed away. Outnumbered by reformers, Leeser wanted to strengthen the Orthodox influence by postponing further action. His proposal was ignored, and the conference continued after he left. Leeser's unexplained early departure was clearly a tactical error, because the group had discussed only the platform, the first of the three items on its published agenda. Liturgy and education, both controversial subjects, remained to be considered. With Leeser out of the way, Wise and Lilienthal had an opportunity to further their moderate Reform agenda.[99] It is easy to see why Leeser later claimed that the whole conference had been choreographed from Cincinnati.

Wise was appointed head of committees to formulate a uniform American liturgy and to deal with ritual and legal questions. Lilienthal chaired a committee formed to submit a plan for the establishment of an ongoing synod, meant to be the highest authority on Oral Law in the country. He hoped that a synod, made up of seventy members, at least one-third clergy, would meet once every three years and that the resolutions of this body, unlike a conference, would be religiously obligatory.[100] That the synod's rulings would be religiously binding was a more traditional position than even Lilienthal's 1847 *beth din* in New York. Given his views about personal autonomy, this stance indicates how powerfully Lilienthal wanted unity among the factions.

Lilienthal, also chairman of the school committee, emphasized the weakness of the Jewish education system and its reliance on catechism and a limited knowledge of Bible, the prayer book, and Hebrew. The committee members also worried that American Jewish education was not producing its own rabbis, preachers, or cantors. After debating the relative merits of religious and public school education, a committee was set up to consider the question further. Lilienthal asked that educators throughout the United States communicate their views to him, emphasizing that the education of the next generation was of the highest importance to guaranteeing the future of Judaism.[101]

Lilienthal was proud of the Cleveland conference because, by making the Bible and Talmud the bases for change, the platform was broad enough to include the full range of viewpoints. He held that the conference had been more successful than the German rabbinical conferences of the 1840s, whose influence on the congregations was minimal. Further, the Cleveland conference would accomplish more than the dry historical investigations of Frankel's seminary in Breslau, whose *Wissenschaft* studies were largely scholarly and theoretical.[102] Lilienthal had already begun asserting his spiritual independence from the German Jewish leadership by insisting that they could learn from American efforts.[103] Lilienthal believed that the conference had resolved animosities of many years' standing. "The members of the most different parties departed as friends; though differing in opinions, all were convinced that each and every one of the members present had but the welfare, the success and prosperity of Judaism at heart."[104] Even Leeser, annoyed with the work of the conference after he left, withheld judgment, saying, "If the gentlemen I met last week are honest in their attachment to the Bible and Talmud, their reform must be harmless, since they can thus introduce nothing for which they cannot present to the world reasons based upon *authority*."[105]

If the leaders of the conference believed that peace and unity had been achieved through their efforts, that illusion was quickly shattered. Critical reactions flooded the offices of the *Occident*, the *Asmonean*, and the *Israelite* from throughout America and Europe, making it clear that the conference actually caused an intensification of rifts that would never be fully bridged. Wise recalled years later that Lilienthal, as secretary of the conference, received the brunt of the attacks, many of them bitter and personal. He was called names and accused of terrible things. Quietly and skillfully, he met their sharp arguments with reason and the hope for reconciliation.[106]

The Orthodox attacked Lilienthal and Wise indirectly through their assault on Leeser. Dr. Morris Raphall of New York and other Orthodox leaders censured Leeser for compromising with the reformers. Raphall resented the leadership claims of the "mid-western yokels" who wanted to dictate to the more established eastern communities.[107] Abraham Rice declared that he had no sympathy for the so-called "Cincinnati *Beth Din*." Judaism did not need a new platform, he asserted; its platform was revealed thousands of years ago on Mount Sinai.[108] The Orthodox, in their criticism of Leeser, picked apart every word of the propositions, claiming he had been duped. As late as May 1856, Leeser still defended the compromise, saying that if the Orthodox were dissatisfied with the result, it was their fault for not attending the conference.[109] Finally, as a result of the violent attacks he experienced, Leeser moved further to the right. He eventually characterized the meeting as worse than a failure and its platform deceptive. "[It was] little better than a mere trap, contrived, as we thought and still think, to make all reforms lawful on assumed Orthodox principles."[110]

Lilienthal, representing the Cincinnati moderates, countered the attack of the right in an article in the *Israelite*. The right had unreasonably characterized Cleveland's platform as frivolous heresy, contemptible ignorance, and egotistical humbug.[111] He argued that the substantive issues between them centered on different understandings of the nature of Jewish law. Lilienthal treated the Talmud as an evolving, heterogeneous mixture of human and divine elements. Progress was justified if it followed the same process of halakhic precedents by which rabbinic literature had developed after the Talmud's compilation.[112] In sum, Lilienthal viewed the Talmud as a "Reform" document in its own time and the rabbinic tradition that flowed from it as a continuation of the systematic, historical development of Judaism. In contrast, the Orthodox maintained that the rabbinic tradition was a conservative mechanism for passing down divinely ordained practices.[113]

In a series of letters published in the *Occident* and *Israelite*, Leeser and Lilienthal delineated their divergent views of the relationship of Jewish law to history. Leeser refused to believe that Jewish law should change or that prohibited acts were now lawful, simply because some supposedly learned man had tried to demonstrate that the change was justified, not by divine decree but by the "silent action of the age."[114] He suggested that the spirit of the religion needed improvement, but not by conforming to the spirit of the age.[115] Leeser held that the spirit of the age was irrelevant to religious practice.

Lilienthal argued that historical trends were central. History was not a collection of unrelated events but rather a series of logical causes and effects in which each nation was influenced by the rest of the world.[116] For example, Lilienthal characterized the medieval period as an age dominated by the Catholic Church, during which reason was subjugated to fixed and unchangeable dogmas. Jews participated in this zeitgeist, creating an extensive codification of law, which dictated all of Jewish life in the same way that canon law did for Catholics. As the medieval age gave way to the age of Reformation, reason began to reassert itself, and eventually even the insular Jewish culture was affected. The final stage, beginning with the French Revolution, furthered this progression of the universal spirit of reason. Jewish Reform, which reflected this general historical trend, was a legitimate offspring of the spirit of the age.[117]

Lilienthal was influenced by Hegel's philosophy of history, characterizing history as a continuous process of perfection. Hegel had argued that "spirit, and the course of its development, is the substance of history."[118] Lilienthal shared Hegel's optimistic view in the inevitable victory of the spirit, but unlike the Protestant philosopher, he believed that Judaism rather than Christianity was the epitome of the religion of reason that would ultimately triumph.[119]

Leeser had not had the university training necessary to grasp the abstract significance of the Hegelian system. He admitted as much in a response to Lilienthal, pointing out that he was neither a rabbi nor a doctor of philosophy. He asked Lilienthal to drop for once that system of mystification (Gentile philosophy), which used many words and said little or nothing. To Leeser, the spirit of the age was frivolous and irreligious. Furthermore, it was a human, limited spirit that could not compare with divine revelation as a standard for truth.[120]

Lilienthal saw Leeser's views as hopelessly reactionary. He warned Leeser, "While nearly all men advanced in age and led by endeared customs and habits stay with your party, almost the entire rising generation will join that of the Reformers."[121] Recognizing that the gap between their perspectives was unbridgeable, Lilienthal concluded that the Cleveland conference had served only to clarify the issues that separated traditionalists like Leeser from his point of view.

Wise and Lilienthal's unity platform also encountered a damaging salvo from the left at the hands of David Einhorn of Har Sinai Temple in Baltimore. A fellow Bavarian, Einhorn was a radical Reform scholar who had participated in the German rabbinic conferences in 1845 and 1846 and had recently arrived in the United States.[122] He issued a protest, signed by members of his new congregation, that attacked the conference. Because many Jews no longer accept talmudic law, he argued, it could not be a unifying basis for resolving the problems of modern Judaism.[123] Einhorn advocated abolishing much of traditional practice and law. Asserting that American Jewry must escape from the powerful grasp of the Talmud, he warned, "Keep a strict watch on hierarchical movements which would again forge its chains, though under the charming lullabies of peace, now in the guise of dogmas, and ere long by a *Minhag America*."[124] The last was a pointed attack on Wise's liturgy by the same name.

The editors of the *Israelite* at first characterized the protest as rash, frivolous, and misguided, revealing the ambitions of a few, but clearly a more serious response was also necessary.[125] They challenged Einhorn's assumption that American Jewry was ready for radical Reform. It hadn't worked in Europe, despite the efforts of the rabbinic conferences, and Einhorn was mistaken if he believed that the situation would be different in America. They reminded Einhorn of what they had learned the hard way: "The Israelites who . . . came over to America were all of the rural districts in Germany, where at that time orthodoxy was reigning supreme. They brought no ideas, no desire for a reform over to this country, but being poor and hence obliged to direct their undivided attention to gaining a livelihood."[126] When German Jews formed their own congregations, they were based on strict Orthodoxy. Up to the present day, they asserted, 99 of 100 congregations rejected the slightest changes in the services, much less his "deistical schemes." Reform could succeed only if it was based, not on idealistic, ultraradical theory, but on a realistic understanding of the people's needs and the slow pace of liturgical changes in America, nurtured by careful education.[127]

The *Israelite* editors also questioned the arbitrariness of Einhorn's reforms; he advocated throwing out almost all of biblical and talmudic law, while retaining circumcision and Saturday Sabbath observance. Either the choice of what to keep was up to every individual, or some standard had to be found. They argued, as Lilienthal had against the Orthodox, that the Talmud, scientifically understood, was the ideal standard on which to base reforms.[128]

Lilienthal and Wise also addressed the philosophical issue of personal autonomy at the center of Einhorn's attack. The radical reformer had expressed the fear that using the Talmud as the basis for Reform would reestablish the authoritarian structure of traditional Judaism in America. To Einhorn, this seemed to contradict the principles on which the United States was based.[129] Although Lilienthal and Wise cherished the American system and the freedom it offered, for them individual freedom did not mean wholesale rejection of tradition but rather that choices had to be made on the basis of a deep knowledge of Jewish law and history.

The Cleveland conference had, as in the case of the traditionalists, succeeded only in sharpening the ideological split between moderate and radical reformers. Moderates such as Wise and Lilienthal tended to be more pragmatic in their approach, linking a gradual Reform with American values. The radicals emphasized German culture and language as the basis for a more theoretically driven Reform (despite Einhorn's polemical invocation of American freedom in his argument). Central to Wise and Lilienthal's disagreement with traditionalists such as Leeser and radical reformers such as Einhorn was their analysis of the needs of American Jewry. Wise and Lilienthal insisted that the moderate Reform position best reflected the realities of American Jewish life, which required a pragmatic balance of modernity with the traditional orientation of this group.

Foreign periodicals also followed the progress of the Cleveland conference, calling it the "American Provisional Sanhedrin." News of their ambitious agenda reached Rabbi Ludwig Philippson, who reacted with skepticism and annoyance.[130] The *Allgemeine Zeitung des Judenthums* devoted two lengthy discussions to its proceedings, especially taking offense at the phrase "all Israelites agree" with regard to the status of the Talmud. They called the platform a fiasco and approvingly printed Einhorn's protest.[131]

Rabbi Dr. Leopold Stein, a Reform leader from Frankfurt, was especially harsh, calling Wise a traitor and scornfully rejecting the "provisory Sanhedrin."[132] Lilienthal must have been particularly disturbed by the virulence of the attack by his old mentor Philippson and by Stein, also a reformer whom he respected. He responded in an open letter to the editor and to Stein defending the conference's desire to include all viewpoints and concluding that its platform was an honest attempt to find middle ground.[133]

The bitter polemical debates took a toll on Lilienthal, especially the harsh personal attacks that he endured. Although he tried to respond to every attack with reasoned arguments, he felt deeply wounded. Wise recalled the effects on Lilienthal. "He was too sensitive and honorable a man not to feel wounded and mortified. The fact is, he was very sensitive; every abuse pierced his heart. He saw many of his colleagues in that Conference intimidated, and became finally so sick of the aimless and useless controversy, that he not only did not publish the proceedings, but dropped the pen altogether."[134] In disgust, Lilienthal discontinued his associate editorship of the *Israelite* in the summer of 1857.

Another key desideratum of Lilienthal and Wise's national agenda was the education of Jewish leaders. Lilienthal had long bemoaned the fact that the American Jewish community was not producing educated teachers and religious leaders. If the religion was going to survive and flourish in America, institutions to train leaders were a necessity.[135] The effort to professionalize the rabbinate in America mirrored the midcentury national proliferation of theological seminaries, which addressed the need of many Christian denominations to establish American-trained leadership.[136] Toward that end, during the busy fall of 1855, Lilienthal worked with Wise to establish Zion College, an institute of higher Jewish education.

Jewish leaders launched the idea for an independent institution for higher Jewish education in New York even before Lilienthal had moved to Cincinnati. In late May 1855, the "Zion College Association of New York" was formed at a meeting at Temple Emanu-El. A vice-president of the organization, Lilienthal was one of a committee of five that drafted the preliminary resolution for the group.[137] Similar associations were formed in Cincinnati, Cleveland, Louisville, and Philadelphia with the idea of joint sponsorship of a school. In August 1855, the Cincinnati branch considered a plan by Wise to create a preparatory college, modeled on Lilienthal's New York boarding school, which would teach Jewish, classical, scientific, technical, and mercantile subjects.[138] At the September meeting the association resolved to open the college as soon as possible. Local boosters enthusiastically offered to meet all of the first year's expenses, regardless of the contributions of the other Zion association branches, so that, against Wise's better judgment, the school opened that fall. Concerned that the other Zion associations or even the majority of Cincinnati Jewry had not yet been brought on board, he feared that the move was premature.[139] The opening of Zion College was celebrated by a banquet that raised $800; the festivities were attended by Cincinnati's elite, which included the governor of Ohio and two judges. The college boasted a student body of fourteen, including two Christians and a faculty of five professors. Subjects taught at the college were Hebrew, English, German, mathematics, history, geography, and archaeology. Lilienthal, who taught classical languages and literature, asked for no payment.

Within a few weeks the efforts of the two rabbis came under bitter attack by New York leaders who felt that they had been excluded from the process of founding and organizing the school. Calling Cincinnati's action a breach of the covenant under which all other associations were formed, the New Yorkers dissolved their branch of the Zion collegiate association.[140] Critics accused the Cincinnati leaders of being opportunistic in setting up a school that would serve their ideological viewpoint. Orthodox rabbi Bernard Illowy was particularly critical of their efforts. These protests came on the heels of the Cleveland conference, which had polarized the various types of reformers, as well as traditionalists. Ultimately, however, communal apathy and lack of financial support caused Wise and Lilienthal to abandon the school.[141] Despite excellent results at the first annual public examinations, Zion College received virtually no support from communities beyond Cincinnati and lasted little more than one year.[142] Once again, the national agenda of the Cincinnati rabbis was sabotaged by the ideological rivalries of the period.

Exasperated by the failure of the Cleveland conference and Zion College, Lilienthal retreated from the national scene. He continued to work hard on his synagogue agenda: bringing Reform to Bene Israel's ritual practices and creating a successful school. The progress of Reform at Bene Israel was never smooth because Lilienthal encountered resistance to his innovations from the sizable traditionalist group that remained even after the break that created Shearith Israel. The *Occident* reported that, in the summer of 1856, Lilienthal retreated from his earlier stand on the observance of Tisha B'Av by attending the service and advising his congregation to fast. Although the *Occident* was probably using the incident to embarrass the rabbi, his reversal pointed out a real conflict being played out in Bene Israel. In a candid series of articles in the *Israelite*, the rabbi explained his quandary. The conservative party told him he had gone too far, too fast, and as a result they threatened to remove their support from him and the synagogue. The

Reform group had hired him to take a firm stand and make a clean sweep of outmoded traditions, yet he now seemed to have second thoughts. They warned him to "go on, or we'll get tired of you and your ministry, and your best and warmest friends will desert you."[143]

Within his synagogue, Lilienthal was especially critical of the reformers who avoided services and even the general meetings during which Reform measures were debated. He blamed the lack of progress on their apathy, complaining that they seemed inspired only by efforts to abolish old traditions. When he offered replacements for old rituals, the reformers looked at him with contemptible pity, as though he were advocating a return to Orthodoxy. They seemed to want a religion with minimal ceremony, but Lilienthal warned that Judaism had to keep its particularity to fulfill its messianic purpose—of bringing all people to monotheism and defeating heathenism.[144]

The rabbi complained that the reformers never came to the synagogue other than on the High Holy Days, so they were not present to support the changes they advocated. The traditionalists, who came regularly, participated in the services and gave weekly contributions to the synagogue, felt comfortable with the old traditions, and rejected any disruption of their habitual worship patterns. Lilienthal suggested that the conflict was partly generational, because it was usually the older members who favored the more conservative approach. The younger people were kept away by their consuming interest in financial matters, which made spiritual concerns secondary.[145]

Assimilatory pressures militated against Lilienthal's efforts to attract the younger members. Sunday laws made it difficult for Jews to do business on that day, so there was strong incentive for Jewish merchants to work on Saturday. Lilienthal and Wise attempted to alleviate the competition by getting all the Jewish merchants to close on Saturday. Launching a campaign in November 1859, they got the signatures of a number of prominent Jewish leaders, including those of Bene Israel, but, after some temporary compliance, the effort failed.[146]

As he was trying to balance the demands of the Reform and traditional camps within his own synagogue, Lilienthal had to weather a scathing personal attack in March and April 1857 from the Orthodox rabbi Bernard Illowy, then in Syracuse. The two men had once been friendly. Lilienthal had welcomed Illowy on his arrival to New York several years earlier. Illowy admired Lilienthal's talent, intelligence, and dedication. They also shared an interest in *Wissenschaft*. However, during a recent visit the two had quarreled over Lilienthal's increasingly liberal views on Jewish law. In the *Occident*, Illowy ridiculed Lilienthal for having returned to the observance of Tisha B'Av but still rejecting the second-day observance of festivals. Accusing him of gross hypocrisy, he reminded Lilienthal of his inaugural sermon in New York in which he had committed himself to the Code of Jewish Law. He pleaded with Lilienthal to remain within the traditional camp.[147] Illowy's pleas were useless; Lilienthal had spent years arriving at his well-considered Reform views.

Lilienthal successfully overcame a challenge by the traditional faction in his synagogue to abolish the choir. The *Israelite* reported that only 22 voters out of 200 favored the move. With its usual hyperbole the paper announced that the Orthodox had gone home saying, "Our time is over."[148] Perhaps as a result of this vote, the rabbi felt emboldened to propose further Reform measures. When, in a sermon in January 1860, he advocated changes in the service, the board encouraged him to elaborate on his recommendations.[149] No further mention of these proposals can be found in the minutes during this period.

At the same time Lilienthal endured some unpleasant incidents at his synagogue. In July he was accused of violating Jewish law by eating nonkosher food. Lilienthal pleaded not guilty because, though he admitted to eating the food, he had believed it to be kosher. The witnesses accepted his explanation and he was exonerated.[150] Two weeks later the *Israelite* reported that a large group of influential members of Bene Israel had gathered to express their admiration and respect for their rabbi. At that meeting the president remarked on the malicious persecution that the rabbi had suffered during the past year, indicating that the recent accusation was one of a series of attacks, as the president said, to break him down. He wanted Lilienthal to know that he had the devotion and respect of not only the members of the synagogue but also the wider Cincinnati community. The leadership feared that he would leave them; apparently Lilienthal had received pressing offers from congregations in the East. Therefore the board thought it necessary to let him know the high approbation they had for him. They praised his patience in navigating the conflicts between the various factions while pursuing his progressive course. They also lauded the scholarship and theological sophistication with which he proposed "well-timed alterations of many ceremonies of our ritual."[151] The president offered him a gift of $400 in gold as a testimonial of their regard and friendship. The rabbi responded with a highly emotional speech that brought tears to many. Although the leadership expressed support for the rabbi's Reform agenda, in practice it would be years before they would implement it.

Lilienthal also struggled in these years to create an effective educational institution for his synagogue. Noyoth Institute, the day school that had begun to flourish under Lilienthal, eventually succumbed to a variety of pressures. Lilienthal had raised standards by testing the children on a monthly basis and reporting the results to the board.[152] He set up rules, hired and fired teachers, and ran the public examinations, incorporating dramatic presentations and displays of the children's work. The school board invited outside examiners to assist the superintendent.[153]

The problem was not the quality of the school or even its size, which increased to 118 students, but rather the large number of nonpaying and half-tuition students.[154] Because the synagogue would not subsidize the school, the school board was forced to try various fund-raising approaches, such as an annual banquet to cover the deficit. The dinner succeeded in covering a good portion of the debt, but it did not put the institution on a fully solvent basis.

Despite continuing financial concerns, in 1857 the school board worked with Lilienthal to develop a curriculum for commercial subjects. That year, too, one of the school's teachers accused Lilienthal of embezzling money meant for wood and fuel. The school board investigated and ascertained that the charge was false, demanding that the accuser apologize to their rabbi. When he refused, they voted unanimously to discharge the teacher.[155]

In early November 1857 Lilienthal had to travel to Europe on short notice. The *Israelite* made apologies on his behalf that he had not even had time to say goodbye to his friends. Expected back in ten to twelve weeks, the Jewish community became anxious when he failed to return on time. Finally in early February Lilienthal came back, with an exciting story to tell. The ship, the *Ariel*, which he had boarded at Le Havre, encountered heavy storms and, after struggling for fifteen days, put into an Irish harbor. The rabbi went immediately to Liverpool and caught another steamer. Meanwhile, no one in Cincinnati had heard any news about the original vessel. According to the *Israelite*, the *Ariel* and Lilienthal were the only topics of conversation for two weeks among the Jews of Cincinnati. The *Israelite* concluded, "The incident proved how numerous the doctor's friends and admirers are in this city. Thank God he arrived safely to the bosom of his family and among his flock, who together with his numerous friends, have suffered much for the two past weeks."[156]

Because the rabbi was in Europe, the yearly examination was rescheduled for March 1858. This successful event was attended by a number of local dignitaries.[157] In April 1858, the day school's financial statement revealed a deficit of at least $500. The school board decided to lower salaries and to stop accepting nonpaying students, inadequate measures because less than half the students paid full tuition.[158] In late August the deficit remained about the same. Jacob Seasongood, the president, moved that the day school be discontinued because it could not support itself and because many of the students who had previously paid full tuition had withdrawn.[159] He advocated the establishment of a supplementary religious school under the control of the congregation. In November 1858, the synagogue board voted formally to discontinue the primary school, although it lingered on until August 1859.[160]

Having already been thwarted on the national level, Lilienthal now faced frustration in his own congregation. Neither his Reform nor his educational agendas had succeeded. The high hopes that had energized his first years in Cincinnati had been dashed. Further, this man of peace, so easily offended by personal attacks, had been the brunt of many at the hand of congregants, teachers in his school, and the Jewish periodicals. Wise recalled that Lilienthal became sick at heart. He became so profoundly disillusioned, Wise claimed, that he stopped reading Jewish literature entirely.[161] But unlike his earlier period of disillusionment in New York, Lilienthal did not give up the rabbinate. With six young children to support, he needed to keep his job.[162] Lilienthal was forced, once again, to find a new way of being a rabbi that allowed him to keep his integrity and afforded him the respect he craved. The solution that he arrived at would transform the face of the American rabbinate. Turning his back on parochial Jewish issues, Lilienthal threw his energies instead into the communal life of Cincinnati.

6

Creating the New American Rabbi

Facing one of the lowest periods in his career, Lilienthal turned his attention to another area of great personal interest—the civic life of Cincinnati.
Isaac M. Wise gives us insight into his friend during this difficult period in
his rabbinate. "A man with the mind, energy, culture and refinement of Dr.
Lilienthal can not possibly remain inactive. He must do something for the
public good. Turning his attention from Jewish affairs, he attached himself more closely to public affairs."[1] Retreating from the Jewish world that
had afforded him such grief, Lilienthal willingly and energetically devoted
himself to communal causes. According to Wise, Lilienthal pursued public
service in any capacity that he thought was compatible with his office as a
rabbi. He made communal service a major part of his rabbinate. Wise commented on the significance of this innovative approach. "He was popular
and influential in the city of Cincinnati and far beyond its confines, more
so, perhaps than any rabbi ever was in America."[2]

This new approach to Lilienthal's rabbinate matched the aspirations
of Congregation Bene Israel. It wanted to project the most positive image of a Jew to the broader world. Bene Israel's president, Julius Freiberg,
pronounced, "Our members seem to have but one aim before them, that of
elevating our beloved Congregation and Judaism in the eyes of all men."[3]

Through his transformed rabbinate, Lilienthal elevated the congregation's image. As Lilienthal gained more respect and influence in the broader community, they basked in his achievements.

The transformation of his role as rabbi in the general society coincided with his growing disillusionment with the fractious world of internal Jewish politics. Lilienthal left that realm to his friend Wise. However, Lilienthal needed a new ideological basis for his innovative approach to the role of the American rabbi. He found it in an intensified embrace of American patriotism. As Wise notes, "He loved and admired everything that was American. For a number of years patriotism was the principal topic of his conversation and the main subject of his sermons. There was such an abundance of eloquence and vehemence in his address, that he easily impressed his ideas and feelings upon every person."[4] This patriotism was an American version of Lilienthal's earlier embrace of the Haskalah belief in the progressive, even messianic nature of the state. In Germany Lilienthal had believed that the state would help regenerate the Jewish community. In Russia he had pinned his hopes for the modernization of Jewish education on the good intentions of the tsar and his ministers. Deeply disappointed by the failure of both governments to fulfill their redemptive role, Lilienthal now invested the same hope in America.[5]

In essence, Lilienthal was hoping to make a Jewish contribution to the development of an American civil religion. In a nation of immigrants who adhered to many religious traditions, a public faith was needed that could serve as a vehicle for national self-understanding. To unify this diverse nation, a civil religion developed, complete with its own beliefs, symbols, and rituals.[6] Formulated in the early years of the republic by founding fathers immersed in Enlightenment ideology, the civil religion was neither sectarian nor Christian in content, yet it borrowed heavily from biblical imagery. The founders identified America with the metaphorical Israel as both a "Promised Land" and a "Light to the Nations." The Declaration of Independence and the Constitution were the sacred scriptures of this ideology; Washington was the Moses who led his people out of the hands of tyranny.[7]

Lilienthal wrote poetry, preached, and acted out the principles of this civil religion. In 1857 he published a collection of poems, *Freiheit, Frühling, und Liebe*, that took many of its themes from the ideals of the Revolutionary War.[8] Written and published in the German language to appeal to German American immigrants, the poems celebrated the spirit of America's founding. The first section, "Freiheit" (freedom), included poems such as "Unsure Flagge," "Washington," "Mount Vernon," "Lexington," "Der Obelisk auf Bunkerhill," and "Der Vierte Juli 1776." Lilienthal wrote of the blood of heroes that guaranteed the country's freedom and of the flag that had inspired men to victory. The last poem in the "Freiheit" section presented an assessment of America in 1857. "It is accomplished, a lad now stands as a giant among the nations. The wish, which was only an ideal, you have realized before all the world."[9] This was an ideology that Lilienthal could embrace without any conflict with Judaism. As he propounded it to his congregation, he was furthering the goal of their Americanization. Finally, the ideology established common ground between Lilienthal and his Christian neighbors.

The transformation and expansion of Lilienthal's role as an American rabbi occurred over a number of years. Looking back in 1870, when Lilienthal was president of a national song festival and president of the Medical College of Cincinnati, a somewhat amused Lilienthal commented on his own changed profession. "What a chameleon are circumstances not making out of an American Rabbi?"[10] Lilienthal makes it clear that he served these organizations as a rabbi and representative of the Jewish community. "I, the Rabbi, again shall confer the degree of Doctor on twenty students of Medicine."[11] Never downplaying or hiding his profession, Lilienthal immersed himself in communal service. Often starting in traditional Jewish areas of concern, he later branched out into their secular counterparts.

One of Lilienthal's ongoing commitments was to education. Having made his name as a Jewish educator in Russia and New York, Lilienthal never completely turned his back on Jewish education. He abandoned his early commitment to the day school format as he became increasingly devoted to the idea of Americanizing young Jewish immigrants through nonsectarian public schools. In place of day schools, Lilienthal and his congregation put their energy into a supplementary school that met on Saturdays and Sundays. This format was successful, and the student body grew. By 1869 there were 125 students in the school, and that number grew to 225 by 1881.[12] The school was divided into four levels. Lilienthal instructed the oldest children in reading and translation of Hebrew, Hebrew grammar, and Jewish history, eventually even adding biblical and postbiblical history in the light of modern scholarship.[13]

In 1874 the rabbi copied the pattern of Christian religious periodicals of his time when he introduced a children's newspaper, the *Hebrew Sabbath School Visitor*.[14] Distributed to the entire school on Saturdays, the paper's purpose was both to instruct and to amuse the students with a blend of moralistic fiction, articles on Jewish holidays, Bible stories, jokes, anecdotes, and riddles. Woodcuts illustrated the text. The tone of the writing was paternalistic and saccharine (by modern standards), meant to be read to the children by teachers in the religious school to whom occasional pedagogical remarks were addressed. The paper's subscriptions kept expanding, boasting readers as far away as Potsdam, Pennsylvania.[15] This paper had serious pedagogical aims, teaching the doctrines of Judaism and encouraging morality. Lilienthal also inculcated a love for American institutions, particularly during the centennial year, with articles on the Declaration of Independence, the flag, and so on.

> And who should more rejoice, should be more grateful than we Israelites? In this year, one hundred years ago, our fetters were broken, our chains were loosed, and the signal of human freedom was given, and, in truth, it resounded throughout the world.... Therefore young Israelites, young Americans, rejoice and be grateful. Promise it, that you will forever be loyal and true to your country; that you will try to become citizens, worthy of the blessings our Constitution bestows on all classes of the nation.[16]

Although Lilienthal used every opportunity in his congregational school and from the pulpit to inculcate this love of America, he knew that the most effective Americanization of his German Jewish immigrant congregants would come through nonsectarian public education.

Lilienthal first confronted the public school issue when he chaired the committee on education at the Cleveland conference. Split on the issue of whether to favor public or parochial schools, the committee voted to solicit statements from rabbis and teachers throughout the country to prepare a position paper for the next synod.[17] After the Cleveland conference, Lilienthal's retreat from theological and polemical debate was mirrored by a secular shift in his pedagogical interests. According to Wise, "The natural sciences appeared to him [Lilienthal] to contain all that is worth knowing."[18] This intensified commitment to secular learning, combined with Lilienthal's desire to Americanize Jewish youth, helps explain his conversion to the cause of public school education.

By 1860 Lilienthal was such a strong supporter of public schools that he ran successfully for the Cincinnati school board. Both the Democrats and Republicans nominated him. He would serve on that body for thirteen years, during which he worked to make the public schools free of sectarian influence.[19] Lilienthal served as a member of the standing committees on study and classification and on textbooks and school libraries. He also worked to improve the local high schools. Lilienthal took his responsibilities on the school board seriously.[20] Lilienthal was so well regarded that when he moved to a new neighborhood, he was easily elected to the board in his new ward and given a big party by his former board colleagues.[21]

Lilienthal also helped shape the curriculum and teaching methods in the schools through a book that he co-authored with Reverend Robert Allyn, *Things Taught: Systematic Instruction in Composition and Object Lessons*.[22] Lilienthal had proposed the idea to the superintendent while serving on a curriculum committee.[23] The purpose of this graded primer was to develop the students' ability to observe, compare, and combine ideas to express themselves in writing. Using short stories and poems as models, the primer provided exercises to develop fundamental writing skills; the curriculum then moved on to present a basic outline of the plant, animal, and mineral kingdoms and exercises to encourage the ability to collect and organize information. The final lessons focused on various aspects of business writing, such as bills of purchase, orders, and advertisements. The book was used in the curriculum for common and intermediate schools for many years. Rejecting dogma and rote memorization, the school board set the goal of cultivating the senses and reasoning powers of its children. This approach dovetailed with Lilienthal's growing commitment to personal autonomy, as reflected in his writings on Jewish education.[24] Historian of education Stephan Brumberg suggests that this pedagogical approach was an attempt to find a neutral substitute for earlier morality- and theology-based educational materials.[25] In this way, the schools could serve the wide variety of immigrant children without trampling on their religious beliefs, making his pedagogical approach the educational correlate to the American civil religion.

One of Lilienthal's primary motivations for serving on the Cincinnati school board was to work for religiously neutral public schools. The Cincinnati school system, like others in America, had been designed by the Protestant elite to inculcate the values of citizenship and morality. The early regulations of the board stated that "the habits, manners, and morals of the pupils are to be strictly guarded while in school. . . . The moral restraints and obligations of the Bible are to be inculcated as a means of securing good behavior."[26] The curriculum included readings from the King James translation of the Bible and the singing of Protestant hymns. By the late 1830s the Catholic leadership had already begun to challenge Protestant domination of the public schools; Archbishop John B. Purcell again raised the issue in 1855. Protestant elements remained in the curriculum into the 1860s, leading dissatisfied Catholics to flock to parochial schools. Finally in 1869, the competition between the rapidly growing Catholic schools and the public schools began to threaten the latter.[27] In an effort to bring Catholic children back to the public schools, F. W. Rauch, a newly elected Catholic member of the school board, forged a plan with the archbishop's brother to merge the two school systems. To accomplish this end, the schools had to be made religiously neutral; another member of the school board, Samuel Miller, proposed an amendment that would bar the use of all religious books, even the Bible. This proposal touched a raw nerve, prompting intense debate throughout Cincinnati. The Superior Court of Cincinnati issued a restraining order against the school board, setting the stage for *Minor v. Board of Education of Cincinnati*, which attracted national attention.[28]

Lilienthal's views figured prominently in an exchange between Judge Stanley Matthews, one of the Board of Education's attorneys, and Bellamy Storer, a former member of Congress and one of the superior court judges adjudicating the case, both of whom knew Lilienthal personally. Judge Matthews, who would later be an associate justice of the United States Supreme Court, used Lilienthal as an example for his argument that the reading of the New Testament is offensive to Jews. Matthews reminded Storer that for Jews the New Testament was a "sacrilege and blasphemy against God."[29] Storer protested: "Not quite as far as that, because my friend, Dr. Lilienthal, gave me a Syriac Testament a while ago, and said that was the language in which the Savior spoke."[30] That Lilienthal had given Storer a copy of the New Testament in an Aramaic dialect seemed proof that the rabbi did not consider it sacrilege. Judge Matthews, pressing his case that Jews see the New Testament differently from Christians, responded:

> The record of this divine life and death and resurrection is something more to a Jew than an ordinary history: it is a blasphemy, sacrilege. And yet, your Honor, would by law, compel the reading of that book, of that record of the sayings and doings of that life, of the manner of that death, of that resurrection, to the children of Jewish parents, or else forbid them to come into the common schools, that belong to them, as they do to your Honor, and to us all equally, or at least tax them equally for the support of schools, in which, by law, their religion and the religion of their fathers is taught to be false, and that they themselves are unbelievers and rejecters of God.[31]

Matthews tried to convince Storer that although Lilienthal was his friend and a learned and liberal man who respected his belief in the New Testament, it was offensive to impose the New Testament on him and his fellow Jews—and their children—in the public schools.

In December 1869, Lilienthal himself began a series of articles in the New York Reform paper, the *Jewish Times*, that discussed what became known as the Bible case. In the articles, Lilienthal spelled out the significance of the controversy in clear, dramatic terms. "We are in the heat of a contest, the decision of which will be of the highest importance to the whole nation. Shall the Bible and singing of religious hymns be retained in our free schools or excluded from them? Shall our schools be free schools, indeed, or shall they be tinged with any kind of sectarianism? This is the question of the day, which is now tried before the Superior Court of this city."[32]

Lilienthal recognized that the crux of the issue was a nonsectarian standard for schools that would foster the separation of church and state. Catholic clergy reviled such a solution as "godless" but also rejected the use of the Protestant version of the Bible. Lilienthal believed that the concern of these Catholic leaders was not to merge the two school systems but rather to divide the tax revenues allocated for the school fund.[33] A few feared a plot by Catholics to destroy the public schools. "Fanatical" Protestant leaders also opposed strict separation, exclaiming from their pulpits, "This is a Christian country, and the Bible cannot be excluded. . . . Neither Infidels nor Catholics shall interfere with the religious spirit of our institutions."[34] Lilienthal characterized the trial as "a regular tournament between modern philosophy and obsolete theology."[35]

While the nation waited for the court's decision, Lilienthal contributed an essay to the *Jewish Times* titled "Is the Bible Fit to Be Used as a School Book?" He suggested that contradictions in biblical teaching and modern science made Scripture problematical as a textbook. He believed that the two viewpoints might be reconciled if one avoided "the dogmatism of theology," but he admitted that his own efforts to write a biblical history for his Sabbath school that reconciled science and religion had so far been unsatisfactory.[36] In a subsequent piece, Lilienthal laid out his vision of a nonsectarian, modern society.

> Our progressive civilization is neither Jewish nor Christian. It is something greater, something broader than all these sectarian terms, it is divine and providential. It is as deep and beneficial as God's unfathomable wisdom. . . . In the gradual development of all human faculties, every nation has its mission, every religion its task, every individual his duty to fulfill. However diverging the opinions, they still must cooperate for the harmonious execution of the Divine will, which works out the happiness of all members of the human family.[37]

Lilienthal's vision of religious pluralism was part and parcel of his emerging view of civil society.[38]

Although the decision was 2 to 1 against the civil view in the superior court, Judge Alphonso Taft, in an important dissenting opinion, argued forcefully that religious equality required governmental neutrality. "Between all forms of religious belief the State knows no difference."[39] During the wait for the appeal in the Ohio Supreme Court, the battle shifted to the upcoming elections for school board. At a pre-election rally, Lilienthal articulated the supremacy of the state over the church. He was an American first and then a Jew, and he hoped that others would place their loyalty to the state before their Christianity.[40] He summarized his stance.

1. Bible or no Bible, our children will visit the public schools. Our Sabbath schools and synagogs [sic] give us ample room and time to impart to them the required religious instruction.

2. No division of the school fund, no matter under what pretext it may be demanded.

3. Not a penny out of the public funds for the support of any sectarian institution, be it for charitable or educational purposes.

4. No union of state and church, under any shape and form whatsoever.[41]

According to Lilienthal, the city voted by a margin of 3,000 against retention of the Bible in the public school. Even so, through various legal maneuvers, the pro-Bible forces managed to achieve a majority of four members on the next school board. The Ohio Supreme Court eventually vindicated the rabbi's position in 1872 when it unanimously overturned the lower court's ruling, setting aside the original injunction.[42] From 1873 on, there were no more Bible readings or religious opening exercises in Cincinnati schools. Historian Naomi W. Cohen assessed the significance of this decision. "The Cincinnati case was a landmark in the story of American Jews and church-state separation."[43] Lilienthal continued to lead the fight for a strict separation of church and state for the rest of his life. His forcefully articulated position helped to establish the normative Jewish stance on this issue.[44]

Lilienthal's commitment to the public schools extended into the area of higher education. The old collegiate model of higher education, based on the English system of education, was perceived by some contemporary pedagogues as inadequate to meet the demands of increasingly urban and industrial American society. Many mid-nineteenth-century educators trained in German universities advocated implementing the German modern curriculum, which emphasized science, modern languages, and literature. They envisioned an integrated system of state education culminating in advanced studies at a university.[45]

In 1869, Lilienthal participated in the efforts of the Cincinnati school board to form the McMicken University (the precursor of the University of Cincinnati). As a member of the school board with a doctorate from a German university, he had the qualifications to help Cincinnati develop its own institution, but still his prominent role was remarkable given the Christian character of American colleges and universities during this period. The great proponent of the Prussian university ideal, Henry P. Tappan, chancellor of the University of Michigan from 1852 to 1863, strove to establish a nonsectarian school yet assumed that the university would, following the Prussian model, be basically Protestant. The conservative Noah Porter, philosopher and future president of Yale, wrote in 1869 that "American colleges should have a positively religious and Christian character."[46] In the same year the University of California, ostensibly founded on secular principles, was also nonsectarian Protestant. That Cincinnati conceived of a truly secular institution, open to all its citizens, and further chose a rabbi to help create it is a tribute both to its progressive environment and to the general respect that Lilienthal enjoyed.

Lilienthal was appointed to a committee charged with consolidating the various educational funds and organizations into a university that would be closely tied to the school board and to the city council and would offer a free education for all local citizens (nonresidents would pay a nominal fee).[47] Partly as a result of Lilienthal's efforts, the state legislature passed the legislation in April 1870 to create the university. Lilienthal served on its board for nine years, working diligently to hire professors, develop departments, increase funding, and improve facilities and academic standards. Interested in scientific and technological fields, he arranged for some important acquisitions, especially for the school's geological collections.[48] He even chaired board meetings occasionally.[49]

David Philipson, later one of the first rabbinic students at Hebrew Union College, attended McMicken University in its early years. When he enrolled in 1879, it was a modest institution, housed in a single building and boasting only a handful of students and a faculty of six members. Still, Philipson noted that McMicken was the first municipal college in the United States, serving as the capstone of Cincinnati's educational system.[50] Merging his rabbinic and educational vocations, Lilienthal gave the invocation and benediction at the university's first commencement, in June 1878.[51]

Through his service on the school and university boards Lilienthal came into contact with many of the most powerful figures in Cincinnati, including Rufus King and Alphonso Taft. Rufus King, grandson of a Revolutionary War hero, was educated at Harvard and for many years was a leading lawyer in Cincinnati. He served for twelve years as president of the Board of Education. He was also a trustee of Kenyon College and of the University of Cincinnati, director of the Cincinnati Southern and C. H. and D. railroads, and a member of many other organizations.[52] Alphonso Taft was even more prominent. Educated at Yale, he practiced law in Cincinnati beginning in 1840. He was a member of the city council, a delegate to the Republican national convention, and candidate for Congress. He was a judge of the superior court of Cincinnati and ran for governor. In 1876 he was appointed secretary of war under President Grant. His son, William Howard Taft, would become the twenty-seventh president of the United States. Lilienthal worked side by side with these and other prominent members of the Cincinnati elite.

Lilienthal wanted to show the elite of Cincinnati that good Jews made good citizens who were ready to work actively for civic betterment in education, culture, philanthropy, social work, and good government. His rationale for these efforts was based on the struggle for emancipation that Jews had faced in Europe and an appreciation for the unique opportunity that America offered Jews. "We have been deprived too long of human rights and human liberty, that we should not eagerly seize the opportunity of proving to the whole world, that we were treated unjustly and wrongfully, and that we Jews can be as good and worthy citizens as the members of any denomination."[53] Lilienthal helped establish the pattern for a Jewish elite in Cincinnati civic life. Jonathan Sarna and Nancy Klein, in *The Jews of Cincinnati*, describe this elite group. "Local Jews stressed that as good citizens and good Jews they had a mission to work for civic betterment."[54] Lilienthal worked on a variety of fronts in Cincinnati, sometimes continuing the concerns he had pursued in New York but often branching out in new directions. David Philipson said of his Cincinnati career, "[Lilienthal] gave himself without stint and without measure to the service of his coreligionists and his fellowmen. He was a prominent figure in all Jewish public affairs as well as in movements of a larger public interest."[55]

Among the most important of these efforts was Lilienthal's work to improve the system for distributing alms to the Jewish poor. It was his plan to establish a comprehensive benevolent society to coordinate charitable activities for the Jewish population of Cincinnati. In 1856, Lilienthal invited various leaders to his synagogue and proposed a single treasury out of which the poor would be supported. He argued that this would cut down on the annoyance of daily requests for alms and would avoid creating a permanent class of beggars. At a subsequent public meeting, Lilienthal was chosen to be on a committee to both write a constitution for the new Hebrew Relief Society and to collect further contributions. The *Israelite* predicted that the society would succeed brilliantly and, indeed, it set the pattern for later United Jewish Relief efforts. The new organization was a source of pride to his congregation. In a resolution of gratitude in 1860, they credited Lilienthal with developing the system whereby charity was coordinated under a united action of the various Cincinnati congregations.[56]

As he had in education, so too in charitable work, Lilienthal expanded his rabbinate beyond the Jewish community to work with the City Relief Union. Founded in 1848, the Union was one of the oldest charities in the city. Its object was the systematic relief of the poor by providing provisions, clothing, and money to them. The group would collect funds by putting a box at the door of every church. According to the group's constitution, with this system the Union hoped to stop vagrancy and the practice of begging, which wore down the generosity of even the most benevolent.[57] Although the original document had a Christian tone to it, the City Relief Union opened its membership to anyone who was willing to adhere to its constitution. Lilienthal became a director of the citywide group in 1861 and served in that capacity for the rest of his life. The Board of Control met monthly, reviewing and acting on the reports of visitors responsible for the various wards of the city. As in the case of the school board, Lilienthal would rub shoulders with Cincinnati's elite. This work endeared him to rich and poor alike.[58]

Lilienthal also worked to improve the hospitals of Cincinnati, which served both the Jewish community and the city at large. At a time when the Jewish hospital of Cincinnati, the first of its kind in the United States, was foundering, Lilienthal helped to reestablish it, holding board meetings at his temple and serving on the hospital board for years.[59] Just as his charitable work began in the Jewish sphere and later branched out into the broader community, Lilienthal later became involved in the work of other local hospitals. During a cholera epidemic in 1866, Lilienthal was chosen to be a member of a citywide committee to deal with the crisis.[60] On one occasion he gave a speech at a benefit on behalf of the Catholic Good Samaritan Hospital. As noted, Lilienthal also served as president of the Cincinnati Medical School.[61]

Lilienthal was active in many social and cultural organizations, such as B'nai B'rith, a Jewish fraternal organization that helped Jewish immigrants adapt to American life. B'nai B'rith provided them with a sense of belonging and mutual assistance without the religious commitments of a synagogue community.[62] In the first few years Lilienthal supported the local B'nai

B'rith, and in March 1860 he took part in the anniversary festivities for the local Bethel lodge.[63]

Lilienthal also lent a hand to the Young Men's Literary Club, a precursor of the Young Men's Hebrew Association (YMHA), helping to establish its Cincinnati branch shortly after the end of the Civil War.[64] This important communal Jewish organization, which had first appeared in Baltimore in 1854, spread during the late 1850s to Augusta, Buffalo, Cleveland, and Louisville. After the Civil War the movement grew rapidly, in part because of Lilienthal's efforts.[65] Just as B'nai B'rith had helped the German Jewish immigrants adjust to America, the YMHA offered an alternative for the children of immigrants who might have felt uncomfortable with religious organizations but wanted to engage in Jewish cultural and social activities.[66] Although the organization paralleled the successful Young Men's Christian Association, Lilienthal was quick to point out the differences.

> Of course the sphere of action cannot be the same as that of the Christian Young Men's Associations. Our young men have, thank God, no criminals to redeem; no drunkards to reform; no paupers to support, as they are liberally provided for by our benevolent institutions. Their constitution, therefore very appropriately declares that they were organized "for the purpose of cultivating and fostering a better knowledge of the history, literature, and doctrines of Judaism; to develop and elevate our mental and moral character; to entertain and edify ourselves with such intellectual agencies, as we deem fit, and finally and above all, it is our mission to promulgate the sublime and eternal principles of Judaism to the world, and when necessary, to defend, though honorably and peaceably, the faith of our ancestors."[67]

Lilienthal's appeal inspired about a dozen young professional men to form the Cincinnati branch of the Young Men's Hebrew Association. The group met on Sunday afternoons at Bene Israel to hear lectures on Jewish themes.[68] Lilienthal gave several lectures to the group in its early months that helped to launch the organization.[69] At its first anniversary celebration, Lilienthal advocated spreading the movement throughout the nation; he wondered why New York, with its wealth of "eminent Hebrew theologians," had not followed the good example of other cities. In part as a result of his prodding, a New York branch of the YMHA was formed in 1870.[70]

In Cincinnati, the YMHA swelled to more than seventy members. The proceedings sometimes became heated, such as the second anniversary celebration that erupted into a major controversy about Reform. Tempers ran high, and Rabbis Wise and Lilienthal felt the need to respond to the dispute in sermons the following weeks in their pulpits. As a result of the debate, a large number of Christians attended the subsequent meetings. As usual, Lilienthal thought that open discussion of issues was healthy. Encouraged by its own success, the YMHA moved in 1870 to a suite of rooms of its own, which included a large lecture hall, reception room, and reading room. On that occasion, Lilienthal, Wise, and Thomas Vickers, the Unitarian minister, addressed the organization.[71] Off to a strong start, the young organization would eventually play an important role in American Jewish communal life.

Lilienthal did not limit himself only to Jewish cultural and social organizations. When he arrived in Cincinnati, he became a member of the Masons, which had long been a group that welcomed both Christians and Jews. He also joined several clubs dedicated to promoting the German cultural heritage of Jewish and Christian immigrants. For the Allemania club, Lilienthal wrote original poetry to help celebrate the one-hundredth anniversary of Schiller's birth.[72] He became a member of the Cincinnati Turners (Turnverein), whose ranks had swelled in response to the revolutions of 1848. Combining physical fitness and German liberal culture, the Turnverein also was at the forefront of German American antidefamation.[73]

The German immigrants also enjoyed relaxing together during their leisure time. In contrast to their more puritanical Protestant neighbors, the Germans enjoyed a beer on a Sunday afternoon. They also loved theater and music. In 1857 three German singing societies merged to form the Cincinnati Mannerchor. Singing societies became so popular that even the Turners formed a musical ensemble. Lilienthal himself was appointed president of a national German song festival (Sangerfest) in 1870.[74] Lilienthal, who loved music and the arts, relished these social and cultural activities, which afforded him moments of levity and relaxation in his challenging schedule.

German Jews in general made a substantial contribution to the musical culture in Cincinnati. Samuel N. Pike (originally Hecht) settled in Cincinnati in 1844. He married the daughter of a local judge and began a successful liquor business. After hearing Jenny Lind, the "Swedish Nightingale," he was determined to become wealthy enough to build an opera house where she could perform. In February 1859, Pike opened the first opera house in Cincinnati, which was at that time the largest and most beautiful in the country.[75]

Reaching beyond the synagogue, Lilienthal participated in every aspect of social and cultural life in Cincinnati. He had created a wonderful life for himself and his family, which had now grown to seven children.

Widely admired, welcomed into the elite of Cincinnati society, and working for causes in which he fervently believed, the rabbi had found fulfillment in America.

Armed with his civil religious ideology, Lilienthal felt the equal of any American. He showed his comfort and confidence in America when he defended Jewish equality in an outspoken manner. Lilienthal served the function of a prophet for the civil religion, nurturing its growth and chastising authorities when they failed to realize its sacred vision.[76]

When, in November 1856, Governor Samuel P. Chase of Ohio addressed a Thanksgiving proclamation to the "Christian People" of his state, Lilienthal complained that other denominations were excluded.[77] Lilienthal and Wise commented in the *Israelite*, "We are heartily tired of protesting every year against these illiberal and unconstitutional proclamations."[78] Chase was a liberal politician with close ties to the Jewish community, so Lilienthal was careful in his criticism. Although he thought sure that the governor had used the term in a generic sense, he urged him to widen his Thanksgiving proclamation to include Jews. The governor responded graciously, saying that he never had any intention of wounding the sensibilities of his Jewish constituents when he used the customary phrase "as becoming a Christian People." Reaffirming his support for religious and civil liberty and equality, he looked forward to the day when the barriers between brethren would disappear.

Jews also thought that their equal status was threatened when the Christian majority scheduled public events on the Jewish Sabbath. Although Christians resented Jews who wanted to conduct their businesses on Sunday, they routinely forced Jews to violate their Sabbath to participate in these events. In a sharply worded article Lilienthal and Wise complained that the school board showed little respect for Jews when they scheduled the examination for promotion to intermediate and high schools on the Jewish Sabbath. If the board truly wanted to make the public schools accessible to all religious denominations, why did they force Jewish children to violate their Sabbath? In the same piece they criticized the Republican Party for holding their state convention on Saturday. Was it ignorance, they wondered, or willful obstinacy that caused the Jews to be ignored?[79]

Jewish leaders also responded aggressively to Christian proselytizing efforts in the years before the Civil War. For Jewish leaders proselytization particularly violated the values of civil society when missionaries portrayed the emancipation that Jews enjoyed in this country as a gift intended to bring about mass conversion. Few Jews converted to Christianity during this period, but Jewish leaders resented the negative image of Judaism propagated by the missionaries and their tactics of preying on the most vulnerable members of the Jewish community—immigrants and the poor, sick, and ignorant.[80] The struggle against missionaries became for them an expression of Jewish self-affirmation as well as a defense of the American civil religion.

Missionaries claimed that the Jewish prophets in the Hebrew Bible had predicted various details of the birth and life of Jesus; this argument had been widely used in Christian polemics since the Middle Ages. In the article "Spiritualists and Christianity," Lilienthal systematically analyzed twelve instances of Old Testament prophecies that missionaries claimed were fulfilled by Jesus; finally he concluded, "I find no allusion in the Old Testament to any isolated circumstance that happened at the birth or during the life of Jesus."[81]

Another strategy Lilienthal used to bolster Jews against the missionaries was to compare the "irrationality" of Christian doctrine to the "rationality" of Judaism. In "Reply to the Christian Apologete," he criticized the doctrine of the Trinity. Jews had too much talent in arithmetic, he claimed, to believe that "One is Three" and "Three is One." If church scholarship had not succeeded in explicating this mystery from the Council of Nicea until the present time, how could Jews be expected to subscribe to it? He suggested that doctrines such as the belief in an incarnate God born of a virgin were evidence of the heathenism still implicit in Christianity. For Jews, God is a spirit that neither is born nor dies. Given these "irrational elements," Lilienthal concluded that the Christian missionary was wrong when he claimed that the Jews were ripe for conversion to Christianity.[82]

In another piece for the *Israelite*, Lilienthal described a conversation with some Christian women who had visited Bene Israel to hear him speak. After the service they asked him if Jews believed that their Christian souls would be saved. Lilienthal explained that according to Jewish doctrine, the pious adherents of every denomination would earn a place in the Kingdom of Heaven. He quoted Jesus's words to them to prove the centrality of ethical behavior to salvation, adding that, in Jewish theology, a redeemer like Christ was unnecessary. He concluded that Judaism was clearly the superior religion, both with regard to rationality and love.[83]

Lilienthal delivered a scathing sermon attacking Christian revival meetings during the spring of 1858. He noted that the community, suffering from a lack of consumer confidence because of a financial crisis the previous year, was turning to revival and prayer meetings to cope. Calling these measures inadequate to the emergency, Lilienthal suggested instead that the economy would revive when honest politicians were elected and when heads of banks, railroads, and public institutions were men of integrity. Only when corruption, vice, and crime were replaced by rule of law and justice, he argued, would there be a meaningful resolution to the economic crisis.[84]

According to Lilienthal, the Catholic Church was one of the most serious foes of American liberal values. This strident anti-Catholicism apparently flies in the face of Lilienthal's usual conciliatory approach to opposing viewpoints. It is likely that the frustrating experiences of his youth in Catholic Bavaria and the reactionary role of the Catholic Church in European politics, especially its opposition to Jewish emancipation, colored his position. Lilienthal's view also can be understood in the context of the religious debate that had crystallized in Cincinnati. On one side were the conservative forces, represented to a large extent by the growing number of Catholics. One source estimated that by 1859 there were twenty-four Catholic churches and chapels in the city.[85] On the liberal end of the spectrum were the Unitarians, who had first established themselves in 1829 and claimed Alphonso Taft and other local leaders as members. In the midst of harsh polemical exchanges between clergy representing the two groups, Lilienthal felt a great affinity with the Unitarians and was provoked to take up the fight against "Roman Ecclesiastical Tyranny."

In one incident some local priests refused to grant absolution to Catholic servant girls because Jewish families employed them. These girls were told they should leave these families without delay. Lilienthal called this an act of fanatical bigotry and an insult to all men, to American institutions, and to the spirit of humanity. He warned Archbishop Purcell that if his priests continue to take this position, the Jewish merchants would discharge the thousands of Catholic workmen working in their businesses. Purcell, he charged, would be responsible for the disastrous consequences that would result. Fortunately, the Catholics backed down.[86]

Another episode reveals a lighter side to Lilienthal's antipathy toward Catholics in Cincinnati. Although it is possibly apocryphal, the story matches what we know about Lilienthal's personality. At a public dinner, Archbishop Purcell noticed that Lilienthal was not eating the food, because it wasn't kosher. He turned to the rabbi and asked, "When will you eat with us?" Lilienthal is said to have replied, "At your wedding."[87]

In 1858, Lilienthal was at the forefront of expressions of indignation when news reached the United States of an Italian Jewish child, Edgar Mortara, who was secretly baptized by his Catholic nurse, forcibly taken from his parents' home, and placed in a Catholic institution for the education of converts.[88] Lilienthal's open letter to the Jewish people of the United States anticipated the later responses of Isaac Leeser and other Jewish leaders to this outrage. Lilienthal asserted that "the forced abduction of the child of Mr. Mortara in Rome, Italy, by order of the Catholic clergy, has created throughout the civilized world a cry of horror and indignation. Religious liberty is set at naught by the fanaticism of the Roman Inquisition."[89] Lilienthal called on American Jews to hold public protests and to send petitions to the government, following the lead of French, Sardinian, and German Jews. He organized a meeting of Cincinnati's Jews at his synagogue in October 1858, the first of many in the United States, where a petition was sent to the secretary of state, to be forwarded to the papal representative to the United States.[90] The disorganized Jewish efforts to get the administration to apply pressure on the papacy failed, but the incident shows that Lilienthal was willing to take a leadership role in the defense of Jewish rights internationally.

In another international issue, Lilienthal played an important role in the local efforts to protest the ratification of a treaty between the United States and Switzerland. Under the Swiss constitution, only Christians were guaranteed religious freedom; even foreign Jews could be denied entry and commercial privileges in its various cantons. Consequently, American Jewish merchants did not have the rights that American Christians enjoyed when doing business in Switzerland. Although the anti-Jewish clause was eliminated from the 1855 draft, individual cantons still discriminated against American Jews. In 1857, an American Jewish merchant was ordered to leave the canton of Neuchâtel, sparking protests in cities throughout the United States.[91] In Cincinnati, Lilienthal signed a petition inviting local Jews to a meeting to discuss the treaty; at that meeting Lilienthal was appointed to a committee of five to draw up a memorial to the president.[92] In October 1857, a group that included Isaac Mayer Wise (but not Lilienthal) presented their concerns to President Buchanan and received assurances from the president that the matter would be resolved. Not until 1874, however, when Jews won legal equality in Switzerland, were visiting American Jews guaranteed their rights in that country.[93]

Lilienthal covered international politics in the *Israelite* for many months, during which he chronicled what he believed to be "a steady improvement of the condition of our coreligionists in the largest portions of Europe."[94] His concern for Jews around the world contradicts the stereotype that reformers rejected a sense of ethnic solidarity. Scanning the foreign journals, Lilienthal offered detailed summaries of the status of Jewish rights in France, England, Holland, Portugal, Spain, Switzerland, Prussia, Scandinavia, Turkey, and even in the Orient and Africa. He expressed optimism on the accession of Alexander II to the throne of Russia, on the Jewish policies of Napoleon III, and on the decision of the sultan of Turkey to improve the standing of that country's Jews. He pointed with pleasure to minor concessions toward the Jews in Austria and was pleased to report progress in his native Bavaria, where residence restrictions and limitations on the Jews' ability to practice certain trades were abolished. Lilienthal proclaimed, "The Jews were put on equal footing with their Christian fellow-citizens in all places in which Jews are living."[95] Seeing evidence of progress, he asserted, "Time will never roll backwards, Onwards! is the watchword that rules all movements of the human race."[96] Liberalization was not automatic, however, and Lilienthal admitted that serious opposition to the full emancipation of Jews in Europe still remained.

Yet Lilienthal believed in the ultimate victory of reason and freedom over despotism. In his letters to Isaac Leeser, he had affirmed that human history was "an unceasing reform, and a never-stopping development to a higher degree of perfection."[97] All Jews would someday experience that millennial time of liberation and equality. Although the United States was moving toward that ideal faster than any other country, Lilienthal often quoted the adage "Vigilance still remains the price of liberty."[98] Exercised locally, nationally, and internationally, this involvement in Jewish rights became a central element in Lilienthal's new Americanized rabbinate.

The Civil War presented Lilienthal with perhaps the greatest challenge to his faith in the American civil religion. The strife that tore apart the country threatened to undermine its most profound values. Lilienthal reflected later that the period was "the gloomiest in the history of our country; it was as if the sun of liberty were setting forever! Monarchs were rejoicing, but the nations were desponding; kings and their myrmidons were shouting, 'The people's government is a vision and delusion,' but nations were despairing—the last hope of the regeneration of the human race seemed to be lost forever."[99] In one of his poems, Lilienthal praised the Union.

> *Die Union ist ein Zauber,*
> *Der unser Land unschlunget.*
> *Ein Ring voll wunderkraften*
> *Den Keine Nacht bezwinget.*
> *[The Union is a magic,*
> *by which our land is undefeated.*
> *A circle full of miraculous power*
> *that no night can conquer.]*[100]

In the months before the war, Lilienthal preached a number of sermons on the urgency of preserving the Union. Downplaying the differences between North and South, he searched for ways to reconcile the two regions.[101] Living in Cincinnati, close to the slave state of Kentucky and the abolitionist centers of the North, the disagreement between the two regions was an immediate and concrete reality. Always the peacemaker, he sought to find a middle ground that would keep his beloved adopted country from being destroyed by a tragic war.

In the debate over slavery, American rabbis could be found on either side. Morris Raphall of New York tried to show that the Bible justified slavery, whereas David Einhorn of Baltimore insisted that until the Negro was free, Jews and other minorities were profoundly threatened. Isaac M. Wise objected to the fanaticism of Protestant abolitionists; although he did not approve of slavery, he did not want to see the debate resolved through bloodshed.[102] Lilienthal's position was close to that of his friend Wise in the years running up to the war. As he explained, "We hated the Radicals; we shunned their society; we abhorred the thought of abolition—all that we aimed at, all that we were striving for, was the confinement of slavery to its then territorial limits."[103] Although he thought that slavery was immoral, Lilienthal defended the right of the Southern states to determine their own economic system.[104] Cincinnati was a gateway into the slave states; it had powerful commercial interests in the South. At the same time, Cincinnati was a crucial center for the Underground Railroad that helped many slaves to escape to freedom. The city enthusiastically welcomed President Lincoln, who visited on his way to Washington in February 1861, but in April Cincinnati also elected a Democratic mayor who ran on a platform of deference and concessions to the South.[105]

With the attack on Fort Sumter the city's ambivalence dissipated; only a small minority supported the South. Citizens of all backgrounds formed military companies to fight on the Union side.[106] When the war broke out, Lilienthal threw his support to the Union, which infuriated a Mr. Cohen in New Orleans, who scrawled the following message over a picture of the rabbi that he had formerly displayed on his wall: "Sir: Since you have discarded the Lord and taken up the Sword in defense of a Negro government, your picture that has occupied a place in our Southern home, we return herewith, that you may present it to your Black Friends, as it will not be permitted in our dwelling."[107] The former admirer, now a Confederate soldier, called Lilienthal a demagogue and threatened, "I shall be engaged actively in the field and should be happy to rid Israel of the disgrace of your life."[108] Mr. Cohen misunderstood the rabbi's stand, because Lilienthal became antislavery only after Lincoln's Emancipation Proclamation. In his victory sermon at the end of the war, Lilienthal would confess to being ashamed that he had not had the moral courage to oppose slavery from the beginning, waiting until it was national law to accept the need for abolition. He now admitted that slavery was an "everlasting blemish."[109]

Jews enlisted in the armies of both the Union and the Confederacy, a breakthrough in Jewish military participation in America. Almost 8,000 Jews served in the ranks of the Union and Confederacy, giving rise to a call for Jewish chaplains.[110] In the South there was no legal barrier to this, but federal law still stipulated that chaplains must be ordained Christian ministers. The law was tested in September 1861 when Michael Allen, a student of Isaac Leeser, was made chaplain of a cavalry unit. (Allen had also studied Jewish law with Lilienthal while he was in New York.) Allen served as chaplain for the soldiers of all faiths during a two-month career that was cut short by the actions of a zealous YMCA worker. When he reported to the army hierarchy that Allen was neither Christian nor an ordained clergyman, the chaplain quit rather than face the dishonor of dismissal.[111] Meanwhile Colonel Max Friedman, who commanded a regiment made up largely of Jews, chose Rev. Arnold Fischel, lecturer at Congregation Shearith Israel in New York, as their chaplain-designate to challenge the law. Fischel, a representative of the Board of Delegates of American Israelites, mobilized that organization's support. Through publicity, petitions, and the lobbying efforts of the Board of Delegates, they countered the opposition of fundamentalist Protestant groups. After Fischel met with President Lincoln, legislation was introduced in Congress (and passed in July 1862) that authorized the appointment as chaplain of any "regularly ordained minister of some religious denomination" who had "the proper recommendations and qualifications."[112]

The role that Lilienthal and Wise played during the last phase of this controversy was colored by partisanship because they were angered by the Board of Delegates claim that the Board represented all American Jews. Although Lilienthal and Wise strongly supported the cause of Jewish chaplaincy, they thought that the Board, which was primarily an East Coast traditionalist group, did not represent them. They wrote editorials in the *Israelite* and *Sinai* in which they attempted to undermine the credibility of the Board of Delegates. Especially damaging to the cause was the protest that Lilienthal and five other rabbis published in January 1862 in newspapers in Washington, Philadelphia, and New York. The rabbis proclaimed, "While the undersigned . . . pray Congress repeal the clause (or clauses) of a bill (or bills) by which regularly ordained ministers of our persuasion are denied their constitutional right to officiate as Chaplains in the Army or Navy of the United States, they consider it their duty in behalf of truth to protest against the assumption of titles and functions by the so-called 'Board of Delegates.'"[113] They insisted that the Board of Delegates did not represent their congregations, nor any others in America. According to Bertram Korn, Congress could have used this protest as an excuse to withhold support from Fischel's candidacy, but it chose to overlook the challenge. It is a testament to the intensity of the rivalry that split Jewish leadership during this period that they were not able to put aside their personal and religious differences to support Fischel's cause.[114]

The Civil War brought latent American anti-Semitic tendencies to the fore. The media exploited ancient stereotypes to accuse unpatriotic Jews of profiting from the war by providing "shoddy" (reclaimed wool, which was often of inferior quality) supplies to the troops. The term *shoddy* became repeatedly associated with shady Jews in such diverse periodicals as *Harpers's Weekly*, *Vanity Fair*, and the *New York Tribune*.[115] The Cincinnati Jewish community, so important in the clothing industry, did not escape the accusations that they were involved in the manufacture of shoddy merchandise at the expense of the war effort. Indeed, when Wise was considered a candidate for state senator, the *Cincinnati Daily Enquirer* implied that if he ran, he would get the help of "the Shoddy contractors."[116]

The war had created a tremendous demand in the North for Southern cotton and in the South for war materiel, manufactured goods, medical supplies, gold, and silver. Speculators and traders made millions of dollars on illegal commerce that met these demands. At every geographic point of contact between the two sides, Jews were blamed for smuggling. A reporter in Covington, Kentucky, just across the border from Cincinnati, accused the Jews: "The people whose ancestors smuggled for eighteen centuries smuggle yet."[117] In a misguided attempt to address the problem in December 1862, General Grant issued his infamous General Order 11, which expelled all the Jews from the military department of Tennessee. Grant or his subordinates blamed the Jews of the area for the profiteering. Grant ordered the expulsion of all Jews from the entire department in twenty-four hours in what has been called the "most sweeping anti-Jewish regulation in all of American history."[118]

A victim of this expulsion, Cesar Kaskel informed Jewish communities and newspapers, telegraphed the president, and went to Washington to protest this order. Stopping off in Cincinnati, he conferred with Lilienthal and Wise, who decided to appeal to the president themselves. Arriving in Washington, they discovered that Kaskel had met with Lincoln, who had immediately rescinded the order. The delegation decided to thank the president personally for his prompt assistance. According to Wise's account in the *Israelite*, the delegation, with Lilienthal at their head, arrived in Washington at about 5 p.m. By 8 p.m. the same evening, they were ushered into the president's office. They had a private, frank, and open thirty-minute discussion during which the delegation thanked the president for his swift action. Lincoln expressed surprise that General Grant issued so ridiculous an order. He criticized it for condemning an entire group for the sins of a few, declaring that he made no distinction between Jew and Gentile and felt no prejudice toward any group.[119] Pleased with the meeting, Lilienthal and his group hoped to influence Congress to go on record against this bigotry and intolerance, but the Republicans believed it was more important to protect their most successful general than to condemn an injustice. Wise commented, "Sorry we are to say that Congress did not think proper to be as just as the President is."[120]

Lilienthal was active on the home front as well. The Hebrew Relief Union of Cincinnati, which he helped to create, was the sole support for a number of local Jewish orphans and widows created by the conflict. Unable to meet their commitments, the organization got a boost when Lilienthal and the other local rabbis appealed for support at an emergency meeting.[121] In addition, in his role as a director of the citywide relief union, Lilienthal worked hard to bring relief to those in need. As he recalled, "During the long, bloody war, I was working every day, dispensing charity to the good people who needed it among the soldiers' families."[122] In the aftermath of the war, Lilienthal continued to work through the Cincinnati Relief Union to help the returning soldiers remake their lives.[123]

The crisis of the Civil War called forth new themes in the American civil religion: death, sacrifice, and rebirth. Abraham Lincoln not only formulated its meaning but also embodied it in his own person. The Gettysburg Address gave redemptive meaning to the terrible sacrifice of the soldiers who had given their lives for the nation. Called the New Testament of civil religion, the address employed Christian symbolism of death and rebirth without explicit Christian referents.[124] Lilienthal expressed these new motifs in the series of speeches he gave to his congregation at the end of the war.

In his Union Victory address, the rabbi recalled those days of agony and national misery, from the news of the secession of the Southern states to the end of the long war to reestablish the Union. The division had mocked America's holiest symbols: Bunker Hill, Independence Hall, Washington's grave, and the flag. Lilienthal declared, "Long was the struggle, terrible the sacrifices, numerous the disappointments; but 'Onward, always onward!' was the war cry of the army, the prayer of the nation."[125] What is striking in the address is the lack of any reference to the Passover holiday, during which the speech was given. Certainly an obvious parallel could be made between the ancient festival of freedom and the victory celebration, but Lilienthal focused only on the moment's meaning from an American point of view. Forgotten was his enmity toward General Grant, whom he now called a hero. According to the rabbi, the Union army was one of the greatest military powers in the world. He remembered the many fallen heroes who had made this day possible, quoting the psalmist, "They that sow in tears will reap in joy." In the language of sacrifice and redemption he declared, "With millions of lives and millions of treasure, we have brought a sacrifice for our national existence, and morally atoned and morally redeemed we are standing before the astonished and amazed world."[126] Lilienthal portrayed the victory as the next historical step after the French Revolution toward the emancipation of the human race, proclaiming, "We have fought and conquered for the nations all over the world, for by our victories we have reinstated labor in all its pristine and becoming dignity."[127] He implored his congregants to follow the lead of the president, saying, "Let there be no hatred, no vengeance against the South. Let the leaders feel the majesty of the law; but to repentant rebels give pardon, mercy, and brotherly love."[128] He ended with a prayer of thanks that the sun of liberty again shed its warmth over the entire nation.

> Great God! We thank thee for the home,
> This bounteous birth land of the free!
> Where wanderers from afar may come
> And breathe the air of liberty.[129]

It was a speech of thanksgiving, joy, and patriotism. The rabbi and his congregation went home in a jubilant mood, unaware that the president had been shot that evening. When Lilienthal heard the news the next morning, he rushed to the telegraph office to get the latest details. In shock, he was at first unable to believe that the president had been assassinated. After the truth sank in, he recalled, "Tears began to relieve our stupefaction."[130] His reaction was to quote the lament of King David over his son Abner: "Indeed, a great man has fallen in Israel."[131] In a sermon to his congregation on April 22, 1865, Lilienthal called Lincoln "the first laborer president," because he rose from poverty to the presidency, proving the reality of American equality. From his perspective, the freeing of the slaves symbolized that the laboring classes all over the world were now emancipated.[132] Lilienthal praised Lincoln for his undying love of the Union. Earning the reverence and love of the people through his sincerity, simplicity of heart, and down-to-earth shrewdness, Lincoln had become a man of superior destiny. His death helped the nation to understand even more fully the meaning and value of the country's institutions by showing that the machinery of government transcended even the death of the man who had come to represent its highest values.[133] "[Lincoln had] closed his life with an act of unexampled magnanimity and clemency by dismissing the armed leaders of the rebellion to their homes, that they might return to peace and equal rights in the country they had deluged with blood. Let us profit by his almost divine example."[134] Lilienthal urged his listeners to avoid vengeance and the suspicion of widespread conspiracy. They should trust in the law of the land to bring the criminals to justice. He concluded that, although Lincoln was now a martyr, he died preserving the Union, and all Americans must take up and faithfully execute his legacy.[135] Lilienthal, invoking the imagery of sacrificial martyrdom, was helping to create religious meaning for himself and his congregation even as the events were unfolding.

Meanwhile, the war had accelerated the pace of Americanization among all immigrant groups. As Bertram Korn writes, Jews and others had earned their stake in the country. "[By] enduring the hardships of battle, burying sons and husbands and friends, participating in the multifarious welfare activities of the homefront, taking sides in political arguments— these and a thousand other aspects of life in a nation at war with itself Americanized the large immigrant population at a much more rapid rate than that of more peaceful times."[136] No longer strangers in the new land, many American Jews looked to their leaders to merge their adopted country's values to those of their tradition. Lilienthal, as much as any other rabbi of his time, created that synthesis.

In the years after the Civil War many of Lilienthal's public utterances continued to reflect American civil religious values. At the occasion of the laying of the cornerstone of a new temple building in Indianapolis in December 1865, Lilienthal noted that the occasion also marked the first Thanksgiving after the war. As the nation again enjoyed peace and unity, he hoped that the temple would "rise to its future glory, a powerful witness to truth and liberty, to progress and reform."[137]

In the postwar years, Lilienthal continued to move his rabbinate in new directions, especially in the area of interfaith relations. In 1865 the young minister Rev. E. Rexford met Lilienthal. Writing to David Philipson many years later, he remembered how Lilienthal had inspired him to move from what he characterized as "the lowlands of one of the narrowest of Christian sects" to "the higher grounds and broader visions of liberal religious thinking."[138] Lilienthal, by that time, had developed a universal, humanist view far beyond the moderate Reform views he had espoused in the mid-1850s. "He was everybody's brother. His life was lived beyond the limits of sects, and creeds, and was builded [sic] up in the midst of the Humanities.

In those regions, too, he found the Divinity. He would have scorned the thought of being a mere Sectarian. He was a good Jew, but he regarded that as only a stepping stone toward Manhood. . . . The best religion was the Religion that develops the noblest and best types of men and women."[139] Rexford described Lilienthal as an established figure in Cincinnati, yet an approachable man who seemed to instinctively understand the anxieties of younger men finding their way. Lilienthal's empathy came from his own long struggle to embrace a liberal position. He was the sworn enemy of religious exclusiveness and intolerance. Wise suggested that Lilienthal came to reject most traditional theology.[140] Indeed, in a speech celebrating the proposed opening of Hebrew Union College on May 22, 1874, Lilienthal would observe that most theology had become antiquated in the light of modern science, criticism, and reason. He thought that true religion was winning out over "blind faith" in the process.[141]

Lilienthal had become so theologically radical in his last years that he even rejected the divine origin of the Bible, as seen in an article in his scholarly periodical, the *Hebrew Review*. "We know and admit that the Bible, and especially the Mosaic books, are composed of various parts, written and collected at various times. There are legendary parts, historical, legal and dogmatical parts; there are poetical, devotional and homiletical parts, belonging to different times, different periods of Jewish history. They have neither claim nor title to equal value or lasting importance. A large part— nay, the largest part of the Mosaic books . . . have lost all practical significance."[142]

Lilienthal found a great affinity with local Unitarians, who had recently split into two factions: a conservative group led at that time by Rev. A. D. Mayo and a radical party who chose Rev. Thomas Vickers as their leader in 1867.[143] The more liberal group, members of the First Congregationalist (Unitarian) Church were, according to the *Israelite*, "an assembly of persons in advance of any established church having the most radical platform in religion."[144] Lilienthal found in Vickers, who was also a product of a German university, an intellectual equal. The *Israelite* enthusiastically welcomed the new minister. "[Vickers] preaches Hegel and Strauss and prays Kant. Listening to him, I fancy sometimes to attend the lecture of some of the boldest German thinkers."[145]

Historian Benny Kraut explained the affinity of the Reform Jews and Unitarians. Unitarians had rejected many of the traditional doctrines of Christianity, most important, the central notion of the Trinity, which brought them closer to Judaism. Unitarians and Reform Jews also shared a belief in the perfectibility of humanity. This notion of perfectibility harmonized well with the German idealist conception of *Bildung*, embraced by the German Jewish middle class. Further, the two groups were united in their fight for "a politically secular democratic America against the forces of sectarianism and evangelical Christianity."[146] Finally, they shared the ideal of a religion consonant with reason and progress and "the imminent arrival of a religion of humanity."[147]

The closeness between Lilienthal and Vickers opened up the opportunity to engage in a pioneering interfaith dialogue. In March 1867, Lilienthal and Vickers exchanged pulpit visits. Lilienthal's talk at the Unitarian church was titled "The Free Church in the Free State." According to the *Cincinnati Gazette*, a large group assembled in Hopkins Hall, home of the First Congregational Society, to witness this groundbreaking event.[148] After opening hymns Lilienthal prayed for an end to racial and religious bigotry and fanaticism and for the triumph of reason and truth, righteousness and perfection. Although he had longed for the opportunity for many years, he was embarrassed that he had not had longer to prepare an address for this enlightened and liberal audience. He chose his theme based on the words of the great Italian nationalist Count Cavour: "Chiesa libera in libero statu" (a free church in a free state).[149] Lilienthal lauded the American principle of the separation of church and state and hoped that Europe would learn to apply it as well. Vickers preached subsequently at Bene Israel, expressing regret for the many centuries of Christian fanaticism that had caused the Jews so much suffering. He called Christianity a transformed Judaism, the religion of Moses put into Hellenistic form. He referred to Jesus as a mythic figure. The reporter thought that the exchange was nothing short of miraculous. The first of its kind in history, their pulpit sharing captured international attention, with articles in German and French newspapers.[150]

This pulpit exchange underlined how significantly Lilienthal had grasped the changed realities of Jewish-Christians relations in America. In the Middle Ages many Jewish authorities had considered Christianity a form of idol worship. Therefore they ruled that Jews were forbidden to be in any way involved in church services.[151] This attitude was codified in Jewish law and is held to be true to this day in some circles.[152] However, a countervailing view argued that Christians actually worship the same God as Jews, which they associate with Jesus. By the eighteenth century a more tolerant interpretation of Christianity became prevalent. Moses Mendelssohn emphasized the common humanity of all men in his argument for tolerance. By the nineteenth century Jewish preachers emulated famous Christian leaders in sermon style; some of the Christian leaders visited the German synagogues to offer young Jewish preachers hints and guidance on effective oratorical style.[153] Lilienthal, taking advantage of the openness at the liberal end of the religious spectrum in Cincinnati, seized the opportunity to make interfaith history by exchanging pulpits.

Lilienthal came to earn the title the "Broad Church Rabbi," on one occasion volunteering to take over the duties of the minister during the latter's absence.[154] He continued to preach frequently in non-Jewish pulpits and even at Christian funerals.

David Philipson called this aspect of Lilienthal's ministry "the most striking service he performed, a service quite unique in his day and generation."[155] He asserted that Lilienthal did much to foster the spirit of good will in the community and to bring to Christians a better understanding of Judaism. Through these exchanges, Lilienthal, perhaps more than anyone else, contributed to the local conviction that Cincinnati was "a city of mutual good will and understanding where Jews and Christians interacted freely."[156]

During and directly after the war Lilienthal continued to work to reform his congregation. Despite its avowed support for his position, it was not until April 1863 that the board finally acted on the rabbi's proposals that linked Reform to relocating the synagogue to a more suitable neighborhood.

> We have witnessed that our present service is not at all linked to the spirit of the age, and not such as is likely to impress the minds of the rising generation . . . and while we do not wish nor would we like to advocate any change in the fundamental principles of the Mosaic religion, we are of the opinion that an entire change of our mode of service is essential and necessary. Resolved that we recommend to use our energies to build a temple with all the necessary improvements viz., family pews, an organ, a choir, etc. and the Temple to be located in a more suitable part of the City."[157]

Despite this unequivocal show of support for Lilienthal's agenda, these ideas were stalled in committees for over two more years, as resistance to the changes persisted. Finally, in late October 1865, the congregation agreed to adopt the triennial cycle for reading the Torah (a system whereby the Torah is read over a three-year period), to read the prophetic portion in English or German, to buy a melodeon to accompany the choir, to add English and German prayers, and to delete negative references to the Diaspora.[158] The next year the board reaffirmed their full support for the Reform course taken by their rabbi and underlined their satisfaction with a $1,000 new year's gift.[159] The congregation had, in theory, turned a corner and now supported their rabbi's program. Yet it would take another crisis before they actually instituted the changes.

By 1864, Pepi Lilienthal had contracted tuberculosis. Each summer she was forced to leave Cincinnati for several months to avoid the heat. In a letter to his children in August of that year the rabbi described her condition. "Oh, if we only had some of your rainy weather! The heat has been unbearable for the past four days. . . . Mother suffers intensely from these conditions; she is weak and depressed and has no appetite. She also sleeps very badly at night. As soon as it rains and the dust is laid, Dr. Rosenfeld wants me to take her out-of-doors. God give us rain, and I will do everything in my power to get her on her feet."[160] Over the next years the rabbi nursed his wife and, following the doctor's orders, sent her out of town each summer in the hope of prolonging her life. On September 1, 1867, Lilienthal's beloved wife, Pepi, died at the age of 46. He had known her since she was 16 year old. His deep love for his wife, evident to all who knew them, was expressed in several poems in his book *Freiheit, Frühling und Liebe*, especially in the two selections "Mein Ideal" and "Meine Frau."[161] They reveal a sentimental side to this rather formal man.

> *Ich habe oft gesonnen*
> *Was du mir angethan*
> *Das ich gar nimmer anders*
> *Als nur dich lieben kann.*[162]
> *[I have often pondered / what you have done to me. / There is no one else / I can love other than you.]*

Lilienthal admits to having known many beautiful women, but none had Pepi's charms. He concludes the poem by calling her his talisman, the wife of his heart and spirit.

The loss was made even more difficult because Lilienthal was left the sole parent of a large, young family. Recapitulating the situation in his own youth when his mother had died young, one of Lilienthal's daughters, 15-year-old Esther, shouldered the responsibilities of caring for the younger children and managing the household. Nor was Lilienthal well off at the time; he was forced to accept money from his children to help pay the $200 for Pepi's monument. In his thank you letter to his children he added, "I, too, cannot honor the memory of our dear departed one enough; I would have given my heart's blood for her, and I therefore accept the gift for your sakes. . . . It will always be a satisfying memory to know that you have contributed toward her monument."[163] Losing Pepi affected Lilienthal profoundly. His friend Wise recalled, "When his beloved wife died, who was a gem, he was for a long time unlike his former self. His sweet humor was gone and returned not for years. Often have I wept with him."[164]

Added to this burden was Lilienthal's continued frustration with the lack of progress at Bene Israel toward his goals of a new temple and more thorough reform. In December 1867, Lilienthal was invited to deliver a lecture at Temple Emanu-El in New York while on a visit to his brother Samuel, who also had recently lost his wife. That temple, searching for an English lecturer to work alongside their rabbi Samuel Adler, immediately expressed their interest in hiring Rabbi Lilienthal.[165] Over the next month the two parties conducted negotiations over the length of the contract, salary, and job title. With regard to job title, Lilienthal was willing to take a position subordinate to Adler, even at this stage of his professional career, if he were given the title minister. Lilienthal made another trip to New York to clarify his position with Adler and to resolve his differences with the Temple Emanu-El board.[166]

Meanwhile, Lilienthal felt compelled to notify Bene Israel of his intentions in a sermon in late January 1868. His offer to resign was not accepted. At the next board meeting on March 5, the rabbi presented a personal, heartfelt letter in which he tendered his resignation. He attributed his decision to leave to the loss of his adored wife. "My house stands desolate, the companion of my studies, the advisor in my efforts is gone . . . and my children were now motherless."[167] To Philip Heidelbach and Jacob Seasongood, Bene Israel's wealthiest members, he wrote, "I feel it, I cannot be happy in Cincinnati; every nook and corner reminds me of my loss. I am undermining my health and doing injury and wrong to my children."[168] A few days later Lilienthal wrote to President Freiberg, "I cannot help it. I have struggled all night, in vain. I cannot be happy anymore in Cincinnati. Please call a meeting of the congregation and have my resignation accepted."[169] He told the board it would comfort them to be reunited with his brother and his family in New York. In his letter to the board on March 15, Lilienthal also mentioned other concerns "which in this for me so painful hour, I avoid mentioning, having stated them repeatedly from the pulpit. They are known to you all."[170] Clearly Lilienthal was frustrated about the lack of progress on the new building and reforms. He offered to help with the process of finding a new rabbi, because his new appointment was not to begin until August. The board again refused to accept the resignation, saying that to do so would "materially impare [sic] the congregation."[171] They set up a committee of officers to meet with the rabbi. Even though Lilienthal had by then agreed to Temple Emanu-El's terms, he delayed notifying them of his acceptance. Finally the Bene Israel board accepted his resignation on March 17. After that meeting, a number of local Cincinnati communal leaders, led by Judge Bellamy Storer, intervened. Acknowledging the tremendous loss that the rabbi's departure would mean to his congregation as well as to the community at large, the group asserted:

> The Doctor has so essentially aided us, in the education of our youth, by his devotion to his duties on the School board, and has moreover become so identified with our philanthropic institutions, in all that serves to aid the poor and homeless, that we cannot part with him, without the expression of our high esteem for his moral worth, as well as his profound scholarship. May we hope that his resignation may be recalled, and our community still be permitted to enjoy the benefit of his learning and noble character.[172]

In a dramatic move, Judge Storer invited the Bene Israel board to his home for a special meeting on March 24, after which the rabbi withdrew his resignation, apparently because he had received concessions that persuaded him to stay. While the details of this meeting were not recorded in the minutes, it is clear that the lay leadership promised to deliver on the long-delayed reforms and the new building. They also increased his salary by $1,000.[173] Lilienthal apparently never notified Temple Emanu-El of his decision, despite numerous letters from that congregation. They found out about it through a notice in the *Israelite* and formally declared the office of English minister to be vacant.[174]

Although the concessions that Lilienthal received at the March 24 meeting affected his decision to stay, the crucial factor may have been less tangible: an outpouring of support and love from his congregation and from the most prominent members of the broader Cincinnati community that did much to assuage his sense of personal loss.[175] On their side, the Bene Israel community, when faced with the loss of their leader, finally committed themselves to his agenda. Committees were empowered to act, money was raised, and in June 1868, the cornerstone was laid. When the new temple was dedicated in August 1869, the congregation ushered in a new era of Reform. The change was not simply a product of upward mobility but a direct result of Lilienthal's personal influence and his standing in the community. Over the thirteen years since he had arrived in Cincinnati, he had grown into a leader of great importance, with an ideology that spoke effectively to his acculturated congregation.

By the 1870s, after Isaac Leeser, Abraham Rice, and others of that first generation of American Jewish leadership had died, Lilienthal became the elder statesman of the Jewish clergy. Respected by all parties, the Jewish papers frequently called him "venerable." Even his appearance reinforced his stature, as his niece Sophie recalled. "Max Lilienthal's distinguished appearance made him an outstanding figure wherever he went. In later years his fine features were framed by snow-white hair, which he wore rather long; he had a singular sweetness of disposition which, combined with wisdom endeared him to all who knew him."[176] Having emerged as a local and national leader, respected by Christians and Jews, Lilienthal found himself in an ideal position to play a pivotal role in the creation of the central institutions of American Reform Judaism.

7

The Quest to Unite American Jewry

The decades following the Civil War were characterized by economic growth and by the revolutionary changes wrought by industrialization and urbanization. In the Northern states there was prosperity, a sense of power, and a spirit of buoyant confidence. Industry expanded rapidly and cities grew at an unprecedented rate.[1]

The optimism of the period encouraged churches and synagogues to replace old, outgrown buildings with expensive new structures.[2] In August 1869, Congregation Bene Israel dedicated its own beautiful new temple, and its rabbi gave a joyous speech marking the fulfillment of a decade-old dream. "God bless America for this glorious redemption. . . . Sunning ourselves in the golden rays of human and universal liberty we have ceased our wailings and cries of sorrow, and our prayers and psalmodies are full of thanksgiving and wishes for the welfare of the whole human race."[3]

The postwar period was also characterized by a huge new influx of immigrants that far surpassed earlier rates. German immigration, spurred by the promise of an expanding economy, jumped to 130,000 per year between 1866 and 1873. German Jewish immigration also surged, forming a second wave that increased the Jewish population from 150,000 in 1860 to 280,000 by 1880.[4] Mostly middle class and urbanized, these German Jews were better educated and more identified with German culture than the earlier wave had been. In addition, by 1870, at least twenty rabbis who had trained at German universities held rabbinic positions in America. They would infuse a new dose of German Jewish liberal thought into the ideological struggles of the 1870s and 1880s.[5]

Liberal Jewish intellectuals found a hospitable environment in late nineteenth-century America, characterized as the golden age of liberal theology in the United States. Liberal Protestantism, which had experienced a long, slow development in America (particularly among Congregationalists in the Northeast, Northern Methodists, Episcopalians, Presbyterians, and Northern Baptists), reached the height of its influence in the decades after the Civil War.[6] Widespread belief in the immanence of God in the world and human nature led to a humanistic optimism embraced alike by liberal Protestants, Jews, and even some Catholics.[7] Reform Jewish leaders, finally finding support for their liberal ideology in broadly based American religious values, energetically resumed their campaign for the changes they had been advocating for decades.

In the late 1860s Lilienthal and Wise returned to the national agenda that they had put aside after the double debacle of the Cleveland conference and Zion College in 1855: creating a national union for American Jewry and a seminary to train rabbis. It could not have been easy for Lilienthal to return to these controversy-laden issues, being by nature adverse to the kind of polemics and personal attacks that characterized the debates over these issues in the past. Nevertheless, the increasing need for unity to build institutions for American Judaism drew him back to the task. His recent successes at his congregation most likely bolstered his confidence, and his standing both nationally and in Cincinnati's civic life put him in an excellent position to mediate between the factions.

The polemical clash that erupted after the Cleveland conference of 1855 created a long enduring split in the Reform camp.[8] One camp, led by David Einhorn and Samuel Adler, advocated a radical approach, eliminating many of the customs and rituals that made Judaism distinctive. What would remain was a pure philosophical core of ethical monotheism, inspired by the prophetic tradition. These doctors of theology, deeply influenced by the German intellectual orientation, wanted to purify Judaism for an elite constituency. The other camp, under the leadership of Wise and Lilienthal, advanced a more moderate approach. Changes were to be made gradually, as the congregations were ready for them, and they were to be presented and justified, at least during the early period, by reference to traditional sources. Although Wise and Lilienthal also wished to bring Judaism into harmony with Enlightenment-based principles and often spoke of eliminating out-of-date rituals and customs, their American experience had taught them that changes could not be legislated without the consent of their congregants. As reformers, they were willing to proceed at a slower pace, focusing more on unity and less on ideological concerns than their German colleagues.

By the late 1860s and early 1870s the theological differences between the two groups had in fact narrowed. What continued to separate the two camps were issues of organizational strategy. Einhorn and Adler were exclusivists, meeting only with fellow rabbi doctors, whereas Wise and Lilienthal were inclusive, inviting all Jewish ministers, regardless of training, under their umbrella. They also solicited the cooperation of lay leadership for the practical wisdom they would bring to their projects. Lilienthal and Wise had learned that in the voluntaristic synagogues of America, lay support was crucial for success.

More than anything else, however, the split represented a clash between the two dominant personalities of the period: Isaac Mayer Wise and David Einhorn. Wise represented everything that Einhorn rejected; he did not have a doctorate and hence was not part of the highly educated elite, and he was popular and charismatic, appealing to the masses successfully through his periodical, the *Israelite*. Einhorn fought back in his less successful paper, *Sinai*, and later in the *Jewish Times*, edited by his lifelong friend Moritz Ellinger.[9] Wise and Einhorn attacked each other in print, challenged each other's leadership, and took evident pleasure in blocking each other's projects.

Lilienthal returned to the polemical arena in an effort to mediate this division. He had a foot in each camp; although he was a pragmatic and ardent Americanizer, he was also part of the elite German-university-trained group of rabbis and shared many of their values. Indeed, as noted, Lilienthal and Einhorn had attended the same yeshiva in Fürth and the University of Munich. The *Jewish Times* identified Lilienthal as one of their own. "The Rev. Dr. Lilienthal, of Cincinnati, had in his sermons and official acts unhesitantly pronounced in favor of radical Reform measures."[10] Rabbi Bernard Illowy, a traditionalist who had spent several years at Cincinnati's Congregation Shearith Israel, claimed that Lilienthal was more radical than Einhorn. "Wise was conservative, but pressure exercised upon him by his colleague, Dr. Lilienthal, and a few other Rabbis of radical tendencies" pushed him to the left.[11]

These positions did not stop Lilienthal from working closely with Wise, however, because the pragmatic approach of the two friends stressed practical achievements over abstract theology. Reform rabbi Aaron Hahn of

Cleveland confirmed that although Lilienthal was liberal and enlightened in his views and aims, he was no radical reformer.[12] "Radical" and "moderate" in this period referred to differences of strategy rather than theology. Time and again, Lilienthal urged both sides to avoid personal attacks, believing that they should tolerate differences to work for shared goals such as a union, a college, and improved Jewish education. The establishment of these institutions in America was his paramount concern.

In 1866, shortly after the end of the Civil War, Wise wanted to initiate a call for another rabbinic conference. Lilienthal cautioned delay, recognizing that the rift between the camps of Einhorn and Wise had not yet healed. Nevertheless, Wise, impatient as ever, began to agitate for a national meeting in the *Israelite*. Lilienthal, who insisted on the presence of ordained and university-trained rabbis, therefore set out to mend fences with Einhorn's group.[13]

While Lilienthal was engaged with his correspondence, Wise was working on another track. In March 1869 Wise called for a broadly based conference of Hebrew ministers, teachers, lay leaders of congregations, and representatives of the Young Men's Hebrew Associations[14] to set up a publication society, harmonize the efforts of congregations, and, rather vaguely, "elevate Judaism." As the responses began trickling in by the end of April, Wise made it clear that he hoped to avoid the mistakes of the 1855 Cleveland conference by letting others lead; indeed the laity would run the conference, with rabbis and ministers present only in an ex officio status. By May Wise had gotten commitments from eleven congregations and was well on his way to his goal of twenty congregations. Throughout the summer more congregations joined, so that by the end of the High Holy Days, success seemed assured. The New York–based *Jewish Messenger* commented, "The fact that a conference will be called at an early day, through the intervention of Drs. Wise and Lilienthal, and Mr. Mack [president of Bene Yeshurun] and others appears to be now well established."[15] The paper was pleased with the broad platform and the geographic diversity of the participants.

Eighteen congregations had already expressed their support when, on the brink of success, the leaders abandoned the conference in deference to a rabbinic meeting in Philadelphia organized by Einhorn, which was to begin on November 3, 1869. Wise later expressed the view that Einhorn's group had purposely tried to thwart his efforts. "We understood well that this call, intentionally or unintentionally, was calculated to counteract and frustrate the convention called through the columns of this paper."[16] Wise was forced to choose between widening the breach between the parties by going forward with his own conference or postponing it to attend the rabbinic meeting in Philadelphia.

In fact, the *Jewish Times* had already announced the Philadelphia conference in the late spring of 1869.[17] Both conferences were successfully recruiting attendees throughout the summer, but Einhorn's decision to meet in November was probably due to the likelihood that Wise would soon succeed in holding his own more broadly based conference. Once the date for the Philadelphia conference was set, Wise tried to learn indirectly if he would be invited. According to Rabbi Illowy's recollection, Lilienthal's contribution to this effort was crucial. "Lilienthal persisted and after many and long diplomatic negotiations and many promises that Wise would be deferential and submissive, a conference was arranged to be held in the city of Philadelphia in the fall of 1869."[18] Despite the limitations placed on Wise, the invitation meant acceptance into the elite circle of rabbis with doctorates, and in the end Wise could not resist the temptation to attend.[19]

Einhorn set the agenda for Philadelphia in advance. As Wise later noted, "Every proposition not embraced in the printed pamphlet was treated with a sort of contempt, for which we cannot account."[20] Wise, who arrived late, played a passive role for the most part. In a contemptuous description, the *Jewish Times* later claimed, "[Wise] listened with the docility and attention of a pupil and had sagacity enough not to betray his rabbinical ignorance by too lively a share in the discussion."[21] Lilienthal, claiming that "official business" kept him from attending, expressed his full support for the conference and requested that his name be recorded in its list of members.[22]

In good German academic style the conference began by establishing seven principles that distinguished Reform from traditional Judaism, rejecting bodily resurrection, a personal messiah, and the priesthood and embracing universalism and the use of the vernacular in worship.[23] The rabbis then turned to practical issues concerning marriage, divorce, and circumcision. Before the conference Lilienthal had submitted a lengthy set of proposals to the group advocating the harmonization of Jewish marriage and divorce law with that of the state.[24] This issue was critical in the struggle for Jewish emancipation in Europe from the time of Napoleon's Sanhedrin. Could Jews harmonize their religious law with the law of the land? Could they be full participants in modern society?[25] Although emancipation did not have to be won in America, where citizenship was a given, Jews still felt a need to harmonize religious and civil law.

When the subject turned to circumcision, Wise ventured into the discussion. He favored the radical suggestion that circumcision was not necessary for conversion to Judaism. Einhorn opposed him on grounds that Jewish law required circumcision. Seemingly, their positions on this issue were reversed, with the radical reformer citing Jewish law to support a traditional view. Their difference really reflected Wise's inclusive versus Einhorn's exclusive approach to membership in the Jewish community. Wise wanted to make it easier to become Jewish; Einhorn wanted to retain circumcision to protect Judaism from foreign elements.[26]

This difference emerged again at the end of the meeting. Wise advocated the inclusion of lay leadership in the next conference. Einhorn dismissed the idea, saying that the laity was not "advanced enough" to be included. Without the tactical support and academic stature of Lilienthal behind him, Einhorn's group outmaneuvered Wise on this proposal. Perhaps as a conciliatory gesture, the radical reformers appointed Wise and Lilienthal to set up the next conference in Cincinnati.

Despite his misgivings, Wise tried to put a positive spin on the Philadelphia conference, embracing both its declaration of principles and its suggested changes to Jewish civil law. Although he saw himself as a centrist, he praised the radical position for its value as a vanguard, pointing the way forward.[27] Later, as criticism increased from the traditionalists, Wise withdrew his support for the decisions of the conference. Particularly controversial was the conference's position that English and German prayers should replace some of the traditional Hebrew liturgy. Correspondents to the *Israelite* charged that these proposals "would ultimately destroy any vestige of our nationality as Israelites."[28] Historian Michael Meyer notes that the Philadelphia conference was out of touch with the majority of congregations, which abhorred radicalism. When Wise understood this, he moved to distance himself from the radicals and thus treated the Philadelphia conference as a one-time event.[29]

Within a few months of the Philadelphia conference, Lilienthal and Wise decided to organize a congregational convention, even though this move meant breaking their promise to Einhorn's group not to set up a rival conference. Other moderates, notably Adolph Huebsch of New York, faced with revising the liturgy of his own congregation, pressed for the conference to revise Wise's liturgy, *Minhag Amerika*.[30]

Lilienthal played an active role in the work on liturgy and ritual at this conference, which took place in Cleveland in June 1870. The body took moderate stands, including the declaration that Sabbath observance must not be moved away from Saturday.[31] The deliberations went slowly and, because the weather was uncomfortably hot, the group adjourned, promising to meet again in New York in October to continue the revision of the prayer book.

In spite of Lilienthal's attempt to placate the radicals, the *Jewish Times* was furious, labeling the Cleveland conference "a conscious falsehood."[32]

Charging Wise with hypocrisy and equivocation, the paper called Wise "the Barnum of the Jewish pulpit."[33] Lilienthal, Huebsch, and others escaped unscathed, because invariably Wise served as a human lightning rod for all the critics' hostility.

Responding to these attacks in the aftermath of the conference, Lilienthal tried to finesse the matter in a letter to the *Jewish Times*. Defending their conference, he claimed that its scope was limited to a revision of Wise's prayer book.

> In order not to come in collision whatsoever with the Philadelphia conference, and to avoid any ill-feeling and misunderstanding . . . the prayer book question had not been touched by the Philadelphia Conference and was therefore a question fairly open for discussion and action. For the reason first stated, no question acted upon by the Philadelphia Conference or under consideration by the same was either mentioned or approached.[34]

Actually, the prayer book revision was not a side issue but central to the conflict, because Einhorn had a rival liturgy that competed with Wise's. Both men trumpeted the distribution of their books, printing the names of the congregations that adopted their liturgies in the *Israelite* and the *Jewish Times*.

The moderate group reconvened in New York in October 1870.[35] They unanimously elected Lilienthal as their president, perhaps because he was less offensive to the radical reformers than Wise. Still hoping to make peace with Einhorn's group, the conference attendees had formed a committee for reconciliation, but the radicals refused to come. While recognizing the failure of the effort, Lilienthal urged the reconciliation committee to continue to try to make peace. Offering to join in its efforts, he argued that moderate and radical Reform were not so far apart. The need for consolidated action to address the central problems facing American Jewry made reconciliation crucial.[36]

Lilienthal addressed the radical leaders' animosity toward Wise by denying that one man could dominate American Judaism. The time of personal rule had passed, he argued, and every effort had to be made to work in a united fashion to accomplish the work of glorifying American Judaism, its ministry, and its congregations.[37] The committee received his remarks enthusiastically and resolved to renew its efforts to achieve unity.

The New York conference's only serious clash was over a proposal to change the name of the prayer book. This may have been an attempt to defuse radical concerns over Wise's power, but Wise took it as a personal attack, positing that the revision of his *Minhag Amerika* was the central purpose of the conference. The title of this liturgy was his trademark. He walked out in protest, and it took the efforts of Rabbi Huebsch and others to bring him back. This rather childish behavior was not unusual for Wise at these meetings.

The liturgical work of the conference progressed slowly, in part because the members got sidetracked into discussions of other issues—Indiana's divorce laws, a proposal submitted by Lilienthal to abolish the second day of Rosh Hashanah, and Wise's plan to set up a rabbinic college. The pretense that the group was concerned only with liturgical reform was dropped. It was clear that the participants saw themselves as the rabbinic body of American Jewry, and they agreed to convene another conference the following year in Cincinnati.

Wise was now upbeat, even though the revisions of *Minhag Amerika* were still not complete.[38] Meanwhile Lilienthal took advantage of his good relationship with the *Jewish Times* to publish a letter of reconciliation with Einhorn's faction shortly after the conference ended."Dear TIMES, except [*sic*] my sincere thanks for the conciliatory remarks with which you closed your report on the conference. You were perfectly right in stating that the men assembled there cared more for a reconciliation and union of all the Reform rabbis than for any other business. . . . Let us take a calm and considerate review of the situation."[39]

This time Lilienthal addressed the competition between Einhorn's and Wise's prayer books head on, saying the issue was secondary compared to the greater one of unity. He pointed out that Einhorn and Temple Emanu-El's Rabbi Adler did not use the same prayer book and that his congregation, Bene Israel, had used a combination of the Adler, Einhorn, and Wise liturgies on Yom Kippur. Arguing that the choice of liturgy should be left up to each rabbi and congregation, he assured the radicals that the moderate congregations earnestly wished for a union.[40] This letter was classic Lilienthal, stressing pluralism and tolerance of differences. He differed from the ideologically pure radicals mainly in his insistence that the highest value was the achievement of larger common goals.

Einhorn's faction did not share Lilienthal's pluralistic, pragmatic vision. As usual they focused their attack on Wise, whom they blamed for the antagonism between the factions. Moritz Ellinger, editor of the *Jewish Times*, suggested that, in the interest of harmony, it would have been better to leave out the question of a uniform prayer book. If the members of the New York conference really wanted peace and union, he added, all they needed to do was return to the agenda of the earlier Philadelphia conference. Only then would the two groups be reconciled.[41]

Wise had no intention of returning to the platform of the Philadelphia conference when he called for another conference in the *Israelite* in April 1871, to be held in Cincinnati in June; nor would this conference focus on the limited agenda of revising *Minhag Amerika*.[42] The aim of this conference was to establish the institutions that Wise and Lilienthal thought were vital to American Jewry. The *Israelite* listed almost thirty participants, including ministers and lay delegates representing midwestern, southern, and eastern congregations.[43] This eclectic mix of leadership shows how far this Cincinnati conference diverged from the elitist strategy of Einhorn's group. Its regional diversity counteracted the claim that they represented only the western congregations. Its organizers hoped that the conference would itself become an established institution, working for the "benefit and progress of Judaism."[44]

At the opening session, Lilienthal, the outgoing president (and soon to be elected the next vice-president of the group), laid out a wide-ranging list of the tasks before them: finishing the prayer book, establishing a rabbinic college to train American rabbis, formulating a common curriculum for Sabbath schools, creating a Hebrew publication society, sponsoring circuit rabbis to preach to smaller congregations, and arranging that future conventions incorporate the presentation of scholarly papers.

This speech was in fact a blueprint for establishing a viable institutional structure for American Judaism: a national union, a rabbinic seminary, and a professional organization for rabbis. Lilienthal was outlining the goals that he, Wise, and the late Isaac Leeser (who died in 1868) had been striving toward since the late 1840s. Now, with the broad lay and rabbinic consensus established in the previous Cleveland and New York conferences, these crucial building blocks for a self-sustaining American Jewish community seemed within reach.

Most important, in Lilienthal's view, was the need for an American rabbinic college. "The subject which demands our most serious consideration is the establishment of a Rabbinical college. Congregations are building temples and are in need of ministers as soon as they will be finished. Most of them want ministers able to preach in the English language. . . . We therefore are bound to raise ministers in our own country, able to preach and teach in the English language, and educated under the auspices of our free American institutions."[45] Lilienthal thought that the best hope for a seminary lay in establishing a relationship with McMicken University, which Lilienthal was also involved in founding at this time. He was confident that congregational support for a rabbinic school would materialize, especially in the West and Southwest.

As Lilienthal was aware, the radical reformers were moving to form their own seminary in New York at this time. Lilienthal acknowledged and welcomed their efforts in his address. "We do not doubt, that the Hebrew congregations in the East, and especially in the city of New York, where so much wealth and talent is congregated, will also open a Seminary for the institution and education of ministers for our flourishing congregations."[46] In fact, Lilienthal suggested a joint committee to establish a curriculum for both seminaries. Unfortunately, the conference committee on reconciliation had to report their inability to resolve "some personal differences of opinion . . . between the gentlemen of the conference, held in Philadelphia in 1869, and the members of this conference."[47]

With Lilienthal's opening speech, the Cincinnati conference began the work of creating these permanent institutions, including a yearly conference of rabbinic and lay leaders and a union of congregations. The proposed structure of union membership, requiring that congregations pay dues on a per member basis, anticipated that of the future Union of American Hebrew Congregations. The members also wrestled with the issue of whether member congregations needed to adhere to "reformed principles." They decided in favor of this criterion.

A curriculum for the proposed seminary, formulated by Rabbis Wise, Lilienthal, Huebsch, and others, was also presented at the conference. The rabbinic program they recommended was grounded in traditional Judaic studies: Bible and commentaries, Hebrew and Aramaic languages, Mishnah, Talmud, and Midrash. Advanced students would also be exposed to modern German biblical scholarship that would draw on archaeology and philology. This curriculum would become the model for the courses at Hebrew Union College, which would place a strong emphasis on the study of traditional texts along with critical methodology.[48]

Completing its work, the conference declared itself to be a permanent institution called the Union of Israelite Congregations of America and announced that it would hold the next meeting in Chicago the following year. Wise, with his usual dramatic flair, proclaimed, "A chapter of Jewish History was made in one week, which is calculated to open a new and promising future to American Judaism."[49] Although he was right that the work of the Cincinnati conference would be the basis for the future institutions of Reform Judaism, he could not have foreseen the convoluted path that would lead to their creation.

The furious radical reformers were contemptuous of the results of the Cincinnati conference, believing that Wise's sole purpose was to thwart Einhorn's plans.[50] The *Jewish Times* focused on a liturgical debate, glossed over in the *Israelite* account. In the course of a discussion of the High Holy Days liturgy, Wise had denied that the doctrines of personal redemption and reconciliation with God were authentic Jewish beliefs. He was supported by Jacob Mayer, who went so far as to reject the notion of a personal God. After a heated debate, the majority strongly rejected their positions. Wise again exhibited impulsive behavior by temporarily storming out of the room.[51] The *Jewish Times* seized on this incident to ridicule Wise. "According to the philosopher Isaac M. Wise, Judaism knows no personal God, the God of Abraham, Isaac, and Jacob is a mere ethereal essence, as conceived in the world-redeeming brains of Isaac M. Wise."[52] Derisively they suggested that Wise must have had his own divine revelation because this understanding of God could not have come from the Bible itself. They called the conference a farce and a desecration of God's name.[53]

One week later, prominent eastern rabbis, spanning the ideological spectrum from radical reformers such as Adler and Einhorn to traditionalists such as Benjamin Szold, declared that denial of the existence of a personal God was both a blasphemy and slander upon Judaism and that allowing anyone with such beliefs to prepare a prayer book was an absurdity. The signatories seriously distorted the debate, missing the point that it was not Wise but Mayer who had made the offensive statement denying a personal God. They also incorrectly claimed that "scarcely a voice was heard in opposition," contrary to the report in the *Jewish Times* itself.[54] Nevertheless, the protest created such an uproar of indignation that the broad achievements of the conference—laying a foundation for a union and a college— were eclipsed.

As in the past, Lilienthal stepped in to restore calm and clarity. In an article in the *Jewish Times* he claimed that the conference had tabled these liturgical issues to focus on more important concerns. Admitting that Wise's and Mayer's remarks were "inconsiderate expressions," he still insisted that they had the right of free speech and were alone responsible for their positions. Refuting the charge that there was little opposition to these views, he reported that after the two expressed their opinions, a stormy debate ensued, ending when the conference voted almost unanimously to table the discussion. He reminded readers of the *Jewish Times* that "our aim and purpose was and must be A UNION OF ISRAELITE CONGREGATIONS."[55] He admonished readers to be more tolerant. "Let us learn how to forget and forgive mistakes; let us stand united as a band of brethren, working for the same good and holy cause, and a bright future will be in store for the young Judaism of America."[56] In response, the *Jewish Times* called Lilienthal's defense "lame" and laid responsibility for the remarks of Wise and

Mayer on the whole conference, declaring that "Conference, prayer book, congregational union, all sink into insignificance when the ground-work of our religion had been assailed and attacked."[57]

Although he was tired of the bitter recriminations, Lilienthal tried once more to bring reason to the charged situation. He heatedly denied that the conference was "the clique of Rev. Dr. Wise. . . . [It was rather] a body of independent men, who have the interests of Judaism as much at heart, as anybody you may name."[58] Unable to comprehend why the "episode" had caused so much trouble, he assured the *Jewish Times* readers that plans for a union, a seminary, and the other noble intentions of the conference would continue, regardless of the paper's attempt to derail them.

Wise also claimed to be at a loss to understand why an unimportant episode that had merely been touched on during the last day of the conference could cause such controversy. Charging that enemies of the conference had seized on this incident to prove that the members of the group were atheists, he launched into a garbled discussion of various theological systems that posited an impersonal view of God.[59] Later he insisted that personal malice was behind the protest, ironically pointing out that the same group who had accused him of not being Reform enough in 1855 was now protesting that his theology was too radical. Wise lashed out at those rabbis who conducted services on Sunday, banished Hebrew from the service, ate pork, and smoked on the Sabbath yet "assume the surplice of holy inquisition, to wrap themselves in the long gown of unholy hypocrisy."[60]

The vindictiveness of the *Jewish Times* attack was an indication of the level of animosity between the rival leaders, but it also revealed the clash of two basically incompatible viewpoints: American ideological pragmatism and German ideological purity. For Lilienthal and Wise the theological debate over the nature of God was unimportant because their focus was on the practical agenda of establishing American religious institutions. To the radicals, whose German academic orientation was all-important in shaping their perspective, philosophical principles were primary. In Philadelphia Einhorn had established his premises before addressing practical problems. From his point of view, if the Cincinnati conference was based on blasphemous first principles, then all the institutional plans were insignificant. The *Jewish Times* and the radical bloc, scaring off many of Wise's rabbinic colleagues, succeeded in derailing the institutional plans of the Cincinnati leaders temporarily so that the Chicago conference, planned for June 1872, never occurred.

Wise and Lilienthal did not give up. Frustrated with the combination of arrogance and timidity in his rabbinic colleagues, Wise confided to Adolph Huebsch, his close friend and a fellow rabbi from Bohemia, that they had made a conscious decision to shift their tactics. "I've given up the idea of advancing and putting new life into American Judaism through rabbis and their ilk. . . . In a year I will tell you whether this strategy is the better one."[61] They sensed that support for the union and seminary was growing among the laity, especially in western congregations frustrated by the lack of native-born clergy and teachers. The institutional framework for a union, rabbinic college, and professional organization conceived by the Cincinnati conference was subsequently resurrected by the lay leadership of Wise's and Lilienthal's synagogues.

The origins of the Union of American Hebrew Congregations (UAHC) can be traced directly to a call issued in October 1872 by Moritz Loth, the president of Bene Yeshurun, in his annual congregational address. Loth, a prosperous Cincinnati merchant, had been a key player in the earlier conferences and a signatory to the call for the second conference in Cleveland. He was pleased with the material success of American Jewry in the 1860s but declared that building temples was not enough. He asked the various congregations of Cincinnati to appoint committees to call a general conference of congregations to establish a union whose purposes would be the following: to establish a Jewish theological faculty, to publish proper books for Sabbath schools, and to adopt a code of laws to uphold circumcision, Saturday Sabbath observance, kosher slaughtering, and dietary laws. More conservative than his rabbi, Isaac Mayer Wise, Loth feared that unchecked reforms would be disastrous to Judaism.[62] His agenda was traditional enough to attract even the Orthodox congregations of Cincinnati.

Wise was pleased with his president's initiative, declaring that it was in harmony with his deepest wishes, but he counseled that the "limits of reform should be left up to Rabbis."[63] The *Jewish Times*, still hostile to Wise, gleefully characterized the proposal as "a protest against the tendencies pursued by the Cincinnati reformers, and a repudiation of the 'renowned preacher' and 'speculative theologian' occupying the ministerial chair of the congregation in question."[64] In this they were partly right, because Loth reflected the more conservative impulse in Cincinnati congregations that Lilienthal and Wise had been struggling with for almost twenty years.

There must have been behind-the-scenes negotiating on this issue, because by the time the organizers brought the first convention to order in July 1873, they had removed all ideological requirements, whether traditional or Reform. According to historian Steven Fox, the UAHC constitution was intentionally written to appeal to both Orthodox and Reform constituencies, perceiving itself as an umbrella organization for all American Jewish congregations.[65] The new organization welcomed "any Hebrew

Congregation in the United States, lawfully organized," requiring only that they choose representatives and pay dues on a per member basis.[66]

Another potentially divisive element in the original call was its regionalism, inasmuch as it only invited congregations in the South, West, and Midwest. The *Jewish Times* was angry, claiming that New York had been excluded, because the call ignored an existing society in New York formed to establish a Hebrew college. Predicting failure for the conference, the paper snidely remarked, "Whatever has been done so far, whatever organization has been in existence, is to be abandoned at the bidding of the Convention of Cincinnati; for from Cincinnati is to go forth the law and the redemption of American Israel."[67] The *Jewish Messenger*, a New York–based paper with a traditional religious orientation, was similarly annoyed, pointing out that the Board of Delegates of American Israelites, which could have served as the basis for a union, had been ignored.[68]

Again, we can surmise that behind-the-scenes negotiations ensued because, by the time of the July 1873 meeting, the Union welcomed all congregations in the United States. It declared, "We, the delegates representing the various congregations of the South and West . . . do hereby cordially request our sister congregations throughout the United States to cooperate with us for the purpose of forming a more perfect union of congregations."[69]

In this way, the Union mirrored the pattern of American Protestant denominations that, by the mid-nineteenth century, had created nationwide bodies governed by congregational representatives. Like their Christian counterparts, the founders of the UAHC were determined to avoid doctrinal disputes. "Union meant setting aside differences in ritual or theology in order to unify all Jewish congregations in practical projects."[70] Lilienthal and Wise, avid Americanizers, had long been advocates of this pragmatic approach.

The ninety-seven delegates, representing thirty-four synagogues, gathered in Melodeon Hall in Cincinnati, a large public auditorium often used for concerts, from July 8 to July 10, 1873. Representatives of congregations from as far away as Atlanta and Chicago, Houston and Galveston, Charleston, West Virginia, Natchez, Mississippi, and St. Joseph, Missouri, gathered for this historic occasion.[71] Led by President Moritz Loth of Bene Yeshurun and Vice-President Julius Freiberg of Bene Israel, the conference crafted a constitution for the new organization. An executive board was formed, of which a majority were Cincinnati natives who continued to meet after the conclusion of the event in the boardrooms of Wise's and Lilienthal's synagogues.[72] By the time of the next conference, held July 14–16, 1874, in Cleveland, the Union had almost doubled its size to fifty-six congregations.

By the end of the decade it had almost doubled its membership again.[73] The UAHC had quickly fulfilled its goal of uniting American congregations, without regard to sectionalism or ideological differences. It eagerly tackled challenges such as building a rabbinic seminary, creating a system of circuit preaching to reach congregations without rabbis, distributing Isaac Leeser's translation of the Bible (in conscious imitation of the American Bible Society in New York), and strengthening Sabbath schools.

Contemporary observers tended to regard the founding of the UAHC as the result of an entirely lay initiative. The *Jewish Messenger* commented, "What the clergy have failed to do, the laymen are striving very faithfully to begin and to advance."[74] At the first annual conference of the Union, temporary president Sigmund Mann made a similar point, comparing their conference with the 1855 Cleveland conference at which only clergy attended. "Today," he noted, "the practical businessmen of this land are here assembled."[75] Historians tend to concur with this assessment. As Steven Fox writes in his history of the UAHC, "Prior to 1873, all attempts to unite American Israelites were made by rabbis. Having failed, the rabbis were forced to stand aside and allow the laity to proceed."[76] But to what extent were Wise and Lilienthal actually on the sidelines? Was this lay initiative a challenge to rabbinic leadership?

In fact, lay participation in the conferences had always been part of Lilienthal and Wise's plans. At the Cleveland conference in 1855 Lilienthal had advocated a permanent synod made up of one-third clergy and two-thirds lay leadership, believing that the practical skills of the laity would balance the scholarship of the rabbis.[77] Similarly, at the Cincinnati conference in 1871 the lay leaders were invited to be voting members of the proceedings. Their influence behind the scenes in the origins of the UAHC is evident in the fact that the Union's key early leaders were Moritz Loth and Julius Freiberg, presidents of Bene Jeshurun and Bene Israel, respectively. Furthermore, all UAHC executive meetings were held at either Bene Israel or Bene Jeshurun, and for the first five years of its existence Hebrew Union College would essentially be a ward of these two congregations, holding all its classes and board meetings on their premises. Although Wise and Lilienthal deliberately chose to step back and cede the initiative for a union to lay leaders, much of their agenda remained intact.

Since the 1840s the two rabbis had advocated the need for a union, a rabbinic school, and strengthened Sabbath schools. They were willing to take a subordinate role to accomplish these ends. Paradoxically, by relinquishing direct control, the two leaders achieved virtually everything they had worked so long for.

In the process, they also discovered the formula for resolving the long-standing lay-rabbinic power struggle that had plagued their early years in America. The laity would establish a union whose principal purpose was to provide institutional and financial support for a rabbinic seminary. The rabbis would run the school and establish a scholarly and professional organization to support its graduates to raise the standards and stature of the American rabbinate. All subsequent American Jewish denominations would replicate this relationship between laity and rabbinate.

When Loth called for a conference in 1872, he made it clear that his primary concern was to create an American-trained rabbinate. "We must have Rabbis who possess the ability to preach and expound eloquently the true text of our belief. Such Rabbis we can only have by educating them, and to educate them we must have a 'Jewish Theological Faculty.'"[78] Lilienthal and Wise may have played subordinate roles in the founding of the UAHC, but they were central to the formation of Hebrew Union College.

Lilienthal was involved with the development of Hebrew Union College on several levels, helping to create the structure of the college, prepare its curriculum, build the library, and teach its students, for whom he also acted as a mentor. At the first annual conference of the UAHC, in July 1874, Lilienthal was named to the Board of Governors of the proposed school. By July of the next year, the Board of Governors promised that the preparatory department of Hebrew Union College would open on or before October 1875. Timing was crucial because Henry Adler, a wealthy lay leader, had offered the school a gift of $10,000 with the stipulation that it be used within three years.[79] The Board of Governors worked diligently and submitted a code of regulations by which the school would be administered.

The job of preparing a curriculum for the school fell to the rabbinic members of the Board of Governors: Lilienthal, Wise, and Solomon Wolfenstein. The three followed the same pragmatic, unifying strategy that had shaped the UAHC. Wise declared that the school would impose no "isms or schisms" but rather would assemble the finest faculty possible to introduce both Reform and Orthodox students to the treasures of Israel's literature. Their motto was "Justice to all and offence to none."[80]

Wolfenstein later told an amusing story that illustrated the dynamics of those early meetings.

> We met a consecutive number of Sundays at Cincinnati. . . . Our meetings were very animated as a rule. Lilienthal and myself agreeing and Wise opposing us. . . . It was on one of those occasions when Lilienthal, lighting a fresh cigar, broke out in a laugh, in which he liked to indulge so heartily, and turning to me exclaimed: "Wolfenstein,

you are a fool and I am another. We quarrel with Wise, and neverthe-less, he will do as he pleases." He was certainly right.[81]

Wolfenstein and Lilienthal argued for more of a scholarly and theoretical emphasis, whereas Wise wanted to emphasize traditional Jewish studies and practical courses for rabbis. In the compromise curriculum the school would not offer *Wissenschaftlich* courses until the third and fourth years. Later, Wolfenstein would return as an examiner for the school and remark, "I did not find much of the program we had carried out."[82]

In their efforts to craft a curriculum for the new school, the rabbis turned to existing European models.[83] The Jewish Theological Seminary of Breslau, founded by Zacharias Frankel in 1854, combined biblical and rabbinic literature with history, Hebrew grammar, philosophy, ethics, and modern *Wissenschaftlich* studies. Also included were practical courses for the modern rabbi in pedagogy and homiletics. With varying emphasis, the same was true of the Liberal Hochschule established by Abraham Geiger in Berlin in 1872. Even Berlin's Rabbiner Seminar für das Orthodoxe Judenthum combined traditional texts with historical studies.[84] All three of the European seminaries also required the completion of a doctorate at a secular university as a prerequisite for ordination. This goal was beyond the reach of the American school, but the Hebrew Union College would require an undergraduate degree.[85] Lilienthal was realistic about the differ-ences between European and American students. "The student in Europe is used to spend [*sic*] ten to twelve years in preparatory schools and the fin-ishing universities before dreaming of entering the arena of active life. We, in this country are of quite another disposition; life, real, active, earnest, attracts the attention and engages the energy even of our youth."[86] Lilien-thal recognized that a balance had to be struck between the sophisticated course of study in philology, history, philosophy, and other "scientific" dis-ciplines needed to train modern rabbis and the "national temper" of the school's future students.

Lilienthal never abandoned his quest for more *Wissenschaft*, or mod-ern critical scholarship, in the school. At the 1875 UAHC conference, dur-ing which the curriculum for the first four years of study was presented, he gave a lengthy address arguing for the need to harmonize the school's program with scholarly trends in Europe. Beyond his own commitment to this program of study, Lilienthal wanted to use a *Wissenschaft*-oriented curriculum to create a rapprochement between the Cincinnati school and both Reform scholars on the cutting edge in Europe and New York's radical reformers. Wise, concentrating on the classical heritage, wanted to make the school and its graduates acceptable to traditional congregations. For a while the Hebrew Union College managed to balance these opposing trends and, in its first decade, came to be accepted by both reformers and traditionalists.[87]

The Hebrew Union College opened on October 3, 1875, in the vestry rooms of Bene Israel after an impressive ceremony held at Wise's Bene Jeshurun.[88] Its student body of ten, mostly of high school age, met in the afternoon in a single class after public school was over. Lilienthal worked hard to raise the level of what was really little more than an intensive religious school, instituting the system of regular monthly examinations he had used years before in his private school.[89] By the UAHC annual meeting in 1876, the Board of Governors reported an increase in the number of students to seventeen and recommended that Lilienthal be added to the faculty.[90] Lilienthal accepted the invitation and taught without compensation from 1876 until his death. Initially asked to teach a course in ancient Jewish history, he later taught courses on other periods of Jewish history as well. Throughout this time, he remained active on the curriculum, examination, and disciplinary committees.

Commenting on the preparatory program, Wise recalled that students were not always well behaved in the first years. "There sat the wise men of Israel, namely the good old teacher Solomon Eppinger and fourteen noisy boys, most of whom had come only to kill time and at the command of their parents. Four of them wanted to study; ten wanted to make noise."[91] Wise also referred to the problem in his 1875 annual report. "At the beginning some difficulties were experienced in enforcing a proper discipline, but they were soon overcome without rigorous means, merely by moral suasion and personal attention, exercised by the teachers, and supported by Rev. Dr. Lilienthal, and the President."[92]

Another source of disruption was the presence of two young women in the class, one a grandchild of the instructor, Solomon Eppinger, the other Wise's niece. According to David Philipson, "The boys rather resented the presence of these girls" and played practical jokes on them.[93] These incidents may have been part of the motivation for a plan to open a ladies' seminary. Moritz Loth proposed this in his 1877 annual report. "In order to offer the daughters of Israel the same opportunity of obtaining a Hebrew and Classical education, including music and the arts . . . I respectfully and earnestly recommend the adoption by this council of measures which will call into existence a Young Ladies' Hebrew Seminary."[94] Lilienthal was on the committee to put this idea into effect, but it never materialized.

Lilienthal was a mentor for the young students. David Philipson recalled the influence of the older man on him in his autobiography, *My Life as an American Jew*. He remembered the many Friday evenings he spent as a guest in the Lilienthal home, celebrating the Sabbath with them. As he had in New York, the rabbi helped create a feeling of extended family for the students in the young school.

The high point of Lilienthal's involvement in the Hebrew Union College came in April 1881 when a new college building was completed and the school could finally leave the basements of the two large Cincinnati Reform synagogues. The Union had purchased a three-story mansion in a fashionable part of the city and converted it into a school building with a library, classrooms, and chapel.[95] Lilienthal offered a prayer at the dedication ceremony, thanking God for inspiring the Israelites of America to create the Union of American Hebrew Congregations, which in turn had endowed Hebrew Union College. "We have been asked to dedicate in their name this splendid building to the noble purpose of educating ministers and instructing them as servants of the Most High, the Holy One, Father of the whole human race."[96] Especially meaningful to Lilienthal was the merging of Jewish and American values "on this virgin soil of human liberty [so that] they may teach the Sacred doctrines of civil and religious liberty."[97]

With each year the UAHC gained more congregations, and the successful opening of Hebrew Union College also boded well.[98] Eventually the New York rabbinic leadership, both the traditionalists and the radical reformers, seeing the wisdom of supporting the new institutions, began a cautious process of reconciliation.[99] Eastern newspapers—the *Jewish Times*, representing Einhorn's faction, and the *Jewish Messenger*, representing the traditionalists—were initially skeptical of the UAHC and school, not least because they had felt excluded by the regional bias of Moritz Loth's original call. They were still annoyed that their institutions, such as the Board of Delegates, had been ignored by the Union.

Lilienthal sounded one of the first conciliatory notes in a speech to the UAHC annual conference in July 1875.

> I am a man of peace, and am sure I express the unanimous sentiment of this large assembly if I assert that we are tired of the wrangling and quarreling of some of the ministers of this country. The Congregations want peace and harmony; let the ministers, the preachers and teachers of peace, set the good example of extending the brotherly hand of reconciliation. If mistakes have been made, and they have been made, it is no use of denying it, let them be forgotten. . . . Let us show the world we are first in soliciting harmony and in advocating reconciliation in fostering mutual good will.[100]

Lilienthal particularly hoped that the two branches of Reform would cooperate in the Hebrew Union College. Lilienthal's speech elicited loud cheers, after which the UAHC unanimously adopted his resolution.

The radicals, however, showed no signs of cooperating. To the contrary, in January 1876, the *Jewish Times* announced plans for their own convention of congregations that would erect an "Institution for Jewish Science and Theology." The article explicitly cited the example of their western brethren, whose energy had brought about the opening of Hebrew Union College.[101] Over the next few months the *Jewish Times* agitated for the conference, set for May 1876. The list of rabbinic participants represented the major scholars of the young country, ranging from radicals such as Samuel Adler, David Einhorn, and Kaufmann Kohler, to moderates such as Adolph Huebsch, to traditionalists such as Marcus Jastrow, Sabato Morais, and Benjamin Szold.[102] With Hebrew Union College barely opened and struggling to maintain itself, this powerful bloc of rabbis was serious competition.

That this disparate group of rabbis was able to cooperate even to a limited extent is evidence of a change within the eastern leadership, which had been brought together under the auspices of the Board of Delegates of American Israelites. This organization, formed by Isaac Leeser and Samuel Isaacs in 1858 to respond to the Mortara affair, was originally a moderate traditionalist organization dedicated to Jewish antidefamation. The founders also hoped that the Board of Delegates would address wide-ranging issues, such as the improvement of Jewish education, professional standards for clergy, charity, and aid to the sick and immigrant groups.[103] Leeser had hoped that the Board of Delegates would become the basis for a national union of congregations.

In the first years, avowedly Reform congregations were conspicuously absent from the Board of Delegates ranks. But the religious makeup of the group changed as the emphasis of the organization narrowed to the fight for Jewish rights. Reformers, who had been deterred by the traditionalist emphasis in earlier projects, felt free to associate with its new direction. Some key members of the Board of Delegates became more hospitable toward Reform, including Myer Isaacs (son of Samuel Isaacs, the founder). By the mid-1870s the reformers had gained a majority. The organization emerged as a meeting ground for traditionalists and radical Reform leaders.[104]

The easterners were also united in their distrust of Wise, who, they thought, liked to portray himself as the lone champion of Jewish learning in America. They remained scornful of "that college of Wise's" and rebuffed his requests for contributions from the New York congregations. They resented Wise's grandiosity when he, they claimed, spoke about the young school as if it were "the grandest institution of Jewish learning ever established in the world since the time of Johanan ben Sacchai [sic]."[105]

Soon after the East Coast convention, the UAHC met in Washington, D.C., to commemorate the country's centennial; again it was Lilienthal who tried to foster peace by speaking about the proposed New York school in a positive vein. He praised the effort to open another school, declaring that there was plenty of room for more than one seminary in America. He urged the UAHC to back a resolution congratulating the founders of the New York school and wishing them success.[106] His conciliatory effort inspired the UAHC to form a committee whose purpose was to confer with the Board of Delegates of American Israelites and formulate a plan for concerted action. The committee's proposal ultimately used some of the same language as Lilienthal's original resolution.[107]

The cause of unity was helped by the fact that some of the men active on the Board of Delegates were now also members of the UAHC. These reformers saw the benefit of a merger between the two groups, although the traditionalists feared that the merger would lessen their influence.[108] Despite his qualms, Mayer Sulzberger, a traditional lay leader, agreed to address the council at the 1876 UAHC convention in Washington on behalf of the Board of Delegates. Although the actual merger would take two years to finalize, the groups agreed to cooperate on a project to collect statistics on American Jewry.[109]

In the meantime, the New Yorkers did open the Hebrew Theological Seminary, which, by March 1877, boasted twenty-five students. Its faculty consisted of Moses Mielziner, a fine Talmudist, and one other teacher. As late as June 1877, the supporters of the new school still resisted efforts to unite with Hebrew Union College.[110] Sensing that their reticence was based on their distrust of him, Wise commented in the *Israelite* that these gentlemen erroneously believed that he monopolized all the power in the UAHC.[111]

At the annual meeting of the UAHC in June 1877, the joint committee was able to report progress on a plan that would make the Board of Delegates an arm of the UAHC. Lilienthal's rabbinic friend Solomon Wolfenstein, a member of the merger committee, was delighted by the prospect of a truly national organization that would transcend parties and regions.[112] The final details of the merger were worked out by the time of the UAHC annual conference in July 1878, when the two sides celebrated an unprecedented moment of American Jewish unity. Moritz Ellinger, editor of the *Jewish Times*, recounted how pleasant it was to see men who had warred against each other for years shake hands and converse in friendship. During the banquet Ellinger offered a toast: "No East, no West should now divide our common religious interests. We are one people, we are brethren, let us join hands."[113]

Although Einhorn had fought Wise since he had come to America, in the last year of his life he became a member of the Board of Governors of Hebrew Union College. The Hebrew Theological Seminary in New York was transformed into a preparatory school for the Cincinnati rabbinic school. In 1879, Lilienthal was one of three rabbis appointed to examine the New York school. Some of the traditionalists, such as Frederick de Sola Mendes, served as examiners for the Cincinnati school. The *American Hebrew*, which represented the views of the traditionalists, praised the college in the following terms: "For framing minds of such tendencies the Hebrew Union College possesses possibilities, which only require efficient co-operation and encouragement from the American Jewish public, to develop into a permanently fruitful institution."[114]

In 1881, when the new college building was opened, the *American Hebrew* called it "an event in Jewish history" that was achieved by intrepid men despite many obstacles.[115] Lilienthal's quarter-century-old dream of a unification of the liberal and moderate wings of American Jewry had, for the moment, been achieved.

Even before the final reconciliation had taken place, Lilienthal initiated efforts to fulfill his last major goal: an organization of rabbis and scholars.[116] He thought that if rabbis and ministers met regularly in a congenial atmosphere, they would be able to solve many of the important problems facing modern Judaism by, in his words, "harmonizing religion and science, practical life with tradition, and silencing the antagonistic voices of atheism and pessimism."[117] Having been involved in many polemical battles over the years, Lilienthal had no illusions about the substantive differences between the various parties, but he believed that only "from controversy will the truth be created."[118]

At the annual UAHC conference in July 1877, Lilienthal announced, "The undersigned beg leave to inform your honorable body that they have united for the purpose of starting a Jewish Literary Association, consisting both of ministers and laymen."[119] He hoped that the group would share information on ancient and modern Jewish literature, especially from the perspective of German scholarship. The group would discuss theological questions, organize lectures, publish a quarterly, and afford access to the latest scholarly views to the students at Hebrew Union College who could not read German.[120] Beyond this explicit agenda, Lilienthal wanted to use scholarship to raise the professional level of the American rabbinate. As the organization developed, this more general purpose became clearer.

The UAHC leadership that Lilienthal was addressing was painfully aware of the need to raise standards among American clergy. The Union's founding purpose was to establish a seminary dedicated to the education of American-trained ministers and teachers. Many of the congregations, particularly in the sparsely settled regions of the West, had to function without any trained leadership. As a stopgap measure the organization tried to set up a system of circuit rabbis who could preach at small congregations every three or four weeks. The UAHC was also concerned about rabbis without credentials who "imposed" themselves on congregations.[121] President Loth advocated a system whereby rabbis would record their credentials in a book held by the Executive Board of the Union. This would also protect legitimate rabbis from "the perils of slander."[122] These proposals reflect the low standards and the chaotic state of the field in which Lilienthal, Wise, and a few other success stories obscured the fragile stature of the majority of Jewish clergy.

A year later, at the 1878 annual conference in Milwaukee, the Rabbinical Literary Association was formally organized; a constitution was adopted, and an executive committee was appointed. Lilienthal, the chairman, promised "to complete the organization before July 1879, when the association will meet in New York to elect permanent officers and begin its work."[123]

The New York meeting attracted rabbis from across the spectrum from the traditionalist camp to the radical reformers. Lilienthal was elected president. Lilienthal also took advantage of his stay in New York to meet with Samuel Isaacs, editor of the *Jewish Messenger* and of *Hebraica*, a publication that Lilienthal hoped to merge with the quarterly that the Rabbinical Literary Association would produce.

During 1878, Lilienthal had been corresponding with prominent scholars in Europe, including Ludwig Philippson of Bonn, Adolph Jellinek of Vienna, and Heinrich Graetz of Breslau, who all agreed to be honorary members of the new group. Jellinek, a prominent scholar and rabbi, promised to help the association acquire a valuable library. Graetz, the noted historian of the Jewish people, suggested that the literary association join hands with a similar group established by the Alliance Israelite in Paris to jointly sponsor prizes for essays in Jewish scholarship and develop textbooks on Jewish theology.[124] This correspondence fulfilled Lilienthal's wish for Jewish scholars in Europe and America to collaborate on a rabbinic course of study. Almost forty years earlier a naïve Maskil had contacted some of these same scholars in the hope of bringing modern education to Russian Jewry. Now a mature, respected leader of American Jewry, Lilienthal readily attained their cooperation for his rabbinic organization. The response must have been gratifying.

The next year, in Detroit, the first convention of the Rabbinical Literary Association took place. According to Lilienthal, "During the whole meeting, it was not once necessary to call any speaker to order; everyone, it appears, knew exactly his place and duty. . . . It was on the whole, one of the most pleasant and most dignified meetings we have attended."[125] The discussions, open to the public, were energetic but cordial. The rabbis heard a variety of papers, such as "The Law," "Pedagogics in Sabbath Schools," and "Theology in the Age of Criticism."[126] Lilienthal thought that the meeting promised "the happy dawn of peace and concerted effort among [American Jewry's] teachers."[127] Wise, who had a history of turbulent behavior at these conferences, attended with a good deal of trepidation. Later, he acknowledged that the meeting's success was due to his friend. "The venerable leader [Lilienthal] has again taught us the lesson of peace."[128]

The conference focused on much more than literary and theological discussions. Committees were formed to create curricula and textbooks for Sabbath schools and to encourage the institution of weekday prayer services. Commissions were also formed to consider myriad halakhic issues that were controversial within American Jewry, from kashrut, marriage, and divorce laws to funeral rituals. The commissions were to gather and present all the pertinent historical and literary material on these issues.[129] By considering these practical areas of Jewish ritual life, the conference consciously went beyond its function as a literary discussion group and revealed its intention to become a rabbinic union. The question arose, Could they take the next step of ruling on the legal issues they were studying? To examine this issue, they set up a further commission to decide whether a rabbinic court or synod would be compatible with the stated purposes of the Rabbinical Literary Association.[130] Lilienthal had addressed this issue directly in his opening remarks: "We do not, and cannot claim, as at present constituted, any legislative authority."[131] He was not sure whether such authority was even advisable in America, where the autonomy of each congregation and its leadership was so important, but he left the door open for the possibility. The commission on a synod, made up of Wise, Kaufmann Kohler (Einhorn's son-in-law and successor at Temple Beth El in New York), Gustav Gottheil of Temple Emanu-El in New York, and James Gutheim, Gottheil's associate rabbi, was asked to report back at the next annual conference.

A commission on "the duties of the Rabbi and His Position in the Congregation" furthered revealed the intention of the Rabbinical Literary Association to move beyond its purpose as a literary group. Given the chaotic conditions that rabbis and congregations faced, particularly in the West, it was important to these leaders to create guidelines regulating this relationship. This focus on rabbi-congregation relations was perhaps the most important element in the association's attempt to professionalize the rabbinate.

The *Hebrew Review*, the quarterly journal of the Rabbinical Literary Association, reported these proceedings in detail, along with the texts of the papers delivered at the conference. Lilienthal, who edited this periodical, sent the journal to all association members and other subscribers.[132] He also noted that some German and French articles were being translated for subsequent issues.

Predictably, as traditional rabbis read the proceedings, they were angered by some of the more controversial issues the group raised. The *American Hebrew*, a newspaper representing the traditionalists in New York, had initially lauded the formation of the Rabbinical Literary Association and its "energetic president," but it reacted strongly to the publication of Wise's paper on "The Law" in the *Hebrew Review*. The traditionalist newspaper called for Wise's resignation as president of Hebrew Union College, arguing that if Wise really believed that only the Ten Commandments were unchangeable law, then it was hypocritical for him to teach at a school that emphasized the study of traditional texts. The paper actually misinterpreted Wise's article, which argued that the Decalogue was the basis for all Jewish law.[133]

The traditionalist group may have been wary of Lilienthal's organization in any case, because its sole representative on the original board, Frederick de Sola Mendes, withdrew sometime after the 1879 meeting. Clearly, Lilienthal had not achieved the broad-based unity he had hoped for, but as usual he remained optimistic.

> We heartily welcome the criticism on the articles in the *Review* published by the weekly Jewish Press. It reflects the various shades and opinions which now prevail in Judaism. The chaos which hangs over many a vital question can be dispelled only by a discussion and an earnest exchange of ideas. In this era of transition it is the only means of securing harmony for the future. As long as personalities are avoided, and only the case in question is argued, success will finally be secured.[134]

The number of attendees at the second meeting of the Rabbinical Literary Association, held in Chicago in July 1881, grew to almost thirty. As a conciliatory gesture toward the more traditional clergy, a banquet, sponsored by Congregation Bene Shalom, held in honor of the conference was strictly kosher.[135] Nevertheless, the harmony that had pervaded the first gathering was broken on several other occasions. The first outburst came over the issue of whether a synod should be established. Samuel Hirsch, the radical reformer who had hosted the 1869 Philadelphia conference, denounced Wise's advocacy of such a gathering, beginning with reasoned arguments but drifting into a personal attack on Wise.[136] Some leaders, distrusting Wise and the power he already wielded through the college and UAHC, feared a synod would only add to his control of American Reform. Wise appealed to Lilienthal to stop the attack. When Lilienthal was unable to do so, Wise left the hall and Lilienthal adjourned the session.[137]

At the same conference a paper presented by Moritz Ellinger, "Ancient and Modern Rabbis," elicited more fireworks. Ellinger, not a rabbi himself, discussed the new and increased responsibilities of the modern rabbinate. He suggested that the number of capable rabbinic leaders had decreased and that many rabbis lacked enthusiasm for their work. Rabbi Emil Hirsch (son of Samuel Hirsch and a son-in-law of David Einhorn) angrily rejected the negative characterization, blaming the demoralization of American rabbis on autocratic lay leadership. This time Lilienthal was able to turn the controversy in a productive direction, with a resolution making the professionalization of the rabbinate a major focus of the Rabbinical Literary Association.

The association formed a committee to consider establishing a "mutual protective and aid association" for Jewish ministers. A fund, created by annual contributions, would help sick or unemployed members with no other means of support. Another committee was appointed to formulate regulations for the engagement of ministers and to define the responsibilities of clergy and congregations to each other.[138]

A continuation of the efforts of the previous convention, the work of these committees represented the beginnings of a union to provide mutual support for its members. Historian Alan Silverstein has suggested that these efforts of Reform leaders to create standards, mutual support, and formalized clergy-congregation relationships in the rabbinate in the 1880s followed a broader shift in American society. Protestant ministers sought to transform their vocation into a profession in a desire for more status within a growing culture of professionalism that had spread since the Civil War. They formed literary and professional groups and worked hard to raise the standards for clergy training.[139] Lilienthal, ever attentive to American trends, also followed the lead of these professional societies, which established codes of ethics and standardized expectations for their members in the late nineteenth century.[140] The Rabbinical Literary Association was the first attempt at a national rabbinic professional union in America.[141] It also predated any similar organization in Europe by decades.

Securing the professional status of the rabbi was a cause close to Lilienthal's heart. Having served in the American rabbinate for thirty-five years, longer than any other rabbi in America, Lilienthal had ample experience with the early power struggles between the lay and rabbinic leadership that had made the careers of all the first rabbis in America so challenging. He had also created a new model for the American rabbi with his service to the broader community. Although he had personally found job security and satisfaction through a lifetime contract and a substantial salary, many other rabbis still suffered from low salaries, lack of status, and job insecurity. Lilienthal hoped the professional organization would be "the crowning point of the years I have spent in my holy and responsible office."[142]

Lilienthal poured considerable passion and energy into the Rabbinical Literary Association in his final years. In the process he established the basis for what would become the Central Conference of American Rabbis, the third important pillar of Reform Jewry. Although he had taken a backseat to his friend Wise in the creation of the UAHC and Hebrew Union College, here Lilienthal, who had successfully figured out what it meant to be a rabbi in the American environment, took the lead.

8

Legacy

Lilienthal remained vital and active in the full range of his professional, civic, and educational projects. His life in Cincinnati was rich, surrounded by family and friends. His youngest daughter, Victoria (b. 1861), then in her late teens, presided over his home. He referred to her as "my Vicky." It was in those days that he hosted the rabbinic students of Hebrew Union College, as well as the elite of Cincinnati society, on Friday evenings.

Lilienthal's older children were creating lives of their own. The daughters found husbands. Eliza (b. 1846) married Leopold Werner, who owned a large cloak manufacturing business in New York. Esther (1853) married a Mr. Heavenrich and moved to Saginaw, Michigan.[1]

The Lilienthal sons all went on to careers in business and banking. The family became involved in the network of the German Jewish elite of New York and San Francisco. The rabbi worked hard to advance the financial security of his children. He believed that the economic future of the United States was in the rapidly multiplying opportunities for those engaged in business. He used his relationship with prominent Cincinnati businessmen, such as Bene Israel's president, Julius Freiberg, to obtain positions for his children and nephews. He also used his connection with the Seligman family to help his children in both New York and San Francisco.[2]

His sons were close friends with the sons of his brother Samuel. They went into business together and used their connections to help each other. In 1871 Lilienthal wrote to Theodore to suggest that the extended family form a small bank on the model of the Seligmans or Rothschilds. Nothing came of it at that time.[3] However, in 1880 the sons of Max and Samuel Lilienthal formed the Lilienthal Pact.[4] Max's son, Jesse Lilienthal, a Harvard-trained lawyer, first suggested the measure to the other sons and cousins. The pact was meant to create "a common fund for the benefit of all, subscribing thereto, and by the union of all their resources, to be better able to prosecute their several undertakings to a successful termination . . . [and] to protect and make more complete the unity that has heretofore characterized them in their associations."[5] The pact was to remain in force until January 1904, when it would be divided among the survivors or their heirs. The pact worked remarkably well, financing business ventures and the purchase of homes. Although they never achieved the kind of wealth of the Seligmans or Rothschilds, the pact allowed the extended family to "live both comfortably and well for almost twenty-five years."[6]

Trip to San Francisco

One of Lilienthal's brother's sons, in whose career Lilienthal was particularly instrumental, was Ernest, Samuel and Caroline's third son. Lilienthal suggested that Ernest come to Cincinnati to study law and then got him a position at one of the prestigious law firms in Cincinnati.[7] After being admitted to the bar, Ernest decided that he wanted to be a merchant. Again Max reached out to his friend Julius Freiberg, the head of Freiberg and Workum, a wholesale liquor distributor. Ernest opened up a San Francisco branch of the company with Max's endorsement for the credit line. The firm did well and expanded. Other Lilienthal children joined the company. Ernest became an important businessman in San Francisco as his company became the largest wholesale liquor firm in the West.

Ernest met and fell in love with Bella Sloss, daughter of the wealthy San Francisco merchant Louis Sloss. After a lengthy courtship, the Sloss family agreed to the match. The wedding was scheduled for May 1876, and there was no question that Lilienthal would be invited to co-officiate with Rabbi Elkan Cohn of Temple Emanu-El of San Francisco.[8]

The 62-year-old rabbi was happy to celebrate the wedding of his beloved nephew. However, he also relished the opportunity to explore the exciting West where some of his family were making homes. This trip was possible because Lilienthal would not have to take the slow and hazardous route of the early pioneers. Just seven years earlier, in 1869, the first transcontinental railroad had been completed, making the trip relatively quick and comfortable. Lilienthal and his brother Samuel took the Union Pacific to Utah, the Central Pacific to Oakland, and finally a ferry to San Francisco.[9]

Reading Lilienthal's account, published in a series of articles in the *American Israelite* (June 2 and 9, 1876), we encounter a man still enthusiastic about new experiences. The details of his account recall his rich essays on life in Russia, written for the *Israelite* in the 1850s. He comments exuberantly:

> We live in an age of progress. Though Ecclesiastes says, "There is nothing new under the sun." Did you ever hear that a minister traveled three thousand miles to perform a marriage ceremony? . . . I went from Cincinnati to San Francisco to perform the holy ceremony at the wedding of my nephew, Mr. Ernest Lilienthal, with Bella, the daughter of Louis and Sarah Sloss, a prominent member of the Alaska Fur Company.[10]

Lilienthal described the many states that they passed through, commenting on the Jewish brethren he encountered on the way. On his arrival in Ogden, Utah, he noted that Jews were considered Gentiles there. Taking a side trip, he wondered at the beauty of the Great Salt Lake and Salt Lake City, where he visited the Mormon Tabernacle, capable of seating 15,000 people. He also made it a point to find out about the small Jewish population of Salt Lake City. Returning to Ogden, Samuel and Max prepared for the forty-eight hour trip to San Francisco. Lilienthal described the mountains of the Sierra Nevada range and the arrival in Sacramento, where he and his brother were greeted warmly by their sons Philip and Leo.[11]

Lilienthal also marveled at their accommodations in San Francisco. "Our sons and nephews had engaged rooms for us in the Palace Hotel, the largest and finest in the world—the Grand Hotel of Paris not excepted. It occupies an entire block of ground, 344 by 265 feet, and is seven stories high. The entrance and court are of surpassing grandeur and beauty; it is another wonder of California."[12] The rabbi was staggered by the number of both Jewish and Christian millionaires in California.[13] The wedding itself reinforced his impression of the incredible wealth generated by the Gold Rush. It is described in detail in *Ernest Reuben Lilienthal and His Family*. Suffice it to say that the wedding was sumptuous. A pavilion and tent, built especially for the occasion, covered the entire lawn of the bride's parents' home. The wedding dinner menu was printed in gold letters on white silk. It made no attempt to conform to kashrut. The first course was oysters, and a later course featured frog legs. No one seems to have made any comment about this issue. Louis and Sarah Sloss built the wedding couple a three-story home. Ernest presented his bride with a set of solitaire diamond earrings.[14]

While in San Francisco, the rabbi created a stir when his old friend, Rev. E. Rexford, now in San Francisco, invited him to preach before an "immense audience" at his Unitarian church. Lilienthal commented at that time:

> I always cheerfully seize the opportunity of stating before a Christian audience the sublime doctrines of our religion. For Christians they are a "terra incognita." . . . The masses in general hear Judaism decried so much, either in the pulpit, or in the Sunday School, that a fair and impartial judgment can scarcely be expected. Hence, I always seize the opportunity whenever offered to preach in churches and to speak on Judaism and its liberal tendencies.[15]

Speaking at churches had become commonplace for Lilienthal in Cincinnati, but this unprecedented event caused a great sensation in San Francisco.

The return trip was made in luxury. The young married couple joined Lilienthal and his brother in "one of Mr. Pullman's new Palace Cars."[16] The young couple were on their way to the Centennial Exposition in Philadelphia for the honeymoon. Ernest's biographer notes, "We may be sure that Rabbi Max, to whom the Declaration of Independence had become another holy book, instructed them well as to the significance of the Centennial."[17] The somewhat amusing scene in which Lilienthal lectured the young couple, trapped on a lengthy train trip with him, on the meaning of the Declaration of Independence showed that he never lost that religious wonder about the core American symbols. Apparently the new bride and groom did not resent sharing the car with Lilienthal and Samuel on the beginning of their honeymoon. O'Neill reports that Bella was glad to have time to get to know the two elder Lilienthal men, because there had not been time to get acquainted during the prewedding preparations.[18]

From these episodes in the rabbi's later life we can see certain continuities with his lifelong preoccupations. Lilienthal's fascination with travel and learning about different people was intact from his earliest youth. His interest in the conditions of the Jewish people wherever he went remained as well.

We also see a pronounced emphasis on material well-being. Lilienthal wanted his family to be well-off (although he was not personally interested in a luxurious lifestyle) and worked hard to ensure this. According to O'Neill, "Max, because of his contacts with big businessmen, had foreseen the growth of American business and its far-reaching effects on the status of the family."[19] This theme had already been sounded in Lilienthal's letters from Russia to his family. He had closely followed international financial trends and had urged his family members to immigrate to the United States.[20] In his private school in New York, Lilienthal willingly gave up the ideal of a classical humanistic education to accommodate the realities of the German immigrants whose children stopped their education in their early teens to begin earning a living.

As he became more liberal, Lilienthal sided with the Jewish merchants of Mantua who wanted to abolish the second day of Jewish festivals in the Diaspora because it was detrimental to their business interests. In his 1854 *Asmonean* article Lilienthal declared that Reform helped to reconcile a contradiction between "the necessities of active life and the dead forms of religion."[21] For Lilienthal the seeming contradiction between a spiritual life and a successful business life was reconciled through Reform Judaism. It allowed the businessman to avoid the hypocrisy that Lilienthal saw among the traditionalists in his community who had two kinds of *Shulhan Arukh*, one for home and one for abroad.[22] Reform allowed them to embrace the commercial spirit of the time without ambivalence.

Lilienthal's enthusiastic patriotism comes through in a late letter to his son Philip. In 1877, soon after his inauguration, President Hayes visited Cincinnati. Lilienthal delivered the welcoming address as the new president arrived at the train station. Lilienthal proudly told his son, "He immediately came up to me first of all, and the only one, and grasping my hand, said: 'Dr. Lilienthal, I am very happy to meet you.'"[23]

Lilienthal described how he rode in the first carriage after the president's. Mrs. Hayes greeted him and treated him like an old friend. During the president's speech, Lilienthal told his son that he stood at the president's side and was acknowledged by him. He told his son that he had received daily compliments from his address.[24] This letter recalls the many letters Lilienthal sent home to his family from Russia. Then he had regaled his father, brother, and fiancée with his encounters with ministers and the emperor. In this late letter we can still hear the starry-eyed youth, awed by attention from state officials.

Eighteen-eighty was a year of great fulfillment for this elder statesman of American Judaism. In June Lilienthal marked the twenty-fifth anniversary of his rabbinate at Bene Israel. The synagogue prepared a gala celebration for their beloved leader. The *American Israelite* reported, "At 10 a.m. the organ grandly pealed forth Beethoven's Anthem,[25] as Dr. Max Lilienthal, surrounded by his children and the officers of his congregation, entered the Temple. The interior of the latter was splendidly festooned with wreaths of evergreen."[26] Wise, in his tribute to his old friend, summed up his impact on Cincinnati.

> Dr. Lilienthal has become a blessing in our community for peace, good will and the progress of humanitarian feelings and principles. . . . I could speak of the God-blessed work which Dr. Lilienthal has accomplished in the twenty-five years in this congregation, in this temple, in this school for religious instruction, in the board of Education, and the University, even at the head of a medical college of this city. I could speak of the God-blessed work of the honored man done in and for the Hebrew Union College, for the Union of American Hebrew Congregations, for the charities and benevolent institutions of our city.[27]

Surrounded by his children, his adoring congregation, and admiring rabbinic colleagues, Lilienthal could feel the satisfaction of a man whose long struggle to create a new model for the American rabbinate had come to fruition.

In 1882 the American Jewish community chose Lilienthal to make an arduous trip to Russia with Moritz Ellinger on a mission of support for Russian Jewry. Saddened by the news of anti-Jewish repression of the tsarist government following the assassination of Alexander II, Lilienthal felt compelled to address the condition of his coreligionists.[28] These developments depressed him so much that a despairing tone entered his last sermons and writings.[29] Still, Lilienthal held out the hope that these retrogressions were only a brief aberration. "But this storm will pass away. The Jew knows it. . . . And he will succeed, for adaptability is one of his recognized characteristics. He will throw off the stained rags of the pariah and don the toga of the free citizen, of the free man, in the noble and proud sense of the word. He will never surrender his abiding faith in a better future of the human race."[30]

Lilienthal's friends convinced him to postpone the arduous trip, originally scheduled for midwinter, until the summer of 1882.[31] That would have been a remarkable trip for the rabbi, revisiting the place where his career had been launched. Yet as he prepared, his health gave out. His demise came quickly, according to the *American Israelite*.

On Saturday evening, April 1st, Dr. Lilienthal was cheerful and lively, complaining only of a trifling oppression in the chest but displaying to calling friends more or less of his gracious manner and fine humor, retiring to rest at about eleven o'clock. After midnight, or rather on Sunday morning at about four o'clock, he was attacked suddenly by a paralytic stroke, affecting the whole of the left side of his face and body.[32]

His family, living as far away as New York and San Francisco, hurried to his side. During the few days that he lingered, he was able to recognize them sporadically. Although his body was paralyzed, he retained the power of speech, conversing with them in French, German, and English.[33] Lilienthal died peacefully on April 5, 1882, at the age of 67, surrounded by his brother, his children, and many admirers.

Lilienthal's funeral was the largest Cincinnati had ever seen. The *American Israelite* gave a full account.

> Sunday, April 9, 1882, will ever be a memorable day in the annals of Cincinnati, for upon it was committed to mother earth all that remained of him, whose name had become our household word. . . . The day began dark and gloomy, as if heaven itself joined in the general weeping; but at about 10 o'clock the clouds rolled away and bathed the solemn concourse in a flood of April sunshine. The bells upon the city towers had not ceased chiming the hour of nine when the main doors of the Temple were thrown open to admit the funeral cortege.[34]

The simple pine coffin was draped in black but the room was almost overwhelmed by the numerous floral offerings. The thousands who attended the service were a measure of Lilienthal's impact on Cincinnati and wider American Jewry. Adolph Moses of Louisville, who gave the first oration, wondered aloud, "Where is the sage, the amiable counselor and friend of the truth and the needy?"[35] Following a musical interlude, Wise spoke, requiring a few moments to compose himself and dry his tears. He was devastated by the death of his co-worker, whom he tenderly referred to by his Hebrew name, Menachem.

> I lament the loss of the man who has brought us all nearer to one another in the kindness of his heart by his pleasant and conciliatory words and his restless work in the vineyard of humanity and broth-

erly love. . . . With all of you I feel the loss we sustain by the death of this Rabbi in Israel, who was a banner-bearer in our midst, a Captain of the Host of the Lord, a harbinger of peace, whose vacant place in the ranks of our champions cannot easily be filled.[36]

The most emotional moment came as Wise finished his address.

But better than all do I know what I have lost, with whom I have lived and toiled, suffered and hoped, prayed and struggled these thirty-six years. Therefore, I can not speak, for I can not yet think; therefore I can only lament and weep. . . . Forgive me, I can do no better. Forgive me, my eyes are sore, my heart aches; forgive my faults and short-comings. Be an angel of peace and consolation in heaven above as thou hast been on earth below.[37]

After Wise spoke, there was silence in the large congregation, broken only by sobs. Next to speak was Lilienthal's old friend, the Unitarian minister Thomas Vickers, with whom Lilienthal had made history through their pulpit exchange. Now rector of the University of Cincinnati, Vickers focused primarily on Lilienthal's contribution to public education. Finally Rabbi Aaron Hahn of Cleveland spoke of Lilienthal's role as peacemaker within the factions of American Jewry. At the end of the services the immense group marched slowly out of the temple. The *American Israelite* reported that the procession was so long that it took a full hour for the entire group to pass by. In the funeral cortege many organizations in which Lilienthal had served were represented, including the lay leadership of the local synagogues, the Forresters, the University Board, the Board of Education, the Young Men's Hebrew Association, the Allemania Club, the German Pioneer Association, the City Relief Union, the Institute of Technology, the Board of Governors, students, and faculty of the Hebrew Union College, and the Cleveland Orphan Asylum. Perhaps 2,000 mourners gathered for the burial service in the cemetery. After the Kaddish was recited, Wise reverently dropped the first shovels full of dirt into the open grave. Each member of the family followed. At the end of the burial service the large crowd slowly left the cemetery.

Max Lilienthal had lived to see the accomplishment of his major goals for American Judaism. The Union of American Hebrew Congregations had been founded on a solid basis and was expanding its membership yearly. Hebrew Union College was well established and accepted by the spectrum of American Jewry from radical reformers to traditionalists. And the Rabbinical Literary Association, which Lilienthal had personally brought into being, had begun the process of uplifting the profession and providing support for its members.[38]

LEGACY

Max Lilienthal traveled vast distances in his active, rich, and exciting life—both geographically and spiritually. No other rabbi of his era served in that capacity from St. Petersburg to San Francisco. He also intellectually traversed the ideological spectrum from Orthodoxy to radical Reform as he struggled to reconcile the tensions between Jewish tradition and modernity throughout his career. As his nephew Ernest commented, "Max suffered in himself the whole transition from the old orthodoxy to reform."[39] Like the hero of a nineteenth-century bildungsroman, his life was marked by constant change and searching.

Unfortunately for anyone wanting to document that spiritual journey, Lilienthal was reticent about revealing his internal processes. Unlike his friend Wise, he produced no autobiography. However, based on insights of friends and through the observation of various recurring trends, it is possible to reconstruct that long, arduous spiritual journey.

The basic theme of Lilienthal's entire life was the need to reconcile opposites. The conflict between tradition and modernity was established in his childhood. When Lilienthal was still a child, he attended the strictly Orthodox yeshiva in Fürth. His *rosh yeshivah*, Rabbi Wolf Hamburger, had taught that the study of secular subjects was like the evil woman of Proverbs: "None who go to her will return again" (Proverbs 2:19). For Hamburger, secular learning was like a female temptress who would seduce you, given any exposure to her. Rabbi Hamburger chose to close his school rather than introduce government-mandated secular studies.

The rabbi had identified the assimilatory pressure inherent in modernity. The Enlightenment vision of a unified world, based on reason, had an underlying coercive message to ethnic and religious minorities: conform. Both legal and societal pressures demanded homogenization. Modern education threatened traditional ways of thought, but the state also demanded social and behavioral change—different clothes, occupations, and ways of worship to earn equal rights. European Jews responded along a continuum from full accommodation to resistance to modernity.[40]

Lilienthal's parents had already made the choice to embrace modernity when, at the time of his birth, they moved to Munich, away from the traditional setting of their native valley of Schnaittach-Huttenbach. The cosmopolitan environment of the Bavarian capital brought the family into contact with modern and liberalizing trends. Like other wealthy middle-class

German Jews, the Lilienthals chose to embrace the ideology of Haskalah. Believing that a secular education was the guarantor of a successful future, Max's parents exposed their son to a thorough humanistic education from his earliest home tutoring. Lilienthal's studies at the University of Munich continued this process of immersion in secular studies and *Wissenschaft* methodology, infused with the spirit of *Bildung*—self-creation. He was taught to question assumptions and to apply scientific methodology.

Trying to work out his inner conflict, the young scholar became fascinated with the reconciliation of opposites. This is why he was drawn to study Alexandrian Jewry in his dissertation. He explained in the introduction that he was attracted to the topic because the community reconciled heathenism (Greek philosophy) and monotheism. It was through the dialectical confrontation of these opposites that a new, more sophisticated Judaism emerged.

The tension between traditionalism and modernity became painful for Lilienthal when he returned to the Orthodox Würzburg yeshiva to gain the expertise necessary to receive rabbinic ordination. His letters to his fiancée Pepi during this period reveal the turmoil he underwent readjusting to that traditional environment. In his first sermons he bemoans the current strife over Reform issues and articulates his lifelong theme of peace and toleration of differences.

In Russia Lilienthal saw how far he had already traveled along the path to modernity when he compared himself to the profoundly traditional Russian Jews. He commented in letters home that he felt thrust back several centuries as he entered the Jewish towns of the Pale. Believing fervently in maskilic messianism, Lilienthal worked mightily to reconcile the vast chasm between the shtetl Jews and modernity through compulsory secular studies, thereby hoping to help the suffering masses of Russian Jews earn emancipation.

Arriving in New York, Lilienthal struggled to adjust to a new country, a new language, a chaotic immigrant Jewish community, and three fractious traditional German congregations who did not really want him to assert leadership. In his inaugural sermon he called on the reformers and traditionalists to resolve their differences on the basis of Jewish law. Still a traditional Jew, he told the readers of the *Allgemeine Zeitung des Judenthums* that Reform was needed in Europe only to help earn emancipation and was not relevant in free America. He reported to the paper, whose readers included prominent reformers, that "Germany's reformatory aspiration, which has its roots . . . in the striving for emancipation, likewise finds little approval here, since men are free from the outset."[41] At this point, it would seem that Lilienthal saw Reform more as a strategy that European Jewry was forced to adapt, not as an ideology with value in its own right.

The inner shift began in Lilienthal after he left his pulpit in 1847. Bitterness over the backwardness and resistance of the traditional German immigrant community to his modernizing agenda led him to temporarily leave the rabbinate. Inspired by the revolutionary fervor of 1848 and freed by the financial and spiritual autonomy he had achieved by the success of his private school, Lilienthal moved left along the spectrum. Yet when he declared that the bridge to the past had been broken in his Lichtfreunde address, he still worried about what had been lost. "We yearn for the old certainty, for the old unity, for the old peace and ask ourselves: 'What has the tearing apart produced?'"[42] Lilienthal used his maskilic and *Wissenschaft* background to make sense of the changes, both in the world and within himself. Science justified the break from the past, he declared.

In 1854 Lilienthal's *Asmonean* articles revealed that he had discovered a positive content and purpose for Reform Judaism. Reform (informed by *Wissenschaft*) allowed Jews to adapt to the modern world by differentiating the essence of Judaism from the historical accretions of centuries that developed into outmoded customs. By the time he had his exchange with Leeser in 1856 concerning the zeitgeist, he had come to believe that modernity was inevitable. Individuals participated in vast historical trends beyond their ability to control. Each generation worked out and expressed the spirit of their age. The legalism of the medieval period had given way to the contemporary spirit of reason and science expressed in Judaism as Reform.

Lilienthal's writing is infused with the spirit and methodology of both maskilic history and *Wissenschaft*. Were the reformist tendencies in his modern education becoming actualized in him, now that the conditions were right? Perhaps it was the combination of *Wissenschaft* and American conditions? Lilienthal argued that Reform was necessary to help maintain an authentic Judaism, in harmony with the spirit of the time and American conditions. Reform could help the immigrants, struggling for financial success, to practice Judaism without resorting to hypocrisy. Reform would also address the problems of apathy that afflicted congregants who saw little relevance in traditional Judaism as they tried to adjust to American life.

The rabbi used American civil religion to serve as a bridge between his maskilic and American values. Both views shared the premises of the Enlightenment: the belief in reason, the power of education, the freedom of the individual, and the promise of equality under the law. As Lilienthal retreated from traditional theology, he replaced it with an American patriotism infused with general religious symbolism. In this way he also helped his immigrant congregation to become both modern and American at the same time.

Over the years, Lilienthal gave up those aspects of his earlier faith that conflicted with his Americanism. In New York in his Lichtfreunde speech and in his *Asmonean* articles he had railed against materialism that threatened Jewish spirituality. Early on in New York, Lilienthal grudgingly accepted the fact that Jewish education was limited by the pragmatic nature of American life. He also complained that the drive to succeed financially was keeping the younger generation away from the synagogue. By the end of his life he fully embraced materialism. He imparted business advice to his children, encouraging them to enter fields where they could become financially secure.

Lilienthal also struggled early on in Cincinnati with those reformers who wanted to do away with much of Jewish particularism. Although they seemed to want a religion with minimal ceremony, he warned that "Judaism had to keep its particularity in order to fulfill its messianic purpose—of bringing all people to monotheism and defeating heathenism."[43] By the end of his life, Lilienthal had embraced a universalist approach that allowed him to equate his beliefs with those of the Unitarians. The messianic dream of one shared monotheistic faith would be realized in the new promised land of America.

Yet even Lilienthal was willing to set some limits on the assimilatory forces of modernity. He served as a prophet for the American civil religion, berating politicians who forgot to include Jews in their Thanksgiving proclamations and criticizing school officials who wanted to use the Bible in public school or who scheduled important events on Saturdays. He also attacked missionaries who tried to lure his congregants away from the practice of Judaism, even asserting Judaism's superiority. He would adjust his Judaism to America, but America had to fulfill its ideals by treating every religion equally. Having learned his lesson well in Russia, he repeatedly reminded his audiences that vigilance remained the price of liberty.[44]

So, was it American influences that pushed Lilienthal into radical Reform ideology? If that were the case, then rabbis such as Bernard Illowy would have had to follow suit. Illowy, who held a doctorate from the University of Budapest and was a former teacher of secular subjects in a Hungarian gymnasium, was certainly imbued with *Wissenschaft* values. He had also been exposed to American Jewish life for many years, serving pulpits in New York, Syracuse, Baltimore, St. Louis, New Orleans, and Cincinnati. He maintained his Orthodox stance to the end of his life. Even Wise, who had a similar background of university and rabbinic study, never moved from his moderate Reform position after many years in America.

There are no simple answers to the question of what motivated Lilienthal to travel the long ideological road from Orthodoxy to radical Reform.

Both his German background and American experiences were factors. Ultimately, however, the reason Lilienthal changed came down to his individual makeup. He had to find a solution to the tension between tradition and modernity that matched his need to reconcile opposite points of view. He could not tolerate as much dissonance between his Judaism and the modern world as others could. He was less of a resister to the seductions and pressures of modernity than Illowy and other traditionalists.

Lilienthal was obsessed with the need for peace in the Jewish world. As a rabbinic candidate in Germany, he condemned the acrimony resulting from the debates between reformers and traditionalists. In Russia he tried to bridge even larger differences between the Mitnagdim, Hasidim, Maskilim, and the Russian government. He argued for peace in his New York congregation and repeated the call in Cincinnati during the first Cleveland conference. The only thing that could have motivated Lilienthal to return to the polemical battles in the early 1870s was the desire to achieve peace between the various Reform factions to create a union of congregations, a rabbinic seminary, and a professional union.

Each time Lilienthal put himself forward to foster peace in the service of greater good for the Jewish community, he was deeply hurt by personal attacks (except in the 1870s, when his efforts were finally successful). Each time he suffered these disappointments and defeats, he temporarily withdrew into himself, and when he emerged, he had moved closer to the zeitgeist and had given up more of the tradition. Why he moved further left as a result of these incidents is not clear. Perhaps he was more sensitive to attacks from the traditional front. However, unlike his friend Wise, who seemed to relish a good fight and did not mind a little name-calling, Lilienthal took these attacks personally. As much as Lilienthal claimed to embrace a dialectical approach to progress, he seemed much happier promoting a peaceful acceptance of contradictory points of view. Indeed he was often called a prince of peace in his last years. Speaker after speaker at his funeral pointed to this as his most identifiable trait.[45]

The unity that Lilienthal and Wise had achieved by the late 1870s proved ephemeral. Lilienthal's dream of an American Jewish community that could tolerate differences in doctrine and practice and work together was unrealistic. By the mid-1880s the polarizing forces had intensified. The result was the permanent division of American Judaism into denominational movements. On the one hand, the Reform movement, under the leadership of Kaufmann Kohler, took an increasingly radical direction. On the other hand, the traditionalists began defining themselves and their concerns in a way that led to the creation of their own rabbinic school, the Jewish Theological Seminary.[46] Most scholars agree that two events were critical in precipitating the split: the "trefa banquet" of 1883 and the Pittsburgh platform of 1885. In both episodes, Lilienthal's diplomatic skills were sorely missed.

The first incident was meant to be the joyous conclusion of an epochal moment, the first ordination of American-trained rabbis from Hebrew Union College. In July 1883, amid tremendous excitement, Jewish leaders from all over the country assembled to celebrate the occasion, which also coincided with the tenth anniversary of the Union of American Hebrew Congregations. David Philipson recalled the excitement of the first ordination in the United States, calling the moment ecstatic.[47] The feeling shifted dramatically when the caterer for the celebratory dinner that followed served (out of ignorance) littleneck clams, crab, and shrimp salad and mixed milk and meat—all contrary to Jewish dietary laws. Some traditionalists walked out immediately. According to Michael Meyer, Wise had not been a party to this breach of kashrut. However, the faux pas brought into focus the substantive differences among the early supporters of Hebrew Union College.[48] Several traditional rabbis, such as Marcus Jastrow and Frederick de Sola Mendes, who had been an official examiner at the college, immediately distanced themselves from the reformers. Mendes complained, "Does the eleventh chapter of Leviticus form any part of the college edition of the Pentateuch?"[49] Rather than being conciliatory, Wise made jokes about Jews who were obsessed with "stomach Judaism." His defensive reaction at this critical juncture helped launch what would later result in the Conservative movement.[50]

When the traditionalists found a new spokesman in Alexander Kohut, who had recently arrived in New York from Hungary, it was Kohler and not Wise who responded with a spirited defense of Reform. Their debate hearkened back to the Leeser-Lilienthal exchange in 1856 that had crystallized the traditional and Reform positions for an earlier generation, but the spectrum had shifted to the left. Kohut captured the middle ground that had once been Lilienthal and Wise's, arguing for what he characterized as a golden mean between "rigid Orthodoxy" and "heartless Reform." Although allowing for change, Kohut asserted that authentic Judaism was based on an unbroken chain of law, reaching back to Moses. Kohler answered with the radical Reform position, describing Judaism as a religion of reason, premised on freedom and individuality and progressively revealed in each generation. Jews, he claimed, had matured beyond a dependence on law. The debate between the two scholars sharpened the ideological issues separating the two camps. American Jewry was moving away from the model of a theologically diverse union that Lilienthal had espoused.[51]

Meanwhile Kohler was also confronting a challenge from the left. Most Reform rabbis emphasized universalism in their characterization of modern Judaism. Lilienthal himself had said, "We know that the best religion is humanity, the best divine service, love thy neighbor as thyself; the motto which we inscribe on our banner is the common brotherhood of man."[52] In the 1870s and 1880s some liberal Jews and Christians began to see Unitarianism as identical to Reform Judaism because it too defined itself as the "religion of humanity."[53] Was it only a matter of time before the two would be united in a common universal faith? Reform rabbis felt compelled to underline the fundamental differences between the two liberal creeds.

Other Reform Jews were drawn toward the universalist doctrines of movements such as Ethical Culture. Denying the continued need for Jewish particularism and pushing the ethical and universalistic trends in Reform to their extremes, Felix Adler, son of Rabbi Samuel Adler of Temple Emanu-El in New York, founded the Ethical Culture Society in 1877. Jewish liberal intellectuals were attracted to Adler's popular lectures. He too forced Reform to define the boundary issues that justified a continuation of Judaism.

To clarify where Reform stood, both with regard to the traditionalists and to threats from these universalist movements, Kohler called the Pittsburgh conference in November 1885. Even though the conference elected Wise president, Wise's influence was minimal. Rabbi W. Gunther Plaut noted, "To be sure, the famed Isaac Wise of Cincinnati was elected President, which was a wise political move. For while the Cincinnati rabbi's ego was served, his theology was not. When the platform was adopted, his ideas had crumbled in defeat, and the far more radical philosophy of Einhorn, represented by Hirsch and Kohler, had carried the day."[54]

Against the universalists the Pittsburgh platform asserted the importance of the preservation and defense of Judaism and of the mission of the Jewish people as priests of the one God. Although the platform acknowledged much in common with the "modern era of universal culture of heart and intellect," there was still a distinct need for Jewish particularity.[55] Against the traditionalists it asserted that the system of Jewish law had been necessary only during its national period in Palestine, in order to train the people for their mission to spread "ethical monotheism." Now only the moral laws—and those ceremonial laws that, in their view, elevated and sanctified the modern Jew—were still binding. The authors of the Pittsburgh platform explicitly rejected the dietary laws and the priestly code as well as the notions of bodily resurrection and Heaven and Hell as the "abodes for everlasting punishment and reward."[56] The platform defined the classical position of Reform Judaism for its time.

Whatever Wise's private misgivings, he hailed the platform as a "Declaration of Independence."[57] The traditionalist leader Kohut bitterly asked, "Independence from what?" and answered his own question: "Independence from Judaism."[58] Wise threw himself enthusiastically into the polemical fray, defending the platform as if it were his own. He claimed that Reform Jews were now "the orthodox Jews in America" because Reform represented "the overwhelming majority of all American Jewish citizens." He warned the traditionalist group that they would have to join the reformers or remain isolated.[59]

The Pittsburgh platform served to finalize the split between the traditionalists and the reformers. Within months, Sabato Morais, Alexander Kohut, and others founded the Jewish Theological Seminary of America. Sabbath observance, dietary laws, Hebrew language, and resettlement of the Land of Israel were among the defining concerns of their program, which eventually gave rise to the Conservative movement.[60] It would be this movement that helped to Americanize the millions of traditional Eastern European immigrants.

Yet to say that Lilienthal's impact was transitory would also be incorrect. The educational, social, and benevolent institutions he helped to form, both in the Jewish and the general community, became models for other later efforts. Although the Union of American Hebrew Congregations and Hebrew Union College never fulfilled their original purpose as all-embracing institutions, they continue to serve as an umbrella for an important segment of American Jewry, namely, Reform Judaism. All the other American Jewish denominations have emulated the organizational model that Lilienthal helped to establish—a national congregational union, a rabbinic college, and a rabbinic organization—for their key institutions.

Lilienthal's most important historical contribution was the creation of a model for a post-emancipation rabbinate. In doing so, he was furthering, in the cultural realm, the same impulse to bridge opposites that he had attempted ideologically. The German Jewish immigrants were caught between the desire to retain their cultural identity and assimilate into the general American culture. According to Mark Bauman and Arnold Shankman, they wanted acceptance from the dominant group within the adoptive society, in which they felt marginal. "Ethnic brokers" bridge the gap between the two cultures in order to help their community find a place within the general society."[61] This was the role that Lilienthal crafted for himself in Cincinnati. With the freedom and equality that only America offered, he broke down the distinction between rabbi and civic leader. He became a community activist in education, culture, charitable causes, and interfaith work without renouncing his profession. In doing so, he fulfilled the congregation's hope to project "as positive an image of the Jew as possible."[62] By the late 1870s the congregation's president happily reported that Bene Israel's position "had attained an 'enviable eminence.'"[63]

Lilienthal's immediate successor failed in the attempt to replace him. The English-born Raphael Benjamin (1846–1906) had been recruited from Melbourne, Australia. He was young, had a background in education, and was a good speaker. However, "his conception of the rabbinate turned out to be narrowly congregational, rather than broadly communal as Lilienthal's had been. . . . He refused, however, to be drawn into the many outside activities that carried with them the status that Bene Israel's congregants wanted their rabbi to have."[64] Benjamin, an effective rabbi in the modern European style, could not give Bene Israel the "enviable eminence" they had come to expect.

Jacob Rader Marcus noted that "in a number of respects Lilienthal, who also taught at the College, was a prototype of the typical Hebrew Union college graduate of the late nineteenth and early twentieth century."[65] It was David Philipson, one of those early graduates and a great favorite of Lilienthal, who continued his mentor's rabbinic approach. According to Sarna and Goldman, "Philipson soon took up where Lilienthal had left off. Modeling his career upon that of his beloved predecessor, he became active in the general community, especially in cultural, philanthropic, and civic affairs. . . . Once again congregants could now bask in their rabbi's reflected glory."[66] In his autobiography, *My Life as an American Jew*, Philipson describes the wide range of his activities, far surpassing anything a European rabbi could have imagined. In 1911 alone Philipson spoke at the Evolutionists Society, the Presbyterian Brotherhood, and the Norwood Literary Society. He preached at the Universalist church and attended the American Society for the Judicial Settlement of International Disputes.[67] He was also active in the Central Conference of American Rabbis, chairing the committee that revised the *Union Prayer Book*, railed against anti-Semitism and breaches of the wall between religion and state, and testified before Congress on the issue of Zionism.[68] Philipson continued Lilienthal's model of a rabbi as "ethnic broker."[69] Like his mentor Lilienthal, he attempted to bridge the gap between the Jewish community and the general society.

In their article analyzing this phenomenon, Mark Bauman and Arnold Shankman trace the career of another Hebrew Union College graduate of the generation after Lilienthal, David Marx. Marx served as an ethnic broker for Atlanta's Jews in a career that spanned half a century. Like Lilienthal, he undertook three tasks: "leading the Temple firmly into the camp of Reform Judaism, making his congregation more socially conscious and active, and serving as ambassador to Atlanta's Christian Community."[70] Marx worked with orphans, kindergartens, Jewish charities, and the National Council of Jewish Women. He volunteered as a chaplain at the federal penitentiary in Atlanta. He was an officer for the local chapter of the Red Cross, the Tuberculosis Association, the Boy's Club, and the Arts Alliance and helped to found a hospital and the Atlanta Community Chest. Also like Lilienthal, he was a superpatriot (especially during World War I) and spoke about patriotic subjects at civic events.[71]

As generations of rabbis graduated from Hebrew Union College and spread out over the country to serve Jewish communities, many of them continued Lilienthal's modern American model for the rabbinate, expanding the profession in ways that would have been inconceivable in nineteenth-century Europe.

It is impossible to conclude this book without asking an obvious question: If Lilienthal's career and contributions are so significant, why has he been virtually forgotten? Wise noted in his "Reminiscences" in the *Hebrew Review*, "I could write a book on Dr. Lilienthal and not exhaust the subject, but I could not do it now. It is too soon; my heart aches."[72] Wise never found the time or the will to write that book.[73] Gradually the memory of Lilienthal faded, eclipsed by the legacy of Wise's long career and lasting achievements. In the years that followed, however, Wise would sorely miss the guidance of his dynamic and savvy colleague. In that time he ran Hebrew Union College and participated in all the major developments of Reform Judaism, but he was outmaneuvered by Kohler and the other radical reformers. The movement at the end of the nineteenth century did not reflect his vision. I cannot help but think that he lost much of his political effectiveness without the sophisticated support of his longtime friend. Perhaps this is why Wise never fulfilled his promise to write the biography of his beloved Menachem.

For his part, Lilienthal had made the choice to cede the spotlight to his friend. He was glad to take the role of Wise's aide-de-camp. He could not tolerate the vicious personal attacks that came with leadership. Wise seemed to revel in them. If he had been told that Wise would be remembered as *the* founder of American Reform Judaism, my guess is that he would have given a hardy laugh and been happy for his friend.

Notes

Preface

1. Sarna, *American Judaism*, xviii.
2. Philipson, *Max Lilienthal*. See also Ruben, "Max Lilienthal," for a review of the secondary literature on Lilienthal.
3. Philipson, *Oldest Jewish Congregation in the West*.
4. O'Neill, *Ernest Reuben Lilienthal*; and S. Lilienthal, *Lilienthal Family Record*.
5. Ginsburg, "Max Lilienthal's Activities in Russia"; Etkes, "Compulsory Enlightenment"; Meyer, "German Model"; and Stanislawski, *Tsar Nicholas*.
6. Merowitz, "Max Lilienthal."
7. Temkin, "Rabbi Max Lilienthal."
8. Silver, "Rabbi Max Lilienthal."
9. Sherman, "Bernard Illowy." See also Sussman, *Isaac Leeser*.
10. Meyer, *Response to Modernity*, 238; Cohen, *Encounter with Emancipation*, 174.

Chapter 1

1. This lengthy full name was found in an autobiographical sketch that Lilienthal handed to Minister Uvarov upon his arrival in St. Petersburg; cited in Ginsburg, "Max Lilienthal's Activities in Russia," 42. Lilienthal gave his date of birth as November 6, 1814. Gordon O'Neill recorded the date as November 3, 1814 (O'Neill, *Ernest Reuben Lilienthal*). That date was supported by S. Lilienthal, *Lilienthal Family Record*, 5. However, the Judah L. Magnes Museum has a Torah binder made from Lilienthal's circumcision cloth that reads, "Menachem, called Mendl, ben Judah Loeb Schnaidack, born under a good sign on Thursday, 3rd Marheshvan 5575 (October 17, 1814)" (the cloth was the gift of Mr. and Mrs. Theodore Lilienthal, Judah L. Magnes Museum 80.83). For a discussion of the contradictory statements made by Lilienthal himself, see Merowitz, "Note on the Dating," 78–79.

2. See Kilian, *Die Jüdische Gemeinde in München*, 110.

3. O'Neill, *Ernest Reuben Lilienthal*, 3.

4. Israel, *European Jewry*, 40–41.

5. See Meyer, *German-Jewish History*, v. 2, 11.

6. S. Stern, *Court Jew*, esp. 227.

7. J. Katz, *Out of the Ghetto*, 20–21.

8. S. Lilienthal, *Lilienthal Family Record*, 1; Israel, *European Jewry*, 44, 187.

9. S. Lilienthal, *Lilienthal Family Record*, 1; S. Stern, *Court Jew*, 32–33; and O'Neill, *Ernest Reuben Lilienthal*, 3. Apparently, the court abrogated the exclusive arrangement when they allowed other purveyors to settle in Bavaria, resulting in a loss of business and much bitterness on the part of the Seligmann family. Sophie Lilienthal, "Lilienthal Familie, Schnaittach," Leo Baeck Institute Manuscript A, 632 2099.

10. S. Lilienthal, *Lilienthal Family Record*, 1; and S. Stern, *Court Jew*, 164. According to Stern, Jews were especially effective in procuring precious metals because of their good trade relations with Poland.

11. S. Lilienthal, *Lilienthal Family Record*, 2.

12. Meyer, *German-Jewish History*, v. 2, 11, 19.

13. Meyer, *German-Jewish History*, v. 2, 268.

14. Meyer, *German-Jewish History*, v. 2, 101.

15. Meyer, *German-Jewish History*, v. 2, 23. See also Harris, "Bavarians and Jews," 5.

16. Sheehan, *German History*, 321.

17. O'Neill, *Ernest Reuben Lilienthal*, 7.

18. Meyer, *German-Jewish History*, v. 2, 28.

19. Diner, *A Time for Gathering*, 16.

20. Rürup, "Emancipation," 81. See also Richarz, "Jewish Social Mobility," 75.

21. Sterling, "Jewish Reaction," 103.

22. Meyer, *German-Jewish History*, v. 2, 204–7.

23. J. Katz, *From Prejudice to Destruction*, 92–104.

24. Meyer, *German-Jewish History*, v. 2, 36. See also Sheehan, *German History*, 449.

25. Meyer, *German-Jewish History*, v. 2, 37–38.

26. Rohrbacher, "Hep Hep Riots," 23–24.

27. Rohrbacher, "Hep Hep Riots," 31.

28. S. Lilienthal, *Lilienthal Family Record*, 5–6. It is not clear if the fire was related to the anti-Semitic riots.

29. I. Fishman, *History of Jewish Education*, 77. See also Meyer, *German-Jewish History*, v. 1, 184–85.

30. Ginsburg, "Max Lilienthal's Activities in Russia," 42.

31. Mosse, *Jews in the German Economy*, 34, 67. Mosse listed the Seligmanns among those forty or fifty families throughout Germany that made up the elite.

32. Taylor, *Hegel*, 4–7. See also Gay, *The Enlightenment*; and Darnton,

George Washington's False Teeth.

33. Feiner, *Jewish Enlightenment,* 7.

34. Feiner, *Jewish Enlightenment,* 7. For some other sources on the Jewish Enlightenment, see Sorkin, *Transformation of German Jewry;* Zinberg, *A History of Jewish Literature,* vols. 8 and 10; J. Katz, *Tradition and Crisis;* J. Katz, *Out of the Ghetto;* Meyer, *Origins of the Modern Jew;* and Pelli, *Age of Haskalah.*

35. See Altmann, *Moses Mendelssohn.*

36. Feiner, *Haskalah and History,* 38.

37. Sorkin, *Transformation of German Jewry,* 66.

38. Barzilay, "Early Responses," 521.

39. Sorkin, *Transformation of German Jewry,* 86.

40. Ruben, "Max Lilienthal," 24.

41. Schorsch, "Emergence of the Modern Rabbinate," in his *From Text to Context,* 32.

42. Schorsch, "Emergence of the Modern Rabbinate," 32.

43. Ginsburg, "Max Lilienthal's Activities in Russia," 42; O'Neill, *Ernest Reuben Lilienthal,* 9.

44. O'Neill, *Ernest Reuben Lilienthal,* 9; S. Lilienthal, *Lilienthal Family Record,* 4. Sophie gives December 31 as the date of death. A tombstone placed on her grave much later by "her children in North America" marked her death as January 9, 5585 (1825).

45. The extant sources are unclear as to the chronology.

46. Philipson, *Max Lilienthal, American Rabbi,* 8. For more on the Fürth yeshiva, see Meyer, *German-Jewish History,* v. 1, 212, and v. 2, 96.

47. S. M. Lowenstein, *Mechanics of Change,* 13.

48. For conditions at these traditional Ashkenazic yeshivas, see I. Fishman, *History of Jewish Education,* esp. 122–23; and Philipson, *Max Lilienthal,* 141.

49. Meyer, *German-Jewish History,* v. 1, 211–12.

50. Meyer, *German-Jewish History,* v. 2, 96.

51. Scharfman, *The First Rabbi,* 31. Rabbi Salomon Titkin claimed that a university education disqualified a man for the rabbinate. Schorsch, "Emergence of the Modern Rabbinate," 13.

52. Meyer, *German-Jewish History,* v. 2, 98.

53. Not every rabbi who was exposed to modern studies became a reformer. Rabbi Bernard Illowy received his ordination from Rabbi Moses Schreiber in Pressburg and then received his doctorate degree from the University of Budapest. Throughout his later career in the United States, he remained a traditionalist. Illoway, *Sefer,* 12–13. Even Moses Schreiber has some exposure to secular studies.

54. Sorkin, *Transformation of German Jewry,* 15–17.

55. Ringer, *Education,* 36.

56. See Sorkin, "Wilhelm von Humboldt," 63.

57. See Bruford, *German Tradition,* 1, 16–17. See also Paulsen, *German Universities,* 52.

58. Schorsch, "Emergence of Historical Consciousness," 415–17.

59. Schorsch, "Emergence of Historical Consciousness," 415–17.

60. Ginsburg, *Max Lilienthal's Activities in Russia*, 42.

61. Ginsburg, *Max Lilienthal's Activities in Russia*, 48.

62. Schorsch, "Emergence of the Modern Rabbinate," 39–41.

63. O'Neill, *Ernest Reuben Lilienthal*, 13.

64. Sorkin, "Wilhelm von Humboldt," 63.

65. M. Lilienthal, "My Travels in Russia," 204.

66. Philipson, *Max Lilienthal*, 7n5.

67. Ginsburg, *Max Lilienthal's Activities in Russia*, 42.

68. *Hebrew Review* 2 (1881–82): 184.

69. Ginsburg, *Max Lilienthal's Activities in Russia*, 42.

70. Ginsburg, *Max Lilienthal's Activities in Russia*, 43. See also Ringer, *Education*, 35–36.

71. M. Lilienthal, "Ueber den Ursprung," 6.

72. M. Lilienthal, "Ueber den Ursprung," 12.

73. M. Lilienthal, "Ueber den Ursprung," 8, 13, 15, 18.

74. S. Lilienthal, *Lilienthal Family Record*, 55.

75. Philipson, *Max Lilienthal*, 8; and Ginsburg, *Max Lilienthal's Activities in Russia*, 42.

76. Undated letter from Max Lilienthal to Pepi Nettre, Munich, Collection of Max Lilienthal Letters, Judah L. Magnes Museum, no. 2.

77. S. Lilienthal, *Lilienthal Family Record*, 14.

78. S. Lilienthal, *Lilienthal Family Record*, 14.

79. M. Lilienthal, "My Travels in Russia," 233.

80. Altmann, "The New Style of Preaching in Nineteenth-Century German Jewry," in his *Essays*, 192–97. For instance, the great preacher Isaac Noah Mannheimer openly acknowledged his debt to the Christians: "We are pupils and disciples of these masters of the art of preaching" (Altmann, *Essays*, 194–95). For examples of Mannheimer's sermons, see Mannheimer, *Gottesdienstliche Vorträge*.

81. Meyer, *Response to Modernity*, 101.

82. Altmann, "New Style of Preaching," 201.

83. M. Lilienthal, *Predigten*, 8. For Christian trends, see Altmann, "New Style of Preaching," 208–12.

84. M. Lilienthal, *Predigten*, 19.

85. M. Lilienthal, *Predigten*, 36–37.

86. M. Lilienthal, *Predigten*, 31.

87. Altmann, "New Style of Preaching," 220.

88. M. Lilienthal, *Predigten*, 17.

89. Many years later Max still adhered to the opinion that the pulpit was an inappropriate medium for critical scholarship. See *Israelite* 2 (August 10, 1855): 36.

90. M. Lilienthal, *Predigten*, 9. This would be a constant theme in Lilienthal's writing for the rest of his career.

91. M. Lilienthal, *Predigten*, 11. The occasion for the sermon was the second day of the festival of Shavuot, which commemorated the giving of the Law on Mount Sinai.

92. M. Lilienthal, *Predigten*, 12.

93. M. Lilienthal, *Predigten*, 13–14. The only hint of liberal leanings is found in an omission in the sermon. Lilienthal never mentioned the traditional belief in a personal messiah who would usher in the messianic kingdom. In a remark in "My Travels in Russia," he ridiculed the credulous messianism of a Russian Jewish soldier (164).

94. Kilian, *Die Jüdische Gemeinde in München*, 378. For the discussion of the fight over the introduction of the choir, see pages 123–24.

95. Schorsch, "Emergence of the Modern Rabbinate," 39–40.

96. Schorsch, "Emergence of the Modern Rabbinate," 14.

97. O'Neill, *Ernest Reuben Lilienthal*, 9. See also S. Lilienthal, *Lilienthal Family Record*, 7.

98. Philipson, *Max Lilienthal*, 9.

99. For a discussion of Philippson, see Shargel, "Ludwig Philippson"; Philippson, "The Philippsons," 102–4; and Zinberg, *A History of Jewish Literature*, v. 10, 160–69. For Lilienthal's description of him, see a letter to his brother Samuel Lilienthal in Philipson, *Max Lilienthal*, 143.

100. Werner, *A Voice Still Heard*, 206–7. Werner claims that Isaac M. Wise later used Mannheimer's liturgy as the basis for *Minhag America* (318n14). See Chapters 4 and 6 in this book. See also Rosenmann, *Isak Noa Mannheimer*; and *Jewish Encyclopedia*, s.v. "Isaac Noah Mannheimer."

101. Later, Lilienthal would claim that his research led the scholar Adolf Jellenik (1823–93) to the important discovery that the *Zohar* (the classical text of Spanish Jewish mysticism) was written in the thirteenth century by Moses de Leon rather than by second-century rabbi Simeon ben Yohai. See *Asmonean* 10 (June 9, 1854): 62. See also Lilienthal's "Notice Biographique" in Ginsburg, "Max Lilienthal's Activities in Russia," 43.

102. Philipson, *Max Lilienthal*, 15. The letter requested "a German-Jewish rabbi trained in the spirit of 'pure Enlightenment.'" Stanislawski, *Tsar Nicholas*, 58. Count Uvarov's position is translated variously as minister of education, of public instruction, and of national enlightenment.

103. Philipson, *Max Lilienthal*, 159, from his 1855–57 sketches in *The Israelite* titled "My Travels in Russia."

104. Aschheim, *Brothers and Strangers*, 19.

Chapter 2

1. Lincoln, *Nicholas I*, 85.

2. Lincoln, *Nicholas I*, 289.

3. The boundaries of the Pale were not clearly delineated until the 1835 statute. See Klier, *Imperial Russia's Jewish Question*, 9. Also see Stanislawski,

Tsar Nicholas, 36.

4. Stanislawski, *Tsar Nicholas*, 16–31, esp. 22.

5. Stanislawski, *Tsar Nicholas*, 43. See also Nathans, *Beyond the Pale*, 39–40. Lilienthal documents the group of wealthy Jewish entrepreneurs in his article "Sketches of Jewish Life in Russia #2," *Occident* 5 (December 1847): 441–46, esp. 445. One of the group's members, Israel Halperin, a banker and financier, was made part of Lilienthal's 1843 commission to modernize Jewish education.

6. M. Lilienthal, "My Travels in Russia," 261.

7. Feiner, *Haskalah and History*, 157. Feiner notes that the image was more optimistic wish than a reality.

8. Zipperstein, *Jews of Odessa*, 46.

9. Zipperstein, *Jews of Odessa*, 46–47.

10. Stanislawski, *Tsar Nicholas*, 58.

11. Max Lilienthal to Loew Seligmann, October 25, 1839, in S. Lilienthal, *Lilienthal Family Record*, 15; and Max Lilienthal to Samuel Lilienthal, December 12–24, 1840, in S. Lilienthal, *Lilienthal Family Record*, 25. Compare with M. Lilienthal, "My Travels in Russia," 160.

12. Max Lilienthal to Samuel Lilienthal, December 12–24, 1840, in S. Lilienthal, *Lilienthal Family Record*, 25; and M. Lilienthal, "My Travels in Russia," 160.

13. Max Lilienthal to Samuel Lilienthal, December 12–24, 1840, in S. Lilienthal, *Lilienthal Family Record*, 25; and M. Lilienthal, "My Travels in Russia," 160.

14. Altmann, *Essays*, 193–94.

15. Max Lilienthal to Samuel Lilienthal, December 12–24, 1840, in S. Lilienthal, *Lilienthal Family Record*, 25. See also Meyer, *Response to Modernity*, 55.

16. Meyer, *Response to Modernity*, 60–61.

17. Meyer, *Response to Modernity*, 67–70.

18. Max Lilienthal to Samuel Lilienthal, December 12–24, 1840, in Philipson, *Max Lilienthal*, 143. In his memoirs Lilienthal says that the name of the ship was the *Kamtschaka*. The original letter gives the name as the *Nicolai*.

19. Max Lilienthal to Samuel Lilienthal, December 12–24, 1840, in Philipson, *Max Lilienthal*, 144; and M. Lilienthal, "My Travels in Russia," 160–61.

20. Max Lilienthal to Loew Seligmann, October 25, 1839, in Philipson, *Max Lilienthal*, 133.

21. Max Lilienthal to Loew Seligmann, November 1, 1839, in Philipson, Max Lilienthal, 135; and M. Lilienthal, "My Travels in Russia," 161.

22. Although Lilienthal does not say so, this fortress was probably the massive Peter and Paul Fortress, located on the banks of the Neva River.

23. M. Lilienthal, "My Travels in Russia," 164–66.

24. M. Lilienthal, "My Travels in Russia," 161–62. Philipson suggests further evidence of Lilienthal's level of observance. In an October 25, 1839, letter to his father, Lilienthal says he has only a half-hour to write (S. Lilienthal, *Lil-*

ienthal Family Record, 15). Philipson interprets that to mean that the Sabbath was coming so Lilienthal had to finish the letter quickly (see Philipson, *Max Lilienthal*, 133).

25. Philipson, *Max Lilienthal*, 217.

26. Philipson, *Max Lilienthal*, 204.

27. M. Lilienthal, "My Travels in Russia," 168–71.

28. Max Lilienthal to Loew Seligmann, November 1, 1839, in Philipson, *Max Lilienthal*, 135.

29. Philipson, *Max Lilienthal*, 190.

30. Philipson, *Max Lilienthal*, 197.

31. Lilienthal wrote to his brother Samuel (December 12–24, 1840) that he had seven meetings with Uvarov, from whom he secured both "his personal good will, but also his fatherly interest." He told Samuel that he had asked Uvarov about the issue of the right of citizenship as part of his commission from his congregation in Riga. Philipson, *Max Lilienthal*, 144.

32. See Sorkin, *Transformation of German Jewry*, 66–67.

33. Schneersohn, *Tzemach Tzedek*, 17. The characterization of Lilienthal as one who had abandoned Judaism reveals the bias of the writer. However, it represents a common view that Lilienthal was being manipulated by the crafty, conversion-motivated minister and his tsar. Despite its anti-Lilienthal prejudice, this source gives a colorful, if biased picture of some of the important incidents involved in his mission.

34. Zinberg, *History of Jewish Literature*, v. 11, 74, 80. See also Dubnow, *History*, v. 2, 50–52. This portrayal is supported by Nicholas Riasanovsky in his *Nicholas I*, 70–72. Stanislawski disputes the conversionist implications of this so-called "secret memorandum" (Stanislawski, *Tsar Nicholas*, 67). He also denies that it was any more or less secret than any other official document in Russia.

35. Stanislawski, *Tsar Nicholas*, 60–61.

36. Stanislawski, *Tsar Nicholas*, 63.

37. Stanislawski, *Tsar Nicholas*, 62.

38. Stanislawski, *Tsar Nicholas*, 66. This reappraisal of Uvarov is supported by his recent biographer, Cynthia Whittaker, who portrays the minister as supportive of Jewish causes. She says that even if his ultimate goal may have been conversion, because civilization, religion, and citizenship were correlated for him, he never acted in the spirit of blatant anti-Semitism. Whittaker, *Origins*, 202–7.

39. Zinberg, *History of Jewish Literature*, v. 11, 82.

40. M. Lilienthal, "My Travels in Russia," 201.

41. M. Lilienthal, "My Travels in Russia," 217–18.

42. M. Lilienthal, "My Travels in Russia," 219–20.

43. M. Lilienthal, "My Travels in Russia," 220. Also see Henriksson, *Tsar's Loyal Germans*, ix, x, 1, 2.

44. M. Lilienthal, "My Travels in Russia," 221; Max Lilienthal to Loew Selig-

mann, November 1, 1839, in Philipson, *Max Lilienthal*, 135.

45. M. Lilienthal, "My Travels in Russia," 224–25.

46. M. Lilienthal, "My Travels in Russia," 225–26.

47. M. Lilienthal, "My Travels in Russia," 235.

48. M. Lilienthal, "My Travels in Russia," 226–27. Max Lilienthal to Loew Seligmann and Isaac Nettre, September 16, 1840, in Philipson, *Max Lilienthal*, 138–39.

49. M. Lilienthal, "My Travels in Russia," 234, 240–41.

50. See Zinberg, *History of Jewish Literature*, v. 11, 75–76.

51. Max Lilienthal to Pepi Nettre, February 21, 1840, in Philipson, *Max Lilienthal*, 136–37.

52. Meyer, *Response to Modernity*, 39. See also Petuchowski, "Manuals."

53. Meyer, *Response to Modernity*, 39–40.

54. Max Lilienthal to Samuel Lilienthal, December 12, 1840, in S. Lilienthal, *Lilienthal Family Record*, 28.

55. Max Lilienthal to Samuel Lilienthal, December 12, 1840, in S. Lilienthal, *Lilienthal Family Record*, 28.

56. Philipson, *Max Lilienthal*, 235–36.

57. Max Lilienthal to Loew Seligmann and Isaac Nettre, September 16, 1840, in S. Lilienthal, *Lilienthal Family Record*, 19.

58. Max Lilienthal to Loew Seligmann and Isaac Nettre, September 16, 1840, in S. Lilienthal, *Lilienthal Family Record*, 23.

59. Max Lilienthal to Pepi Nettre, March 3, 1840, in S. Lilienthal, *Lilienthal Family Record*, 17–18.

60. Max Lilienthal to Loew Seligmann and Isaac Nettre, September 16, 1840, in Philipson, *Max Lilienthal*, 137–41.

61. M. Lilienthal, "My Travels in Russia," 243–44; Stanislawski, *Tsar Nicholas*, 59.

62. M. Lilienthal, "My Travels in Russia," 244–45.

63. The actual money that he was paid is unclear. Philipson's translation of the amount is in dollars. Sophie Lilienthal's version uses the terms *thalers* and *florins*. Neither was the currency in Bavaria at the time. The original letter, found at the Judah Magnes Museum, uses the letter G, which presumably refers to guldens, a currency used in southern German regions during the period. In any case, the salary seems to have been quite low.

64. Max Lilienthal to Pepi Nettre, August 22, 1841, in S. Lilienthal, *Lilienthal Family Record*, 33.

65. M. Lilienthal, "My Travels in Russia," 244–45; Stanislawski, *Tsar Nicholas*, 59; Max Lilienthal to Loew Seligmann and Isaac Nettre, September 16, 1840, in S. Lilienthal, *Lilienthal Family Record*, 23. Lilienthal seemed a little more sanguine about the position in a December 12–24, 1840, letter to his brother Samuel, in S. Lilienthal, *Lilienthal Family Record*, 24–30. By then, however, he had already been invited to return to St. Petersburg. He chose not to mention this to his brother for reasons that are unclear. Nor does he write

about the trip in his January 3, 1841, letter to Pepi Nettre, Judah L. Magnes Memorial Museum.

66. Stanislawski, *Tsar Nicholas*, 43–48. Other elements in Kiselev's reforms included requiring rabbis to have secular training, outlawing traditional Jewish dress, and abolishing the *kahal* and the tax it collected from its members (*korobka*). See also Lincoln, *Nicholas I*, 188–90, for a discussion of Kiselev's reform of the state peasants.

67. Stanislawski, *Tsar Nicholas*, 63. Vilna's leaders included Nisan Rosenthal, Hirsh Zvi Katzenellenbogen, and Israel Gordon.

68. Lincoln, *Nicholas I*, 59, 69–71.

69. M. Lilienthal, "My Travels in Russia," 246–47. Unfortunately Lilienthal does not tell us what Uvarov said to reassure him.

70. *Allgemeine Zeitung des Judenthums* 6 (1842): 603. See also Philipson, "Max Lilienthal in Russia," 828–29; and Stanislawski, *Tsar Nicholas*, 70–71.

71. According to David Philipson, a groundless rumor began circulating in Germany that the project had been abandoned because progress was so slow. Philipson, *Max Lilienthal*, 26–27.

72. Raisin, *Haskalah Movement*, 171.

73. Philipson, *Max Lilienthal*, 26. Mannheimer and Sulzer in Vienna volunteered to train the young men in preaching and liturgy to prepare them for pulpits.

74. Feiner, *Haskalah and History*, 158.

75. Stanislawski, *Tsar Nicholas*, 72. Stanislawski said that Lilienthal wrote this report after his return to Riga, but this does not accord with Lilienthal's account in "My Travels in Russia" (247–48). Why else would he need to have stayed in St. Petersburg until March 6? Philipson follows Lilienthal's own chronology. Philipson, *Max Lilienthal*, 25–26; and *Allgemeine Zeitung des Judenthums* 6 (October 8, 1842): 603.

76. Philipson, *Max Lilienthal*, 21; M. Lilienthal, "My Travels in Russia," 247–48.

77. M. Lilienthal, "My Travels in Russia," 257–58.

78. Stanislawski, *Tsar Nicholas*, 72.

79. M. Lilienthal, "My Travels in Russia," 258.

80. M. Lilienthal, "My Travels in Russia," 265–66.

81. M. Lilienthal, "My Travels in Russia," 265; and Stanislawski, *Tsar Nicholas*, 73. Despite Lilienthal's promise to Luzzato, the government never paid for Jewish schools. See Lilienthal's report in *Allgemeine Zeitung des Judenthums* 6 (October 8, 1842): 605, for the proposed breakdown of taxes on kosher food that would pay for Vilna's schools. The national plan for the modern schools would be paid by a tax on Sabbath candles.

82. M. Lilienthal, "My Travels in Russia," 293–94.

83. Stanislawski, *Tsar Nicholas*, 73–74. Stanislawski cites the recollections of one of the Maskilim, Benjamin Mandelshtam.

84. M. Lilienthal, "My Travels in Russia," 309–10. See also Stanislawski,

Tsar Nicholas, 74.

85. Vilna's entire Jewish population would not reach 40,000 until the 1880s. *YIVO Encyclopedia of Jewish Eastern Europe*, s.v. "Vilnius."

86. Quoted in Stanislawski, *Tsar Nicholas*, 75. The gist of Mandelshtam's description matches that in Lilienthal's memoirs.

87. M. Lilienthal, "My Travels in Russia," 315–16.

88. M. Lilienthal, "My Travels in Russia," 317–20.

89. M. Lilienthal, "My Travels in Russia," 324. See also Stanislawski, *Tsar Nicholas*, 75–76.

90. Stanislawski, *Tsar Nicholas*, 329–30.

91. Stanislawski, *Tsar Nicholas*, 332; M. Lilienthal, "My Travels in Russian," 334.

92. *Allgemeine Zeitung des Judenthums* 6 (1842): 602–11. For the order itself, see pages 609–10. In the article Lilienthal also quashed a rumor that the entire undertaking had been abandoned (604).

93. Stanislawski, *Tsar Nicholas*, 76–77. See Zinberg, *History of Jewish Literature*, v. 11, 87–88.

94. Zinberg, *History of Jewish Literature*, v. 11, 87–88.

95. Bartal, "Mordechai Aaron Günzburg," 139–40.

96. Lederhendler, *Road to Modern Jewish Politics*, 135.

97. Feiner, *Haskalah and History*, 193. For details of Lilienthal's relationship with the Maskilim, see also Etkes, "Compulsory Enlightenment," esp. 280–99.

98. M. Lilienthal, "My Travels in Russia," 331. Philipson claims that this propagandist tour was a triumphal march. Philipson, *Max Lilienthal*, 31. Some of the stops had this quality; others were fraught with tension, controlled by the presence of his police escort.

99. M. Lilienthal, "My Travels in Russia," 331.

100. M. Lilienthal, "My Travels in Russia," 350. For the threats behind Lilienthal's discussions, see Stanislawski, *Tsar Nicholas*, 78. Lilienthal told the rabbi that Uvarov and Kiselev were the only ministers urging this enlightened approach. The rest of the government urged punitive measures.

101. M. Lilienthal, "My Travels in Russia," 360.

102. See Philipson, *Max Lilienthal*, 33–35.

103. Wengeroff, *Rememberings*, 73.

104. Wengeroff, *Rememberings*, 74.

105. Wengeroff, *Rememberings*, 74–75.

106. Wengeroff, *Rememberings*, 80.

107. Zipperstein, *Jews of Odessa*, 52.

108. Schneersohn, *Tzemach Tzedek*, 50.

109. Schneersohn, *Tzemach Tzedek*, 51. The children were mirroring the central concern of the traditional community that the modern schools were vehicles for conversion of the Jews.

110. S. Lilienthal, *Lilienthal Family Record*, 4. The claim is found in Schneersohn, *Tzemach Tzedek*, 12–13. I have found no evidence that Lilienthal's

grandfather was an atheist who taught in the Vilna Talmud Torah. According to the memoirs, his grandfather was a major supporter of the Fürth yeshiva.

111. Zinberg, *History of Jewish Literature*, v. 11, 82–94.

112. Zipperstein, *Jews of Odessa*, 52.

113. Zipperstein, *Jews of Odessa*, 84–85.

114. Stanislawski, *Tsar Nicholas*, 78. Lilienthal had invited two prominent Western Jewish leaders, Adolphe Crémieux and Sir Moses Montefiore, to serve as observers, but they declined.

115. *Jewish Times* 1 (January 28, 1870): 3.

116. *Jewish Times* 1 (January 28, 1870): 4.

117. Zinberg, *History of Jewish Literature*, v. 11, 76. See also Lilienthal's praise for Nicholas in *Allgemeine Zeitung des Judenthums* 6 (1842): 602.

118. *Jewish Times* 1 (January 28, 1870): 4.

119. Schneersohn, *Tzemach Tzedek*, 52. This contradicts Lilienthal's memory that Uvarov left town a week into the commission's work. Perhaps he returned to participate later. Schneersohn, *Tzemach Tzedek*, 55.

120. Stanislawski, *Tsar Nicholas*, 79; M. Lilienthal, "The Russian Government and the Russian Jews: My Personal Experience," *Jewish Times* 1 (1870): 4.

121. Stanislawski, *Tsar Nicholas*, 82. The "evil decree" may have been a reference to the ukase.

122. Schneersohn, *Tzemach Tzedek*, 57.

123. Stanislawski, *Tsar Nicholas*, 82, 94.

124. Max Lilienthal to Loew Seligmann and Isaac Nettre, July 1844, in S. Lilienthal, *Lilienthal Family Record*, 45.

125. Stanislawski, *Tsar Nicholas*, 86.

126. Stanislawski, *Tsar Nicholas*, 78–79. See also Philipson, *Max Lilienthal*, 39.

127. Stanislawski, *Tsar Nicholas*, 82–85. After Lilienthal's departure, Nicholas reversed this portion of the law because of his reactionary response to the revolutions of 1848. He forbade the importation of any foreign teachers to keep out the harmful intellectual trends of the West. Stanislawski, *Tsar Nicholas*, 104.

128. Stanislawski, *Tsar Nicholas*, 93, 95.

129. Stanislawski, *Tsar Nicholas*, 95.

130. *Jewish Times* 1 (January 28, 1870): 4. This reason is supported by the report in the Philadelphia Jewish monthly *The Occident* 3 (January 1846): 526. "[Lilienthal] had resigned his office, and quitted Russia, in consequence of having been undeceived respecting the intentions of the Emperor, through his famous Ukase against the frontier Jews." The 1846 formulation, which undoubtedly came from Lilienthal himself, represents the first attempt to make sense of his experience.

131. Max Lilienthal to Pepi Nettre, November 1843, in S. Lilienthal, *Lilienthal Family Record*, 39.

132. Max Lilienthal to Loew Seligmann and Isaac Nettre, July 1844, in S.

Lilienthal, *Lilienthal Family Record*, 44–47. The problem relates to the onerous Matrikel, according to David Philipson. Because Lilienthal had only been a rabbinic candidate in Bavaria, he needed verification from Russia of his official position to qualify to marry. See Philipson, *Max Lilienthal*, 155n25 and 156n26. This is confirmed by a Bavarian document from the Munich municipal archives (EBA 83 1509), found for me by Jonathan Sarna. This handwritten document shows that in May 1845 Lilienthal's father, Loew Seligmann, had to fill out legal forms proving that Lilienthal had a position in Russia (including information about his salary) in order to establish a Matrikel number and thereby gain permission to marry Pepi.

133. Max Lilienthal to Pepi Nettre, late 1844, in S. Lilienthal, *Lilienthal Family Record*, 51.

134. Max Lilienthal to Pepi Nettre, late 1844, in S. Lilienthal, *Lilienthal Family Record*, 51.

135. Max Lilienthal to Loew Seligmann and Isaac Nettre, September 1840, in S. Lilienthal, *Lilienthal Family Record*, 21. Lilienthal discussed several disturbing incidents with the police as well as the high level of vice in the government in "My Travels in Russia," 168–71.

136. Max Lilienthal to Samuel Lilienthal, December 12, 1840, in S. Lilienthal, *Lilienthal Family Record*, 29.

137. Max Lilienthal to Isaac Nettre, July 5–17, 1843, in S. Lilienthal, *Lilienthal Family Record*, 35; and Philipson, *Max Lilienthal*, 151.

138. Max Lilienthal to Loew Seligmann, November 23, 1843, in S. Lilienthal, *Lilienthal Family Record*, 41–42.

139. Max Lilienthal to Loew Seligmann and Isaac Nettre, July 6–18, 1844, in S. Lilienthal, *Lilienthal Family Record*, 46.

140. Max Lilienthal to Loew Seligmann and Isaac Nettre, July 1844, in S. Lilienthal, *Lilienthal Family Record*, 45.

141. Philipson, *Max Lilienthal*, 43. Lilienthal's mentor, Ludwig Philippson, had to defend him in his paper.

142. The statistics come from Stanislawski, *Tsar Nicholas*, 97–101. Cynthia Whittaker, in her biography of Uvarov, sets the end of his ministry in 1849, indicating that he resigned rather than accept the reactionary turn in Nicholas's policies following the revolutionary upheaval of 1848. Whittaker, *Origins*, 3.

143. Whittaker agreed, saying, "Even Lilienthal felt duped and grew to understand that the government had no intention of emancipating the Jews." Whittaker, *Origins*, 206.

144. *Allgemeine Zeitung des Judenthums* 10 (January 5, 1846): 18. In the *Allgemeine Zeitung* in 1848 Lilienthal says, "Nothing remained but the absolute certainty—if God does not intervene—that Judaism will be ruined in Russia." Quoted in Stanislawski, *Tsar Nicholas*, 88. See *Allgemeine Zeitung des Judenthums* 12 (1848): 232. See also *Occident* 3 (January 1846): 525, and *Occident* 5 (August 1847): 252–56, where Lilienthal characterizes the condition of the Jews under the Russian government as "mournful." He also castigates Nicholas

for his conversionary policies.

145. Feiner, *Haskalah and History*, 157.

146. Leon Mandelstamm took over Lilienthal's position in St. Petersburg. Shmuel Fuenn was appointed to Vilna's school district's supervisory staff. In Kiev, Usher Rosenzweig became a consultant for the Jewish crown schools and was made head of the Jewish crown school at Mogilev Podolsk. Lederhendler, *Road to Modern Jewish Politics*, 93.

147. Raisin, *Haskalah Movement*, 199.

148. See Silver, "Rabbi Max Lilienthal," 343–72, for a detailed discussion of the relationship of this experience to Lilienthal's later stand on the separation of church and state.

Chapter 3

1. *Jewish Times* 1 (January 28, 1870): 5.

2. S. Lilienthal, *Lilienthal Family Record*, 53; Max Lilienthal to Isaac Nettre, July 18, 1844, in S. Lilienthal, *Lilienthal Family Record*, 46.

3. Stanislawski, *Tsar Nicholas*, 91.

4. See O'Neill, *Ernest Reuben Lilienthal*, ch. 3, for Samuel Lilienthal's career as a homeopathic physician.

5. Philipson, *Max Lilienthal*, 151. Philipson quotes this letter earlier on page 48.

6. Cohen, *Encounter with Emancipation*, 4–14; Barkai, *Branching Out*, 10–11.

7. See Kisch, "Revolution of 1848." Also see Cohen, *Encounter with Emancipation*, 9–10.

8. *Allgemeine Zeitung des Judenthums* 10 (August 24, 1846): 502–4; 10 (September 14, 1846): 553–55; and 10 (September 28, 1846): 585–86.

9. The classic study of this wave of immigration is Hansen, *Atlantic Migration*. A more recent account is Jones, *American Immigration*. The German immigration has been studied by Walker, *Germany and the Emigration*; Moltmann, *Germans to America*; and Knewson, *Immigrants*. For the German Jewish immigration, see Glanz, "Immigration of German Jews." More recent discussions include Cohen, *Encounter with Emancipation*; Diner, *A Time for Gathering*; and Barkai, *Branching Out*.

10. See Diner, *A Time for Gathering*, 42–49; and Cohen, *Encounter with Emancipation*, 4–12. Katznelson, "Jews on the Margins," 171, discusses the effect of market forces of supply and demand for labor on immigration.

11. Cohen, *Encounter with Emancipation*, 8–12; and Diner, *A Time for Gathering*, 37–39.

12. Hansen, *Atlantic Migration*, 172–73. See also Tyler, *Steam Conquers the Atlantic*, for a history of the development of steamship travel.

13. Ernst, *Immigrant Life*, 12.

14. Ernst, *Immigrant Life*, 13–14.

15. See Foster's account in Erickson, *Emigration from Europe*, 255–57. For a full biography, see McNeill, *Vere Foster*. Also see R. C. Cohn, "Mortality on Immigrant Voyages," 119.

16. *Jewish Times* 1 (January 28, 1870): 5.

17. *Passenger Lists of Vessels Arriving in New York, 1820–1897*. Because of the chaotic conditions surrounding immigration during the period, it is difficult to say with certainty when and on which vessel the Lilienthals traveled to America. A number of possible entries in ships' logs might have recorded their passage. In no cases were the names spelled correctly or the ages accurate. One entry seems most likely because of the date of arrival (early November) as well as the port of embarkation (Le Havre). The Philadelphia Jewish paper, *The Occident*, confirms that the couple passed through Paris on the way to Le Havre to embark for America.

18. Quoted in Tyler, *Steam Conquers the Atlantic*, 96. For more colorful details, see Dickens, *American Notes*, 25–39.

19. *New York Times*, June 23, 1853. Cited in Bretting, *Soziale Probleme*, 39. See also Bogen, *Immigration in New York*, 15–16.

20. *New York Times*, June 23, 1853. Cited in Bretting, *Soziale Probleme*, 39.

21. Bretting, *Soziale Probleme*, 41.

22. Bogen, *Immigration in New York*, 15–16.

23. See Cohen, *Encounter with Emancipation*, 19–22. Also see Diner, *A Time for Gathering*, 58.

24. Ernst, *Immigrant Life*, 20. For a vivid study of New York in the 1840s, see Spann, *New Metropolis*.

25. Ernst, *Immigrant Life*, 46; Diner, *A Time for Gathering*, 89–92. See also Katznelson, "Jews on the Margins," 159–60.

26. Ernst, *Immigrant Life*. See maps on pages 30–31.

27. Dolan, *Immigrant Church*, 37. See also Moltmann, *Germans to America*, 145–51; Thomas et al., *Old World Traits Transplanted*; and Bretting, *Soziale Probleme*.

28. Dolan, *Immigrant Church*, 110.

29. Ahlstrom, *Religious History*, 519. See also Gilbert, *Commitment to Unity*, 11; and Wentz, *Basic History of Lutheranism*, 87.

30. Cohen, *Encounter with Emancipation*, 58. Also see Reissner, "German-American Jews," 94.

31. It was not until about 1850 that Lilienthal began to emphasize English education in his private school.

32. *Allgemeine Zeitung des Judenthums* 10 (January 5, 1846): 18. "Der Name German-Jew ist zum Ehrennamen, zur Bezeichnung der Redlich und Ehrlichkeit hier worden."

33. *Asmonean* 2 (August 6, 1850): 122.

34. *Asmonean* 2 (August 6, 1850): 122.

35. *Allgemeine Zeitung des Judenthums* 10 (January 5, 1846): 18 (my translation).

36. Ahlstrom, *Religious History*, 515–18.

37. Ahlstrom, *Religious History*, 546.

38. Diner, *A Time for Gathering*, 56; Reissner, "German-American Jews," 68.

39. Grinstein, *Rise of the Jewish Community*, 35.

40. Grinstein, *Rise of the Jewish Community*, 50. For the early history of New York, see also Marcus, *Colonial American Jew*; and Marcus, *Early American Jewry*. For the early national period, see Blau and Baron, *Jews of the United States*. Also see Schappes, *Documentary History*.

41. Sarna, *American Judaism*, xviii.

42. Grinstein, *Rise of the Jewish Community*, 472–73. For the location of early synagogues, see pages 32 and 472–73.

43. *Seder Tefilah: The Order of Prayer for Divine Service* (1855). For the history of Temple Emanu-El, see M. Stern, *Rise and Progress*. For more on Merzbacher, see also Meyer, *Response to Modernity*, 237–38.

44. Marcus, *Colonial American Jew*, v. 2, 1063.

45. Gartner, *Jewish Education*, 1. The development of Jewish education is treated later in this chapter.

46. *Asmonean* 2 (May 16, 1850): 29. For further discussion of this situation, see Jick, *Americanization of the Synagogue*, 58–59. Also see Marcus, *United States Jewry*, v. 1, 249.

47. *Occident* 3 (March 1846): 578. See Sussman, *Isaac Leeser*; and Seller, "Isaac Leeser." Also see Davis, *Emergence of Conservative Judaism*, 347–49.

48. Sussman, *Isaac Leeser*, 175–78.

49. Jick, *Americanization of the Synagogue*, 58.

50. *Occident* 1 (June 1843): 137–42; and 3 (January 1846): 521.

51. S. Lilienthal, *Lilienthal Family Record*, 54.

52. *Occident* 3 (January 1846): 525. Lilienthal's own account of the banquet is in his first correspondence to the *Allgemeine Zeitung des Judenthums* 10 (January 5, 1846): 18.

53. Philipson, *Max Lilienthal*, 51. The talk was also announced in *Occident* 3 (December 1845): 471.

54. See Cuddihy, *No Offense*, 26.

55. *Occident* 3 (January 1846): 525. See also Philipson, *Max Lilienthal*, 51.

56. *Occident* 3 (January 1846):, 523. Gutheim, although not an ordained rabbi, would serve congregations in Cincinnati, New York, and New Orleans.

57. Grinstein, "Minute Book," 322–23, 329.

58. Grinstein, *Rise of the Jewish Community*, 89; Protokolle von Emanu-El Congregation Board of Trustees, February 16, 1847; Congregation Shearith Israel, Minutes of the Trustees, October 2l, 1844.

59. By 1847 Merzbacher's salary reached $800 per year. Protokolle von Emanu-El Congregation Board of Trustees, February 16, 1847; Congregation Shearith Israel, Minutes of the Trustees, October 2l, 1844. Lilienthal reported Isaacs's salary in Temkin, "Rabbi Max Lilienthal," 593. Samuel Isaacs (1804–78) was born in Holland and lived for twenty-five years in England until he came

to New York in 1839 to serve Bnai Jeshurun. In 1845 he left to lead the split-off Congregation Shaaray Tefila. In 1857 he founded the weekly *Jewish Messenger.* Schappes, *Documentary History*, 437.

60. Grinstein, "Minute Book," 323, 329. See also Marcus, *United States Jewry*, v. 2, 229.

61. Grinstein, "Minute Book," 323.

62. Grinstein, "Minute Book," 323.

63. Grinstein, "Minute Book," 329. They specify the code *Hoshen Mishpat*, a portion of the *Shulhan Arukh* dealing with the civil code.

64. This possibility is supported by comments in an article in *Allgemeine Zeitung des Judenthums* 10 (July 27, 1846): 448. See also Grinstein, *Rise of the Jewish Community*, 90. Emanu-El's rise was spectacular. Within ten years it would surpass Anshe Chesed and nearly rival Shearith Israel with regard to its financial and social standing.

65. Marcus, *United States Jewry*, v. 2, 233.

66. Grinstein, "Minute Book," 328.

67. *Allgemeine Zeitung des Judenthums* 10 (February 1846), 98.

68. For their location, see Nadel, *Little Germany*, 31–32. The early German district was centered in the Eleventh Ward between Houston and East Fourteenth Streets and Clinton Avenue and the East River. John Lehrmaier's address is on Lilienthal's naturalization record, where he is listed as a witness.

69. O'Neill, *Ernest Reuben Lilienthal*, 26.

70. S. Lilienthal, *Lilienthal Family Record*, 55.

71. O'Neill, *Ernest Reuben Lilienthal*, 26.

72. Wise, *Reminiscences*, 20.

73. S. Lilienthal, *Lilienthal Family Record*, 56.

74. S. Lilienthal, *Lilienthal Family Record*, 56.

75. *Occident* 3 (March 1846): 584.

76. *Occident* 3 (March 1846): 584.

77. *Occident* 3 (March 1846): 586.

78. *Occident* 3 (March 1846): 587.

79. *Occident* 3 (February 1846): 574–75. Later, Gutheim would also embrace Reform.

80. See Temkin, "Beth Din," 418.

81. *Israelite* 1 (August 11, 1854): 37–38. David Philipson, Lilienthal's student and first biographer, concurred with Wise's assessment. Philipson, *Max Lilienthal*, 52. Wise has been one of the most thoroughly documented American Jewish leaders. Among his biographies are May, *Isaac Mayer Wise*; Heller, *Isaac M. Wise*; and Temkin, *Isaac Mayer Wise*. Wise attended the yeshiva at Goltsch-Jenikau and later spent two years at the University of Prague and one year at the University of Vienna. Although he attached "D.D." to his name in later years, this degree was never granted by a university. Temkin denied that Wise actually received rabbinic ordination either. Temkin, *Isaac Mayer Wise*, 22–24.

82. *Israelite* 1 (August 11, 1854): 37–38.

83. *Occident* 3 (March 1846): 588.

84. *Occident* 3 (March 1846): 589.

85. *Occident* 3 (March 1846): 589–90.

86. *Occident* 3 (March 1846): 591.

87. *Occident* 3 (March 1846): 592.

88. *Occident* 3 (March 1846): 592–93.

89. *Occident* 3 (March 1846): 593–94.

90. *Occident* 3 (March 1846): 594–95.

91. Grinstein, *Rise of the Jewish Community*, 304–5.

92. Grinstein, *Rise of the Jewish Community*, 304–5.

93. Plaut, *Rise of Reform Judaism*, 212.

94. Plaut, *Rise of Reform Judaism*, 307.

95. Grinstein, "Minute Book," 343–44.

96. Grinstein, *Rise of the Jewish Community*, 308.

97. Temkin, "Rabbi Max Lilienthal," 600.

98. Grinstein, "Minute Book," 338–39. My translated paraphrase follows.

99. Grinstein, *Rise of the Jewish Community*, 289.

100. Plaut, *Rise of Reform Judaism*, 215.

101. Philipson, *Reform Movement*, 218; Plaut, *Rise of Reform Judaism*, 218.

102. Anshe Chesed Trustee Minutes, September 18, 1846.

103. Temkin, "Rabbi Max Lilienthal," 601; and Grinstein, *Rise of the Jewish Community*, 396.

104. Philipson, *Reform Movement*, 218.

105. Grinstein, "Minute Book," 336.

106. Grinstein, *Rise of the Jewish Community*, 181–82.

107. Anshe Chesed Trustee Minutes, November 29, 1846.

108. Anshe Chesed Trustee Minutes, January 3 and 24, 1847.

109. Philipson, *Reform Movement*, 217.

110. Meyer, *Response to Modernity*, 35–36.

111. Philipson, *Reform Movement*, 178.

112. Marcus, *Colonial American Jew*, v. 2, 922–26.

113. Grinstein, *Rise of the Jewish Community*, 272.

114. Grinstein, *Rise of the Jewish Community*, 275.

115. Grinstein, "Minute Book," 331.

116. Anshe Chesed Trustee Minutes, March 3, 1846.

117. Cahen, "Een eigen ziekenfonds voor joden," 145–47.

118. Cahen, "Een eigen ziekenfonds voor joden," 145–47.

119. Wise, *Reminiscences*, 22.

120. *Occident* 4 (February 1847): 553.

121. Anshe Chesed Trustee Minutes, March 24, 1847. The minutes do not specify the nature of Bachman's infraction.

122. Anshe Chesed Trustee Minutes, November 21, 1847.

123. Sarna, "Forgotten Prayer," 431–40.

124. Sarna, "Forgotten Prayer." See also Grinstein, "Minute Book," 338, 341

(February 8 and 16, 1846); and Philipson, *Max Lilienthal*, 54.

125. Friedenberg, *Hear O Israel*, 2–5. See also Marcus, *Colonial American Jew*, v. 2, 971–72.

126. Friedenberg, *Hear O Israel*, 10–17. See also Ahlstrom, *Religious History*, 513. For a contemporary discussion of sermon style, see Baird, *Religion in America*, 192–96. See also von Rohr, *Shaping of American Congregationalism*, 43–44.

127. Friedenberg, *Hear O Israel*, 41.

128. Friedenberg, *Hear O Israel*, 26–27. See Sussman, "Isaac Leeser," 1–21, esp. 8.

129. Max Lilienthal to Samuel Lilienthal, December 12–24, 1840, in Philipson, *Max Lilienthal*, 148.

130. Max Lilienthal to Samuel Lilienthal, December 12–24, 1840, in Philipson, *Max Lilienthal*, 148.

131. *Occident* 3 (January 1846): 523.

132. Wise, *Reminiscences*, 22.

133. Grinstein, *Rise of the Jewish Community*, 275.

134. Wise, *Reminiscences*, 51; Werner, *A Voice Still Heard*, 206–19; Meyer, *Response to Modernity*, 151.

135. Grinstein, *Rise of the Jewish Community*, 274–76

136. Gartner, "Temples of Liberty Unpolluted," 166–67.

137. Kaestle, *Evolution of an Urban School System*, 138, 158. See also Spann, *New Metropolis*, for the religious controversy (29–34) and for the development of public education during the period (257).

138. Cremin, *American Education*, v. 2, 244–45. See also Marsden, *Soul of the American University*, 89. For a discussion of this issue in the Jewish community, see Gartner, "Temples of Liberty Unpolluted," 157–90; Cohen, *Encounter with Emancipation*, 91–96; and Diner, *A Time for Gathering*, 152–53. For the Protestant viewpoint, see Handy, *Christian America*, 35, 8–88; von Rohr, *Shaping of American Congregationalism*, 271; and Baird, *Religion in America*, 146–49.

139. Kaestle, *Evolution of an Urban School System*, 151–53. Also see Ravitch, *Great School Wars*, xiv.

140. Diner, *A Time for Gathering*, 152; Dolan, *Immigrant Church*, 110; Gilbert, *Commitment to Unity*, 16–17.

141. Gartner, *Jewish Education*, 6–7, 30–31.

142. Dushkin, *Jewish Education*, 133; Marcus, *Colonial American Jew*, v. 2, 1065.

143. Grinstein, "History of Jewish Education," 43.

144. Grinstein, "Minute Book," 335 (January 14, 1846).

145. Anshe Chesed Trustee Minutes, January 25, 1846.

146. Grinstein, "Minute Book," 337–38; *Allgemeine Zeitung des Judenthums* 11 (January 4, 1847): 26. See also Merowitz, "Max Lilienthal," 50.

147. Grinstein, "History of Jewish Education," 48.

148. Anshe Chesed Trustee Minutes, October 18, 1846.

149. Grinstein, "Minute Book," 326; Dushkin, *Jewish Education*, 47. See also Gartner, *Jewish Education*, 61.

150. Grinstein, "Minute Book," 351.

151. Merowitz, "Max Lilienthal," 51.

152. Merowitz, "Max Lilienthal," 51.

153. Grinstein, "History of Jewish Education," 48.

154. Cremin, *American Education*, 394.

155. Gartner, *Jewish Education*, 61–62.

156. Anshe Chesed Trustee Minutes, October 31, 1847.

157. Grinstein, *Rise of the Jewish Community*, 233.

158. Merowitz, "Max Lilienthal," 60, citing *Allgemeine Zeitung des Judenthums* 10 (May 11, 1846): 289–90. Merowitz suggests that confirmation also gave the congregations an edge in the competition with Temple Emanu-El.

159. Merowitz, "Max Lilienthal," 60.

160. Grinstein, "Minute Book," 334.

161. Grinstein, "Minute Book," 333–35; Grinstein, *Rise of the Jewish Community*, 250; *Occident* 4 (February 1847): 552.

162. *Occident* 4 (August 1846): 552.

163. *Occident* 4 (August 1846): 259. The *Occident* erroneously announced the confirmation as the first celebrated in America, although the ceremony was conducted in Charleston as early as 1825. Barnet A. Elzass described a confirmation service in the prayer book of the Charleston congregation K. K. Beth Elohim, printed in 1830 in the *Jewish Tribune* 7 (May 18, 1906): 17.

164. *Allgemeine Zeitung des Judenthums* 10 (January 4, 1847): 25.

165. *Occident* 4 (February 1847): 552.

166. *Occident* 4 (February 1847): 555. A Dutch acquaintance of the rabbi sent a letter home in 1848 that mentions the study group, a "Gemara chebra." He reported that the congregation kept Lilienthal so busy that he couldn't keep the group going. Cahen, "Een eigen ziekenfonds voor joden," 145–47.

167. *Occident* 5 (April 1847): 27–34; 5 (May 1847): 93–97; and 5 (June 1847): 142–48.

168. Grinstein, *Rise of the Jewish Community*, 398–400. Grinstein speculates that the enlarged union would have chosen Lilienthal rather than Merzbacher to be their rabbi because Lilienthal was a stronger orator and a superior educator and in better physical health.

169. Grinstein, *Rise of the Jewish Community*, 147–49, 155–56. For a discussion of poverty in New York in the 1840s, see Spann, *New Metropolis*, ch. 4.

170. *Allgemeine Zeitung des Judenthums* 10 (January 5, 1846): 18–20. Also see the report in *Occident* 3 (January 1846): 524.

171. Congregation Shearith Israel, Minutes of the Trustees, December 29, 1845; Grinstein, *Rise of the Jewish Community*, 425; Anshe Chesed Trustee Minutes, November 29, 1846.

172. Wise, *Reminiscences*, 17–18.

173. Wise, *Reminiscences*, 20.

174. Wise, Reminiscences, 20.

175. Wise, *Reminiscences*, 19–20.

176. Wise, *Reminiscences*, 129; *Israelite* 1 (August 11, 1854): 37–38.

177. Temkin, "Beth Din," 413.

178. *Occident* 3 (March 1846): 588, 590.

179. Grinstein, "Minute Book," 323.

180. Jick, *Americanization of the Synagogue*, 118. See *Occident* 5 (May 1847): 110; and Lilienthal's letter to the *Allgemeine Zeitung des Judenthums* translated in Temkin, "Beth Din," 416.

181. *Occident* 5 (May 1847): 107–9.

182. *Occident* 5 (May 1847): 107–9.

183. The main questions of law received from Europe dealt with the difficult issue of *agunoth*, or women unable to remarry because the death of their husband cannot be proved. The letters from America dealt mostly with strange circumstances arising out of intermarriages between young German Jews and non-Jewish wives. See Temkin, "Beth Din," 418.

184. Temkin, "Beth Din," 110–11.

185. Jick, *Americanization of the Synagogue*, 119.

186. Heller, *Isaac M. Wise*, 137.

187. Wise, *Reminiscences*, 55. Lilienthal came to the meeting with an English reader that he had prepared for intermediate classes of Hebrew schools. *Occident* 5 (May 1847): 110.

188. *Occident* 5 (June 1847): 163.

189. *Occident* 5 (August 1847): 259.

190. See, for example, Anshe Chesed Trustee Minutes for September 18, November 29, and December 13, 1846. When Lilienthal was present, the minutes indicate this explicitly.

191. Because we do not have access to the minute books of Rodeph Shalom or Shaarey Hashamayim, we do not know whether Lilienthal was excluded from their meetings.

192. Anshe Chesed Trustee Minutes, May 30, 1847.

193. Anshe Chesed Trustee Minutes, December, 13, 1846.

194. Anshe Chesed Trustee Minutes, January 3, 1847.

195. Anshe Chesed Trustee Minutes, October 10, 1847.

196. Anshe Chesed Trustee Minutes, October 10, 1847.

197. Anshe Chesed Trustee Minutes, May 2, 1847.

198. Wise, *Reminiscences*, 129.

199. Anshe Chesed Trustee Minutes, December 14, 1847.

200. Anshe Chesed Trustee Minutes, December 21, 1847.

201. Anshe Chesed Trustee Minutes, December 21, 1847.

202. Anshe Chesed Trustee Minutes, December 21, 1847.

203. Anshe Chesed Trustee Minutes, February 13, 1848.

204. Grinstein, *Rise of the Jewish Community*, 398. Grinstein further speculated that the other synagogues could no longer afford to pay Lilienthal's salary

and therefore had to disband the union. Grinstein, *Rise of the Jewish Community*, 587n15.

205. *Asmonean* 5 (October 24, 1851): 6

206. Jick, *Americanization of the Synagogue*, 73.

207. Heller, *Isaac M. Wise*, 192.

208. Dolan, *Immigrant Church*, 91.

Chapter 4

1. Temkin, "Rabbi Max Lilienthal," 596–97.

2. Wise, *Reminiscences*, 129.

3. *Allgemeine Zeitung des Judenthums* 16 (February 16, 1852): 92.

4. Merowitz, "Max Lilienthal," 52.

5. *Asmonean* 10 (August 11, 1854): 132–33. The article continues in *Asmonean* 10 (September 1, 1854): 156; and 10 (September 15, 1854): 172–73.

6. Petuchowski, "Manuals," 48, 63. Catechisms were used in American public schools in the 1830s and 1840s as well. See Kaestle, *Evolution of an Urban School System*, 152.

7. Gartner, *Jewish Education*, 6–7. See also Pilch, *History of Jewish Education*, 32. For specific catechisms used in American Jewish schools, see Grinstein, *Rise of the Jewish Community*, 257. For the catechism at Bnai Jeshurun, see Grinstein, "History of Jewish Education," 43.

8. *Asmonean* 10 (September 15, 1854): 172–73.

9. *Asmonean* 10 (September 15, 1854): 172–73.

10. *Asmonean* 10 (September 15, 1854): 172–73. For similar trends in Catholic catechisms and readers, see Dolan, *Immigrant Church*, 114–16. Lutherans also used catechisms in their Sunday schools, especially Luther's *Small Catechism*, brought from Germany. Gilbert, *Commitment to Unity*, 3, 16–17.

11. Chomsky, *Hebrew*, 255; *Asmonean* 10 (September 1, 1854): 156.

12. Grinstein, *Rise of the Jewish Community*, 242–43.

13. Ringer, *Education*, 34. Sorkin points out that Jewish schools in Germany also emulated the *Realschulen* (Sorkin, *Transformation of German Jewry*, 127).

14. Pilch, *History of Jewish Education*, 30–32/. Also see Grinstein, *Rise of the Jewish Community*, 247. Another model may have been secular academies that mixed classical and "realist" subjects and catered to middle-class families who could afford schooling beyond elementary level but whose children were not college bound. Hundreds of these academies were incorporated in New York state between 1841 and 1860. See Good and Teller, *History of American Education*, 67–68, 106–7; Cremin, *American Education*, 427; and Noble, *History of American Education*.

15. *Asmonean* 1 (November 9, 1849): 23.

16. *Asmonean* 1 (November 9, 1849): 23.

17. *Asmonean* 1 (December 14, 1849): 61.

18. Grinstein, "Minute Book," 336 (January 14, 1846); *Occident* 4 (May

1846): 97.

19. *Occident* 8 (November 1850): 52. In Schappes's *Documentary History* (116), we see that 6 was the minimum age in the Spanish-Portuguese Talmud Torah.

20. The advertisement appeared regularly on the last page of the *Asmonean*, a new Jewish weekly; for examples see volume 1, pages 48, 56, 64, and 72.

21. *Asmonean* 3 (April 16, 1851): 204.

22. Nadel, *Little Germany*, 35, 104–5; Grinstein, *Rise of the Jewish Community*, 32.

23. *Asmonean* 3 (April 16, 1851): 204. See also Nadel, *Little Germany*, 35.

24. *Asmonean* 10 (August 11, 1854): 133.

25. Dushkin, *Jewish Education*, 49.

26. *Occident* 8 (November 1850): 424–25. For a biography of this colorful early New York Jewish lay leader, see Sarna, *Jacksonian Jew*.

27. Pilch, *History of Jewish Education*, 39.

28. *Asmonean* 4 (April 16, 1851): 204.

29. *Asmonean* 4 (May 2, 1851): 11.

30. *Occident* 9 (May 1851): 104–5; *Asmonean* 3 (April 16, 1851): 204.

31. The German Catholic community had similar concerns about the practical necessity of learning English to ensure socioeconomic advancement. Like the Jews, they also felt ambivalent about giving up their German cultural heritage. Dolan, *Immigrant Church*, 110.

32. *Occident* 9 (May 1851): 104.

33. *Asmonean* 3 (April 16, 1851): 204.

34. *Asmonean* 3 (April 16, 1851): 204; *Occident* 9 (May 1851): 105.

35. *Asmonean* 6 (September 10, 1852): 197. Merowitz suggested that the music and art courses required an additional fee (Merowitz, "Max Lilienthal," 53).

36. *Asmonean* 10 (September 15, 1854): 173.

37. *Asmonean* 7 (November 19, 1852): 53. For a discussion of discipline, see Pilch, *History of Jewish Education*, 32. See also *Occident* 8 (November 1850): 424–25; and *Asmonean* 4 (May 23, 1851): 37. According to Grinstein, one of the reasons for the decline in Jewish parochial schools may have been their reported laxity of discipline (Grinstein, *Rise of the Jewish Community*, 245).

38. *Asmonean* 6 (September 10, 1852): 197.

39. Pilch, *History of Jewish Education*, 39. Also see Merowitz, "Max Lilienthal," 53.

40. *Asmonean* 1 (December 21, 1849): 71.

41. *Asmonean* 6 (September 10, 1852): 197. After Lilienthal left the city, Loewe's school became more prominent. Grinstein, *Rise of the Jewish Community*, 243.

42. *Asmonean* 3 (February 7, 1851): 124.

43. *Asmonean* 7 (January 7, 1853): 137. Grinstein lists other private schools in his *Rise of the Jewish Community*, 243 and 565n34. The *Asmonean* 12 (July 13, 1855) printed advertisements for other schools.

44. *Asmonean* 4 (May 23, 1851): 37.

45. For instance, Congregation Anshe Chesed, reestablishing its school simultaneously with the founding of Lilienthal's school, was wary about the outlay of funds. Anshe Chesed Trustee Minutes, April 30, May 7, 1848. The minutes for the next months reveal that Anshe Chesed's school was plagued by the constant need for repairs to its building, poor teachers, and an inattentive superintendent. Anshe Chesed Trustee Minutes, January 1, 1850.

46. Gartner, "Temples of Liberty Unpolluted," 169–70; *Israelite* 1 (December 8, 1854): 173. A similar debate occurred among liberals in the Catholic community, where the commitment to parochial schooling was generally stronger. Dolan, *Immigrant Church*, 91.

47. Grinstein, "History of Jewish Education," 190. A similar tendency can be seen in Christian religious education, which, in the face of competition from the public schools, turned increasingly to the Sunday school to impart religious values by the 1850s. See Seymour, *Sunday School.* Henry Barnard, an American educator, wrote in 1865, "Religious instruction has been withdrawn from the common school and entrusted wholly to the home and the church" (Seymour, *Sunday School,* 31). For origins of the Sunday School movement, see Cremin, *American Education,* 66.

48. *Asmonean* 12 (August 3, 1855): 121. For advertisements for the Jewish Academy for Young Ladies at the same address, see *Asmonean* 14 (May 2, 1856): 19. These notices stopped abruptly after *Asmonean* 14 (June 13, 1854): 65.

49. Grinstein, *Rise of the Jewish Community,* 93. Henry probably left New York in the spring of 1857. The last advertisement for the school appeared in the *Asmonean* 15 (April 10, 1857): 201. The *Occident* reported Henry's arrival in San Francisco in August 1857, where he eventually became the minister of Congregation Shearith Israel. *Occident* 15 (November 1857): 407; 16 (October 1859): 606; and 19 (October 1861): 323.

50. Grinstein, *Rise of the Jewish Community,* 245.

51. Anshe Chesed Trustee Minutes, September 19, 1848.

52. *Occident* 6 (July 1848): 214.

53. Grinstein, *Rise of the Jewish Community,* 32; Nadel, *Little Germany,* 30–32; Burrows and Wallace, *Gotham,* 745.

54. Grinstein, *Rise of the Jewish Community,* 364.

55. Grinstein, *Rise of the Jewish Community,* 364. The ruling validated the synagogue's decision in late 1849 to include women choristers. See Anshe Chesed Trustee Minutes, December 2, 1849, and January 20, 1850. For Viennese ritual, see Mannheimer, *Gebete des Israeliten.*

56. Wise, *Reminiscences,* 129.

57. Anshe Chesed Trustee Minutes, August 19, 1949. Choir members were paid by receiving either free seats in the new synagogue (worth $50) or $36 per year for three years (Anshe Chesed Trustee Minutes, November 18, 1849). By December 1849 the synagogue had hired eight paid singers, eight who worked in exchange for seats, and eleven children who received seats for their parents.

58. Anshe Chesed Trustee Minutes, December 2, 1849, and January 20, 1850.

59. The clipping of the article in the *New York Daily Tribune* is included in the Anshe Chesed Trustee Minutes.

60. Anshe Chesed Trustee Minutes, June 16, 1850.

61. Lilienthal officiated at Shaarey Hashamayim and Ahavat Chesed during the High Holy Days in September 1850 and again at Shaarey Hashamayim for Washington's birthday in February 1851. *Asmonean* 2 (September 20, 1850); 2 (October 18, 1850); 3 (November 29, 1850); and 3 (February 21, 1851).

62. Anshe Chesed Trustee Minutes, April 27, 1851.

63. Anshe Chesed Trustee Minutes, October 8, 1851.

64. Anshe Chesed Trustee Minutes, October 8, 1851. Although Lilienthal was called "honorary rabbi," there was no other to share the duties with him. He was given no salary for the honor.

65. Anshe Chesed Trustee Minutes, October 13, 1851.

66. *Asmonean* 5 (October 24, 1851): 6. The paper included a similar resolution by the board of Rodeph Shalom.

67. *Asmonean* 5 (October 24, 1851): 6.

68. Anshe Chesed Trustee Minutes, March 28, 1852.

69. Anshe Chesed Trustee Minutes, August 15, 1852; October 20, 1853; and October 29, 1854.

70. Anshe Chesed Trustee Minutes, August 1, 1853.

71. *Asmonean* 4 (October 17, 1851): 283; *Israelite* 1 (September 29, 1854): 95; *Asmonean* 7 (November 19, 1852): 53; *Israelite* 1 (June 1, 1855): 373; *Asmonean* 10 (June 9, 1854): 63; *Israelite* 1 (November 17, 1854): 149; and *Israelite* 1 (August 28, 1854): 78.

72. *Asmonean* 10 (June 9, 1854): 63.

73. Cohen, *Encounter with Emancipation*, 8–9; Rürup, "European Revolutions," 16–23.

74. Gailus, "Anti-Jewish Emotion," 50–55.

75. Nadel, *Little Germany*, 119–21.

76. Nadel, *Little Germany*, 102.

77. Wise, *Reminiscences*, 81.

78. Wise, *Reminiscences*, 82–83.

79. *Occident* 7 (January 1850): 515.

80. *Occident* 7 (January 1850): 514.

81. *Asmonean* 2 (August 6, 1850): 122.

82. *Asmonean* 2 (August 6, 1850): 122.

83. Rürup, "European Revolutions," 16–18.

84. Marcus, *United States Jewry*, v. 2, 43; Nadel, *Little Germany*, 18; Cohen, *Encounter with Emancipation*, 8–9.

85. Wise, *Reminiscences*, 78–79; Heller, *Isaac M. Wise*, 138–40.

86. Wise, *Reminiscences*, 86.

87. *Occident* 6 (March 1849): 614–15.

88. *Occident* 6 (March 1849): 614–15.

89. *Occident* 7 (April 1849): 12–13. In his *Reminiscences*, Wise claims that this address, which came to be known as "the reform lightning" (87), instigated a number of reform efforts.

90. Graetz, *History of the Jews*, v. 5: 418–19.

91. *Occident* 7 (August 1849): 271.

92. Marcus, *United States Jewry*, v. 2, 311; Greive, "Religious Dissent," 340–52.

93. M. Lilienthal, "Erster Vortrag," 25.

94. M. Lilienthal, "Erster Vortrag," 25–27, 34–35. See also Kisch, "*Israels Herold*," 3–22.

95. Philipson, *Max Lilienthal*, 65. Cited in *Occident* 7 (June 1849): 142.

96. Kisch, "*Israels Herold*," 16.

97. See *Occident* 7 (August 1849): 274, where his letter to the society, written April 4, 1849, is printed.

98. Kisch, "*Israels Herold*," 16–17.

99. Wise, *Reminiscences*, 90.

100. Wise, *Reminiscences*, 91. See also May, *Isaac Mayer Wise*, 83.

101. Wise, *Reminiscences*, 91. This is verified by Sigismund Waterman in his letter to the *Occident* 7 (August 1849): 271.

102. Wise, *Reminiscences*, 92.

103. *Occident* 7 (June 1849): 143–44.

104. *Occident* 7 (August, 1849): 272.

105. *Occident* 7 (August 1849): 272.

106. See Wise's comment in the *Israelite* 1 (August 11, 1854): 37–38.

107. Barkai, *Branching Out*, 17.

108. Barkai, *Branching Out*, 99. See also Temkin, "Beth Din," 418.

109. *Israelite* 1 (August 11, 1854): 37–38.

110. See Marcus, *United States Jewry*, v. 2, 98.

111. Marcus, *United States Jewry*, v. 2, 98.

112. See Feiner, *Haskalah and History*, 38. Feiner delineates a maskilic historical tradition that moves in a separate, parallel path from *Jüdische Wissenschaft* while sharing certain basic assumptions, such as a rationalist approach, belief in the disjunction of modern age from the past, and the Mendelssohn legend (Feiner, *Haskalah and History*, 9). According to Feiner, *Jüdische Wissenschaft* provided a historiography for these general theories (Feiner, *Haskalah and History*, 60). Lilienthal grew up assimilating maskilic attitudes and developed *Wissenschaft* methodology at the University of Munich.

113. *Israels Herold* 5 (April 27, 1849): 34.

114. Feiner, *Haskalah and History*, 39, 57–59.

115. Feiner, *Haskalah and History*, 39, 57–59.

116. See Feiner, *Haskalah and History*, 62, for a discussion of the dissemination of maskilic history throughout the nineteenth century.

117. Ismar Schorsch addressed this issue directly in "Scholarship in the Ser-

vice of Reform," in his *From Text to Context*, 303–33. Gershom Scholem addressed this issue as well in "Science of Judaism," 304–5.

118. Levels of observance are of course relative. Lilienthal's shaved face and modern clothing made him seem a reformer to the traditional Jews of Russia.

119. Schorsch, "Emergence of Historical Consciousness," 419–20. See also Meyer, *Origins of the Modern Jew*.

120. Schorsch, "Emergence of Historical Consciousness," 420. See also Ellenson, *Between Tradition and Culture*, 3; and Ellenson, *Rabbi Esriel Hildescheimer*, 143–45.

121. *Israels Herold* 4 (April 27, 1849), 35.

122. *Asmonean* 10 (June 1, 1854): 53.

123. *Asmonean* 10 (August 4, 1854): 125.

124. *Asmonean* 10 (August 4, 1854): 125.

125. *Asmonean* 10 (August 4, 1854): 125.

126. *Asmonean* 1 (December 14, 1849): 61.

127. *Asmonean* 6 (September 10, 1852): 197.

128. *Asmonean* 7 (January 7, 1853): 137; and 12 (August 3, 1855): 121.

129. Merowitz, *Max Lilienthal*, 54. Lilienthal did become a spokesman for moderate Reform by the time he left New York.

130. *New York Daily Tribune*, May 18, 1850, 2.

131. *New York Daily Tribune*, May 18, 1850, 2. See also Anshe Chesed Trustees Minutes, January 1, 1854.

132. *Asmonean* 10 (July 21, 1854): 108. The triennial reading of the Torah was practiced in Palestine as early as the second century BCE and continued until at least the twelfth century CE.

133. *Asmonean* 10 (August 25, 1854): 149–50.

134. *Asmonean* 10 (June 1, 1854): 53. This issue had already been addressed by reformers in England in 1840 and in Charleston's Reform congregation. See Sarna, *American Judaism*, 85.

135. *Asmonean* 10 (June 1, 1854): 53. See Meyer, *Response to Modernity*, 123.

136. *Asmonean* 10 (June 1, 1854): 53.

137. Meyer, *Response to Modernity*, 87.

138. *Asmonean* 10 (September 1, 1854): 156.

139. *Asmonean* 10 (September 1, 1854): 156.

140. *Asmonean* 10 (July 14, 1854): 100. See Meyer, *Response to Modernity*, 93, for a discussion of Geiger's views.

141. Schorsch, "Emergence of Historical Consciousness," 421.

142. *Asmonean* 10 (June 23, 1854): 77. See also *Asmonean* 10 (June 30, 1854): 85, for Lilienthal's response to Isaac Leeser.

143. Even the modern Orthodox leader Samson R. Hirsch did not believe that customs, no matter how venerable, were necessarily binding in the new age. Meyer, *Response to Modernity*, 78. For a general discussion of the traditional relationship of custom to law, see Urbach, *Yad la-Talmud*, 38.

144. *Asmonean* 10 (June 23, 1854): 77.

145. *Asmonean* 10 (June 23, 1854): 77. Immanuel Etkes argues that this view is also a central characteristic of the Haskalah in general, which became "increasingly conscious of the historical character of the process by which the *halachah* (rabbinic law) took shape" (Etkes, "Immanent Factors," 14). *Minhagim* were seen as "late accretions and the product of unnecessarily strict interpretations."

146. *Asmonean* 10 (June 9, 1854): 62. For this trend in maskilic history, see Feiner, *Haskalah and History*, 33, 97–100.

147. *Asmonean* 10 (June 9, 1854): 63. Lilienthal cited A. Jellinek's pamphlet "Contribution to the History of Kabbalah."

148. *Asmonean* 10 (June 9, 1854): 62. Again Lilienthal betrayed an important Jewish *Wissenschaft* bias in favor of philosophy. Its rationalism was in harmony with the spirit of the times, and its creators, the Spanish Jews, were idealized by these nineteenth-century scholars.

149. *Asmonean* 10 (June 16, 1854): 70. Jewish philosophy should have been vulnerable to the same criticism as mysticism—that is, that it was an alien plant grafted on the biblical essence of Judaism. Lilienthal seemed to be implicitly denying this by claiming that Jewish philosophy had its origins in the Bible itself and therefore partook of Judaism's essence.

150. The Hellenistic period had been the focus of Lilienthal's dissertation.

151. *Asmonean* 10 (August 18, 1854): 142. For other installments, see *Asmonean* 10 (June 30, 1854): 85; 10 (July 21, 1854): 110; 10 (July 28, 1854): 117–18; and 10 (August 11, 1854): 133–34. Some of the *Wissenschaft* scholars that Lilienthal cited were A. Jellinek, N. Krochmal, A. Geiger, and L. Zunz. Lilienthal's list of intellectual heroes mirrors the pantheon set up by the Haskalah, especially his treatment of Maimonides. See Feiner, *Haskalah and History*, 50–60.

152. *Asmonean* 10 (June 16, 1854): 70. This open admiration for the heretic Spinoza was anticipated by one of Lilienthal's models, Moses Mendelssohn. See Altmann, *Moses Mendelssohn*, 34–36, 50–53. For the idealization of Spinoza in maskilic history, see Feiner, *Haskalah and History*, 146–50.

153. *Asmonean* 10 (June 1, 1854): 53–54.

154. *Asmonean* 10 (June 23, 1854): 77.

155. *Asmonean* 10 (June 23, 1854): 77.

156. *Asmonean* 10 (September 1, 1854): 156.

157. Nadel, *Little Germany*, 99. For parallels in the Catholic community, see Dolan, *Immigrant Church*, 7–8.

158. *Asmonean* 10 (June 30, 1854): 85.

159. Temkin, "Beth Din," 418. (Discussed in Chapter 3.)

160. Temkin, "Beth Din," 418.

161. Temkin, "Beth Din," 418.

162. *Asmonean* 10 (September 22, 1854): 181.

163. *Asmonean* 10 (August 4, 1854): 125.

164. *Asmonean* 10 (August 4, 1854): 125.

165. For Moses Mendelssohn's precepts of natural theology, see Meyer, *Ori-*

gins of the Modern Jew, 19–20. See also Altmann, *Moses Mendelssohn*, 29, 249, 341. Also see Mendelssohn, "The Principles of Judaism: A Credo," in his *Jerusalem*, 154–56.

166. *Asmonean* 10 (August 25, 1854): 150.

167. *Asmonean* 10 (August 25, 1854): 150.

168. See *Asmonean* 10 (June 16, 1854): 70; and 10 (June 30, 1854): 94. Lilienthal's long article on Jewish education, written during this period, was discussed earlier in this chapter.

169. *Asmonean* 10 (June 30, 1854): 84.

170. *Israelite* 1 (September 15, 1854): 76.

171. *Israelite* 1 (September 29, 1854): 95.

172. For an overview, see Sarna, *American Judaism*, 73–74. See also Cohen, *Jews in Christian America*, 39–40.

173. Baird, *Religion in America*, 130; Silverstein, *Alternatives to Assimilation*, 9–10.

174. *Israelite* 1 (November 17, 1854): 149.

175. Jonathan Sarna, in Cohen, *Essential Papers*, 29.

176. Anshe Chesed Trustee Minutes, May 13, 1855. The news of the appointment had already been announced in the *Israelite*. *Israelite* 1 (April 27, 1855): 335.

177. *Israelite* 1 (April 27, 1855): 335. The Bene Israel Trustee Minutes indicate that Lilienthal had not yet signed a contract on June 5, 1855, when he met with them in Cincinnati.

178. Anshe Chesed Trustee Minutes, June 24, 1855. There was one further attempt to keep Lilienthal in New York, in the form of a petition calling for another general meeting, which was thrown out on procedural grounds.

179. *New York Times*, April 6, 1882, 2. See the discussion of his school earlier in this chapter.

180. May, *Isaac Mayer Wise*, 145–46.

181. Philipson, *Max Lilienthal*, 59.

182. *Israelite* 1 (April 20, 1855): 323.

183. Bretting, "Little Germanies," 147.

184. *Israelite* 1 (April 27, 1855): 335.

185. *Israelite* 1 (April 27, 1855): 335.

186. *Israelite* 1 (May 11, 1855): 349.

187. Anshe Chesed Trustee Minutes, July 1, 1855, and April 1, 1855. See also the minutes for January 1, 1854.

188. Anshe Chesed Trustee Minutes, April 1, 1855.

Chapter 5

1. Sarna and Klein, *Jews of Cincinnati*, 1ff. For Joseph Jonas's memoir, see his "Moving Westward," 223–35. For another early account, see Samuel Bruel, "Cincinnati Israelitish Institutions," *Israelite* 1 (July 15, 1854): 1.

2. Mostov, "Jerusalem on the Ohio," 61.

3. Sarna and Goldman, "Synagogue-Community," 164–65.

4. Dickens, *American Notes*, 207, 209.

5. Ford and Ford, *History of Cincinnati*, 126–34.

6. Klauprecht, *German Chronicle*, 170.

7. Klauprecht, *German Chronicle*, 170, 179; Toth, *German-English Bilingual Schools*, x.

8. Cohen, *Encounter with Emancipation*, 41. Other general studies of the Cincinnati Jewish community include Michael, "Origins"; and Brickner, "Jewish Community."

9. Mostov, "Jerusalem on the Ohio," 50.

10. Mostov, "Jerusalem on the Ohio," 37.

11. Cohen, *Encounter with Emancipation*, 41, 60–61.

12. Whiteman, "Notions," 309.

13. Sarna and Klein, *Jews of Cincinnati*, 4; Mostov, "Jerusalem on the Ohio," 126–27; Whiteman, "Notions," 311–13; Cohen, *Encounter with Emancipation*, 21; Philipson, "Jewish Pioneers"; and May, "Jews of Cincinnati."

14. Mostov, "Jerusalem on the Ohio," 106.

15. Mostov, "Jerusalem on the Ohio," 111.

16. Mostov, "Jerusalem on the Ohio," 111.

17. Jonas, "Moving Westward," 224.

18. Sarna and Klein, *Jews of Cincinnati*, 4.

19. Jonas, "Moving Westward," 227.

20. For Jonas's complete description, see his "Moving Westward," 230–31.

21. Jonas, "Moving Westward," 147.

22. Sarna and Goldman, "Synagogue-Community," 166.

23. Sarna and Goldman, "Synagogue-Community," 168.

24. Sarna and Goldman, "Synagogue-Community," 172.

25. Wise, *Reminiscences*, 276–77.

26. Samuel Bruel, "Affairs in Cincinnati," *Occident* 13 (December 1855): 458–64. See also Sarna and Goldman, "Synagogue-Community," 173. The cost of the expansion was $40,000.

27. Mostov, "Jerusalem on the Ohio," 168.

28. Wise, *Reminiscences*, 277.

29. Sarna and Goldman, "Synagogue-Community," 173.

30. Wise, *Reminiscences*, 277. Wise published the results of the meeting and contract terms in the *Israelite* 1 (November 17, 1854): 147–48.

31. *Occident* 13 (December 1855): 459.

32. Wise, *Reminiscences*, 283.

33. *Israelite* 1 (April 27, 1855): 335. Lilienthal confirmed that the election had already taken place in his response to Wise in the *Israelite* 1 (May 11, 1855): 349.

34. *Occident* 13 (December 1855): 459.

35. *Israelite* 1 (April 27, 1855): 335.

36. *Occident* 13 (December 1855): 460.

37. Bene Israel Trustee Minutes, May 25, 1855.

38. Bene Israel Trustee Minutes, June 3, 1855. Lilienthal's wish to confer with his wife first was later stricken from the minutes, without explanation.

39. See Philipson, *Oldest Jewish Congregation*, 23; and Wise, *Reminiscences*, 276.

40. Wise, *Reminiscences*, 277.

41. *Hebrew Review* 2 (1881–82): 187.

42. *Hebrew Review* 2 (1881–82): 187.

43. Bene Israel Trustee Minutes, June 10 and 19, 1855. See Chapter 4 for a discussion of these rituals.

44. Bene Israel Trustee Minutes, June 26, 1855.

45. Bene Israel Trustee Minutes, August 1, 1855.

46. *Israelite* 2 (August 10, 1855): 34.

47. *Israelite* 2 (July 27, 1855): 23; *Occident* 13 (November 1855): 360.

48. Schappes, *Documentary History*, 223–35.

49. Philipson, *Oldest Jewish Congregation*, 23–24.

50. Wise, *Reminiscences*, 260. See Chapter 1 for the importance of "edification" in the modernization of German Jewish services.

51. *Israelite* 2 (August 10, 1855): 36.

52. *Israelite* 2 (August 10, 1855): 36. Many legal sources were then analyzed to support the editors' contention.

53. *Israelite* 2 (September 21, 1855): 83; and 2 (October 5, 1855): 102.

54. Bene Israel Trustee Minutes, August 19 and September 16, 1855, and March 23, 1856; *Occident* 13 (December 1855): 460.

55. *Occident* 13 (December 1855): 460.

56. *Occident* 13 (November 1855): 360.

57. *Israelite* 2 (August 10, 1855): 36.

58. *Occident* 13 (December 1855): 461–62.

59. *Occident* 13 (December 1855): 461–62.

60. *Israelite* 2 (August 10, 1855): 38.

61. *Occident* 13 (December 1855): 461.

62. *Occident* 13 (December 1855): 462.

63. *Occident* 13 (November 1855): 369.

64. *Israelite* 2 (October 19, 1855): 115.

65. Philipson, *Max Lilienthal*, 59.

66. Wise, *Reminiscences*, 277.

67. Bene Israel Trustee Minutes, January 25, 1855.

68. Bene Israel School Board Minutes, May 21 and July 1, 1855.

69. Bene Israel School Board Minutes, September 9, 1855.

70. Bene Israel School Board Minutes, October 7 and November 17, 1855; *Israelite* 2 (January 11, 1856): 218.

71. *Israelite* 2 (January 11, 1856): 218.

72. *Israelite* 2 (January 11, 1856): 218; Bene Israel Trustee Minutes, January

4, 1856; Bene Israel School Board Minutes, January 6, 1856.

73. *Israelite* 2 (September 14, 1855): 74–75.

74. *Israelite* 2 (September 14, 1855): 74–75.

75. *Asmonean* 10 (September 15, 1854): 173.

76. *Israelite* 2 (September 14, 1855): 75.

77. *Israelite* 2 (September 14, 1855): 75.

78. For a discussion of the importance of individualism in Reform thought, see Borowitz, *Choices in Modern Jewish Thought*, 244–46.

79. Meyer, *Response to Modernity*, 132.

80. Silverstein, *Alternative to Assimilation*, 35.

81. See Meyer, *Response to Modernity*, 243–44; Cohen, *Encounter with Emancipation*, 175–76; Davis, *Emergence of Conservative Judaism*, 130–32; and Jick, *Americanization of the Synagogue*, 162–63. Also see Temkin, *Isaac Mayer Wise*, 136–49.

82. Illoway, *Sefer*, 2.

83. Heller, *Isaac M. Wise*, 56, 58. See also Temkin, *Isaac Mayer Wise*, 122–23; and Meyer, "In the Days," 11–13.

84. Lafcadio Hearn, quoted in Sarna and Klein, *Jews of Cincinnati*, 50; and May, "Jews of Cincinnati," 941. See also S. Lilienthal, *Lilienthal Family Record*, 56, for a discussion of Lilienthal's personality.

85. Wise, *Reminiscences*, 129.

86. Quoted in Sarna and Klein, *Jews of Cincinnati*, 86. Reprinted from the *St. Louis Jewish Tribune* (1883). See also Illoway, *Sefer*, 5–6.

87. Wise, *Reminiscences*, 307.

88. *Occident* 13 (November 1855): 413.

89. *Israelite* 2 (August 17, 1855): 44.

90. *Israelite* 2 (August 17, 1855): 50; 2 (August 31, 1855): 60; 2 (September 7, 1855): 68; 2 (September 14, 1855): 77; 2 (September 21, 1855): 85; etc.

91. *Israelite* 2 (September 21, 1855): 84.

92. Sussman, *Isaac Leeser*, 197–98.

93. *Occident* 13 (November 1855): 409; Sussman, *Isaac Leeser*, 197.

94. *Occident* 13 (October 1855): 360.

95. *Israelite* 2 (November 9, 1855): 148.

96. *Occident* 14 (May 1856): 75–76.

97. *Occident* 13 (November 1855): 411.

98. *Occident* 13 (November 1855): 414; Wise, *Reminiscences*, 314.

99. Sussman, *Isaac Leeser*, 199. Sussman was unable to account for Leeser's early departure.

100. *Israelite* 2 (November 2, 1855): 140; and 2 (November 9, 1855): 148.

101. *Israelite* 2 (November 2, 1855): 137.

102. *Israelite* 2 (November 2, 1855): 137. Zacharias Frankel, the ideological founder of present-day Conservative Judaism, had developed the Positive-Historical school, which combined *Wissenschaft* with tradition. See Meyer, *Response to Modernity*, 84–89.

103. Barkai, *Branching Out*, 159.

104. *Israelite* 2 (November 2, 1855): 137.

105. *Occident* 13 (November 1855): 414 (italics in original).

106. *Hebrew Review* 2 (1881–82): 1887–88.

107. Jick, *Americanization of the Synagogue*, 163.

108. *Occident* 13 (December 1855): 451.

109. *Occident* 14 (May 1856): 77–78.

110. *Occident* 14 (February 1857): 505.

111. *Israelite* 2 (February 1, 1856): 244.

112. *Israelite* 2 (December 7, 1855): 180.

113. Again we see the influence of Geiger and the *Wissenschaft* approach to rabbinic literature (see Chapter 4).

114. *Occident* 14 (November 1856): 382. See also Cohen, *Encounter with Emancipation*, 175–77; and Sussman, *Isaac Leeser*, 201–2. Leeser and Lilienthal discussed many other issues in their wide-ranging exchange. For more detail, see especially Cohen's treatment.

115. *Occident* 14 (November 1856): 385.

116. Philipson, *Max Lilienthal*, 370.

117. Philipson, *Max Lilienthal*, 371, 377, 382.

118. Philipson, *Max Lilienthal*, 379. See, for instance, Hegel, *Reason in History*, 20.

119. See Lilienthal's translation of Emanuel Hecht's *History of the Israelites*, 118.

120. *Occident* 14 (November 1856): 363–65; and 14 (February 1857): 534–35.

121. Philipson, *Max Lilienthal*, 386–87.

122. For a discussion of Einhorn and his intellectual position, see Meyer, *Response to Modernity*, 244–50. See also Greenberg, "Significance of America."

123. *Occident* 13 (December 1855): 449.

124. *Occident* 13 (December 1855): 450.

125. *Israelite* 2 (November 30, 1855): 173.

126. *Israelite* 2 (February 22, 1856): 268.

127. *Israelite* 2 (February 22, 1856): 268.

128. *Israelite* 2 (February 8, 1856): 253.

129. *Occident* 13 (December 1855): 450.

130. *Allgemeine Zeitung des Judenthums* 19 (September 3, 1855): 464–65. For a discussion of Philippson's attitude toward the American Jewish leadership, see Barkai, *Branching Out*, 159–61.

131. *Allgemeine Zeitung des Judenthums* 19 (November 26, 1855): 622–23; and 19 (December 10, 1855): 634–37. The paper regularly received the *Israelite* and the German-language *Die Deborah*, which was also edited by Wise and Lilienthal. See *Die Deborah* 1 (October 26, 1855): 73; 1 (November 2, 1855): 81; 1 (November 9, 1855): 89; and 1 (December 14, 1855): 129, for "Die Conferenz in Cleveland."

132. See the article "Is Dr. I. M. Wise a Traitor" in *Asmonean* 13 (January 11,

1856): 101; and *Asmonean* 13 (March 28, 1856): 186.

133. *Israelite* 2 (March 28, 1856): 308–9.

134. *Hebrew Review* 2 (1881–82): 188.

135. *Israelite* 2 (November 9, 1855): 148.

136. Cremin, *American Education,* 400. According to Cremin's estimate, there were 22 theological seminaries in 1831, 44 by 1850, and 124 by 1876. See also Marsden, *Soul of the American University,* 80.

137. *Israelite* 1 (June 8, 1855): 379. See Heller, *Isaac M. Wise,* 274–82, for details. Heller is incorrect when he states that the college opened in the fall of 1856 (275). See Wise, *Reminiscences,* 324. Also see Korn, *Eventful Years,* 156–59.

138. Wise, *Reminiscences,* 324; *Israelite* 2 (August 10, 1855): 37; Heller, *Isaac M. Wise,* 280.

139. Wise, *Reminiscences,* 305.

140. The meeting took place on October 28, 1855. See *Occident* 13 (December 1855): 453–55.

141. Davis, *Emergence of Conservative Judaism,* 57.

142. Wise, *Reminiscences,* 334–35. See also Heller, *Isaac M. Wise,* 281.

143. *Israelite* 3 (March 20, 1857): 297–98.

144. *Israelite* 3 (March 27, 1857): 300.

145. *Israelite* 3 (March 27, 1857): 300.

146. *Israelite* 6 (November 6, 1859): 140.

147. Sherman, "Bernard Illowy," 191, 195–96; *Occident* 14 (March 1857): 576–79, and 14 (April 1857): 35–38.

148. *Occident* 6 (November 11, 1859): 150.

149. Bene Israel Trustee Minutes, January 29, 1860.

150. Bene Israel Trustee Minutes, July 15, 1860. As assimilated as the membership was becoming, it still expected their rabbi to maintain strict observance of Jewish law.

151. *Israelite* 7 (July 27, 1860): 26.

152. Bene Israel School Board Minutes, February 17 and April 6, 1856.

153. Bene Israel School Board Minutes, January 25, 1857.

154. See Merowitz, "Max Lilienthal," 55.

155. Bene Israel School Board Minutes, April 26 and May 3, 1856.

156. *Israelite* 4 (November 13, 1857): 145; 4 (February 5, 1858): 246.

157. Bene Israel School Board Minutes, March 20, 1858.

158. Bene Israel School Board Minutes, April 25, 1858.

159. Bene Israel School Board Minutes, August 29, 1858.

160. Bene Israel Trustee Minutes, November 22, 1858, and August 4, 1859.

161. *Hebrew Review* 2 (1881–82): 188.

162. Eliza (1846), Theodore (1847), Philip (1849), Esther (1853), Jesse (1855), and Albert (1859). In 1861 the Lilienthals' last child, Victoria, was born. See O'Neill, *Ernest Reuben Lilienthal,* 30.

Chapter 6

1. *Hebrew Review* 2 (1881–82): 188.

2. *Hebrew Review* 2 (1881–82): 189.

3. Sarna and Goldman, "Synagogue-Community," 177.

4. Sarna and Goldman, "Synagogue-Community," 188.

5. See Silver, "Rabbi Max Lilienthal," 343–47.

6. Bellah, "Civil Religion," 171, 176. See also Albanese, *Sons of the Fathers*; and Ahlstrom, *Religious History*, 383–84.

7. Bellah, "Civil Religion," 176.

8. Cohen, *Jews in Christian America*, 37.

9. M. Lilienthal, *Freiheit*, 9, 41 (quotations are my translations). The last two sections treat springtime and love.

10. *Jewish Times* 1 (January 28, 1870): 6.

11. *Jewish Times* 1 (January 28, 1870): 6.

12. Merowitz, "Max Lilienthal," 56.

13. Mound Street Temple Religious School Accounts, October 12, 1878.

14. Merowitz, "Max Lilienthal," 57. See also Edward L. Cohn, "The Sabbath Visitor: A Child's Paper," May 11, 1961, American Jewish Archives, Max Lilienthal Correspondence, SC-2228. In about 1880 the name of the children's newspaper was shortened to *The Sabbath Visitor*.

15. See *Hebrew Sabbath School Visitor* 1(1) (January 1874); and 1(17) (n.d.): 67.

16. *Hebrew Sabbath School Visitor* 3(1) (January 14, 1876): 4.

17. *Israelite* 2 (November 9, 1855): 148.

18. *Hebrew Review* 2 (1881–82): 189.

19. *Israelite* 6 (March 30, 1860): 307; and 6 (April 6, 1860): 315. Also see Sarna and Klein, *Jews of Cincinnati*, 50. That Protestants still hoped to use the public schools to promote a Christian America is well documented by Handy, *Christian America*, 35–36. See also Cohen, *Jews in Christian America*, 81–85.

20. Sarna and Klein, *Jews of Cincinnati*, 50. For the details of Lilienthal's contribution, see Common Schools of Cincinnati, *Annual Reports for the School Year Ending June 30, 1860*, and following years.

21. *Israelite* 16 (July 23, 1869): 10.

22. Common Schools of Cincinnati, *Annual Reports*; and Sarna and Klein, *Jews of Cincinnati*, 50. Allyn, apparently a local minister, was not a member of the Board of Education.

23. Common Schools of Cincinnati, *Thirty-Third Annual Report*, 11.

24. Common Schools of Cincinnati, "Report of the President" (1866), 18–19.

25. Stephan Brumberg, personal communication, 2005.

26. Hamant, "Religion in the Cincinnati Schools," 239.

27. Hamant estimates that more than a third of the schoolchildren of Cincinnati attended Catholic school in 1869 (Hamant, "Religion in the Cincinnati Schools," 242).

28. There are many discussions of the Cincinnati Bible case, including

Miller, "Public Elementary Schools in Cincinnati"; Perko, "Building Up of Zion"; and Michaelson, "Common Schools." For the implications in the Jewish community, see Cohen, *Jews in Christian America*, 83–85. For a discussion of constitutional issues, see Howe, *The Garden*, 149–61.

29. *Bible in the Public Schools*, 226.

30. *Bible in the Public Schools*, 226.

31. *Bible in the Public Schools*, 226.

32. *Jewish Times* 1 (December 10, 1869): 4. See also Philipson, *Max Lilienthal*, 120–24. That year Lilienthal served on the high school board and so was not directly involved in the case himself.

33. Philipson, *Max Lilienthal*, 124. The Catholic clergy immediately distanced themselves from Rauch and Miller's plan, although many lay Catholics still approved of the change. See Perko, "Building Up of Zion," 105; and Hamant, "Religion in the Cincinnati Schools," 245.

34. *Jewish Times* 1 (December 10, 1869): 4.

35. *Jewish Times* 1 (December 10, 1869): 4; and 1 (December 17, 1869): 6. See also Brumberg, *Religion*.

36. *Jewish Times* 1 (December 24, 1869): 5. Always sensitive to international trends, Lilienthal pointed out that the German reformer Abraham Geiger had posed the same problem at a recent synod. Lilienthal had also consulted his friend Rev. Thomas Vickers of the Unitarian church for help. In raising the problem of reconciling science and the Bible, he anticipated concerns of the last quarter of the nineteenth century when all religions would have to harmonize Darwinism with their doctrines. See Cohen, "Challenges of Darwinism."

37. *Jewish Times* 1 (January 7, 1870): 4. For a similar expression of toleration and religious pluralism, see also M. Lilienthal, *Freiheit*, 131–32. Lilienthal hoped for the day when Catholic, Jew, and Protestant would join hands in reconciliation, when the dishonor of fanaticism would be gone.

38. Michaelson, "Common Schools," 217. For a general discussion of this secularization process, see Berger, *Sacred Canopy*. Also see Cuddihy, *No Offense*, esp. ch. 1 ("The Emergence of Denominational Pluralism"); and Pfeffer, *Creeds in Competition*.

39. Howe, *The Garden*, 150. Also see Cohen, *Jews in Christian America*, 84. For biographical information concerning Taft, see Goss, *Cincinnati*, 222.

40. Michaelson, "Common Schools," 216, quoting a Cincinnati paper, *Commercial*, March 31, 1870.

41. Quoted in Philipson, *Max Lilienthal*, 122.

42. 23 Ohio St. 211 (1872). See also Hamant, "Religion in the Cincinnati Schools," 247.

43. Cohen, *Jews in Christian America*, 85.

44. Matthew Silver is correct when he argues that Lilienthal's experience in Russia provided the background for his passionate stand on the separation of church and state. Lilienthal had experienced firsthand the disastrous effect of government meddling in religious education. See Silver, "Rabbi Max Lilien-

thal."

45. Hofstadter and Smith, *American Higher Education*, v. 2, 475–89. Some of these theorists included Henry Tappan, James Morgan Hart, and Daniel Coit Gilman. See also Spring, *American School*, 149; Cremin, *American Education*; and Marsden, *Soul of the American University*.

46. Marsden, *Soul of the American University*, 108, 125, 143.

47. See Common Schools of Cincinnati, "Superintendent's Report" (1869), 49. The Board of Education also subsidized the university in its early years. For example, see McMicken Board of Trustees, Record of Minutes, February 28, 1871.

48. The donation was from his brother Samuel, whose deceased son Benjamin had studied in the Mining Academy of Freiberg and subsequently died in a mine disaster in Idaho in 1875. See O'Neill, *Ernest Reuben Lilienthal*, 123. See also McMicken Board of Trustees, Record of Minutes, v. 1, December 20, 1875, 535.

49. See, for instance, McMicken Board of Trustees, Record of Minutes, v. 1, June 19, 1876, and v. 2, June 20, 1881, 423.

50. Philipson, *My Life*, 18–19.

51. McGrane, *University of Cincinnati*, 64–66.

52. Ford and Ford, *History of Cincinnati*, 200; Goss, *Cincinnati*, v. 1, 200.

53. *Israelite* 2 (September 14, 1855): 75.

54. Sarna and Klein, *Jews of Cincinnati*, 9–10. See also Cohen, *Encounter with Emancipation*, 109–14.

55. Philipson, *Max Lilienthal*, 60.

56. *Israelite* 3 (September 19, 1856): 94; and 7 (July 27, 1860): 26.

57. Ford and Ford, *History of Cincinnati*, 212; Cincinnati Relief Union, *Constitution and By-Laws*, 3–9.

58. See *Jewish Times* 1 (January 7, 1870): 3; and Philipson, *Max Lilienthal*, 100.

59. *Israelite* 3 (October 17, 1856): 118; and 3 (May 8, 1857): 347. See also Sarna and Klein, *Jews of Cincinnati*, 44.

60. Philipson, *My Life*, 83.

61. Philipson, *Max Lilienthal*, 100; and *Jewish Times* 1 (January 28, 1870): 6.

62. Silverstein, *Alternatives to Assimilation*, 34. See Moore, *B'nai B'rith*, 7–10.

63. *Israelite* 3 (August 8, 1856): 37–38; 3 (August 22, 1856): 55; and 6 (March 9, 1860): 282.

64. *Jewish Times* 1 (December 10, 1869): 5.

65. Rabinowitz, "Young Men's Hebrew Association," 226–31. See also Kraft, *Development of the Jewish Community Center*, 1–2.

66. Silverstein, *Alternatives to Assimilation*, 82.

67. *Jewish Times* 1 (December 10, 1869): 5.

68. *Jewish Times* 1 (December 10, 1869): 5. This arrangement also allowed young professionals, who felt compelled to work on Saturday, to benefit from

Jewish studies.

69. *Israelite* 15 (February 12, 1869): 2. See also *Israelite* 15 (February 26, 1869): 6, for the full text of the lecture.

70. *Israelite* 15 (November 6, 1868): 6; *Jewish Times* 1 (December 10, 1869): 5; Rabinowitz, "Young Men's Hebrew Association," 229.

71. *Israelite* 2 (March 11, 1870): 21. Lilienthal continued to support the group, helping it to reorganize in 1873 and to establish a permanent organization in 1877. Rabinowitz, "Young Men's Hebrew Association," 230.

72. *Israelite* 6 (November 11, 1859): 150; and 6 (March 9, 1860): 282.

73. For the Turners in New York, see Chapter 4.

74. *Jewish Times* 1 (January 28, 1870): 6.

75. *Jewish Times* 1 (January 28, 1870): 6.

76. For parallel attempts to merge American and Catholic values, see Ahlstrom, *Religious History*, 546, 549–54. For Lutheran efforts at Americanization, see Gilbert, *Commitment to Unity*, 11.

77. *Israelite* 3 (November 21, 1856): 154.

78. *Israelite* 3 (November 21, 1856): 154.

79. *Israelite* 3 (July 10, 1857): 4; Cohen, *Jews in Christian America*, 58–64. Also see Handy, *Christian America*, 73–74, for the importance of the Sunday Sabbath observance for the Christian agenda.

80. Cohen, *Encounter with Emancipation*, 67–68; Cohen, *Essential Papers*, 15; and Sarna "American Jewish Response."

81. *Israelite* 2 (April 25, 1856): 340.

82. *Israelite* 3 (August 1, 1856): 30.

83. *Israelite* 3 (August 15, 1856): 45.

84. *Israelite* 4 (April 23, 1858): 334.

85. Ford and Ford, *History of Cincinnati*, 168.

86. *Occident* 18 (April 19, 1860): 23.

87. Tarshish, "Jew and Christian," 579. The story was reported much later, in 1876.

88. For a full discussion, see Kertzer, *Kidnapping of Edguardo Mortara*. Also see Korn, *American Reaction*; Schappes, *Documentary History*, 385–92; and Cohen, *Encounter with Emancipation*, 215–18.

89. Philipson, *Max Lilienthal*, 110.

90. Philipson, *Max Lilienthal*, 110. See also Schappes, *Documentary History*, 386.

91. Cohen, *Jews in Christian America*, 53. See also Cohen, *Encounter with Emancipation*, 101–8.

92. *Israelite* 4 (September 11, 1857): 76; and 4 (September 18, 1857): 85.

93. See Schappes, *Documentary History*, 315–24 and notes.

94. *Israelite* 2 (November 30, 1855): 172.

95. *Israelite* 3 (July 18, 1856): 12–13; and 3 (July 25, 1856): 20.

96. *Israelite* 2 (May 9, 1856): 357.

97. Philipson, *Max Lilienthal*, 379.

98. *Jewish Times* 3 (February 17, 1871): 804–5.

99. Philipson, *Max Lilienthal*, 399. See also Bellah, "Civil Religion," 177.

100. M. Lilienthal, *Freiheit*, 37 (my translation).

101. Philipson, *Max Lilienthal*, 124.

102. Korn, *American Jewry*, 30–31. For a detailed analysis of Wise's views, see Temkin, "Isaac Mayer Wise and the Civil War."

103. Philipson, *Max Lilienthal*, 403.

104. Philipson, *Max Lilienthal*, 403.

105. Goss, *Cincinnati*, v. 1, 206.

106. Goss, *Cincinnati*, v. 1, 207.

107. S. Lilienthal, *Lilienthal Family Record*, 56–57. This passage shows how popular Lilienthal had been throughout the country. As one of only a few ordained rabbis, he was often present at the dedication of new synagogues and other important events in widespread communities. Lithographs of Lilienthal were sold all over the country.

108. S. Lilienthal, *Lilienthal Family Record*, 56–57.

109. Philipson, *Max Lilienthal*, 403–4.

110. This number represents a large increase over the Mexican War, in which just fifty-eight Jews served. See Katznelson, "Jews on the Margins," 177. See also Sussman, *Isaac Leeser*, 223–24; and Sarna, *American Judaism*, 119–20.

111. Korn, *American Jewry*, 68–73.

112. Korn, "Jewish Chaplains," 342. See also Tarshish, "Board of Delegates."

113. Korn, *American Jewry*, 86.

114. Korn, *American Jewry*, 86–87.

115. Bunker and Appel, "Shoddy."

116. Bunker and Appel, "Shoddy," 56.

117. Korn, *American Jewry*, 193.

118. Korn, *American Jewry*, 145. See also Simon, "That Obnoxious Order"; and Stephen V. Ash, "Civil War Exodus."

119. Schappes, *Documentary History*, 474–75.

120. Schappes, *Documentary History*, 475; and Korn, *American Jewry*, 127–28.

121. Korn, *American Jewry*, 128.

122. Morse, "Religious Liberality."

123. For example, see Cincinnati Relief Union, *Seventeenth Annual Report*, 28.

124. Indeed, after his assassination Lincoln was explicitly identified with Jesus. Bellah, "Civil Religion," 177.

125. The speech, titled "The Flag and the Union," is printed in full in Philipson, *Max Lilienthal*, 398–414.

126. Philipson, *Max Lilienthal*, 404.

127. Philipson, *Max Lilienthal*, 406–9. The institution of slavery demeaned the dignity of labor. Lilienthal developed this theme further in his next address. See Philipson, *Max Lilienthal*, 417.

128. Philipson, *Max Lilienthal*, 412.

129. Philipson, *Max Lilienthal*, 414.

130. Philipson, *Max Lilienthal*, 416.

131. Philipson, *Max Lilienthal*, 416. See also Korn, *American Jewry*, 247.

132. Philipson, *Max Lilienthal*, 417. The entire speech is on pages 415–29.

133. Philipson, *Max Lilienthal*, 419–20.

134. Philipson, *Max Lilienthal*, 424.

135. Philipson, *Max Lilienthal*, 427–29.

136. Korn, *American Jewry*, 259. See also Katznelson, "Jews on the Margins," 17. The immigrant Lutherans experienced the same accelerated Americanization process as the Jews. See Wentz, *Basic History of Lutheranism*, 167. The war had the same effect on Catholics, whose service to the country won them a degree of respect undreamed of a decade earlier. Catholics also pointed to their own heroic sacrifices as proof that they too were patriotic and shared a fullhearted love for America. Cross, *Emergence of Liberal Catholicism*, 30.

137. *Israelite* 12 (December 22, 1865): 196.

138. Reverend E. L. Rexford to David Philipson, October 10, 1915, David Philipson Papers, American Jewish Archives, Ms. 35. I want to thank Jonathan Sarna for drawing my attention to this letter. A different picture of Lilienthal emerges from his ideological opponent, the traditionalist Rabbi Bernard Illowy: "Dr. Lilienthal was essentially an aristocrat; his appearance, his manner, bespoke it. . . . Access to him, except to the foremost of his members and a few other select mortals, was not readily had" (Illoway, *Sefer*, 5). This negative portrayal may reflect the falling out between the two former friends when Lilienthal abandoned Orthodoxy (see Chapter 5). The more benign view is corroborated by the family histories. See S. Lilienthal, *Lilienthal Family Record*, 56.

139. Reverend E. L. Rexford to David Philipson, October 10, 1915, David Philipson Papers, American Jewish Archives, Ms. 35. Lilienthal also continued to articulate his version of the American civil religion.

140. *Hebrew Review* 2 (1881–82): 189.

141. From a speech delivered at Bene Jeshurun on May 22, 1874, cited in Philipson, *Max Lilienthal*, 83.

142. M. Lilienthal, "The Jew, A Riddle," *Hebrew Review* 2 (1881): 131.

143. Ford and Ford, *History of Cincinnati*, 164.

144. *Israelite* 13 (March 15, 1867): 6. For the development of these trends, see Hutchison, *Modernist Impulse*. For a general introduction to American Unitarianism, see Ahlstrom, *Religious History*, 391–92, 397–402. See also Albanese, *America*, esp. 133–36.

145. *Israelite* 13 (March 15, 1867): 6. For a discussion of Vickers, see McGrane, *University of Cincinnati*, 81–82. In the 1870s Lilienthal and Vickers worked together to create the University of Cincinnati.

146. Kraut, "Ambivalent Relations," 61. Kraut lists some of the liberal Christian and Jewish clergy who became involved in these exchanges (see 61n8). Wise and other leaders also made clear the important distinctions between the

two religions.

147. Kraut, "Judaism Triumphant," 180.

148. The address, printed in full in the Unitarian periodical the *Radical* 2 (1867): 503, used the *Cincinnati Gazette* as its source.

149. *Radical* 2 (1867): 504.

150. Sarna and Klein, *Jews of Cincinnati*, 50; and *Israelite* 13 (March 15, 1867): 6. See also Tarshish, "Jew and Christian," 579. Foreign articles appeared in *Die Neuzeit* 7 (1867); *Abendland* 4 (1867); and *Archive Israelite* 28 (1867): 394.

151. Jacob Katz, *Exclusiveness and Tolerance*, 13–24. See also Ellenson, *Tradition in Transition*, 146–48. I am grateful to David Ellenson for helping to elucidate these issues.

152. For a popular discussion of the issue, see Schreiber, "My House," where Rabbi Herschel Schachter of Yeshiva University asserts, "A Jew is not permitted to go into a church during prayer service, even to save his life" (80).

153. Altmann, "The New Style of Preaching in Nineteenth-Century German Jewry," in his *Essays*, 196.

154. Sarna and Klein, *Jews of Cincinnati*, 50. Lilienthal substituted for Rev. Spaulding of the Universalist church for two weeks. Philipson, *Max Lilienthal*, 98.

155. Philipson, *Max Lilienthal*, 96.

156. Philipson, *Max Lilienthal*, 96; and Isaac M. Wise's tribute to Lilienthal on the occasion of Lilienthal's twenty-fifth anniversary at Bene Israel (Philipson, *Max Lilienthal*, 70). Also see Sarna and Klein, *Jews of Cincinnati*, 2.

157. Bene Israel Trustee Minutes, April 8, 1863.

158. Bene Israel Trustee Minutes, October 28, 1865; *Israelite* 12 (November 3, 1865): 141. See Philipson, *Oldest Jewish Congregation*, 28.

159. *Israelite* 13 (September 21, 1866): 5.

160. S. Lilienthal, *Lilienthal Family Record*, 69.

161. M. Lilienthal, *Freiheit*, 89–90.

162. M. Lilienthal, *Freiheit*, 90, from "Meine Frau" (my translation).

163. Three older children had left the house already, leaving Esther (15), Jesse (12), Albert (8), and Victoria (6). S. Lilienthal, *Lilienthal Family Record*, 71.

164. *Hebrew Review* 2 (1881–82): 189.

165. Temple Emanu-El Trustee Minutes, December 18, 1867, and January 6, 1868. The congregation's search coincided with the completion of their elaborate new building, for which they raised more than $700,000. Jick, *Americanization of the Synagogue*, 179.

166. Temple Emanu-El Trustee Minutes, January 14, 1868; January 24, 1868; February 23, 1868; and March 10, 1868.

167. Bene Israel Trustee Minutes, March 5, 1868.

168. Max Lilienthal to Philip Heidelbach, Jacob Seasongood, and James Lowman, March 5, 1868, American Jewish Archives, Manuscript Collection, no. 24.

169. Max Lilienthal to Julius Freiberg and the Bene Israel Board, March 8, 1868, American Jewish Archives, Manuscript Collection, no. 24.

170. Max Lilienthal to Bene Israel officers and board, March 15, 1868, American Jewish Archives, Manuscript Collection, no. 24.

171. Max Lilienthal to Bene Israel officers and board, March 15, 1868, American Jewish Archives, Manuscript Collection, no. 24; Temple Emanu-El Trustee Minutes, March 10, 1868. Lilienthal's acceptance letter was dated February 28, 1868.

172. Bene Israel Trustee Minutes, March 22, 1868. Storer's position reinforced the congregation's view of Lilienthal as their invaluable representative to the larger community. This is the same Judge Storer who lectured in the Bene Israel Sunday school and who a year later would rule on the Bible case.

173. Bene Israel Trustee Minutes, March 24, 1868. See also Engel, "Congregation Bene Israel." The details of this meeting were not recorded in the minutes. It is possible that Lilienthal also pressed for the reinstitution of the Sabbath school, because the board acted quickly to reinstate it.

174. *Israelite* 14 (April 10, 1868): 4; Temple Emanu-El Trustee Minutes, April 24, 1868.

175. In the Temple Emanu-El Trustee Minutes for April 16, 1868, is a letter written to that board, dated March 16, in which Lilienthal reveals another factor in his choice. "I know the prejudices existing against me in New York; please assist me by your hearty cooperation in overcoming them."

176. S. Lilienthal, *Lilienthal Family Record*, 56.

Chapter 7

1. See Morrison et al., *Growth of the American Republic*, v. 1, 723–26.

2. See Wentz, *Basic History of Lutheranism*, 174. Also see Jick, *Americanization of the Synagogue*, 178–81.

3. Philipson, *Max Lilienthal*, 67. See also Silver, "Rabbi Max Lilienthal," 371, for the importance of this speech.

4. Barkai, *Branching Out*, 125.

5. Barkai, *Branching Out*, 153–54. See also Silverstein, *Alternatives to Assimilation*, 114–15.

6. Ahlstrom, *Religious History*, 763, 775; Albanese, *America*, 120–25; Hutchison, *Modernist Impulse*, 2.

7. For liberal Catholic trends, see Cross, *Emergence of Liberal Catholicism*; and Dolan, *American Catholic Experience*, 307–16.

8. See Ryback, "East-West Conflict."

9. Temkin, *Isaac Mayer Wise*, 209. See also Meyer, *Response to Modernity*, 255.

10. *Jewish Times* 2 (November 25, 1870): 616–17.

11. Illoway, *Sefer*, 3 and 5. Rabbi Illowy's son Henry added an "a" to the spelling of the family name.

12. *American Israelite* 28 (April 14, 1882): 333.

13. Illoway, *Sefer*, 7.

14. *Israelite* 15 (March 5, 1869): 4; and 15 (April 9, 1869): 4. See Temkin,

Isaac Mayer Wise, 209–10; and Meyer, *Response to Modernity*, 260.

15. *Jewish Messenger* 26 (October 22, 1869): 1.

16. *Israelite* 17 (June 2, 1871): 8.

17. *Jewish Times* 1 (June 4, 1869): 8, 9.

18. Illoway, *Sefer*, 7.

19. Meyer, *Response to Modernity*, 255–56.

20. *Israelite* 16 (November 19, 1869): 8.

21. *Jewish Times* 2 (August 26, 1870): 408; Temkin, *New World of Reform*, 43. Temkin's work contains a complete transcript of the proceedings, translated from the original German. See Temkin, *New World of Reform*, Appendix 9, 105–10.

22. Temkin, *New World of Reform*, 105–10.

23. Meyer, *Response to Modernity*, 256.

24. Temkin, *New World of Reform*, 105–10.

25. See Ellenson, *After Emancipation*, 139–53.

26. *Jewish Times* 1 (November 12, 1869): 6.

27. *Israelite* 16 (November 19, 1869): 8.

28. See, for instance, *Israelite* 16 (December 3 and 17, 1869): 8; and 16 (December 24, 1869): 8.

29. Meyer, *Response to Modernity*, 258.

30. Meyer, *Response to Modernity*, 258–59.

31. Meyer, *Response to Modernity*, 359; Heller, *Isaac Mayer Wise*, 394–95. Radical reformers had been considering a switch to Sunday services, in line with Christian observance.

32. *Jewish Times* 2 (August 26, 1870): 408–9.

33. *Jewish Times* 2 (August 26, 1870): 408–9.

34. *Jewish Times* 2 (August 5, 1870): 358.

35. For a full report, see *Israelite* 17 (November 4, 1870): 8.

36. *Jewish Times* 2 (November 4, 1870): 564.

37. *Jewish Times* 2 (November 4, 1870): 564.

38. *Israelite* 17 (November 18, 1870): 8.

39. *Jewish Times* 2 (November 25, 1870): 612.

40. *Jewish Times* 2 (November 25, 1870): 612.

41. *Jewish Times* 2 (November 25, 1870): 616–17.

42. *Israelite* 17 (April 14, 1871): 8.

43. *Israelite* 17 (June 9, 1871): 8.

44. *Israelite* 17 (June 9, 1871): 8.

45. *Israelite* 17 (June 9, 1871): 8.

46. *Israelite* 17 (June 9, 1871): 8.

47. *Israelite* 17 (June 16, 1871): 8.

48. *Israelite* 17 (June 16, 1871): 8.

49. *Israelite* 17 (June 23, 1871): 8.

50. *Jewish Times* 3 (June 9, 1871): 233.

51. *Jewish Times* 3 (June 16, 1871): 246.

52. *Jewish Times* 3 (June 16, 1871): 248–49.

53. *Jewish Times* 3 (June 16, 1871): 248–49.

54. *Jewish Times* 3 (June 30, 1871): 280.

55. *Jewish Times* 3 (June 30, 1871): 276.

56. *Jewish Times* 3 (June 30, 1871): 276.

57. *Jewish Times* 3 (June 30, 1871): 281.

58. *Jewish Times* 3 (July 14, 1871): 309.

59. *Israelite* 18 (July 14, 1871): 8.

60. *Israelite* 18 (July 21, 1871): 8; and 18 (July 28, 1871): 8.

61. Meyer, "Thank You, Moritz Loth," 30–31. See also Meyer, *Response to Modernity*, 260.

62. *Proceedings of the Union of American Hebrew Congregations*, v. 1, ii.

63. *Israelite* 19 (October 18, 1872): 8.

64. *Jewish Times* 4 (October 25, 1872): 688.

65. Fox, "Road to Unity," 152.

66. *Proceedings of the UAHC*, v. 1, 23.

67. *Jewish Times* 5 (August 22, 1873): 408.

68. Fox, "Road to Unity," 152. The editor of the *Jewish Messenger*, Samuel Isaacs, was one of the founders of the Board of Delegates.

69. *Proceedings of the UAHC*, v. 1, 18. Accusations of regionalism persisted for years, even though the leadership sent this invitation to every congregation in the country.

70. Silverstein, *Alternatives to Assimilation*, 46.

71. *Proceedings of the UAHC*, v. 1, 7–9.

72. *Proceedings of the UAHC*, v. 1, 39–40.

73. Silverstein, *Alternatives to Assimilation*, 48.

74. *Jewish Messenger* (May 29, 1874). Cited in Fox, "Road to Unity," 157.

75. *Proceedings of the UAHC*, v. 1, 28.

76. Fox, "Road to Unity," 157.

77. *Israelite* 2 (November 2, 1855): 140.

78. *Proceedings of the UAHC*, v. 1, i.

79. Fox, "Road to Unity," 145. See also Meyer, *Hebrew Union College*, 17.

80. Ellenson, *After Emancipation*, 285.

81. Temkin, *Isaac Mayer Wise*, 282.

82. Temkin, *Isaac Mayer Wise*, 282.

83. *Hebrew Student* 2 (November 1882): 84–85. Wise specifically cites the two Berlin and the Breslau seminaries as well as ones in Pest and Paris that are connected with academic institutions.

84. Ellenson, *After Emancipation*, 283–84.

85. Ellenson, *After Emancipation*, 286–87.

86. *Proceedings of the UAHC*, v. 1, 185.

87. *Proceedings of the UAHC*, v. 1, 185; and Meyer, *Response to Modernity*, 262.

88. Meyer, Hebrew *Union College*, 18.

89. *Proceedings of the UAHC*, v. 1, 230.

90. *Proceedings of the UAHC*, v. 1, 312.

91. Meyer, *Hebrew Union College*, 19. See also Marcus, "Hebrew Union College," 108–9, for David Philipson's stories of practical jokes.

92. *Proceedings of the UAHC*, v. 1, 230–31. This mild approach to discipline had long been Lilienthal's preference, going back to his early years in New York.

93. Marcus, "Hebrew Union College," 108.

94. *Proceedings of the UAHC*, v. 1, 188–89 and 246–47.

95. Meyer, *Hebrew Union College*, 19.

96. Meyer, *Hebrew Union College*, 19; and *Proceedings of the UAHC*, v. 2, 1064.

97. Meyer, *Hebrew Union College*, 19; and *Proceedings of the UAHC*, v. 2, 1064.

98. See Silverstein, *Alternatives to Assimilation*, 48, for a chart of the UAHC's growth. In 1874, the UAHC boasted fifty-six affiliated congregations, the next year seventy-two, then eighty-one, and so on.

99. See Ryback, "East-West Conflict," 3–25; Fox, "Road to Unity," 145–93; Tarshish, "Board of Delegates," 16–32; and Kohler, "Board of Delegates," 79.

100. *Proceedings of the UAHC*, v. 1, 170.

101. *Jewish Times* 7 (January 28, 1876): 759.

102. *Jewish Times* 8 (May 26, 1876): 200.

103. Tarshish, "Board of Delegates," 16.

104. Tarshish, "Board of Delegates," 30–31.

105. *Jewish Times* 7 (February 17, 1876): 809. The reference is to Rabbi Yochanan ben Zaccai's gathering at Yavneh after the destruction of Jerusalem in 70 CE.

106. *Proceedings of the UAHC*, v. 1, 239–40.

107. *Proceedings of the UAHC*, v. 1, 253.

108. Tarshish, "Board of Delegates," 31; and Davis, *Emergence of Conservative Judaism*, 198.

109. *Proceedings of the UAHC*, v. 1, 245.

110. *Proceedings of the UAHC*, v. 1, 345–46.

111. *Israelite* 28 (June 18, 1877): 4.

112. *Proceedings of the UAHC*, v. 1, 347–48. The publication society was yet another idea that Lilienthal had advocated in his presidential address at the Cincinnati conference of 1871.

113. *Jewish Times* 10 (July 19, 1878): 1.

114. *American Hebrew* 2 (March 19, 1880): 50.

115. *American Hebrew* 6 (April 29, 1881): 121.

116. Regner, "History of the Conference," 2. Heller discussed the organization but focused on Wise (Heller, *Isaac M. Wise*, 439).

117. *American Israelite* (formerly the *Israelite*) 26 (August 1, 1879): 4.

118. *American Israelite* 26 (August 1, 1879): 4.

119. *Proceedings of the UAHC*, v. 1, 387.

120. *Proceedings of the UAHC*, v. 1, 387. This reflected Lilienthal's ongoing concern that the rabbinic students be exposed to German scholarship.

121. *Proceedings of the UAHC*, v. 1, 190.

122. *Proceedings of the UAHC*, v. 1, 190.

123. *American Israelite* 25 (July 19, 1878): 4.

124. *American Israelite* 26 (August 1, 1879): 4.

125. *American Israelite* 27 (July 23, 1880): 28.

126. "Proceedings of the Second Regular Meeting of the Rabbinical Literary Association of America," *Hebrew Review* 1 (1880): 74–96.

127. *Israelite* 27 (July 23, 1880): 28.

128. *Hebrew Review* 1 (1880): 95.

129. *Hebrew Review* 1 (1880): 85–86.

130. *Hebrew Review* 1 (1880): 85–86.

131. *Hebrew Review* 1 (1880): 7.

132. *American Israelite* 27 (October 1, 1880): 108.

133. *Hebrew Review* 1 (1880): 31.

134. *American Israelite* 27 (April 8, 1881): 317.

135. *American Israelite* 28 (July 15, 1881): 20.

136. *American Israelite* 28 (July 15, 1881): 20. For Samuel Hirsch's role in the European Reform movement and important philosophical writings on Reform Judaism, see Meyer, *Response to Modernity*, 72–73.

137. Meyer, *Response to Modernity*, 72–73.

138. *Hebrew Review* 2 (1882): 52–53.

139. Silverstein, *Alternatives to Assimilation*, 128. Also see Scott, *Office to Profession*; and Marty, *Righteous Empire*.

140. Silverstein, *Alternatives to Assimilation*, 127. Also see Bledstein, *Culture of Professionalism*.

141. For other early attempts, see Zola, "Southern Rabbis," 354–72. The Board of Jewish Ministers of Philadelphia met as early as 1861.

142. Philipson, *Max Lilienthal*, 95.

Chapter 8

1. Philipson, *My Life*, 8–9.

2. See S. Lilienthal, *Lilienthal Family Record*, 78–79. There is a letter of introduction to Abe Seligman (no relation) that Max wrote for his son Philip when he moved to San Francisco. He reminded the banker that he had officiated at his confirmation at the Henry Street Synagogue in New York.

3. S. Lilienthal, *Lilienthal Family Record*, 73–74.

4. The complete text of the Lilienthal Pact can be found in O'Neill, *Ernest Reuben Lilienthal*, 70–71.

5. O'Neill, *Ernest Reuben Lilienthal*, 70.

6. O'Neill, *Ernest Reuben Lilienthal*, 72.

7. O'Neill, *Ernest Reuben Lilienthal*, 51. Hoadley, Jackson, and Johnson was the firm at which Lilienthal's friend Alphonso Taft, the father of President Wil-

liam Howard Taft, was a partner.

8. O'Neill, *Ernest Reuben Lilienthal*, 56–63. For a description of the career of Louis Sloss, see O'Neill, *Ernest Reuben Lilienthal*, 31–47; and Kahn, *Jewish Voices*, 105–6.

9. Kahn, *Jewish Voices*, 104.

10. Kahn, *Jewish Voices*, 141.

11. Kahn, *Jewish Voices*, 141–44. Actually Leo was one of Samuel's sons. The family made no distinction between nephews and sons.

12. Kahn, *Jewish Voices*, 144.

13. Kahn, *Jewish Voices*, 490–94.

14. O'Neill, *Ernest Reuben Lilienthal*, 60–62.

15. Philipson, *Max Lilienthal*, 97–98.

16. Philipson, *Max Lilienthal*, 62.

17. O'Neill, *Ernest Reuben Lilienthal*, 62.

18. O'Neill, *Ernest Reuben Lilienthal*, 62.

19. O'Neill, *Ernest Reuben Lilienthal*, 51.

20. Max Lilienthal to Isaac Nettre, July 5–17, 1843, quoted in Philipson, *Max Lilienthal*, 151.

21. *Asmonean* 20 (June 1, 1854): 53.

22. *Asmonean* 20 (August 4, 1854): 125.

23. S. Lilienthal, *Lilienthal Family Record*, 76.

24. S. Lilienthal, *Lilienthal Family Record*, 76–77.

25. "Beethoven's Anthem" probably refers to the "Ode to Joy" from the fourth movement of the Ninth Symphony, often extracted for inspirational moments. Today it is used as the anthem of the European Union.

26. *American Israelite* 27 (June 25, 1880): 4.

27. *American Israelite* 27 (June 25, 1880): 4.

28. Philipson, *Max Lilienthal*, 126. Sophie Lilienthal remembered the motivation for the trip differently. In her account Max and his brother Samuel planned a vacation to visit their old European home and friends. S. Lilienthal, *Lilienthal Family Record*, 77–78.

29. Philipson, *Max Lilienthal*, 126–27.

30. Philipson, *Max Lilienthal*, 127–28.

31. *American Israelite* 28 (April 14, 1882): 332.

32. *American Israelite* 28 (April 14, 1882): 329.

33. S. Lilienthal, *Lilienthal Family Record*, 78.

34. *American Israelite* 28 (April 14, 1882): 329, 332–33.

35. *American Israelite* 28 (April 14, 1882): 332.

36. *American Israelite* 28 (April 14, 1882): 332.

37. *American Israelite* 28 (April 14, 1882): 332.

38. Lilienthal claimed 189 subscribers to his *Hebrew Review* during his presidential address in Chicago in July 1881. *Hebrew Review* 2 (1881): 7.

39. O'Neill, *Ernest Reuben Lilienthal*, 9.

40. See Hess, *Germans*, 7–11, for a recent discussion of the two sides of modernity.

41. Temkin, "Beth Din," 418.

42. M. Lilienthal, "Erster Vortrag," 26.

43. *Israelite* 3 (March 27, 1857): 300.

44. This famous phrase has been attributed to Thomas Jefferson, Thomas Paine, and others.

45. See accounts of the addresses in the *American Israelite* 28 (April 14, 1882): 332–33.

46. Davis, *Emergence of Conservative Judaism*, 200–11.

47. Marcus, "Hebrew Union College," 128.

48. Meyer, *Hebrew Union College*, 41.

49. Cited in Plaut, *Growth of Reform Judaism*, 55.

50. Plaut, *Growth of Reform Judaism*, 55; and Temkin, *Isaac Mayer Wise*, 286. According to Michael Meyer, Wise personally refrained from pork on sanitary grounds and excluded all seafood, except oysters. Meyer, *Hebrew Union College*, 42; Silverstein, *Alternatives to Assimilation*, 116.

51. Silverstein, *Alternatives to Assimilation*, 116. See also Cohen, *Encounter with Emancipation*, 180–85, for the issues in the debate.

52. Philipson, *Max Lilienthal*, 63–64; UAHC convention, 1876.

53. Kraut, "Judaism Triumphant," 181.

54. Plaut, "Pittsburgh Platform," 17.

55. The entire platform is found in Meyer, *Response to Modernity*, 387–88.

56. Meyer, *Response to Modernity*, 388.

57. Plaut, *Growth of Reform Judaism*, 34.

58. Davis, *Emergence of Conservative Judaism*, 228.

59. Plaut, *Growth of Reform Judaism*, 37.

60. Davis, *Emergence of Conservative Judaism*, 216–28. For another view of the significance behind the rise of the Conservative group, see Sarna, *Great Awakening*, 12–13. Sarna places the movement within the context of late nineteenth-century religious revivals.

61. Bauman and Shankman, "Rabbi as Ethnic Broker," 51–52.

62. Sarna and Goldman, "Synagogue-Community," 175.

63. Sarna and Goldman, "Synagogue-Community," 178.

64. Sarna and Goldman, "Synagogue-Community," 179.

65. Marcus, *United States Jewry*, v. 2, 98–99.

66. Sarna and Goldman, "Synagogue-Community," 180.

67. Philipson, *My Life*, 227.

68. Philipson, *My Life*, 297.

69. Bauman and Shankman, "Rabbi as Ethnic Broker."

70. Bauman and Shankman, "Rabbi as Ethnic Broker," 53.

71. Bauman and Shankman, "Rabbi as Ethnic Broker," 54–57.

72. Wise, *Reminiscences*, 190.

73. This task fell to Philipson, whose *Max Lilienthal, American Rabbi* was published on the centenary of Lilienthal's birth.

Bibliography

Correspondence

Lilienthal, Max. Letters (38) written while in Russia, 1839–1844, Judah L. Magnes Memorial Museum.

Lilienthal, Max, to Mrs. Rutherford B. Hayes, June 18, 1876, American Jewish Archives, SC-7244.

Lilienthal, Max. Letters to Board of Bene Israel, March 1868, American Jewish Archives, Ms. Collection 24.

Lilienthal, Max, to Dr. Heinrich Zindorf (7 letters), 1877, American Jewish Archives.

Rexford, Rev. E., to David Philipson, October 10, 1915, David Philipson Papers, American Jewish Archives, Ms. 35.

Schwab, Dr. Isaac, to Max Lilienthal, March 23, 1880, Correspondence File, American Jewish Archives.

Storer, Judge Bellamy, and other Cincinnati dignitaries to Board of Bene Israel, March 1868, American Jewish Archives, Ms. Collection 24.

Minutes

Anshe Chesed, Trustee Minutes, 1844–1855.

Bene Israel, School Board Minutes (Cincinnati), 1855–1882.

Bene Israel, Trustee Minutes (Cincinnati), 1855–1882.

Bene Israel, Vestry Minutes (Cincinnati), 1855–1882.

Congregation Shearith Israel, Minutes of the Trustees (New York), 1844–45.

Protokolle von Emanu-El Congregation Board of Trustees (New York), 1845–1847 (German).

Temple Emanu-El, Trustee Minutes (New York), 1845–47, 1848–1868.

University of Cincinnati (McMicken), Record of Minutes, v. 1 (December 1859–December 1876) and v. 2 (January 1877–April 17, 1882).

Periodicals

Allgemeine Zeitung des Judenthums (Leipzig), 1839–1848
American Hebrew (New York), 1879–1886
American Israelite (Cincinnati), 1854–1886
Asmonean (New York), 1849–1855
Die Deborah (Cincinnati), 1855–1857
Hebrew Review (Cincinnati), 1880–1882
Hebrew Sabbath School Visitor (Cincinnati), 1874–1882
Israels Herold (New York), 1849
Jewish Messenger (New York), 1870–1882
Jewish Times (New York), 1869–1879
Jewish Tribune (New York), May 18, 1906
Nieuw Israelietisch Weekblod (1985)
Occident (Philadelphia), 1843–1850
Sinai (Baltimore), 1856

Primary Sources

Aub, Hirsch. *Predigt bei dem in der Synagoge zu München am 16 Marz 1868.* Munich: C. R. Schurich, 1868.

Baird, Robert. *Religion in America.* New York: Harper & Row, 1970 [1844].

The Bible in the Public Schools: Arguments Before the Superior Court of Cincinnati in the Case of Minor v. Board of Education of Cincinnati *(1870).* New York: Da Capo Press, 1967.

Bogen, F. W. *The German in America or Advice and Instruction for German Emigrants in the United States of America.* New York: B. H. Greene, 1851.

Cincinnati Relief Union. *Seventeenth Annual Report of the Cincinnati Relief Union.* Cincinnati: Times Steam Boat and Job Office, 1866.

———. *Constitution and By-Laws.* Cincinnati: Times Steam Book and Job Office, 1848.

Common Schools of Cincinnati. *Annual Reports for the School Year Ending June 30, 1860.* Cincinnati: Times Steam Book and Job Printing Establishment, 1860.

———. *Thirty-Third Annual Report for the School Year Ending June 30, 1862.* Cincinnati: Times Steam Book and Job Printing Establishment, 1862.

Dickens, Charles. *American Notes, for General Circulation.* Middlesex: Penguin, 1972 [1842].

Grinstein, Hyman. "The Minute Book of Lilienthal's Union of German Synagogues in New York." *Hebrew Union College Annual* 18 (1943–44): 321–52.

Hecht, Emanuel. *Israels Geschichte von der Zeit des Bibel-Abschusses bis zur Gegenwart.* Leipzig: Baumgartner, 1865.

———. *Synopsis of the History of the Israelites from the Time of Alexander the Macedonian to the Present Age,* trans. Max Lilienthal. Cincinnati: Bloch, 1857.

Heller, James G. *As Yesterday When It Is Past: A History of the Isaac M. Wise Temple—K. K. B'nai Yeshurun of Cincinnati in Commemoration of the Centenary of Its Founding.* Cincinnati: K. K. B'nai Yeshurun, 1942.

Hübsch, Julia, ed. *Rev. Dr. Adolph Hübsch, Late Rabbi of the Ahawath Chesed Congregation in New York.* New York: A. L. Goetzl, 1885.

Illoway, Henry. *Sefer Milchamot Elohim: Being the Controversial Letters and the Casuistic Decisions of the Late Rabbi Bernard Illowy.* Berlin: M. Poppelauer, 1914.

Jonas, Joseph. "Moving Westward." In *A Documentary History of Jews in the United States, 1654–1875,* ed. Morris U. Schappes, 223–35. New York: Schocken, 1971 [1843].

Lilienthal, Max. "Erster Vortrag im Vereine der Freunde." *Israels Herold* 4 (April 20, 1849): 25–27, 34–35.

———. *Freiheit, Frühling, und Liebe.* Cincinnati: Bloch, 1857.

———. "Literarische Correspondenz in Literarisches und homiletisches Bleiblatt." *Allgemeine Zeitung des Judenthums* 1 (May–December 1838).

———. *Maggid Yeshuah.* Vilna, 1842.

———. "My Travels in Russia." In *Max Lilienthal, American Rabbi: Life and Writings,* ed. David Philipson. New York: Bloch, 1915.

———. *Predigten für Sabbathe und Festage.* Munich: J. Lindauer, 1839.

———. *Rede am Dankfeste.* Riga: W. F. Hacker, 1840.

———. "Ueber den Ursprung der jüdisch-alexandrinischen Religionsphilosophie." Doctoral dissertation, University of Munich, 1839.

Lilienthal, Max, and Robert Allyn. *Things Taught: Systematic Instruction in Composition and Object Lessons.* Cincinnati: W. B. Smith, 1862.

Lilienthal, Sophie. *The Lilienthal Family Record.* San Francisco: By the author, 1930.

Mannheimer, Isaac Noah. *Gebete des Israeliten.* Vienna: J. Schlesinger's Buchhandlung, 1909.

———. *Gottesdienstliche Vorträge gehalten im israelitsichen Bethause zu Wien im Monate Tischri.* Vienna: C. Gerold, 1876.

McNeill, Mary. *Vere Foster, 1819–1900: An Irish Benefactor.* Newton Abbot, U.K.: David & Charles, 1971.

Mendelssohn, Moses. *Jerusalem and Other Jewish Writings,* ed. and trans. Alfred Jospe. New York: Schocken, 1969.

Morse, Sidney H. "Religious Liberality." *The Radical* 2 (1867): 503–7.

O'Neill, F. Gordon. *Ernest Reuben Lilienthal and His Family.* San Francisco: n.p., 1949.

Passenger Lists of Vessels Arriving at New York, 1820–97. Microcopy 237. Washington, DC: National Archives Microfilm Publications.

Proceedings of the Union of American Hebrew Congregations, vols. 1 and 2. Cincinnati: Union of American Hebrew Congregations, 1873–1874.

Rabbinical Literary Association of America. "Constitution of the Rabbinical Literary Association of America." Cincinnati: Rabbinical Literary Association, 1880.

Stern, Myer. *The Rise and Progress of Reform Judaism: Embracing a History Made from the Official Records of Temple Emanu-El of New York*. New York: By the author, 1895.

Temkin, Sefton D. (trans.). *The New World of Reform: Containing the Proceedings of the Conference of Reform Rabbis Held in Philadelphia in November 1869*. London: Leo Baeck College, 1971.

Wengeroff, Pauline. *Rememberings: The World of a Russian-Jewish Woman in the Nineteenth Century*, trans. Henny Wenkart. Bethesda: University of Maryland Press, 2000.

Wise, Isaac M. *The History of the K. K. Bene Yeshurun of Cincinnati, Ohio*. Cincinnati: Bloch, 1892.

———. *Reminiscences*, 2nd ed., trans. David Philipson. New York: Central Synagogue of New York, 1945.

———. *The Western Journal of Isaac Mayer Wise*. Berkeley, CA: Western Jewish History Center, Magnes Museum, 1974.

Secondary Sources

Ahlstrom, Sydney. *A Religious History of the American People*. New Haven, CT: Yale University Press, 1974.

Albanese, Catherine L. *America: Religions and Religion*, 2nd ed. Belmont, CA: Wadsworth, 1992.

———. *Sons of the Fathers: The Civil Religion of the American Revolution*. Philadelphia: Temple University Press, 1976.

Altmann, Alexander. *Essays in Jewish Intellectual History*. Hanover, NH: University Press of New England, 1981.

———. *Moses Mendelssohn: A Biographical Study*. Philadelphia: Jewish Publication Society of America, 1973.

Aschheim, Steven E. *Brothers and Strangers: The East European Jews in Germany and German-Jewish Consciousness, 1800–1923*. Madison: University of Wisconsin Press, 1982.

Ash, Stephen V. "Civil War Exodus: The Jews and Grant's General Order No. 11." In *Jews and the Civil War: A Reader*, ed. Jonathan D. Sarna and Adam Mendelsohn, 353–384. New York: New York University Press, 2010.

Barkai, Avraham. *Branching Out: German-Jewish Immigration to the United States, 1820–1914*. New York: Holmes & Meier, 1994.

———. "The German Jews at the Start of Industrialization: Structural Change and Mobility, 1835–1860." In *Revolution and Evolution: 1848 in German-Jewish History*, ed. Werner E. Mosse, Arnold Paucker, and Reinhard Rürup, 123–49. Tubingen: Mohr, 1981.

Baron, Salo W. "The Image of a Rabbi Formerly and Today." In *Steeled by Adversity: Essays and Addresses on American Jewish Life*, by Salo W. Baron and Jeanette M. Baron, 147–57. Philadelphia: Jewish Publication Society, 1971.

———. *The Russian Jews Under Tsars and Soviets*, 2nd ed. New York: Schocken, 1987.

Bartal, Israel. "Mordechai Aaron Günzburg: A Lithuanian Maskil Faces Modernity." In *From East and West: Jews in a Changing Europe, 1750–1870*, ed. Frances Malino and David Sorkin, 126–47. Cambridge, MA: Basil Blackwell, 1991.

Barzilay, Isaac. "Early Responses to the Emancipation in Hebrew Haskalah Literature." *Judaism* 38(4) (1989): 517–26.

Bauman, Mark K., and Arnold Shankman. "The Rabbi as Ethnic Broker: The Case of David Marx." *Journal of American Ethnic History* 2(2) (spring 1983): 51–68.

Bellah, Robert N. "Civil Religion in America." In *Beyond Belief: Essays on Religion in a Post-Traditional World*, by Robert N. Bellah, 168–89. New York: Harper & Row, 1970.

Berger, Peter L. *The Sacred Canopy: Elements of a Sociological Theory of Religion*. New York: Random House, 1967.

Billigmeier, Robert Henry. *Americans from Germany: A Study in Cultural Diversity*. Belmont, CA: Wadsworth, 1974.

Blau, Joseph L., and Salo W. Baron. *Early American Jewry*. Philadelphia: Jewish Publication Society, 1964.

———. *The Jews of the United States, 1790–1840: A Documentary History*. New York: Columbia University Press, 1964.

Bledstein, Burton J. *The Culture of Professionalism: The Middle Class and the Development of Higher Education in America*. New York: Norton, 1976.

Bodnar, John. *The Transplanted: A History of Immigrants in Urban America*. Bloomington: Indiana University Press, 1985.

Bogen, Elizabeth. *Immigration in New York*. New York: Praeger, 1987.

Borowitz, Eugene B. *Choices in Modern Jewish Thought: A Partisan Guide*. New York: Behrman House, 1983.

Bretting, Agnes. "Little Germanies in the United States." In *Germans to America: 300 Years of Immigration, 1683–1983*, ed. Günter Moltmann, 145–51. Stuttgart: Institute for Foreign Cultural Relations, 1982.

———. *Soziale Probleme deutscher Einwanderer in New York City, 1800–1860*. Wiesbaden: Steiner, 1981.

Brickner, Barnett R. "The Jewish Community of Cincinnati, Historical and Descriptive, 1817–1933." Ph.D. dissertation, University of Cincinnati, 1933.

Bruford, W. H. *The German Tradition of Self-Cultivation: "Bildung" from Humboldt to Thomas Mann*. Cambridge, U.K.: Cambridge University Press, 1975.

Brumberg, Stephan F. *Religion and the Public School System in Nineteenth-Century America (Anne Bass Schneider Scholar-in-Residence Lecture)*. Adler Seminar in American Judaism, no. 22. New York: Temple Israel, 2002.

Buchler, Joseph. "The Struggle for Unity: Attempts at Union in American Jewish Life." *American Jewish Archives* 2 (June 1949): 21–46.

Bunker, Gary L., and John Appel. "'Shoddy,' Anti-Semitism, and the Civil War." *American Jewish History* 82(1) (1994): 43–72.

Burrows, Edwin G., and Mike Wallace. *Gotham: A History of New York City to 1898.* Oxford, U.K.: Oxford University Press, 1999.

Cahen, Joel. "Een eigen ziekenfonds voor joden in New York." *Nieuw Israelietisch Weekblod* (November 15, 1985), 145–47.

Chomsky, William. *Hebrew: The Eternal Language.* Philadelphia: Jewish Publication Society of America, 1957.

Chyet, Stanley F. "Ohio Valley Jewry During the Civil War." *Historical and Philosophical Society of Ohio Bulletin* 21 (July 1963): 179–87.

Cohen, Naomi W. "Antisemitism in the Gilded Age: The Jewish View." *Jewish Social Studies* 41 (1979): 187–210.

——. "The Challenges of Darwinism and Biblical Criticism to American Judaism." *Modern Judaism* 4 (May 1984): 121–57.

——. *Encounter with Emancipation.* Philadelphia: Jewish Publication Society of America, 1984.

——. *Essential Papers on Jewish-Christian Relations in the United States: Imagery and Reality.* New York: New York University Press, 1990.

——. *Jews in Christian America: The Pursuit of Religious Equality.* New York: Oxford University Press, 1992.

Cohn, Bernhard N. "Early German Preaching in America." *Historia Judaica* 15(pt. 2) (October 1953): 86–127.

——. "Leo Merzbacher." *American Jewish Archives* 4 (January 1954): 21–4.

Cohn, Raymond C. "Mortality on Immigrant Voyages to New York, 1836–1853." In *American Immigration and Ethnicity*, v. 2, *Emigration and Immigration: The Old World Confronts the New*, ed. George Pozzetta. New York: Garland, 1991.

Cremin, Lawrence A. *American Education: The National Experience, 1783–1876.* New York: Harper & Row, 1980.

Cross, Robert D. *The Emergence of Liberal Catholicism in America.* Cambridge, MA: Harvard University Press, 1958.

Cuddihy, John Murray. *No Offense: Civil Religion and Protestant Taste.* New York: Seabury Press, 1978.

Darnton, Robert. *George Washington's False Teeth: An Unconventional Guide to the Eighteenth Century.* New York: W. W. Norton, 2003.

Davis, Moshe. *The Emergence of Conservative Judaism: The Historical School in 19th Century America.* Philadelphia: Jewish Publication Society of America, 1963.

De Santis, Vincent P. *The Gilded Age, 1877–1896.* Northbrook, IL: Harlan Davidson, 1973.

Diehl, Carl. *Americans and German Scholarship, 1770–1870.* New Haven, CT: Yale University Press, 1978.

Diner, Hasia. "A Time for Gathering: The Second Migration." *American Jewish History* 81 (autumn 1993): 22–33.

———. *A Time for Gathering: The Second Migration, 1820–1880.* Baltimore: Johns Hopkins University Press, 1992.

Dolan, Jay P. *The American Catholic Experience: A History from Colonial Times to the Present.* New York: Doubleday, 1985.

———. *The Immigrant Church: New York's Irish and German Catholics, 1815–1865.* Baltimore: Johns Hopkins University Press, 1975.

Dubnow, S. M. *History of the Jews in Russia and Poland: From the Earliest Times Until the Present Day,* v. 2, *From the Death of Alexander I Until the Death of Alexander III,* trans. I. Friedlaender. Philadelphia: Jewish Publication Society of America, 1918.

Dushkin, Alexander. *Jewish Education in New York City.* New York: Bureau of Jewish Education, 1918.

Ellenson, David. *After Emancipation: Jewish Responses to Modernity.* Cincinnati: Hebrew Union College Press, 2004.

———. *Between Tradition and Culture: The Dialectics of Modern Jewish Religion and Identity.* Atlanta: Scholars Press, 1994.

———. "A Jewish Legal Decision by Rabbi Bernard Illowy of New Orleans and Its Discussion in Nineteenth Century Europe." *American Jewish History* 69 (December 1979): 174–95.

———. *Rabbi Esriel Hildescheimer and the Creation of a Modern Jewish Orthodoxy.* Tuscaloosa: University of Alabama Press, 1990.

———. *Tradition in Transition: Orthodoxy, Halakhah, and the Foundations of Modern Jewish Identity.* Lanham, MD: University Press of America, 1989.

Engel, Steve. "Congregation Bene Israel (Rockdale): Historical Changes, 1860–1880." Manuscript, American Jewish Archives, 1988.

Erickson, Charlotte, ed. *Emigration from Europe, 1815–1914: Selected Documents.* London: A. and C. Black, 1976.

Ernst, Robert. *Immigrant Life in New York: 1825–1863.* New York: King's Crown Press, 1949.

Etkes, E. "Compulsory Enlightenment as a Crossroads in the History of the Haskalah Movement in Russia. *Zion* 43 (1978): 264–313 (in Hebrew).

———. "Immanent Factors and External Influences in the Development of the Haskalah Movement in Russia." In *Toward Modernity: The European Jewish Model,* ed. Jacob Katz, 13–32. New York: Leo Baeck Institute, 1987.

Evans, Eli N. *Judah P. Benjamin: The Jewish Confederate.* New York: Free Press, 1988.

Feiner, Shmuel. *Haskalah and History: The Emergence of a Modern Jewish Historical Consciousness,* trans. Chaya Naor and Sondra Silverston. Oxford, U.K.: Littman Library of Jewish Civilization, 2002.

———. *The Jewish Enlightenment,* trans. Chaya Naor. Philadelphia: University of Pennsylvania Press, 2002.

Feingold, Henry L. *Zion in America: The Jewish Experience from Colonial Times to the Present,* rev. ed. New York: Hippocrene Books, 1981.

Feldman, Egal. *Dual Destinies: The Jewish Encounter with Protestant America.*

Urbana: University of Illinois Press, 1990.

Fishman, David E. *Russia's First Modern Jews: The Jews of Shklov.* New York: New York University Press, 1995.

Fishman, Isadore. *The History of Jewish Education in Central Europe: From the End of the Sixteenth to the End of the Eighteenth Century.* London: Edward Goldston, 1944.

Ford, Henry A., and Kate B. Ford. *History of Cincinnati, Ohio.* Cleveland: L. A. Williams, 1881.

Fox, Steven A. "On the Road to Unity: The Union of American Hebrew Congregations and American Jewry, 1873–1903." *American Jewish Archives* 32 (November 1980): 145–93.

Franchot, Jenny. *Roads to Rome: The Antebellum Protestant Encounter with Catholicism.* Berkeley: University of California Press, 1994.

Friedenberg. Robert V. *"Hear O Israel": The History of American Jewish Preaching, 1654–1970.* Tuscaloosa: University of Alabama Press, 1989.

Gailus, Manfred. "Anti-Jewish Emotion and Violence in the 1848 Crisis of German Society." In *Exclusionary Violence: Antisemitic Riots in Modern German History,* ed. Christhard Hoffmann, Werner Bergmann, and Helmut Walser Smith, 443–65. Ann Arbor: University of Michigan Press, 2005.

Gamoran, Emanuel. *Changing Conceptions in Jewish Education.* New York: Macmillan, 1924.

Gartner, Lloyd P. (ed.). *Jewish Education in the United States: A Documentary History.* New York: Teachers College Press, 1976.

———. "Temples of Liberty Unpolluted: American Jews and Public Schools, 1840–1875." In *A Bicentennial Festschrift for Jacob Rader Marcus,* ed. Bertram Wallace Korn, 157–90. New York: Ktav, 1976.

Gay, Peter. *The Enlightenment: An Interpretation,* 2 vols. New York: W. W. Norton, 1977.

Gilbert, W. Kent. *Commitment to Unity: A History of the Lutheran Church in America.* Philadelphia: Fortress Press, 1988.

Ginsburg, Saul. "Max Lilienthal's Activities in Russia: New Documents." *Proceedings of the American Jewish Historical Society* 25 (1939): 39–51.

Glanz, Rudolf. "The Immigration of German Jews to 1880." *YIVO Annual of Jewish Social Science* 2–3 (1947–48): 81–99.

———. *Jews in Relation to the Cultural Milieu of the Germans in America up to the Eighteen Eighties.* New York: Marstin Press, 1947.

———. *Studies in Judaica Americana.* New York: Ktav, 1970.

Glazer, Nathan. *American Judaism,* 2nd ed. Chicago: University of Chicago Press, 1972.

Gleason, Philip, ed. *The Catholic Church in America.* New York: Harper & Row, 1970.

———. *The Conservative Reformers: German-American Catholics and the Social Order.* Notre Dame, IN: University of Notre Dame Press, 1968.

Goen, C. C. *Broken Churches, Broken Nation: Denominational Schisms and the*

Coming of the American Civil War. Macon, GA: Mercer University Press, 1985.

Good, Harry G., and James D. Teller. *A History of American Education,* 3rd ed. New York: Macmillan, 1973.

Goss, Charles Frederic. *Cincinnati: The Queen City, 1788–1912,* 4 vols. Chicago: S. J. Clarke, 1912.

Graetz, Heinrich. *History of the Jews,* v. 5, *From the Chmielnicki Persecution of the Jews in Poland (1648 C.E.) to the Present Time (1870 C.E.).* Philadelphia: Jewish Publication Society, 1946 [1895].

Greenberg, Gershon. "The Significance of America in David Einhorn's Conception of History." *American Jewish Historical Quarterly* 63(2) (December 1973): 160–84.

Greive, Hermann. "Religious Dissent and Tolerance." In *Revolution and Evolution: 1848 in German-Jewish History,* ed. Werner E. Mosse, Arnold Paucker, and Reinhard Rürup, 337–52. Tubingen: Mohr, 1981.

Grinstein, Hyman. *The Rise of the Jewish Community of New York, 1654–1860.* Philadelphia: Jewish Publication Society of America, 1945.

———. "Studies in the History of Jewish Education in New York City." *Jewish Review* 2 (July–October, 1944): 187–201.

Gurock, Jeffrey S. *American Jewish Orthodoxy in Historical Perspective.* Hoboken, NJ: Ktav, 1996.

Hamant, Nancy K. "Religion in the Cincinnati Schools, 1830–1990." *Historical and Philosophical Society of Ohio Bulletin* 21 (October 1963): 239–51.

Hamburger, Ernest. "One Hundred Years of Emancipation." *Leo Baeck Institute Yearbook* 14 (1969): 3–66.

Handy, Robert T. *A Christian America: Protestant Hopes and Historical Realities,* 2nd ed. New York: Oxford University Press, 1984.

Hanley, Mark. *Beyond a Christian Commonwealth: The Protestant Quarrel with the American Republic, 1830–1860.* Chapel Hill: University of North Carolina Press, 1994.

Hansen, Marcus Lee. *The Atlantic Migration, 1607–1860.* New York: Harper, 1961.

Harris, James F. "Bavarians and Jews." *Leo Baeck Institute Yearbook* 32 (1987): 103–17.

Hartz, Louis. *The Liberal Tradition in America: An Interpretation of American Political Thought Since the Revolution.* New York: Harcourt Brace, 1955.

Hatch, Nathan O. *The Democratization of American Christianity.* New Haven, CT: Yale University Press, 1989.

Hearn, Lafcadio. *Barbarous Barbers and Other Stories,* ed. Ichiro Nishizaki. Tokyo: Hokuseido Press, 1939.

Hegel, G. W. F. *Reason in History: A General Introduction to the Philosophy of History,* trans. Robert S. Hartman. Indianapolis, IN: Bobbs-Merrill, 1953.

Heller, James G. *Isaac M. Wise: His Life, Work, and Thought.* New York: Union of America Hebrew Congregations, 1965.

Hennesy, James. *American Catholics: A History of the Roman Catholic Community in the United States.* New York: Oxford University Press, 1981.

Henriksson, Anders. *The Tsar's Loyal Germans: The Riga German Community, Social Change, and the Nationality Question, 1855–1905.* New York: Distributed by Columbia University Press, 1983.

Herring, Basil. *The Rabbinate as Calling and Vocation: Models of Rabbinic Leadership.* Northvale, NJ: J. Aronson, 1991.

Hertz, Emanuel (ed.). *Abraham Lincoln: The Tribute of the Synagogue.* New York: Bloch, 1927.

Hess, Jonathan M. *Germans, Jews, and the Claims of Modernity.* New Haven, CT: Yale University Press, 2002.

Hirshler, Eric (ed.). *Jews from Germany in the United States.* New York: Farrar, Straus & Cudahy, 1955.

Hofstadter, Richard, and Wilson Smith (eds.). *American Higher Education: A Documentary History,* 2 vols. Chicago: University of Chicago Press, 1961.

Honor, Leo L. "The Impact of the American Environment and American Ideas on Jewish Elementary Education in the United States." *Jewish Quarterly Review* 45 (April 1955): 451–96.

Howe, Mark DeWolfe. *The Garden and the Wilderness: Religion and Government in American Constitutional History.* Chicago: University of Chicago Press, 1965.

Hudson, Winthrop S. *American Protestantism.* Chicago: University of Chicago Press, 1961.

Hutchison, William R. *The Modernist Impulse in American Protestantism.* Cambridge, MA: Harvard University Press, 1976.

Israel, Jonathan. *European Jewry in the Age of Mercantilism, 1550–1750.* Oxford, U.K.: Clarendon Press, 1989.

Jackson, Kenneth (ed.). *The Encyclopedia of New York.* New Haven, CT: Yale University Press, 1995.

Jarausch, Konrad. "Die neuhumanistische Universität und die bürgerliche Gesellschaft, 1800–1870." *Darstellung und Quellen zur Geschichte der deutschen Einheitsbewegung in neunzehnten und zwanzigsten Jahrhundert* 11 (1980): 11–58.

Jick, Leon A. *The Americanization of the Synagogue, 1820–1870.* Hanover, NH: University Press of New England, 1976.

Jones, Allen Maldwyn. *American Immigration,* 2nd ed. Chicago: University of Chicago Press, 1992.

Kaestle, Carl F. *The Evolution of an Urban School System: New York City, 1750–1850.* Cambridge, MA: Harvard University Press, 1973.

Kahn, Ava F. (ed.). *Jewish Voices of the California Gold Rush: A Documentary History, 1849–1880.* Detroit: Wayne State University Press, 2002.

Karff, Samuel E. (ed.). *Hebrew Union College–Jewish Institute of Religion at One Hundred Years.* Cincinnati: Hebrew Union College Press, 1976.

Katz, Jacob. *Exclusiveness and Tolerance.* New York: Schocken, 1969.

———. *From Prejudice to Destruction: Anti-Semitism, 1700–1933*. Cambridge, MA: Harvard University Press, 1980.

———. *Out of the Ghetto: The Social Background of Jewish Emancipation, 1770–1870*. New York: Schocken, 1978.

———. *Toward Modernity: The European Jewish Model*. New York: Transaction, 1987.

———. *Tradition and Crisis*. New York: Schocken, 1971.

Katz, Robert L. "David Caro's Analysis of the Rabbi's Role." *Central Conference of American Rabbis Journal* (April 1966): 41–6.

Katznelson, Ira. "Jews on the Margins of American Liberalism." In *Paths of Emancipation: Jews, States, and Citizenship*, ed. Pierre Birnbaum and Ira Katznelson, 157–205. Princeton, NJ: Princeton University Press, 1995.

Kertzer, David I. *The Kidnapping of Edguardo Mortara*. New York: Knopf, 1997.

Kessner, Thomas. *The Golden Door: Italian and Jewish Immigrant Mobility in New York City, 1880–1915*. New York: Oxford University Press, 1977.

Kilian, Hendrikje. *Die Jüdische Gemeinde in München, 1813–1871: Eine Großstandtgemeinde in Zeitalter der Emanzipation*. Munich: Kommissionsverlag, UNI-Druck, 1989.

Kisch, Guido. "*Israels Herold*: The First Jewish Weekly in New York." *Historia Judaica* 2 (1940): 3–22.

———. "The Revolution of 1848 and the Jewish 'On to America' Movement." *Publication of the American Jewish Historical Society* 38 (March 1949): 185–234.

Klauprecht, Emil. *German Chronicle in the History of the Ohio Valley and Its Capital City Cincinnati in Particular*, trans. Dale V. Lally; ed. Don Heinrich Tolzman. Bowie, MD: Heritage Books, 1992.

Klier, John. *Imperial Russia's Jewish Question, 1855–1881*. Cambridge, U.K.: Cambridge University Press, 1995.

Knewson, Margrit B. *Immigrants from the German-Speaking Countries of Europe: A Selective Bibliography*. Washington, DC: Library of Congress, 1991.

Kober, Adolf. "Emancipation's Impact on the Education and Vocational Training of German Jewry." *Jewish Social Studies* 16 (January 1954): 3–32.

———. "One Hundred Fifty Years of Religious Instruction." *Leo Baeck Institute Yearbook* 2 (1957): 98–118.

Kohler, Max J. "The Board of Delegates of American Israelites, 1859–1878." *Publications of the American Jewish Historical Society* 29 (1925): 75–116.

Korn, Bertram Wallace. *American Jewry and the Civil War*. Philadelphia: Jewish Publication Society of America, 1957.

———. *The American Reaction to the Mortara Case*. Cincinnati: American Jewish Archives, 1957.

———. *Eventful Years and Experiences: Studies in Nineteenth-Century American Jewish History*. Cincinnati: American Jewish Archives, 1954.

———. "Jewish 48ers in America." *American Jewish Archives* 11 (June 1949): 3–20.

————. "Jewish Chaplains During the Civil War." In *Jews and the Civil War: A Reader*, ed. Jonathan D. Sarna and Adam Mendelsohn, 335–51. New York: New York University Press, 2010.

————. *Retrospect and Prospect: Essays in Commemoration of the Seventy-Fifth Anniversary of the Founding of the Central Conference of American Rabbis, 1889–1964*. New York: CCAR, 1965.

Korros, Alexandra Shecket, and Jonathan D. Sarna (eds.). *American Synagogue History: A Bibliography and State-of-the-Field Survey*. New York: M. Wiener, 1988.

Kraft, Louis. *The Development of the Jewish Community Center: Purposes, Principles, and Practice*. New York: National Association of Jewish Center Workers, 1967.

Kraut, Benny. "The Ambivalent Relations of American Reform Judaism with Unitarianism in the Last Third of the Nineteenth Century." *Journal of Ecumenical Studies* 23(1) (winter 1986): 58–68.

————. *From Reform Judaism to Ethical Culture*. Cincinnati: Hebrew Union College, 1979.

————. *German-Jewish Orthodoxy in an Immigrant Synagogue: Cincinnati's New Hope Congregation and the Ambiguities of Ethnic Religion*. New York: M. Wiener, 1988.

————. "Judaism Triumphant: Isaac Mayer Wise on Unitarianism and Liberal Christianity." *Association for Jewish Studies* 78 (1982–83): 179–230.

Kurzweil, Z. E. *Modern Trends in Jewish Education*. New York: T. Yoseloff, 1964.

Latourette, Kenneth Scott. *Christianity in a Revolutionary Age: A History of Christianity in the Nineteenth and Twentieth Centuries*, 5 vols. Westport, CT: Greenwood Press, 1958–59.

Lederhendler, Eli. *The Road to Modern Jewish Politics: Political Tradition and Political Reconstruction in the Jewish Community of Tsarist Russia*. New York: Oxford University Press, 1989.

Lincoln, W. Bruce. *Nicholas I: Emperor and Autocrat of All the Russias*. Bloomington: Indiana University Press, 1980.

Lowenstein, Leopold. *Zur Geschichte der Juden in Fürth*. Hildescheim, Germany: Olms, 1974.

Lowenstein, Steven M. "The 1840s and the Creation of the German-Jewish Religious Reform Movement." In *Revolution and Evolution: 1848 in German-Jewish History*, ed. Werner E. Mosse, Arnold Paucker, and Reinhard Rürup, 255–97. Tubingen, Germany: Mohr, 1981.

————. "Governmental Jewish Policies in Early Nineteenth Century Germany and Russia: A Comparison." *Jewish Social Studies* 46 (summer 1984): 303–20.

————. *The Mechanics of Change: Essays in the Social History of German Jewry*. Atlanta, GA: Scholars Press, 1992.

————. "The Pace of Modernization of German Jewry in the Nineteenth Century." *Leo Baeck Institute Yearbook* 21 (1976): 41–56.

Lutz, Charles P. (ed.). *Church Roots: Stories of Nine Immigrant Groups That Became the American Lutheran Church*. Minneapolis, MN: Augsberg, 1965.

Marcus, Jacob R. *The Colonial American Jew: 1492–1776*, 3 vols. Detroit: Wayne State University Press, 1970.

———. *Early American Jewry*, 3 vols. Philadelphia: Jewish Publication Society, 1953.

———. "Hebrew Union College–Jewish Institute of Religion: A Centennial Documentary." *American Jewish Archives* 26 (November 1974): 99–244.

———. *United States Jewry: 1776–1985*, 3 vols. Detroit: Wayne State University Press, 1989.

Marcus, Jacob R., and Abraham Peck. *The American Rabbinate: A Century of Continuity and Change, 1883–1893*. Hoboken, NJ: Ktav, 1985.

Markens, Isaac. "Lincoln and the Jews." *American Jewish Historical Society* 17 (1909): 109–65.

Marsden, George M. *The Soul of the American University: From Protestant Establishment to Established Nonbelief*. New York: Oxford University Press, 1994.

Marty, Martin E. *Pilgrims in Their Own Land: 500 Years of Religion in America*. Boston: Little Brown, 1984.

———. *Righteous Empire: The Protestant Experience in America*. New York: Dial Press, 1970.

Marty, Martin E., and Frederick E. Greenspahn (eds.). *Pushing the Faith: Proselytism and Civility in a Pluralistic World*. New York: Crossroads, 1988.

May, Max B. *The History of K. K. Bene Yeshurun of Cincinnati, Ohio*. Cincinnati: Bene Yeshurun, 1892.

———. *Isaac Mayer Wise: The Founder of American Judaism*. New York: Putnam's Sons, 1916.

———. "The Jews of Cincinnati." In *Centennial History of Cincinnati and Representative Citizens*, ed. Charles Theodore Greve, v. 1, 939–49. Cincinnati: Biographical, 1904.

McGrane, Reginald C. *The University of Cincinnati: A Success Story in Urban Higher Education*. New York: Harper & Row, 1963.

Merowitz, Morton J. "Max Lilienthal (1814–1882): Jewish Educator in Nineteenth-Century America." *YIVO Annual of Jewish Social Studies* 15 (1974): 46–65.

———. "A Note on the Dating of Dr. Max Lilienthal's Birth." *American Jewish Archives* 26 (1974): 78–79.

Meyer, Michael A. "Christian Influence on Early German Reform Judaism." In *Studies in Jewish Bibliography, History, and Literature in Honor of I. Edward Kiev*, ed. Charles Berlin, 289–303. New York: Ktav, 1971.

———, ed. *German-Jewish History in Modern Times*, 2 vols. New York: Columbia University Press, 1997.

———. "The German Model of Religious Reform and Russian Jewry." In *Danzig, Between East and West: Aspects of Modern Jewish History*, ed. Isadore

Twersky, 67–91. Cambridge, MA: Harvard University Press, 1985.

———. *Hebrew Union College–Jewish Institute of Religion: At One Hundred Years*, ed. Samuel E. Karff. Cincinnati: Hebrew Union College Press, 1976.

———. "In the Days of Isaac Mayer Wise." In *Hebrew Union College-Jewish Institute of Religion at One Hundred Years*, ed. Samuel E. Karff. Cincinnati: Hebrew Union College Press, 1976.

———. *The Origins of the Modern Jew: Jewish Identity and European Culture in Germany, 1749–1824.* Detroit: Wayne State University, 1967.

———. *Response to Modernity: A History of the Reform Movement in Judaism.* New York: Oxford University Press, 1988.

———. "Thank You, Moritz Loth: A 125-Year UAHC Retrospective." *Reform Judaism*, fall 1998, 30–39.

Michael, Ann Deborah. "The Origins of the Jewish Community of Cincinnati, 1817–1860." *Cincinnati Historical Society Bulletin* 30 (fall–winter 1972): 155–82.

Michaelson, Robert. "Common Schools, Common Religion?" *Church History* 38 (1969): 201–17.

Miller, Janet A. "Public Elementary Schools in Cincinnati, 1870–1914." *Cincinnati Historical Society Bulletin* 38 (summer 1980): 83–96.

Moore, Deborah Dash. *B'nai B'rith and the Challenge of Ethnic Leadership.* Albany: State University of New York Press, 1981.

Moltmann, Günter, ed. *Germans to America: 300 Years of Immigration, 1683–1983.* Stuttgart, Germany: Institute for Foreign Cultural Relations, 1982.

Morrison, Samuel Eliot, Henry Steele Commager, and William G. Leuchtenberg. *The Growth of the American Republic.* New York: Oxford University Press, 1969.

Mosse, Werner E. *Jews in the German Economy: The German-Jewish Economic Elite, 1820–1935.* Oxford: Clarendon Press, 1987.

Mostov, Stephen G. "A 'Jerusalem' on the Ohio: The Social and Economic History of Cincinnati's Jewish Community, 1840–1875." Ph.D. dissertation, Brandeis University, 1981.

Nadel, Stanley. *Little Germany: Ethnicity, Religion, and Class in New York City, 1845–80.* Urbana: University of Illinois Press, 1990.

Nathans, Benjamin. *Beyond the Pale: The Jewish Encounter with Late Imperial Russia.* Berkeley: University of California Press, 2002.

Nelson, Clifford E. (ed.). *The Lutherans in North America*, rev. ed. Philadelphia: Fortress Press, 1980.

Noble, Stuart G. *A History of American Education.* New York: Rinehart, 1954.

O'Neill, Frederic Gordon. *Ernest Reuben Lilienthal and His Family.* Stanford, CA: Stanford University Press, 1949.

Paulsen, Friedrich. *The German Universities and University Study*, trans. Frank Thilly and William W. Elwang. New York: Scribner's Sons, 1906.

Pelli, Moshe. *The Age of Haskalah: Studies in Hebrew Literature of the Enlightenment in Germany.* Leiden, Netherlands: Brill, 1979.

———. "The Methodology Employed by the Hebrew Reformers in the First Temple Controversy (1818–1819)." In *Studies in Jewish Bibliography, History, and Literature in Honor of I. Edward Kiev*, ed. Charles Berlin, 381–97. New York: Ktav, 1971.

Perko, F. Michael. "The Building Up of Zion: Religion and Education in Nineteenth Century Cincinnati." *Cincinnati Historical Society Bulletin* 38 (summer 1980): 97–114.

Petuchowski, Jakob J. "Abraham Geiger and Samuel Holdheim: Their Differences in Germany and Repercussions in America." *Leo Baeck Institute Yearbook* 22 (1977): 139–59.

———. "Manuals and Catechisms of the Jewish Religion in the Early Period of Emancipation." In *Studies in Nineteenth-Century Jewish Intellectual History*, ed. Alexander Altman, 47–64. Cambridge, MA: Harvard University Press, 1969.

———. *Prayerbook Reform in Europe: The Liturgy of European Liberal and Reform Judaism*. New York: World Union for Progressive Judaism, 1968.

Pfeffer, Leo. *Creeds in Competition: A Creative Force in American Culture*. New York: Harper, 1958.

Philippson, Johanna. "The Philippsons, A German-Jewish Family, 1775–1993." *Leo Baeck Institute Yearbook* 7 (1962): 95–118.

Philipson, David. "The Cincinnati Community in 1825." *Publications of the American Jewish Historical Society* 10 (1902): 97–99.

———. "The Jewish Pioneers of the Ohio Valley." *Publications of the American Jewish Historical Society* 8 (1900): 43–57.

———. "Max Lilienthal." *Central Conference of American Rabbis Annual Convention* 25 (1915): 191–220.

———. "Max Lilienthal, 1815–1882." In *Centenary Papers and Others*, by David Philipson, 149–90. Cincinnati: Ark, 1919.

———. *Max Lilienthal, American Rabbi: Life and Writings*. New York: Bloch, 1915.

———. "Max Lilienthal in Russia." *Hebrew Union College Annual* 12–13 (1937–38): 825–39.

———. *My Life as an American Jew: An Autobiography*. Cincinnati: J. G. Kidd and Son, 1941.

———. *The Oldest Congregation: Bene Israel, Cincinnati—Souvenir of Seventieth Anniversary, 1824–1894*. Cincinnati: Press of C. J. Krehbiel, 1894.

———. *The Oldest Jewish Congregation in the West: Bene Israel, Cincinnati*. Cincinnati: C. J. Krehbiel, 1924.

———. "Personal Contacts with the Founder of the Hebrew Union College." *Hebrew Union College Annual* 11 (1936): 1–18.

———. *The Reform Movement in Judaism*. New York: Ktav, 1967.

Pilch, Judah (ed.). *A History of Jewish Education in America*. New York: National Curriculum Research Institute of the American Association for Jewish Education, 1969.

Plaut, W. Gunther (ed.). *The Growth of Reform Judaism: American and European Sources Until 1948.* New York: World Union for Progress Judaism, 1965.

———. "The Pittsburgh Platform in the Light of European Antecedents." In *The Changing World of Reform Judaism: The Pittsburgh Platform in Retrospect—Papers Presented on the Occasion of the 100th Anniversary of the Pittsburgh Platform, February 1985, and the Proceedings of 1885,* ed. Walter Jacob, 17–24. Pittsburgh, PA: Rodef Shalom Congregation, 1985.

———. *The Rise of Reform Judaism: A Sourcebook of Its European Origins.* New York: World Union for Progressive Judaism, 1963.

Pozzetta, George E. *American Immigration and Ethnicity,* v. 19, *The Immigrant Religious Experience.* New York: Garland, 1991.

Preston, David L. "The German Jews in Secular Education, University Teaching, and Science: A Preliminary Inquiry." *Jewish Social Studies* 38 (spring 1976): 99–116.

Rabinowitz, Benjamin. "The Young Men's Hebrew Association (1854–1913)." *Publications of the American Jewish Historical Society* 37 (1947): 221–326.

Raisin, Jacob S. *The Haskalah Movement in Russia.* Philadelphia: Jewish Publication Society of America, 1913.

Ravitch, Diane. *The Great School Wars in New York City, 1805–1973: A History of the Public Schools as Battlefields of Social Change.* New York: Basic Books, 1974.

Regner, Sidney. "The History of the Conference." In *Retrospect and Prospect: Essays in Commemoration of the Seventy-Fifth Anniversary of the Founding of the Central Conference of American Rabbis, 1889–1964,* ed. Bertram W. Korn, 1–19. New York: CCAR, 1965.

Reissner, H. G. "The German-American Jews (1800–1850)." *Leo Baeck Institute Yearbook.* 10 (1965): 57–116.

Riasanovsky, Nicholas. *Nicholas I and Official Nationality in Russia, 1825–1855.* Berkeley: University of California Press, 1959.

Richarz, Monika. "Jewish Social Mobility in Germany During the Time of Emancipation, 1790–1871." *Leo Baeck Institute Yearbook* 20 (1975): 69–77.

Ringer, Fritz K. *Education and Society in Modern Europe.* Bloomington: Indiana University Press, 1979.

Rohrbacher, Stefan. "The 'Hep Hep' Riots of 1819: Anti-Jewish Ideology, Agitation, and Violence." In *Exclusionary Violence: Antisemitic Riots in Modern German History,* ed. Christhard Hoffmann, Werner Bergmann, and Helmut Walser Smith, 23–42. Ann Arbor: University of Michigan Press, 2005.

Rosenmann, Moses. *Isak Noa Mannheimer: Sein Leben und Wirken.* Vienna: R. Lowit Verlag, 1922.

Rosenwaike, Ira. *On the Edge of Greatness: A Portrait of American Jewry in the Early National Period.* Cincinnati: American Jewish Archives, 1985.

Ruben, Bruce. "Max Lilienthal: Rabbi, Educator, and Reformer in Nineteenth-

Century America." Ph.D. dissertation, City University of New York, 1997.

Rürup, Reinhard. "Emancipation and Bourgeois Society." *Leo Baeck Institute Yearbook* 14 (1969): 67–91.

———. "European Revolutions and Emancipation." In *Revolution and Evolution: 1848 in German-Jewish History*, ed. Werner E. Mosse, Arnold Paucker, and Reinhard Rürup, 1–53. Tübingen, Germany: Mohr, 1981.

Ryback, Martin B. "The East-West Conflict in American Reform Judaism." *American Jewish Archives* 4 (January 1952): 3–25.

Sarna, Jonathan. *The American Jewish Experience*. New York: Holmes & Meier, 1986.

———. "The American Jewish Response to Nineteenth-Century Christian Missions." In *Essential Papers on Jewish Christian Relations in the United States*, ed. Naomi W. Cohen, 21–42. New York: New York University Press, 1990.

———. *American Judaism: A History*. New Haven, CT: Yale University Press, 2004.

———. "A Forgotten Nineteenth-Century Prayer for the United States Government: Its Meaning, Significance, and Surprising Author." Manuscript, Brandeis University, February 14, 1997. Reprinted in *Hesed Ve-Emet: Studies in Honor of Ernest S. Frerichs*, eds. J. Magness and S. Gitin, 431–40 (Athens, GA: Scholars Press, 1998).

———. *A Great Awakening: The Transformation That Shaped Twentieth Century American Judaism and Its Implications for Today*. New York: Council for Initiatives in Jewish Education, 1996.

———. *Jacksonian Jew: The Two Worlds of Mordecai Noah*. New York: Holmes & Meier, 1981.

———. "The Spectrum of Jewish Leadership in Ante-Bellum America." *Journal of American Ethnic History* 1 (1982): 54–67.

Sarna, Jonathan D., and Karla Goldman. "From Synagogue-Community to Citadel of Reform: The History of K. K. Bene Israel (Rockdale Temple) in Cincinnati, Ohio." In *American Congregations*, v. 1, *Portraits of Twelve Religious Communities*, ed. James Wind and James W. Lewis, 159–220. Chicago: University of Chicago Press, 1998.

Sarna, Jonathan D., and Nancy H. Klein. *The Jews of Cincinnati*. Cincinnati: Center for the Study of the American Jewish Experience, and Hebrew Union College Jewish Institute of Religion, 1989.

Schappes, Morris U. (ed.). *A Documentary History of the Jews in the United States, 1654–1875*. New York: Citadel Press, 1952.

Scharfman, I. Harold. *The First Rabbi: Origins of the Conflict Between Orthodox and Reform—Jewish Polemic Warfare in Pre–Civil War America, A Biographical History*. Malibu, CA: Pangloss Press, 1988.

Scheinhaus, Leon. *Ein Deutscher Pioner: Dr. Lilienthals Kulturversuch in Rußland*. Berlin: M. Poppelauer, 1911.

Schneersohn, Joseph I. *The "Tzemach Tzedek" and the Haskala Movement*, trans. Zalman I. Posner. New York: Kehot Publication Society, 1962.

Schofer, Lawrence. "Emancipation and Population Change." In *Revolution and Evolution: 1848 in German-Jewish History*, ed. Werner E. Mosse, Arnold Paucker, and Reinhard Rürup, 63–89. Tubingen: Mohr, 1981.

Scholem, Gershom. "The Science of Judaism: Then and Now." In *The Messianic Idea in Judaism, and Other Essays on Jewish Spirituality*, by Gershom Scholem, 304–13. New York: Schocken, 1972.

Schorsch, Ismar. "Emancipation and the Crisis of Religious Authority: The Emergence of the Modern Rabbinate." In *Revolution and Evolution: 1848 in German-Jewish History*, ed. Werner E. Mosse, Arnold Paucker, and Reinhard Rürup, 205–53. Tubingen: Mohr, 1981.

———. "The Emergence of Historical Consciousness in Modern Judaism." *Leo Baeck Institute Yearbook* 28(1) (1983): 413–437.

———. "Jewish Studies: Jewish Studies from 1818 to 1919." In *Encyclopedia of Religion*, ed. Mircea Eliade, 45–53. New York: Macmillan, 1987.

———. *From Text to Context: The Turn to History in Modern Judaism*. Hanover, NH: University Press of New England, 1994.

Schreiber, Lynne. "My House Shall Be a House of Prayer for All People." *Moment* 30(6) (December 2005): 50.

Scott, Donald M. *From Office to Profession: The New England Ministry, 1750–1850*. Philadelphia: University of Pennsylvania Press, 1976.

Seller, Maxine S. "Isaac Leeser, Architect of the American Jewish Community." Ph.D. dissertation, University of Pennsylvania, 1965.

Seltzer, Robert M., and Norman J. Cohen (eds.). *The Americanization of the Jews*. New York: New York University Press, 1995.

Seymour, Jack L. *From Sunday School to Church School: Continuities in Protestant Church Education in the United Sates, 1860–1929*. Washington, DC: University Press of America, 1982.

Shargel, David. "Ludwig Philippson: The Rabbi as Journalist—An Anthology of His Writings with an Introductory Essay." Ph.D. dissertation. Jewish Theological Seminary, 1990.

Sheehan, James J. *German History, 1770–1866*. New York: Oxford University Press, 1990.

———. *German Liberalism in the Nineteenth Century*. Chicago: University of Chicago Press, 1978.

Sherman, Moshe D. "Bernard Illowy and Nineteenth Century American Orthodoxy." Ph.D. dissertation, Yeshiva University, 1991.

Silver, Matthew. "Rabbi Max Lilienthal: From 'Compulsory Education' to the Separation of Religion and State." *Zion* 71(3) (2006): 343–72 (in Hebrew).

Silverstein, Alan. *Alternatives to Assimilation: The Response of Reform Judaism to American Culture, 1840–1930*. Hanover, NH: University Press of New England, 1994.

Simon, John. "That Obnoxious Order." *Civil War Times Illustrated* 23(6) (October 1984). Reprinted in *Jews and the Civil War: A Reader*, ed. Jonathan

D. Sarna and Adam Mendelsohn, 353–61 (New York: New York University Press, 2010).

Sorkin, David. *The Transformation of German Jewry, 1780–1840.* New York: Oxford University Press, 1987.

———. "Wilhelm von Humboldt: The Theory and Practice of Self-Formation (*Bildung*), 1791–1810." *Journal of the History of Ideas* 44(1) (1983): 55–74.

Spann, Edward K. *The New Metropolis: New York City, 1840–1857.* New York: Columbia University Press, 1981.

Spring, Joel. *The American School, 1642–1990,* 2nd ed. New York: Longman, 1990.

Stanislawski, Michael. *Tsar Nicholas I and the Jews.* Philadelphia: Jewish Publication Society of America, 1981.

Sterling, Eleonore. "Anti-Jewish Riots in Germany in 1819: A Displacement of Social Protest." *Historia Judaica* 12 (October 1950): 105–42.

———. "Jewish Reaction to Jew-Hatred in the First Half of the Nineteenth Century." *Leo Baeck Institute Yearbook* 3 (1958): 103–21.

Stern, Myer. *Rise and Progress of Reform Judaism: Embracing a History Made from the Official Records of Temple Emanu-El of New York.* New York: By the author, 1895.

Stern, Selma. *The Court Jew: A Contribution to the History of the Period of Absolutism in Central Europe,* trans. Ralph Weiman. Philadelphia: Jewish Publication Society of America, 1950.

Stevens, Elliot L. (ed.). *Rabbinic Authority: Papers Presented Before the 91st Convention of the Central Conference of American Rabbis.* New York: CCAR, 1982.

Sussman, Lance J. *Isaac Leeser and the Making of American Judaism.* Detroit: Wayne State University Press, 1995.

———. "Isaac Leeser and the Protestantization of American Judaism." *American Jewish Archives* 38 (April 1986): 1–21.

Tarshish, Alan. "The Board of Delegates of American Israelites (1859–1878)." *Publications of the American Jewish Historical Society* 49 (September 1959–June 1960): 16–32.

———. "Jew and Christian in a New Society: Some Aspects of Jewish-Christian Relationships in the United States, 1848–1881." In *A Bicentennial Festschrift for Jacob Rader Marcus,* ed. Bertram W. Korn, 565–88. New York: Ktav, 1976.

Taylor, Charles. *Hegel.* London: Cambridge University Press, 1975.

Temkin, Sefton D. "A Beth Din in America." In *Perspectives on Jews and Judaism: Essays in Honor of Wolfe Kelman,* ed. Arthur A. Chiel, 409–20. New York: Rabbinical Assembly, 1978.

———. *Isaac Mayer Wise: Shaping American Judaism.* Oxford, U.K.: Oxford University Press, 1992.

———. "Isaac Mayer Wise and the Civil War." In *Jews and the Civil War: A Reader,* ed. Jonathan D. Sarna and Adam Mendelsohn, 161–80. New York:

New York University Press, 2010.

—— (trans.). *The New World of Reform: Containing the Proceedings of the Conference of Reform Rabbis in November 1869*. London: Leo Baeck College, 1971.

——. "Rabbi Max Lilienthal Views American Jewry in 1847." In *A Bicentennial Festschrift for Jacob Rader Marcus*, ed. Bertram Wallace Korn, 581–608. New York: Ktav, 1976.

Thomas, J. William, Robert E. Park, and Herbert A. Miller. *Old World Traits Transplanted: Americanization Studies*. New York: Harper Brothers, 1921.

Tolzmann, Don Heinrich. *German-Americana: A Bibliography*. Metuchen, NJ: Scarecrow Press, 1975.

Toth, Carolyn R. *German-English Bilingual Schools in America: The Cincinnati Tradition in Historical Context*, v. 2 *New German-American Studies*. New York: 1990.

Toury, Jacob. "Types of Jewish Municipal Rights in German Townships: The Problem of Local Emancipation." *Leo Baeck Institute Yearbook* 22 (1977): 55–80.

Trilling, Lionel. *Sincerity and Authenticity*. Cambridge, MA: Harvard University Press, 1972.

Tyler, David Budlong. *Steam Conquers the Atlantic*. New York: Appleton-Century, 1939.

Urbach, Ephraim E. *Yad la-Talmud* [The Halakha: Its Sources and Development], trans. Raphael Posner. Tel Aviv: Massada, 1986.

Veysey, Laurence R. *The Emergence of the American University*. Chicago: University of Chicago Press, 1965.

Vishniak, Mark. "Anti-Semitism in Tsarist Russia: A Study in Government-Fostered Anti-Semitism." In *Essays on Anti-Semitism*, ed. Koppel S. Pinson. New York: Conference on Jewish Relations, 1946.

Von Rohr, John. *The Shaping of American Congregationalism, 1620–1957*. Cleveland: Pilgrim Press, 1992.

Walker, Mack. *Germany and the Emigration, 1816–1885*. Cambridge, U.K.: Cambridge University Press, 1964.

Weiner, Max. *Abraham Geiger and Liberal Judaism: The Challenge of the Nineteenth Century*, trans. Ernest J. Schlochauer. Cincinnati: Hebrew Union College Press, 1981.

Wentz, Abdel Ross. *A Basic History of Lutheranism in America*, rev. ed. Philadelphia: Fortress Press, 1964.

Werner, Eric. *A Voice Still Heard: The Sacred Songs of the Ashkenazic Jews*. Philadelphia: Pennsylvania University Press, 1976.

Whiteman, Maxwell. "Isaac Leeser and the Jews of Philadelphia." *Publications of the American Jewish Historical Society* 48(4) (June 1959): 207–44.

——. "Notions, Dry Goods, and Clothing: An Introduction to the Study of the Cincinnati Peddler." *Jewish Quarterly Review* 53 (April 1963): 306–21.

Whittaker, Cynthia H. *The Origins of Modern Russian Education: An Intellec-*

tual Biography of Count Sergei Uvarov, 1786–1855. Dekalb: Northern Illinois University Press, 1984.

Wolfe, Gerard. *The Synagogues of New York's Lower East Side.* New York: Washington Mews Books, 1978.

Zinberg, Israel. *The History of Jewish Literature*, 12 vols. Cincinnati: Hebrew Union College Press, 1972–78.

Zipperstein, Steven. *The Jews of Odessa: A Cultural History, 1794–1881.* Stanford, CA: Stanford University Press, 1982.

Zola, Gary Phillip. "Southern Rabbis and the Founding of the First National Association of Rabbis." *American Jewish History* 85(4) (December 1997): 353–72.

INDEX

Page numbers in italics refer to illustrations. Subentries have been arranged chronologically.

arba kanfot, 41
Ariel, 158
Aschheim, Steven, 20
Asmonean, 66, 93, 114; Lilienthal's articles in, 116–22, 225, 231, 232
Aub, Hirsch, 17, 18
Aub, Joseph, 10

Baal Shem Tov, 23
Bachman, Joseph, 80
Bahya ibn Pakuda, 119
Baird, Robert, 123
Bamberger, Seligmann, 10
bar mitzvah, 35
Bauman, Mark, 236, 237
Bavaria: Jewish legal status in, 3–4; Judenedikt of 1813, 4, 5; anti-Jewish violence, 5; and question of Jewish emancipation, 5–6; crop failures in 1816 and 1817, 6; educational policy *(Erziehungspolitik)*, 9, 10; establishment of gymnasium and university in 1826, 11–12; abolishment of restrictions against Jews, 178
Beckel, Joseph, 111
ben David, Abraham, 119
Bene Israel, Cincinnati: Broadway Synagogue, *131;* original building, *131;* Mound Street Temple, *132;* establishment of, 137–38; as traditional *kahal,* 138; decline of older congregation, 138–39; election of Wise to serve as rabbi, 139; Noyoth Institute, 139, 143–45, 157–58; Orthodox opposition to Lilienthal, 139–40; Orthodox opposition to mixed choir, 141; board adoption of Lilienthal's reforms, 142–43; Orthodox formation of new synagogue, 143; conflict with Lilienthal, 155–56; commitment to Lilienthal's Reform agenda, 187–88, 190; concessions to Lilienthal, 189–90; dedication of new temple, 193

Bene Yeshurun, Cincinnati: hiring of Isaac Wise as rabbi, 138; unwillingness to share Wise with Bene Israel, 139; Talmud Yelodim day school, 144
ben Haim, Yitzhak, 47, 50, 51–52
Benjamin, Raphael, 237
ben Yohai, Simeon, 119
ben Zeev, Yehudah Leib, 8
Berdichev, 48
Bernays, Isaac, 25
beth din, 65, 73, 88–90
beth hamidrash, 41
Bialystok, 48
Bible, King James translation, 165
Bildung, 10–11, 20, 82, 100, 113, 185–86, 230
Bing, Abraham, 10
B'nai B'rith, 171–72
Bnai Jeshurun: separation from Shearith Israel, 64, 65; New York Talmud Torah and Hebrew Institute, 83
Boarding and Day School for Young Ladies of the Jewish Faith, New York City, 98
Board of Delegates of American Israelites: and controversy over Jewish chaplains in Civil War, 180–81; increasingly more hospitable toward Reform, 212; and Mortara affair, 212; reconciliation with UAHC, 213–14
bodily resurrection, 197
Bogen, F. W., 62
Breslau conference, 77, 78
Brest-Litovsk, 48–49
Bruel, Samuel, 139, 140, 142
Brumberg, Stephan, 165
Brunswick conference, 76–77
Busch, Isidor, 101–2, 109

Caro, Joseph, 147
Castle Garden, 62
catechism, 96, 97, 145
Catholic Good Samaritan Hospital, 171

Enlightenment: German, 3; and human reason, 7, 229; concepts of equality and citizenship, 8

Eppinger, Solomon, 210

Ernest Reuben Lilienthal and His Family, 223

Ethical Culture, 235

Ethical Culture Society, 235

Euche, Isaac: *Toldot Harav*, 113

European revolutions of 1848, 106–8, 112

Evangelical Christians, 123

Ezra, Abraham ibn, 119

Falkenberg, Baron, 26

Feiner, Shmuel, 23

Felsenheld, Herman, 88, 89, 90–91

Fichte, Johann, 11

First Congregationalist (Unitarian) Church, Cincinnati, 185

Fischel, Arnold, 180

Fort Sumter, attack on, 179

48ers, 108

Foster, Vere, 61

Fox, Steven, 205, 207

Frank, Henry, 80

Frankel, Zacharias, 73, 117, 150, 209, 269n102

Frankfurt *Reformfreunde*, 75

Freiberg, Julius, 161, 206, 207, 221

French Revolution, 3

Friedman, Max, 180

Fuenn, Shmuel, 251n146

funeral and burial practices, 77–78

Furness, Henry, 81

Fürth yeshiva, 9–10, 229

Geiger, Abraham, 39, 209, 265n151, 273n36

German American anti-defamation, 173

German Catholic immigrants: bilingual parochial schools, 63, 82; and increase in Catholic population of America, 64; challenge to Protestant domination of public schools, 83, 165;

concerns about necessity of learning English, 260n31

German Enlightenment, 3

German Haskalah, 7, 8, 23, 162, 230

German Hebrew Benevolent Society, 67, 87, 100, 106

German Jacobites, 3

German Jewish immigrants: and personal freedoms, 60–61; dual German and Jewish ethnicity, 63; settlement on lower East Side of New York, 63; demands on educational system, 65–66; expectations for sermons, 81; dissatisfaction with public schools, 82–83; dissatisfaction with Jewish day schools, 83; influx after events of 1848, 108; liberals, or 48ers, 108; pressure to succeed materially, 120; post–Civil War increase in, 193–94. *See also* Jewish immigrants

German Jewish immigrants, Cincinnati: and changed character of city, 136; belief in divine mission, 137; as merchants, brokers, and traders, 137; upward mobility, 137

German Lutheran immigrants, 63, 64

German Maskilim: proposals for modernization of Jewish education, 8; response to Lilienthal's appeal for German Jewish teachers for Russian schools, 40

German modern curriculum, 168–69

German mysticism, 10

German Reform rabbinic conferences, 77, 145–46

German Relief Committee, 107

Germany: anti-Jewish riots of 1819, 6–7; education, 10, 11, 168–69; 1838 edict restricting Jewish citizens, 18

Gettysburg Address, 182

Gnosticism, 119

Gottheil, Gustav, 216

Gottlober, Abraham Baer, 47

Graetz, Heinrich, 215

Grant, Ulysses, expulsion of Jews from military department of Tennessee, 181–82
Gratz, Rebecca, 96
Greene Street Educational Institution, 101
Guenzburg, Aaron, 147
Gunther, W., 235
Günzberg, Mordecai Aaron, 46
Gutheim, James K., 68, 71, 72, 81, 216

Hahn, Aaron, 195–96, 228
halitzah, 77
Halperin, Israel, 50, 244n5
Hamburger, Wolf, 9, 10, 229
Ha-Notein Teshu'ah, 80
Harmony Society, 107
Har Sinai Temple, Baltimore, 152
Haskalah: Russian, 23, 56; vision of education, 74, 82, 145. *See also* German Haskalah
Hayes, Rutherford B., 225
hazzan, 79
Heavenrich, Esther Lilienthal, 95, 221, 271n162
Hebraica, 215
Hebrew Benevolent Society, 87
The Hebrew Language Demonstrated on Ollendorf's Method, 97
Hebrew Relief Union of Cincinnati, 182
Hebrew Review, 185, 217
Hebrew Sabbath School Visitor, 163–64
Hebrew Theological Seminary, New York, 213; transformed into preparatory school for Hebrew Union College, 213
Hebrew Union College, 207, 214, 228, 236; first ordination of American-trained rabbis, 234
Hebrew Union School Society, 84
Hegel, Georg Wilhelm Friedrich, 151
Heidelbach, Philip, 137, 139, 189
Henry, H. A., 102
Henry, Prince of Reuss of Austria, 4
"Hep, Hep" riots, 6

Hessel, Hesekiel, 1
High Holy Days liturgy, 203
Hildescheimer, Esriel, 114
Hirsch, Emil, 218
Hirsch, Jacob von, 6
Hirsch, Samson Raphael, 25, 77–78, 264n143
Hirsch, Samuel, 218
Hirsch, Solomon, 13
Hochheimer, Henry, 147
Huebsch, Adolph, 198, 200, 204, 212

Ibn Ezra, Abraham, 116
Ibn Gabirol, Solomon, 119
Illowy, Bernard, 146, 147, 155, 195, 197, 241n53, 277n138; attack on Lilienthal, 156–57
immigration: Central European immigration to America, 60, 64; transatlantic transport of immigrants, 61–62. *See also* German Catholic immigrants; German Jewish immigrants; German Lutheran immigrants; Jewish immigrants
Isaacs, Myer, 212
Isaacs, Samuel, 68, 81, 83, 96, 103, 212, 215, 253n59
Israelite, 24, 170; Lilienthal's editorial position with, 122–23, 141, 145, 154; support of Lilienthal's agenda at Bene Israel, 141–42; articles supporting Lilienthal's Tisha B'Av stance, 142; "Minhag America" (Lilienthal), 147; Lilienthal's counter to Orthodox attack on Cleveland conference, 151; challenge to Einhorn's criticism of moderates, 152–53; on governor's Thanksgiving Proclamation, 174; Lilienthal's coverage of international politics, 177–78; on Unitarian church, 185; popularity of, 195; and Cincinnati conference of 1871, 200
Israels Herold, 109

Jacobson, Israel, 76

address, 109–11, 231; motivated by trends in American Jewish life, 112, 120–22; and *Wissenschaft*, 114–15, 116–20, 231, 232; and custom of sales of *misheberach*, 116; and reform of liturgy, 116; and second-day festival observance, 116–17; approach based on both Jewish law and *Wissenschaft*, 116–20; belief in bibical law as means for unity, 118; belief in rabbinic law derived from biblical precedents, 118; concept of essence of Judaism, 118; on *minhag*, 118–19; on Kabbalah, 119, 265n148, 265n149; on contributions of Jewish philosophers to philosophy in general, 119–20; on lack of relevance of traditional worship, 121; and Cleveland conference for national unity, 145–55; growing spiritual independence from German Jewish leadership, 150; Hegelian influence, 151; view of relationship of Jewish law and history, 151; view of Talmud as "Reform" document, 151; and Zion College, 154–55

Lilienthal, Maximilien Emanuel (Max): AS NEW AMERICAN RABBI, 161–91: and Christian proselytizing, 123, 175, 232; patriotism, 162, 225, 231; prophet of American civil religion, 162, 167, 174–78, 184, 231; on the Cincinnati bible case, 166–68; commitment to separation of church and state, 167, 168, 186, 273n44; vision of nonsectarian society, 167; establishment of pattern for Jewish elite in civic life, 170; establishment of Hebrew Relief Society, 170–71; director of City Relief Union, 171, 182; and hospitals of Cincinnati, 171; president of Cincinnati Medical School, 171; and B'nai B'rith, 171–72; and Young Men's Literary Club,

172; and Young Men's Hebrew Association (YMHA), 172–73; and Allemania Club, 173; and Cincinnati Turners, 173; and Masons, 173; and national German song festival (Sangerfest), 173; protest of public events on Sabbath, 174; defense of Jewish equality, 174–78; on Christian revival meetings, 175–76; antipathy toward Catholic Church, 176–77; and Edgar Mortara issue, 176–77; protest of Swiss discrimination against American Jews, 177; concern for Jews around the world, 177–78; and the Civil War, 178–84; and slavery issue, 179–80; opposition to Board of Delegates over issue of Jewish chaplains, 180–81; meeting with President Lincoln over Grant's anti-Semitic order, 181–82; and Hebrew Relief Union of Cincinnati, 182; universalism, 184–85, 235; and interfaith relations, 184–87; rejection of most traditional theology, 185; affinity with Unitarians, 185–86; pulpit exchange with Vickers, 186; title of "Broad Church Rabbi," 187; as "ethnic broker," 236; creation of model for post-emancipation rabbinate, 236–37

Lilienthal, Maximilien Emanuel (Max): AND UNITY OF AMERICAN JEWRY, 194–238: efforts to create national union, 194; and Hebrew Union College, 194, 200–201, 202, 208–11; support for lay participation in conferences, 194–95, 207; peacemaker role, 195–96, 203, 216, 228, 230, 233; and Cleveland Conference of 1870, 198–99; and New York convention of 1870, 199–200; reconciliation attempts with Radical Reformers, 200; and Cincinnati conference

Lilienthal, Maximilien Emanuel (Max): AND UNITY OF AMERICAN JEWRY (*continued*) of 1871, 200–204; and creation of permanent Jewish institutions, 202; shift of tactics to lay leadership of congregation, 204–5; peacemaker role, 213; and Rabbinical Literary Association, 214–19; editor of *Hebrew Review*, 217; need to reconcile opposites, 229; legacy, 229–38

Lilienthal, Maximilien Emanuel (Max): SERMONS AND SPEECHES: "Der Herr und sein Name der Einig-Eine," 16; on separation of church and state, 16; "Unsterblickheit," 16; rhetorical technique, 16–17, 81; published sermons from Riga, 34; "The Vocation of the Minister," 71–74; belief in central place of sermon in religious service, 81; sermon at consecration of Anshe Chesed's new building, 103–4, 115; Lichtfreunde address, 109–11, 231, 232; "Essence of Religion," 110; "Parties—Keep Peace!", 121; "About What Are You Quarreling?", 122; sermon attacking Christian revival meetings, 175–76; Union Victory address, 182–83; sermon on assassination of Lincoln, 183–84; speech celebrating opening of Hebrew Union College, 185; "The Free Church in the Free State" (at Unitarian church), 186; speech of reconciliation at UAHC conference of 1875, 211–12

Lilienthal, Maximilien Emanuel (Max): WRITINGS: doctoral dissertation ("Ueber den ursprung der jü dish-alexandrischen Religionsphilosophie"), 13–14, 230; "Sketches of Jewish Life in Russia: A General Survey of the Conditions of the Jews in Russia," 56, 86; "Sketches of Jewish Life in Russia #2, 244n5; articles in *Asmonean* developing Reform ideology, 116–22, 225, 231, 232; "Kabbalah and Philosophy," 119, 265n148, 265n149; "Parties—Keep Peace!", 121; "Jewish Geographical Sketches," 122; "The Jews in Russia Under Nicolai I," 122; editorial position with *Israelite*, 122–23; "The Aim of Our Schools," 145; "Minhag America," 147; "The Reformers Want to Uproot All!", 147; *Freheit, Frühling, und Liebe* (poetry), 162–63, 188; *Things Taught: Systematic Instruction in Composition and Object Lessons* (Lilienthal and Allyn), 165; articles in *Jewish Times* on the Cincinnati bible case, 166–68; "Is the Bible Fit to Be Used as a School Book?", 167; "Reply to the Christian Apologete," 175; "Spiritualists and Christianity," 175; coverage of international politics in *Israelite*, 177–78; article in *Hebrew Review* rejecting divine origin of Bible, 185; infused with maskilic history and *Wissenschaft*, 231. See also *Allgemeine Zeitung des Judenthums*, Lilienthal's writings for

Lilienthal, Maximilien Emanuel (Max): PHOTOGRAPHS OF: at age 12, *127*; c. 1860s, *127*; photo defaced by Southerner, *133*, 179

Lilienthal, Maximilien Emanuel (Max): PERSONAL LIFE: engagement to Pepi Nettre, 14, 15, 19; marriage, 59; move to America, 59–64; death of wife, 188–89; efforts to ensure financial security of children, 221–22, 224–25; trip to San Francisco, 222–24; death and funeral, 227–28

Lilienthal, Philip (son), 105, 223, 225, 271n162

Lilienthal, Samuel, 7, 12, 13, 24, 55, 60, 71, 105, 223, 274n48; photograph of, age 11, *128*; photograph of, as adult,

273n36

Vilna Jewish community: Orthodoxy, 23, 41; schools, 42–43

Voltaire, 113

Von Hardenberg, Prince Karl August, 4

Von Humboldt, Wilhelm, 4, 11

Wallerstein, Prince, 24

Washington, George, 162

Waterman, Sigismund, 111

Wengeroff, Pauline, 48–49

Werner, Eliza Lilienthal, 95, 221, 271n162

Werner, Leopold, 219

Wessely, Naphtali: "Words of Peace and Truth," 8, 113

Westphalia, emancipation of Jews, 4

Whittaker, Cynthia, 245n38, 250n142

Wise, Isaac M., 72–73, 79, 94; on Lilienthal's preaching, 81–82; relations with Lilienthal, 87–88, 146–47; *Reminiscences,* 87–88, 89, 238; and establishment of *beth din,* 88–90; *Minhag Amerika,* 89, 198, 200; on events of 1848, 107; plan for national convention for uniting Jewish congregations, 108–11; "Principles of Mosaic Religion," 110; as rabbi of Bene Yeshurun, Cincinnati, 116; and *Israelite,* 122; on Lilienthal's move to Cincinnati, 124–25, 139, 140–41; as rabbi of Bene Israel, Cincinnati, 139; institution of choir and organ at Bene Yeshurun, 141; and Cleveland conference of 1855, 145–55; and Zion College, 154–55; on Lilienthal's focus on public affairs, 161; on Lilienthal's patriotism, 162; on governor's Thanksgiving Proclamation, 174; protest of public events on Sabbath, 174; and protest of Swiss discrimination against American Jews, 177; on slavery, 179; opposition to Board of Delegates over

issue of Jewish chaplains, 180–81; meeting with President Lincoln over Grant's anti-Semitic order, 181–82; on Lilienthal's loss of wife, 188–89; support for inclusion of lay leadership in conferences, 194–95, 198, 204–5; and Einhorn, 195; call for rabbinic conference in 1866, 196–97; on circumcision, 197; and Cleveland conference of 1870, 197–99; and Philadelphia conference of 1869, 198; *Minhag Amerika,* 200; and Cincinnati conference of 1871, 201–4; shift of tactics to lay leadership of congregation, 204–5; and formation of Hebrew Union College, 208–10; on Hebrew Union students, 210; Eastern establishment distrust of, 212–13; and Rabbincal Literary Association, 216; paper on "The Law" in *Hebrew Review,* 217; on Lilienthal's impact on Cincinnati, 226; at Lilienthal's funeral, 227–28; moderate Reform position, 232; jokes about "stomach Judaism," 234; and Pittsburgh conference, 235, 236; education, 254n81

Wissenschaft, 11, 112, 263n112; Lilienthal and, 12–13, 114–15, 116–20, 209, 231; distinction between *minhag* and Halakha, 118

Wolf, F. A., 11

Wolfenstein, Solomon, 208–9, 213

Wrede, Count, of Bavaria, 4

Würzburg yeshiva, 10, 15

yarmulke, 41

Yiddish language, 23

Yom Kippur, 117

Young Hegelians, 113

Young Ladies' Hebrew Seminary, 210

Young Men's Christian Association, 172

Young Men's Hebrew Association (YMHA), 172, 196; New York branch, 172; Cincinnati branch, 172–73

Young Men's Literary Club, 172

Zaddik, Joseph ibn, 119
Zeitgeist, 107, 119, 151, 231, 233
Zinberg, Israel: *History of Jewish Literature*, 29–30, 50

Zion College, 154–55, 194
"Zion College Association of New York," 154
Zohar, 119
Zunz, Leopold, 39, 265n151